THE MANY FACES OF GIFTEDNESS

Lifting the Masks

Alexinia Young Baldwin
University of Connecticut

Wilma Vialle
Wollongong University

Wadsworth Publishing Company
I(T)P® An International Thomson Publishing Company

Belmont, CA • Albany, NY • Boston • Cincinnati • Johannesburg • London
Madrid • Melbourne • Mexico City • New York • Pacific Grove, CA
Scottsdale, AZ • Singapore • Tokyo • Toronto

Education Editor: Dianne Lindsay
Assistant Editor: Tangelique Williams
Marketing Manager: Becky Tollerson
Project Editor: Jerilyn Emori
Print Buyer: Barbara Britton
Permissions Editor: Robert Kauser
Production: Sara Dovre Wudali, Gustafson Graphics
Designer: Timothy J. Conners
Copy Editor: Linda Ireland
Cover Design: Margarite Reynolds
Illustrator and Cover Image: Myriam Mickhail, University of Wollongong
Compositor: Gustafson Graphics
Printer: Webcom Ltd.

Printed in Canada
2 3 4 5 6 7 8 9 10

For more information, contact Wadsworth Publishing Company, 10 Davis Drive, Belmont, CA 94002, or electronically at http://www.wadsworth.com

International Thomson Publishing Europe
Berkshire House
168-173 High Holborn
London, WC1V 7AA, United Kingdom

International Thomson Editores
Seneca, 53
Colonia Polanco
11560 México D.F. México

Nelson ITP, Australia
102 Dodds Street
South Melbourne
Victoria 3205 Australia

International Thomson Publishing Asia
60 Albert Street
#15-01 Albert Complex
Singapore 189969

Nelson Canada
1120 Birchmount Road
Scarborough, Ontario
Canada M1K 5G4

International Thomson Publishing Japan
Hirakawa-cho Kyowa Building, 3F
2-2-1 Hirakawa-cho, Chiyoda-ku
Tokyo 102 Japan

International Thomson Publishing Southern Africa
Building 18, Constantia Square
138 Sixteenth Road, P.O. Box 2459
Halfway House, 1685 South Africa

Library of Congress Cataloging-in-Publication Data
The many faces of giftedness : lifting the mask / [edited by]
   Alexinia Young Baldwin and Wilma Vialle.
       p. cm.
   Includes bibliographical references.
   ISBN 0-7668-0006-7
   1. Gifted children—United States. 2. Gifted children—
Australia. 3. Gifted children—Case studies. I. Baldwin,
Alexinia Y. II. Vialle, Wilma.
BF723.G5M36 1999
371.95—dc21   98-10691

stakeholders—government bodies, schools, teachers, and families—to ensure that this occurs.

The governmental bodies responsible for education need to ensure that policy statements are not simply rhetoric but are accompanied by mandates. The policies related to gifted education must reflect the diverse ways in which giftedness may be demonstrated. They must explicitly describe the ways in which giftedness may be masked and provide guidelines for school systems and teachers to employ. Further, if policies are to become more than mere rhetoric, they need to be accompanied by a range of support mechanisms, particularly through the provision of financial resources. For example, in Australia, all states have policies related to the education of gifted students, but there is no policy at the federal level. In addition, the policy recommendations at state level have not been matched by the systematic provision of resources for the professional development of teachers or for providing resourcing special programs for students.

Teacher training institutions have a significant role in the preparation and ongoing professional development of teachers. Gifted education is not the province of a small cadre of teachers but is the responsibility of all teachers. It is essential that all undergraduate training encompass at least some compulsory study of giftedness that includes the broader approaches to giftedness that we have described herein. It remains an intriguing phenomenon that the energy that pertains to other areas of special education is often absent for gifted children. In Australia, for example, all teacher trainees must study special education for at least one fourteen-week semester, but no similar mandate exists for the study of the needs of gifted children. A similar lack of attention to the gifted in undergraduate teacher education programs in the United States can also be found. We would maintain that such minimal training is a fundamental cornerstone on which more appropriate educational programs may be built.

Schools need to develop their own policies on gifted education, in line with the system's policies, but reinterpreted to respond to the specific context in which the school is located. Again, it is essential that the school administrators endeavor to ensure that policies are translated into practice within each classroom and within the school's organization. In the spirit of this book, we emphasize the need for schools to recognize the heterogeneity of gifted students and, therefore, the need to reflect such diversity by developing a range of strategies and programs. We need to move away from the notion of *the* gifted program, singular, to a plurality of diverse offerings to meet the particular needs of the gifted students within the school. We also recommend that a coordinator be appointed to oversee the identification of and programming for gifted students. In larger schools, the establishment of a committee may be necessary.

The identification of giftedness remains a central and controversial issue for schools to address. Intelligence quotient (IQ) testing has been pivotal in the selection procedures for the majority of gifted programs in the past; further, teacher recommendations have often been predicated on IQ-based notions of giftedness. While these approaches have some utility, they continue to disadvantage the students described in this book. Further, narrowly based perceptions of giftedness have resulted in educators not recognizing students' abilities because of their preoccupation with the sensory, physical, or emotional challenges faced by the students. This preoccupation leads to their adopting a deficit approach to the education of those students rather than developing the students' intellectual strengths. Therefore, it is absolutely vital that multifaceted approaches to identification are developed to reflect the diversity to be found in gifted populations and that involve a team of people. Central to such an undertaking is finding ways to improve the observational skills of teachers and encouraging them to probe more deeply into the ways that students reason, rather than focusing on the "correctness" of students' answers. It also needs to be recognized that identification is an ongoing requirement.

Teachers make a difference. They remain the most significant element in the education of our students. It is clear, therefore, that teachers must develop an understanding of diversity that embraces the strengths in difference rather than condemning difference as a deficit to an ill-defined norm. Teachers must be assisted in the development of positive attitudes toward gifted students and the challenges they present in the classroom. It is important for teachers to realize that the existence of separate programs for the gifted does not eradicate the teachers' responsibility to teach for giftedness no matter what class they teach. All teachers must be prepared to adapt their strategies and programs for the gifted students in their classes. Teachers must also be willing to adopt an advocacy role for their gifted students. As the case studies in this book demonstrate, many gifted students have depended on one or two teachers who recognized their abilities despite the masks and advocated for them.

Families, too, need to provide emotional and cognitive support to their gifted children. This may mean that they undertake an advocacy role to ensure that their children's needs are recognized and met. One way in which families may accomplish the broader goal of appropriate education for gifted students is through membership in gifted organizations such as the National Association for Gifted Children (NAGC) in the United States, the Australian Association for the Education of the Gifted and Talented (AAEGT) in Australia, as well as the state and regional organizations and affiliates in both countries.

Difference is not another word for *deficit*. The deficit-approach models for the education of students from special populations have disadvantaged countless individuals at a cost to individuals and society. It is now imperative, as we embrace the new millennium, to cease making the mistakes of the past and to recognize and value the strengths that diversity offers our community. The masks to giftedness must be lifted by educators at all levels if the important goal of ensuring that all children reach their potential is to be realized.

INDEX

Page numbers listed in bold refer to illustrations.

This book is dedicated to the memory of my parents,
Mr. & Mrs. King Young, Sr., and to my daughter, Carlita Rose
Baldwin. It is also dedicated to the African-American students
of the Enrichment class in Birmingham, Alabama, who helped
me lift their masks to reveal their giftedness, and inspired me
to seek answers to the concerns of this book.

ALEXINIA YOUNG BALDWIN

To the friends who continue to stimulate me with their ideas
and support, to good wine, to my family, and
to the children who will make our tomorrows,
I dedicate this book.

WILMA VIALLE

Contents

Foreword

Every now and then a book comes along that adds a new dimension to the genre. This book is such an addition. Issues that have only been touched upon or sprinkled throughout the literature on the gifted and talented have been brought together under one cover for researchers, policy makers, and practitioners who want to investigate important concerns about gifted students who also experience learning disabilities, cultural differences, sensory and physical disabilities, and other challenges that place them at risk in educational settings. The cross-cultural perspective also allows the reader to gain a broader viewpoint about giftedness than ordinarily would be possible from books that focus on concerns within a single nation or culture. This point of convergence on both nontraditional student populations and the ways in which different cultures deal with the concept of giftedness makes for both interesting as well as informative reading.

Although the editors have compiled chapters that delve into new territory on disabilities and culture, they also have selected material that confronts the long-standing issues and controversies that surround the field. The nature/nurture controversy, the conflict between excellence and equity, issues related to identification and programming alternatives, and the always-debated concern about the definition of giftedness are only a few of the "hot topics" around which the various chapters have been constructed. The focus of each chapter is a particular disability or cultural perspective; however, the several writers are in general harmony about the direction they think the field of gifted education should be headed. Thus, a theme emerges that includes moving from a mono to a multidimensional perspective of giftedness; that services to gifted students should be flexible, comprehensive, and inclusive of authentic approaches to instruction; that increased attention should be given to the multiple roles that technology can play in effective education; that multiple criteria are essential in matters related to identification; and that in order to fully understand the true nature of giftedness, we must look behind the masks that hide the abilities of young people who are physically, emotionally, linguistically, or culturally challenged. Some of the chapters also provide a historical perspective ranging from the nineteenth-century contributions of persons such as Galton, Lombroso, and Binet to present-day conceptions of human ability that are reflected in the work of Gardner, Sternberg, Gallagher, Passow, and others. Similarly, overviews of legislative and policy initiatives point out milestones that mark the growth of national support, particularly in Australia and the United States.

One of the features of this book that is especially appealing is the use of case studies to illustrate in a deep and personal way the realness of the various disabilities. In order to develop the instruction support systems and the policy decisions that will foster success in young people whose disabilities place them at risk, it is necessary to get to "know" them beyond generic descriptions and statistical representations. Several of the chapter authors bring us face-to-face with young people who are wearing the masks that hide their true potential. These case studies bring to our attention in a profound way the need for more flexible identification procedures, more effective teacher training, more diversified services, and a greater societal awareness of persons whose potential is hidden behind the disabilities that mask their strengths and uniqueness.

It seems quite clear that at this time there are no simple answers to the wide range of issues and challenges that are brought to our attention in this timely and thought-provoking book. But the issues are brought before us, as promised, by lifting the masks that hide the kinds of disabilities and cultural challenges that cause many gifted students to go unrecognized and underserved. The psychological, educational, and situational contexts that surround the persons who are the subjects of this book are in much clearer focus. The book will surely generate new theories, research, and practical ways of addressing the target population. It is a worthwhile, promising, and very interesting task that deserves the continued attention of the educational and psychological communities.

During the thirty years that I have known and worked with Alexinia Baldwin, she has always sought to address the more complex and elusive tasks that define and extend the parameters of our field. This book is an extension of the pioneering quest that characterizes her work and the work of Wilma Vialle, who has collaborated with her in the development of this book.

Joseph S. Renzulli
The Neag Professor of Gifted Education and Talent Development
The National Research Center on the Gifted and Talented
The University of Connecticut

Preface

This book had its genesis in the research, teaching experiences, and the heart and soul of the first editor, Alexinia Baldwin, and was complemented in thought and scholarship by the second editor, Wilma Vialle. Our summary experiences have shown us that many individuals who possess exceptional intellectual qualities are overlooked due to the masks that hide their abilities. These masks have often been present among individuals of particular cultural or ethnic groups and among those who are sensory or physically challenged, those who are learning disabled and emotionally challenged, and those who have linguistically or politically different backgrounds.

Our experiences as researchers in the area of education of the gifted have shown us that this issue is an international one, and we believe that the cross-cultural perspective of these concerns will open the eyes of a universe of decision makers regarding the need to lift these masks.

This book does not propose to be all-inclusive, and the chapters are organized in the manner in which the authors, who are scholars from Australia and the United States, felt best conveyed their perspectives. We believe that the central tenet of diversity, which is the theme of this book, should be reflected in the ways the authors present their ideas. Therefore, we have not "homogenized" the chapters by insisting that the individual authors present their ideas in identical formats; rather, we have encouraged them to tell their stories in the way that best suits them. Many of the inclusions in the chapters are from personal experiences, whereas others rely heavily upon the data and personal research activities available on the topic. Just as our title indicates, there are many faces to giftedness, and there are many faces to the manner in which each chapter is presented.

The book is organized into five parts with each part representing a particular mask. There are chapters under each part that address some aspect of the particular mask. Each represents an area of challenge and is accompanied by a descriptive mask. Part I, Social and Cultural Challenges, is the Kaleidoscopic Mask; Part II, Learning Disability, is the Mysterious Mask; Part III, Sensory and Physical Challenges, is the Hidden Mask; Part IV, Autism, is the Silent Mask; and Part V, Emotional Disturbance, is the Beguiling Mask.

It is our hope that readers of this text will look at the meaning of gift-edness and its reflection in individuals who fall into the categories of this book and change their attitudes toward, and knowledge of, the possible masks that hide giftedness.

Acknowledgments

There are several persons we would like to recognize for their assistance in completing this book. Ms. Myriam Mickhail of the University of Wollongong, Australia, interpreted each part of this book with an abstract drawing that communicated the message of each part. Our respective university deans—John Paterson, University of Wollongong, Australia, and Charles Case, University of Connecticut, Storrs, Connecticut, USA—allowed us an opportunity to work togeth-er by providing space, technical assistance, time, and encouragement. We are also grateful to Dr. Joseph Renzulli who applauded our efforts and agreed to write the foreword. Last, but not least, our thanks to the authors who responded to our requests and worked hard to help us complete the book and to the following reviewers who gave us critical feedback that helped us make the finished product stronger:

Yvonne Carnellor
University of Wollongong

Abbey Block Cash
State University of New York at
   Albany

Eva Diaz
University of Connecticut

Natalia Gajdamaschko
University of Georgia

Mary Frances Hanline
Florida State University

Mary Henthorne
Western Wisconsin Technical
   College

Pat Kelley
Texas Tech University

Deslea Konza
University of Wollongong

Amy Sue Reilly
Auburn University

Dorothy Sisk
Lamar University–Beaumont

INTRODUCTION
Potential That Is Masked

When will we also teach them who they are?
We should say to them—
You are unique—You are a marvel
In this whole world there is no one like you and
There will never be again.

Pablo Casals

The many faces of giftedness have stimulated much discussion and controversy within the fields of psychology and education. The first questions to be asked are, What is giftedness? Is it inherited or acquired? Is it a rare characteristic in a chosen few or is it present in all human beings? Is it a narrow concept or does it encompass a multiplicity of abilities and skills? Although we know that the definitive answers to these questions will not be finally determined in this text, we feel that our research and years of experience in the fields of education and psychology support our thesis that there are many faces of giftedness (as we define it) that are often masked by physical, social and/or economic challenges. As Willard-Holt (1994) has stated, "recognizing intellectual talent in these children and subsequently developing it can enrich our lives as well as theirs. . . . Gaining a new perspective of giftedness and its many forms of expression will thus help educators to broaden their perspective and seek to develop the talents of more of our children" (p. ix).

The purpose of this text, then, is to explore a number of these challenges or masks using primarily an American (USA) and Australian perspective. In so doing, we hope to reveal the gifted potential that the masks have concealed. Indeed, we would argue that the time is long overdue for these masks to be lifted. It is important, therefore, that readers of this book view the stated situations and recommendations of each part of the book through the prisms of giftedness and intelligence in their historical and contemporary forms, as outlined by the authors. Readers will be able to get a perspective of the various masks as juxtaposed against the historical development of the concept of giftedness in the public schools and communities of the United States of America, Australia, and the totalitarian government of the former Soviet Union.

HISTORICAL PERCEPTIONS OF GIFTEDNESS/INTELLIGENCE

The Ancient Greek philosopher Plato was among the first to comment on the intellectual differences that exist among people. His observations led him to conclude that such differences are the result of inherited differences. While Plato argued for specialized training for the best and brightest in that society—what he described as "men of gold"—on the basis of merit, in practice, the future leaders were members of the wealthy patrician classes. Thus, for Plato and others of that era, the status quo was maintained because an individual's level of intelligence was considered to be an inborn characteristic.

Inevitably, thoughts on the nature of intelligence led to desires to measure the capacity. Early attempts linked physical brain size with intellectual capacity. Thus, the phrenologists of the eighteenth and nineteenth centuries such as Franz Joseph Gall and Johann Spurzheim mapped the functions and capacities of the brain by observing and measuring the bumps on the human cranium. In many respects, the pioneering work of the phrenologists was the forerunner to more recent neurological studies of brain specialization.

Although the term *giftedness* was not found as frequently in earlier literature as it is in contemporary writings, Lombroso and Galton influenced, through their writings, the underlying concept of giftedness that can still be found in the literature today.

Writers such as Lombroso (1891) perpetuated the readily accepted myth that genius and insanity are inextricably linked. Children with intellectual gifts were thus regarded with distrust and often discouraged from developing their talents.

Diametrically opposed to Lombroso was Francis Galton (1869) who studied the tendency of genius to run in families. His publication, *Hereditary Genius*, propounds this viewpoint and uses statistics to provide evidence that intellectual gifts are inherited. In arguing for the nurturing of intellectual gifts, he became an important voice in presenting a more positive view of the gifted in the nineteenth century than that presented by Lombroso. Galton suggested the use of anthropometric tests to measure intelligence. These included, among others, the following: (1) keenness of vision and hearing, (2) dynometric pressure (that is, a measure of force expended by an individual or muscular strength), (3) reaction time, and (4) word association.

Similarly, James McKeen Cattell (1890) devised mental tests that included measures of strength, reaction time, and sensory discrimination. Nevertheless, distrust of the "genius" was still prevalent in the nineteenth century. Typifying highly intelligent children as socially maladjusted is an attitude that has persisted into the twentieth century and no doubt still has its proponents today.

Twentieth-Century Developments
The turn of the century heralded a critical moment in intelligence testing with the work of Alfred Binet and Théophile Simon. Unlike his predecessors, Binet (1908) theorized that children learn from their cultural environment and that their intellectual functioning is determined by familiarity with particular materials in that environment. For Binet, then, intelligence was not an inborn characteristic, and he did not regard his measurements as a method for ranking students. The tests that were included in the Binet-Simon battery attempted to measure superior faculties and included the following: (1) memory, (2) the nature of mental images, (3) imagination, (4) attention, (5) comprehension, (6) suggestibility, (7) aesthetic feelings, (8) moral feelings, (9) muscular strength and will power, and (10) motor skill and perceptual skill in spatial relations.

Much of the controversy surrounding IQ and giftedness during the twentieth century has centered on the assumptions that intelligence is an inherited, unitary, measurable quality. From the middle of this century, theorists have debated the singularity versus plurality of intelligence. In particular, theorists have differed on whether or not there is a g factor in intelligence as proposed by Charles Spearman (1929). The g specifies the abstract reasoning power a person has and is consistent across all domains.

Following Spearman's work, Louis Thurstone (1938) proposed that intelligence was not unitary but multidimensional and comprised seven, relatively independent, capacities or "primary mental abilities." J. P. Guilford (1967) went even further in hypothesizing his "structure-of-intellect" model that included one hundred and fifty separate ability factors.

Since the 1980s, theories of intelligence have multiplied, and although they have different emphases, they highlight a broader conceptualization of the nature of intelligence. Two influential theories have been Gardner's (1983) theory of "multiple intelligences" and the triarchic theory posited by Sternberg (1985). The latter emerges from the information-processing perspective on human learning and contains three subtheories that seek to specify the precise mechanisms and processes involved in intelligence. Gardner's theory also calls for a more pluralistic account of intelligence. He defined intelligence as *"the ability to solve problems, or to create products, that are valued within one or more cultural settings"* (Gardner, 1983, p. x). In a controversial approach to the topic, Gardner has suggested that all individuals possess not one but at least seven relatively discrete intelligences that include linguistic, logical-mathematical, spatial, musical, bodily-kinesthetic, interpersonal, and intrapersonal intelligences.

Although there are numerous differences among Gardner's multiple intelligences theory, Sternberg's triarchic theory, and Guilford's structure-of-intellect model, they all challenge traditional formulations of intelligence as follows:

- Intelligence is not a single or fixed trait.
- Intelligence is "teachable."
- Intelligence is culture-dependent.
- Intelligence involves both internal and external factors. In other words, the individual's inherited intellectual potential is activated, enhanced, or hindered by their interaction with the environment.

Relationship Between Intelligence and Giftedness

The relationship between *giftedness* and *intelligence* has varied throughout the twentieth century. From a position early in the century in which the terms were used to indicate a certain score on an IQ test, we have moved to a position during the latter part of this century when the construct of giftedness has been expanded to encompass fields of endeavor beyond the scope of traditional views of intelligence (see Figure I–1).

Developments in the United States of America

Lewis M. Terman (1926, 1947, 1959) pioneered the field of empirical research into giftedness with his longitudinal studies conducted from

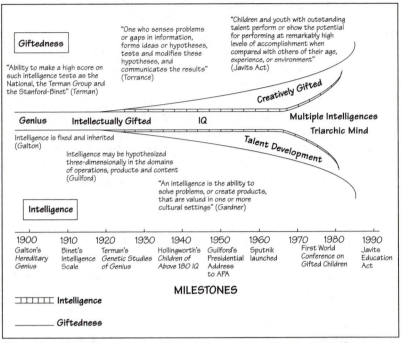

The figure contains the following labels:

Giftedness

"Ability to make a high score on such intelligence tests as the National, the Terman Group and the Stanford-Binet" (Terman)

"One who senses problems or gaps in information, forms ideas or hypotheses, tests and modifies these hypotheses, and communicates the results" (Torrance)

"Children and youth with outstanding talent perform or show the potential for performing at remarkably high levels of accomplishment when compared with others of their age, experience, or environment" (Javits Act)

Creatively Gifted

Genius   Intellectually Gifted   IQ   Multiple Intelligences

Triarchic Mind

Intelligence is fixed and inherited (Galton)

Talent Development

Intelligence may be hypothesized three-dimensionally in the domains of operations, products and content (Guilford)

"An intelligence is the ability to solve problems, or create products, that are valued in one or more cultural settings" (Gardner)

Intelligence

1900	1910	1920	1930	1940	1950	1960	1970	1980	1990
Galton's Hereditary Genius	Binet's Intelligence Scale	Terman's Genetic Studies of Genius		Hollingworth's Children of Above 180 IQ	Guilford's Presidential Address to APA	Sputnik launched	First World Conference on Gifted Children		Javits Education Act

MILESTONES

⊤⊤⊤⊤⊤⊤ Intelligence

———— Giftedness

Figure I-1 The historical relationship between intelligence and giftedness

1925 to 1951. Although some criticism has been leveled at the selection processes determining the sample, it is widely recognized that his findings represent a significant turning point in the attitude toward gifted education on a worldwide basis, but particularly in the United States. His conclusion that gifted children are every bit as well-adjusted socially as their nongifted peers has been supported by a great deal of subsequent research into the topic.

Since Terman's study, education of the gifted has fluctuated according to the perceived needs of the society. An emphasis was placed on "excellence" whenever there was a pressing need for special skills and talents, such as in the period immediately following the second world war. When the crisis abated, other educational needs took precedence. The introduction of universal, comprehensive education brought with it concerns for those disadvantaged by their cultural, socioeconomic conditions or mental capacity. With the egalitarian thrust that developed in Western society, special provision for those already blessed with intellectual gifts was seen as not only unnecessary but also totally undesirable. The concept of equal opportunity for all, a desirable educational aim, was too frequently confused with equal educational provision. At the same time, the belief also developed that in order for children to be socially well-adjusted, they should be promoted through the school system on the basis of age rather than academic attainment. These two beliefs militated strongly against the provision of special programs for the gifted. During this time, also, little thought was given to considering students who were physically, mentally, or socio-economically challenged or culturally diverse, for programs for the gifted.

After a burst of enthusiasm following the Terman studies and the predictable downturn of interest in education of the gifted, there was a renewed interest in gifted education sparked by the Russian success with Sputnik in 1957. Since the USA regarded itself as the most progressive country in the world, there was a concern that the Soviet Union had moved ahead. It was concluded that the reasons for the USA's lack of success rested in its failure to develop the abilities in its most gifted students. The race was on to be first again, and much money was provided for developing programs for the gifted. The fear of being outstripped by the Russians, then, caused Americans to demand emphasis on excellence in education, particularly in the fields of science and mathematics.

The University of Chicago's Experimental School for the Gifted and the Leta Hollingworth's school in New York served as examples, during the twenties and thirties, of what could be done for children who were gifted. Although some minorities were included in programs for the gifted, little attention was given to the active pursuit of locating children from minority groups. The Cleveland Major Works Program was one program that looked at minorities and worked to give African-American students a chance to develop their abilities. Out of these schools came research that helped educators make decisions regarding selection and education of students. States such as New York, California, and Illinois were among the few that had institutions and groups that organized programs for the gifted and had official legislation pertaining to the education of the gifted.

Many centers were funded to develop appropriate curriculum for science and mathematics. With this expenditure of money came objection from some parents and community members who wanted the definition of gifted expanded to enable the inclusion of more students.

Advocates such as James Gallagher, Harry Passow, Dorothy Sisk, Abraham Tannenbaum, William Vasser, and Joseph Renzulli pushed for the development of specialist teachers of the gifted. Universities that had programs for the development of trained teachers and researchers, along with advocate organizations such as The Association of the Gifted (TAG) as a division of the Council for Exceptional Children (CEC), put pressure on the federal government to pass legislation that would provide federal monies for the study and development of programs for the gifted. The Javits Bill of 1972 was the first legislation created for education of the gifted. The Marland report, which supported the Javits Bill, included in it an expansion of the definition of giftedness. The areas defined were creativity, performing arts, and leadership ability. These established a mindset for those who worked to provide programs for the gifted. This mindset would carry through to the nineties. Multidimensional assessment techniques were advocated for all programs; however, in practical terms, there was little change in the conception of giftedness as a high IQ score and high academic achievement. This report became a significant milestone in the USA's subsequent research and policy in gifted education. It also made a marked impact on developments in Britain and Australia. Arising from the landmark Marland report came the Leadership Training Institutes developed by Irving Sato and David Jackson. These training institutes helped states to organize for legislation and the training of specialist teachers.

As Treffinger and Feldhusen (1996) have stated, "a new conceptual framework for the field of gifted education has been emerging from many sources since the mid-1980s" (p. 183). These authors cite the move toward a different paradigm for gifted. This paradigm has been developing out of the lack of defensible constructs for gifted education and the feeling that there is a lack of recognition of those populations of students who are socially, economically, or physically challenged. Children from various cultural groups are also included in this population. The decrease in funding from the federal government and a move toward equity in education (interpreted to mean the same for all) spawned the rhetoric that advocated the retention of gifted students in the regular classroom.

During the early nineties, funding from the federal government again provided research monies for the development of research centers. These centers were designed to complete research along many dimensions of what was referred to as education of the "gifted." Although much work emerged out of these centers and concomitantly funded educational programs, there have still persisted questions of equity of service to all students.

The mid-nineties heralded a diminution of monies to support programs for the gifted. With the swing to the right of the new majority party of the federal government, talk of eliminating various aspects of the Department of Education challenged the two strongest professional organizations—The Association of the Gifted (TAG) and the National Association for Gifted Children (NAGC)—to influence the legislators to maintain proper funding for the gifted. In the midst of this divergence in thinking about giftedness, the paradigm that started in the mid-eighties gained much credibility. The *Roeper Review* published an article by Francoys Gagné (1995) that was entitled "From Giftedness to Talent: A Developmental Model and Its Impact on the Language of the Field." This article was one of many that posited a need for the differentiation between the concepts of giftedness and talentedness. Both refer to human abilities and both refer to and define abilities that are above that of the general population. Gagné has suggested that the differentiation has as its foundation two extreme poles of the developmental process. He cited these as natural abilities and systematically developed abilities. Additionally, a special issue of the *Journal for the Education of the Gifted* featured a critical appraisal of gifted education as seen by several authors. In Gallagher's (1996) summary "Critique of the Critiques" of gifted education featured in the issue, it was proposed that the comments made by the various authors "could be boiled down to several important questions:

- Is there such a thing as giftedness?
- If there is such an entity, can we find students who possess it or them?
- If we can find such children, can we provide them with quality differentiated services?
- Is it morally right or correct that we put such programs or services into action?" (p. 234)

The USA, as the forerunner in the concept of giftedness, must address these questions whether or not a new paradigm is being developed. The World Council for the Gifted and Talented will need to address these questions also, with the cultures that are represented within its membership. Our look at the historical perception of giftedness by the educators and researchers in the USA and Australia addresses one aspect of the questions Gallagher has posed: If there is such an entity, can we find students who possess it, or them? We feel that there is such an entity, whether it is called giftedness or talentedness, that is not readily observed in students who are represented in the topics of this book.

Developments in Australia

Developments in Great Britain, the United States of America (USA), and Australia have largely paralleled each other, although Australia has lagged somewhat behind the other two in the development of policy and implementation of programs.

Secondary schools in Australia were originally conceived to cater for the more academically able students. From 1940 onward, however, a number of policy changes occurred in education that radically altered the composition of students in Australian secondary schools. These changes included raising the minimum leaving age, the abolition of school fees, and the reappraisal of external examinations, all of which contributed to removing the selective intake of schools in favor of the democratic notion of universal schooling (Braggett, 1985).

Between 1943 and 1947, Tasmania led the other states in abolishing the system of grade promotion by virtue of academic attainment in favor of promotion based on age. This dramatic change signaled an important shift in the thinking of the time: that students should be grouped with their social peers was deemed preferable to the alternative of grouping based on ability and achievement. It was inevitable that the next step in educational developments witnessed the emergence of the comprehensive school. Secondary schools were now faced with the challenge of catering for a much wider heterogeneous grouping than at any time in the past, and in the attempt to adjust to these changes, the needs of individuals at each end of the academic scale were largely ignored. Braggett (1985) encapsulates the outcome of this movement, thus: "a degree of mediocrity resulted when average quality was stressed at the expense of intellectual rigor" (p. 298). In the process of adjusting to meet the needs of students with average and below-average ability, there was an often-stated assumption that the more able could "look after themselves."

The 1960s and early 1970s were a time of financial hardship for schools as the effects of the postwar baby boom were felt in an unprecedented growth in school enrollments. At the same time there was a marked increase in retention rates that was unmatched by financial provision for adequate expansion of resources and buildings. Additionally, demand outstripped the supply of trained teachers, and therefore, the number of inadequately trained personnel in schools increased markedly. In this climate of great educational change, it is hardly surprising that the needs of gifted children were pushed further into the background as schools struggled to face the challenges provided by the economic hardship occasioned by the greatly increased secondary school population.

The Australian Labor Government of Whitlam attempted during the mid-seventies to redress the "ills" of preceding years by injecting funds into a wide range of social services including education, and the emphasis in schools shifted to programs to help disadvantaged students. To ensure equal opportunity in the educational sphere for these students, special funds were made available. While the focus remained on raising the attainments of low achievers to the norm, there was a concomitant "holding back" of those with potential to be *high achievers* (a term used to designate giftedness).

To counter this thrust, in the mid-1970s, the voices of some Australian educators (notably the N.S.W. Ministerial Committee into Gifted Education 1975–1997; Professor K. B. Start, Inspector H. P. Waller 1975–1976; Dr J. Eedle; and R. Day) began to question whether the efforts to provide for low achievers had brought about a new disadvantaged group. They believed that gifted and talented children had attained the status of disadvantage because lack of special provision in curriculum was preventing them from developing to their full potential. At the same time there were those who feared a return to selectivity and elitism, and thus strongly resisted any attempts to explore the needs of gifted and talented children.

During this dichotomous era, the World Council for the Gifted and Talented was organized by Henry Collins of England. This organization played a role in heralding the importance of the worldwide need to attend to the needs of the gifted. Australia's representation at the first conference held in 1975 in London subsequently gave impetus to and legitimized the gifted education movement in this country. Most states independently established investigations into the status of gifted education in their schools. In New South Wales, a Ministerial Committee was established to review selective high schools. In 1977 the committee reported "that the talented were possibly the most disadvantaged group in schools for they generally did not receive sufficient stimulation to achieve their full potential" (Braggett, 1985, p. 299). In Victoria, the Gifted Children's Task Force was established after much lobbying from a number of concerned individuals, including H. P. Waller. The continuation of this lobbying eventually prompted the Victorian Director-General of Education, Dr. Shears, to seek the inclusion of the topic of "the education of gifted children" as an agenda item for the 1976 meeting of the Australian Education Council. To meet this request, position statements were sought from each state as a background to future discussions (Braggett, 1985).

Although no formal outcomes emerged from the Australian Education Council, there was nevertheless a heightened awareness and growing acceptance of the notion of specialized provision for gifted children. All states and territories in Australia continued to explore the issues and developed their own philosophical stance. With the exception of Victoria, all states and territories formally released policy statements on gifted education by 1985.

In 1988, a report was tabled by the Senate Select Committee on the Education of Gifted and Talented Children. Among its recommendations, this report called for the issuance of a Commonwealth statement in support of educational provision for gifted students, for teacher training opportunities, and for the establishment of a research center on giftedness. None of these recommendations have been implemented in any systematic fashion, and provisions for gifted students remain at the ad hoc whim of state and territory departments and committed individuals.

The biennial meeting of the World Council for the Gifted and Talented was held in Sydney in 1989 which further legitimized attention to the gifted, and a flurry of activity at the school level resulted. At the state level, however, developments have continued to wax and wane. In New South Wales, for example, there has been a resurgence of selective schools and specialist classes at the same time that a restructuring in the education system has abolished the ministerial committee on gifted education and cut funding to special programs for students, in-service provisions, and research initiatives.

All states currently have policies on the education of gifted students, but, as indicated, rarely are these matched with appropriate funding for in-service workshops for teachers or resources to maintain special programs for gifted children. At the national level, there is still no policy for the education of gifted students, although the Australian Association for the Education of Gifted and Talented is currently engaged in advocating for such a policy at the government level.

CONCLUSIONS

We believe that there exists a hard-to-define quality (known as intelligence and most often equated with giftedness) in all human beings that gives them the ability to process information, acquire skills, and produce products within specific domains at a much higher level than those of the average population. We also believe that these abilities can be found in all ethnic or racial groups and that environment, social mores, and physical and emotional challenges, as well as political restrictions, can influence the display of this ability. The extensive work of Baldwin in the design of processes for locating and developing potential talent among various ethnic and racial minorities is a precursor to the concept that there are many variables that mask the inherent qualities that are equated with giftedness. Similarly, Vialle's work with educationally disadvantaged groups has confirmed the value of a broader perspective on the nature of intelligence as well as giftedness.

Just as Binet's search for assessment strategies for children who were mentally disabled led him to design a protocol for finding children who were highly able mentally, our search for a deeper meaning of giftedness has led us to lift the masks that have hidden potential giftedness in many segments of society. With a clear understanding and recognition of the historical and contemporary permutations of intelligence and giftedness, we wish to direct our readers to a broader perception of these two areas of human interaction. Our focus is to lift the masks that have hidden the exceptional abilities of particular groups in our society: those with learning disabilities, sensory impairments (blind, deaf), cerebral palsy, autism, and/or emotional disturbance; those who are regarded as culturally different (Australian indigenous, socioeconomically disadvantaged, and limited facility of dominant English language); and those of a totalitarian society.

Our work is based on the assumption that:

- Giftedness can be expressed through a variety of behaviors.

- Intelligence is a broad concept that goes beyond language and logic to encompass a wide range of human abilities.

- Carefully planned subjective assessment techniques can—and should—be used effectively along with objective measures of giftedness.

- All populations, including those who are physically, economically, [politically], or emotionally challenged, have gifted children who exhibit behaviors that are indicative of giftedness (Baldwin, 1984, p. 3).

REFERENCES

Baldwin, A. Y. (1984). *Baldwin identification matrix for the identification of gifted and talented.* New York: Trillium Press.

Binet, A. (1908). Le developpement de l'intelligence chez les enfants. *L'Annee Psychologique.*

Braggett, E. J. (1985). *Education of gifted and talented children: Australian Provision.* Canberra, Australia: Commonwealth Schools Commission.

Burks, B. S., Jensen, D. W., & Terman, L. M. (1930). *Genetic studies of genius: Vol. III. The promise of youth.* Stanford, CA: Stanford University Press.

Cattell, J. M. (1890). Mental tests and measurements. *Mind(15),* 373–381.

Cox, C. (1926). *Genetic studies of genius: Vol. II. The early mental traits of three hundred geniuses.* Stanford, CA: Stanford University Press.

Gagné, F. (1995). From giftedness to talent: A developmental model and its impact on the language of the field. *Roeper Review, 18*(2), 103–111.

Gallagher, J. (1996). A critique of critiques of gifted education. *Journal for the Education of the Gifted, 19*(2), 234–249.

Galton, F. (1869). *Hereditary genius.* New York: D. Appleton.

Gardner, H. (1983). *Frames of mind.* New York: Basic Books.

Guilford, J. P. (1967). *The nature of human intelligence.* New York: McGraw-Hill.

Lombroso, C. (1891). *The man of genius.* New York: Carland. (English translation, 1984)

Spearman, C. (1929). *The abilities of man.* New York: Macmillan.

Sternberg, R. J. (1985). *Beyond I.Q.* New York: Cambridge University Press.

Terman, L. M. (Ed.). (1926). *Genetic studies of genius: Vol. I. Mental and physical traits of a thousand gifted children* (2nd ed.). Stanford, CA: Stanford University Press.

Terman, L. M., & Oden, M. H. (1947). *Genetic studies of genius: Vol. IV. The gifted child grows up.* Stanford, CA: Stanford University Press.

Terman, L. M., & Oden, M. H. (1959). *Genetic studies of genius: Vol. V. The gifted group at mid-life.* Stanford, CA: Stanford University Press.

Thurstone, L. L. (1938). *Primary mental abilities.* Chicago: University of Chicago Press.

Treffinger, D., & Felhusen, J. (1996). Talent recognition and development: Successor to Gifted Education. *Journal for Education of the Gifted, 19*(2), 181–193.

Vialle, W. (1991). *Tuesday's children: A study of five children using multiple intelligences theory as a framework.* Unpublished doctoral dissertation, University of South Florida.

Vialle, W., & Perry, J. (1995). *Nurturing multiple intelligences in the Australian classroom.* Melbourne, Australia: Hawker Brownlow Education.

Willard-Holt, C. (1994). *Recognizing talent: Cross-case study of two high potential students with cerebral palsy. (CRS94308).* Storrs, CT: National Research Center on the Gifted and Talented.

Social and Cultural Challenges: The Kaleidoscopic Mask

PART 1

CHAPTER

1

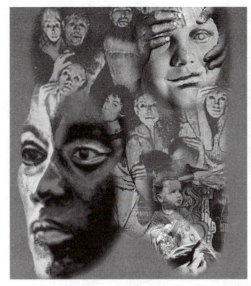

AFRICAN-AMERICANS: USA

For too many years, differences in the definition of what giftedness meant were centered around four basic concepts that all personnel in this field were expected to keep in mind. Those concepts were that some gifted students were more conforming, some were less conforming, some were concerned with ideas, and some more concerned with things and people. Within these concepts it was said that one could find the gifted social leader, the high-achieving and studious student, the rebel, and the creative intellectual. In spite of the appearance of an extended definition of giftedness, the selection of these students depended upon the score that would be made on the IQ test. However, from more recent studies and research by Sternberg (1985), Gardner (1983), and others, it has become quite clear that a large segment of the population (especially African-Americans) is still being overlooked because the IQ criteria for giftedness has failed to validate their giftedness or their potential for giftedness. We are now aware through this research that giftedness has many faces and can be represented in ways other than a single IQ score.

Whereas other chapters in this Part 1 will discuss the indigenous culture of Australia, and the challenged non–English speaking students of Australia and America, this chapter will focus on one minority, the African-American who has been socially and economically disadvantaged.

In March 1989, the United States Department of Education Office of Planning, Budget and Evaluation issued a report titled *No Gift Wasted: Effective Strategies for Educating Highly Able, Disadvantaged Students in Mathematics and Science*. At the time of this document's publication, minority students were underrepresented in programs designed to serve gifted and talented students. Although at that time minorities made up thirty percent of public school enrollment, they represented less than twenty percent of the gifted and talented programs. Among these students only four percent performed at the ninety-fifth percentile or above on standardized tests. These and other statistics prompted the funding of a project to identify successful efforts by districts and schools to serve highly able, economically disadvantaged students, and to foster their achievement in mathematics and science. Techniques found at the various sites indicated that processes used to uncover or "unmask" the ability of these students included: (1) a preselection process such as the activity-based assessment, (2) encouragement of students to develop and display their skills and abilities over an extended period of time in order to increase their prospects for admission into a gifted and talented program, and (3) the use of multiple criteria rather than a single measure. The instruction and support system for these students provided an environment that fostered success.

The efforts of personnel and researchers in the field of education of the gifted have continued to be presented with a dilemma when faced with questions regarding the lack of African-Americans and other minorities in programs for the gifted. The process for looking philosophically and historically at the situation in order to make a judgement has stimulated many writers to posit certain beliefs regarding this issue. (Note: The use of *African-American, Black,* and *Negro* will be used in the context of the quotes. Through the years, the correct nomenclature has changed to more appropriately designate the origin or nature of the group.)

Cook and Baldwin (1979) wrote that

> [w]hile there is a dearth of research and writing on the gifted of the black population, black Americans have historically asserted that there are among them those whose talents and gifts should be identified and nurtured. Foremost among twentieth century advocates of this persuasion was W. E. B. DuBois. Although he articulated an educational philosophy proposing that all blacks should receive an education that would permit them to make their daily bread at an honest skilled job, DuBois' theory of the "Talented Tenth" more accurately became the heart of his philosophy. This

theory in large measure establishes him as father of gifted education for blacks. (p. 388)

The historical background of the African-American in America with its
societal and often economic impact has placed these students in an
unequal position of recognition within the programs for the gifted.
Historical factors and continuing research on identification and education of the gifted play an important role in understanding the rationale
for a concerted effort to lift the masks that currently obscure the existence of giftedness among this population of students. For instance, the
nineteenth-century African-American landscape painter Robert Scot
Duncanson is just being recognized as a great artist and honored by the
Smithsonian's National Museum of American Art. Other great inven-
tors, scientists, and performing and graphic artists who went unrecognized as students who were gifted are just too numerous to list here.

PERSPECTIVES ON THE ROLE OF CULTURE

In an attempt to understand differences, there have been many efforts
to look at the effects of culture, societal attitudes, and language on the
lack of inclusion of African-Americans in programs for the gifted. This
effort by Ogbu (1992) has included research around the world focusing
particularly on groups such as the aborigines of Australia, and
language-different students such as those included in this publication.

Ogbu describes two different types of minority. His descriptions
help readers and researchers to get another perspective on the effects
each of these categories might have on the within-group attitudes
about programs for the gifted. He posits that these groups are *voluntary*
and *involuntary*. He explains that if you came to the United States voluntarily, you would see yourself as part of the American dream and
therefore would attempt to do all of the things necessary to become
successful in this societal milieu. However, if your journey here was
involuntary, or you had your native land taken away from you, there
would be a tendency for you to resist the values of the mainstream culture. Ogbu goes on to say that success of the minority student depends
largely upon the attitude of the dominant society.

[M]ere cultural and language differences cannot account for the
relative school failure of some minorities and the school success
of others. Minority status involve[s] complex realities that affect
the relationship between the culture and language of the minority and those of the dominant groups and thereby influences the
school adjustment and learning of the minority. (p. 362)

Perhaps the resistance among some African-American students to
be identified as gifted is because those characteristics determined to
be indications of giftedness are deemed to be the important ones of

the dominant society—the group that represents those responsible for the involuntary migration to this country. Therefore, as descendants of this involuntary group, there perhaps remains a resistance to accept this academic classification.

Fordham (Fordham & Ogbu, 1986) has expressed this concern also by suggesting that academic excellence is often considered as identifying too strongly with beliefs and values of the dominant society. This often causes conflict within the student because there is a desire not to become raceless. Although Fordham indicates that her research has shown that Black students often feel that success means giving up their identities and becoming a part of the indigenous culture, I wonder whether her message is that adolescents should not attempt to achieve in this culture while maintaining the roots of their own culture.

Banks (1989) has suggested that the culture of the United States overlaps many cultures without diluting the role each plays in the development of the individual. He explains that

> [a] nation as culturally diverse as the United States consists of a common-overarching culture, as well as a series of microcultures. These microcultures share most of the core values of the nation-state, but these values are often mediated by the various microcultures and are interpreted differently within them. . . . Afro-Americans and Hispanic Americans who have not experienced high levels of cultural assimilation into the mainstream culture are much more group-oriented than are mainstream Americans. These students experience problems in the highly individualistic learning environment of the school. (p. 10)

Ogbu's research has focused attention on the societal variables that foster "masks" among African-American students. These masks are due to a lack of understanding regarding giftedness and intelligence. This lack of understanding is quite evident in writings by Herrnstein and Murray (1994) in their book *The Bell Curve: Intelligence and Class Structure in American Life*. They have included in their list of six conclusions regarding intelligence, two that have caused many researchers to question these conclusions: "5. Properly administered IQ tests are not demonstrably biased against social, economic, ethnic, or racial groups; and 6. Cognitive ability is substantially heritable, apparently no less than 40 percent and no more than 80 percent" (pp. 22–23).

The conclusions of these two authors are based on culture and race differences. They have used statistical data in an attempt to draw a relationship between these data and changes in American society along with concomitant predictions for the future. In an attempt to bolster their conclusions, these authors have addressed each of the arguments used to explain why there is a difference in the scores of blacks and whites by focusing on the fallacies in each of the arguments. One of those arguments addressed is "motivation to try." They have recounted the arguments as stated below and have pointed out the weaknesses as they see them.

> Suppose that the nature of cultural bias does not lie in predictive validity or in the content of the items but in what might be called "test willingness." A typical black youngster, it is hypothesized, comes to such tests with a mindset different from the white subject's. He is less attuned to testing situations (from one point of view), or less inclined to put up with such nonsense (from another). Perhaps he just doesn't give a damn, since he has no hopes of going to college or otherwise benefiting from a good test score. Perhaps he figures that the test is biased against him anyway, so what's the point. Perhaps he consciously refuses to put out his best effort because of the peer pressures against "acting white" in some inner-city schools. [Their conclusion follows.]
> The studies that have attempted to measure motivation in such situations have generally found that blacks are at least as motivated as whites. (pp. 282–283)

This conclusion highlights the lack of understanding of the impact society can have on the individual child.

In Hunsaker's (1995) discussion of the gifted metaphor, he indicated that the distribution of gifts, according to his historical presentation of the role culture plays in designating giftedness, is dependent upon the society's cultural connection with this phenomenon. He says that:

> This is a problem that we ourselves have not dealt with adequately. We continue to be burdened with a political struggle between excellence and equity. While progress has been made, gifted programs continue to be filled with students from middle-class, and mainstreamed backgrounds. The implication is clear that we must conceive of giftedness in a more global, inclusive way, focusing perhaps more on performance than on status indicators such as IQ test scores. (p. 264)

Kitano (1991) has written, "Ideally, issues of effective identification, instruction, and curriculum practices for culturally diverse gifted students would be resolved by reference to the research literature" (p. 5). However, little of this research exists. Much of what exists argues that certain behaviors of groups, particularly African-Americans, are predictive of school failure. Very little attention has been paid to within-group differences, and consequently *all* the generalizations by Herrnstein and Murray are placed on all members of this group. New models must be devised. Kitano has suggested that assimilation and cultural pluralism constitute two philosophical views affecting educational practices for culturally diverse gifted students. Table 1–1 summarizes these views and subsequent expectations.

Table 1–1 Summary of assimilationist and pluralist perspectives

	Assimilationist	*Pluralist*
Source of underachievement	within child based on culture and experience; need for intervention aimed at deficits	within system or within interactions between system and child; need for empowerment of child
Purpose of Schooling	transmission of mainstream values toward maintenance of core culture	understanding many cultural perspectives toward creation of a society that values diversity
Identification	standardized assessment	alternative assessment, nonbiased assessment, multiple measure assessment
Instructional Processes	focus on individual achievement; helping child fit the school	focus on democratic structures; changing school to fit the child
Curriculum	problem solving and critical thinking applies to mainstream culture and history	problem solving and critical thinking applies to culture and history of many groups; building skills to transform society

Note. From "A Multicultural Educational Perspective on Serving the Culturally Diverse Gifted," by M. K. Kitano, 1991, *Journal for the Education of the Gifted, 15*(1), p. 15. Reprinted by permission of Dr. Lawrence Coleman.

IDENTIFICATION AND PLACEMENT CONCERNS

Identification and placement continue to be concerns of educators. Federal funding criteria that require the inclusion of minorities have brought these concerns to the attention of many researchers. There have been many suggestions regarding the "best" instrument to use; however, much depends upon the attitudes of those who are making the placement decisions and the way giftedness is defined. Many school districts define giftedness one way, but the criteria for placement and the instruments used for selection are not congruent with the definition. A review of research and practice reveals the concern in this area.

The Baldwin Identification Matrix (1984) is one of the many tools for helping administrators to select minority students. It is designed to include all of the variables of the definitions as seen in Figure 1–1. The assumptions for the definitions and matrix design (see Figure 1–2) are:

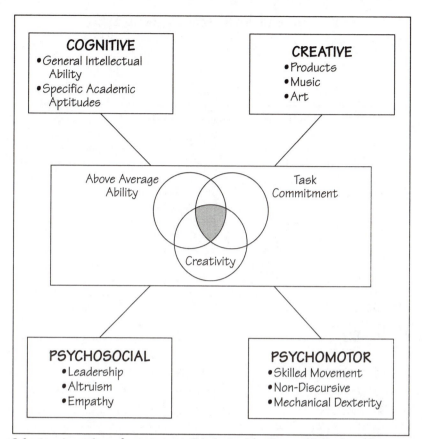

Subcategories under each area are not all-inclusive. The diagram above shows the areas under which the various aspects of human response to stimuli can be grouped. The three-ring illustration shows that the potential or presence of these qualities should be exhibited in the broad area or any of its subcategories, when identifying the child who is gifted. The three-ring circle is reprinted from Renzulli (1979) of the National/State Leadership Training Institute on The Gifted and Talented. Reprinted by permission.

Figure 1–1 Areas of giftedness

Giftedness expressed in one dimension is just as important as giftedness expressed in another.

Giftedness can be expressed through a variety of behaviors.

Giftedness in any area can be a clue to the presence of potential giftedness in another area, or a catalyst for the development of giftedness in another area.

A total ability profile is crucial in the educational planning for the gifted child.

Carefully planned subjective assessment techniques can be used effectively with objective assessment techniques.

BALDWIN IDENTIFICATION MATRIX 2

STUDENT _____ BIRTHDATE _____ AGE _____ SEX___ GRADE ___ DATE_____

Area	Assessment Items	Mode of Score	Data Card Info	RATINGS					B-NA	No. of Items	Raw Score	Area Score (RS + N)
				5	4	3	2	1				
COGNITIVE	1.1 General IQ											
	1.2											
	1.3											
	1.4											
	1.5											
1.	TOTAL COGNITIVE											
PSYCHOSOCIAL	2.1											
	2.2											
	2.3											
	2.4											
	2.5											
2.	TOTAL PSYCHOSOCIAL											
CREATIVE/ PRODUCTS	3.1											
	3.2											
	3.3											
	3.4											
	3.5											
3.	TOTAL CREATIVE PRODUCTS											
PSYCHOMOTOR	4.1											
	4.2											
	4.3											
	4.4											
	4.5											
4.	TOTAL PSYCHOMOTOR											
MOTIVATION	5.1											
	5.2											
	5.3											
	5.4											
	5.5											
5.	TOTAL MOTIVATION											
CREATIVE PROBLEM-SOLVING	6.1											
	6.2											
	6.3											
	6.4											
	6.5											
6.	TOTAL CREATIVE PROBLEM-SOLVING											
	MATRIX TOTALS	Maximum Points For This Matrix										
		STUDENT TOTALS										

Figure 1–2 The Baldwin Identification Matrix
Reprinted by permission of Royal Fireworks Publishing Co., Ltd. of Unionville, NY, from whom the complete *Matrix* is available.

All populations have gifted children who exhibit behaviors that are indicative of giftedness.

Behaviors classified as gifted should be above and beyond the average of a broad spectrum of individuals. (Baldwin, 1984, p. 3)

Cornell, Delcourt, Goldberg, and Bland (1995) said in summarizing their research that

findings of this study pose a challenge to the process of identifying minority-group students for gifted programs. Achievement testing with the Iowa Test of Basic Skills indicated consistent minority group differences among students placed in gifted programs. For example, even though gifted-program students of African-American background scored at or above grade level, white 2nd and 3rd grade students scored approximately 5–6 months higher than African-American students in reading comprehension, and just over 1 year higher in science. (p. 201)

There are many defensible criteria for identifying high-ability students, but no single agreed-upon definition or universal standard. Although problematic for researchers who wish to obtain a homogenous sample of subjects, this is an unavoidable state of affairs given that children can have exceptional abilities in many different areas and that school programs have varied educational standards and goals. (p. 205)

These authors also highlighted other research that concluded that self-concept for white students is quite different from what produces self-concept in African-American students. Academic ability is important for white students, and other cultural variables are important for African-American students as a whole.

Borland and Wright (1994) discussed, in their study, a three-stage screening and identification procedure that identifies Phase I as the screening stage, Phase II as the diagnostic assessment stage, and Phase III as the case study and placement decisions stage. This identification process was for a study titled *Project Synergy*. It was developed by the Department of Special Education and the Leta Hollingworth Center of Teachers College, Columbia University. In phases one and two of the study, standardized, nontraditional assessment, teacher nominations, and parent input were used as indicators of giftedness. Although the project was proven to have validity in that economically disadvantaged students were selected, the researchers described the project as extremely time- and labor-intensive, making its use difficult for school districts.

Mills and Tissot (1995) used the Raven Advanced Progressive Matrices (APM) along with the School and College Ability Test (SCAT) in an effort to clarify the use of the Raven test to help locate minority students with potential.

Differences among ethnic groups were found on the APM, a finding that is consistent with Robinson et al. (1990). It did, however, identify a significantly greater percentage of minority students, many of whom were low-income and low achieving students, than the more traditional measure (SCAT). . . . Why did the APM identify more minority students than the SCAT? One reason may be the different degree of verbal skills necessary to do well on each of the tests. For example, the APM, a nonverbal test, did reasonably well in identifying high potential in children with limited English proficiency. . . . The SCAT, [however,] because of its highly verbal nature . . . was inappropriate for this group. . . . The relationship between the tests and school achievement may, therefore, be a key indicator in equitable identification for both African-American and Hispanic students . . . poor schooling or gaps in their education [were] affect[ing] students' performance on the SCAT. Problems exist regarding the placement of students into programs. (p. 215)

Excelling on the APM, however, does not say that these students are ready for a program that includes high levels of verbal and mathematics skills. Herein lies the placement dilemma and continuing educational concern.

In research by Baldwin & Start (1987) on reaction time, the Button Box (Jensen et al. 1981) was used along with the Raven's Standard Progressive Matrices (SPM). One purpose was to determine whether there was any relationship between scores received by children selected or not selected for the advanced classes (gifted) and the SPM. A second purpose was to determine whether there was any correlation between the means of the SPM scores and the speed of processing information as judged by Response Time/Movement Time (RT/MT). The third question was whether there was any correlation between the selected IQ and achievement test scores (commonly used in this school district) and the SPM.

The subjects of this study were inner city students of a ninety-nine percent African-American and Hispanic school population. Underlying these three purposes was an effort on the researchers' part, to see if the response time process could be used to identify students who were underachieving or not showing their abilities on the usual IQ tests. Another objective was to see if additional data could be secured regarding the inherent problems associated with IQ tests in properly assessing the innate abilities of students from culturally different backgrounds and poor socioeconomic conditions.

Five of the fifty students of this study scored within the eighty to ninety-nine percentile range on the SPM. Two of these students had not been included in the existing classes for the gifted. Both had high SPM scores and average RT/MT scores but low Otis IQ and CAT V&Q scores. It was also found that the SPM tapped skills that were not tapped in the other tests used in the study. The Button Box items were found to explain approximately nineteen percent of the variance of the SPM scores. Whereas one could not, from this study, suggest the use of the Button Box for identification, it can be suggested that the SPM and a combination of other assessment strategies should be used to carefully document the ability of students. This follows the original recommendation of the Baldwin Matrix design.

From the data of the foregoing studies, which represent only a sample of continuing research in this area, it is evident that: (1) successful identification of the gifted among African-Americans cannot be accomplished effectively by the use of one measure (the IQ test); (2) a total profile of abilities must be collected in order to ascertain the strengths and weaknesses; (3) a program for parents is a must in order to foster understanding of the concept of giftedness; (4) nonverbal instruments such as the Raven's (APM and SPM) are beneficial when used with other standardized measures; (5) a positive attitude of administrators and teachers is important in the attempt to locate gifted students of this group; (6) within-group differences defy group generalizations of innate abilities; and (7) to err on inclusion is better than to err on exclusion.

CASE STUDY

As indicated from the preceding discussion, the key to identifying giftedness is based on the following "A" words as suggested by Frasier (1993): ATTITUDES regarding ability to achieve; screening procedures that limit ACCESS, focusing on the IQ as the "sine qua non" in the ASSESSMENT process; and emphasizing curriculum ACCOMMODATIONS rather than curriculum ADAPTATIONS. Lifting the KALEIDOSCOPIC MASK involves a combination of societal and educational awareness of the depth of understanding necessary for changes to be made.

The masks for several black students in a southern town were lifted when an experiment in the design of a gifted program was instituted by the Board of Education of this school district. The initial achievement and IQ scores of these students ranged from 100 to 180 with the median score for the group being 118. Several of these students, when selected, were operating on grade level (grade 4), but some were seriously underachieving, while only a few were operating above grade level. The usual IQ cutoff for admission to gifted programs was 130, and only three of these students would have been included if there had not been an advocate for their inclusion. After working with the students in a stimulating environment, the students blossomed into achievers who would defy the predictions made by the authors of The Bell Curve. If, however, these students had not experienced the challenge that was offered them, they could have possibly been placed at the lowest level of education or professional success. In fact, one student who met the author of this chapter after reaching adulthood indicated that he had become fed up with a school that did not challenge him with materials, ideas, and resources to which he could relate. He had planned to quit school as soon as possible and join a gang. His inclusion in the class for the gifted challenged his mind. He is now an attorney, having completed his degree from Princeton and Howard universities. Additional information on these students can be found in Baldwin (1977).

The next case study reflects the confusion within a gifted child's mind about the perceptions he has received through the media and access to literature and family experiences. It also addresses the resistance factor among African-American students as expressed by Fordham (1988). It points out how early environmental factors set the stage for the uncertainty about the role of one's own culture versus those things considered the purview of the dominant culture. Although this story is recorded as an event of the early seventies, the events of the nineties unfortunately still reflect this story's message as can be experienced throughout the United States. It is a story titled *The World Through Mark's Eyes*, as told by Cynthia N. Shepard (1972).

I would like you to know my son Mark, who is now five years old. Although he has not yet attended kindergarten, he can both read and write, and can accurately identify colors and forms with an acuity beyond his years. He collects American flags, and pictures and ceramics of our national emblem, the eagle. He learned from somewhere on his own initiative the Pledge of Allegiance, which he recites with deep fervor. He only asked me the definitions of those difficult words: indivisible, liberty, justice. My precious, precocious Mark is very proud of his white, Anglo-Saxon heritage. But, he's black: a beautifully carved and polished piece of black American earth.

You may debate with me whether I should have taught him from birth that he is black. Instead, I invite you to see the world through Mark's eyes. Mark learned to read when he was three years old—books based on the white American style of life with pictures of blond, blue-eyed suburbia, with decent interspersing of browns and brunets—but no blacks. He watched the "educational" newsreels on television, which for him reinforced the rightness of whiteness. The man in the white hat—beating the black man with a billy club and then kicking him into insensibility—was the good guy. He was the protector of our individual rights. The books said so. Black is the night which Mark fears, vanquished by the white of day. White is the knight on the white horse charging the black stains of daily living, and they all vanish. Black is unwanted, black is weak and easily defeated; black is bad. I took Mark [to the] South with me and placed him in an all-black nursery school during the day. The first evening, when I brought him home, he was in tears, writhing and retching in painful confusion. "Why did you make me go to school with all those Negroes?" Then, just like NOW, I dig! Intellectuality had blocked my insight, creating of me a blind broad and of my black son a white racist. In his innocence—or highest sophistry, you see—he had intuitively perceived race not as color, but as an attitude that he did not exemplify. My arguments to the contrary were completely hushed by his own words: "You said I could be anything I choose, and I choose to be white, I am white." I returned North and searched both public and university libraries for literature with both pictures and narrative with which he might relate. *Little Black Sambo?* Oh no, dear God! Where are the black men of history, the Nat Turners, the Veseys, the Prossers? The uncompromising, unprecedented, unheralded warriors for true democracy? I found a book about John Henry, with all the usual legendary verbiage. But it had pictures—pictures of John Henry as a big black and beautiful baby; pictures of a handsome, adventurous black youth; and then a picture of a dynamic, virile, muscle-bound black man. John Henry, the steel-driving man: a beautiful portrayal of black maleness, bared to the waist, swinging that hammer with all his might. It is with *that* picture that my son finally identified: an uncompromising image of black masculinity. That's what it's all about, baby. I doubled my search for books that pictured black and white children running and laughing together, while black and white mothers shopped and lunched together, while black and white fathers worked and played together. I found a few. Mark had no difficulty identifying me in the pictures, but only recently could he find himself. Eventually, I overheard him speak of himself as a little brown boy, and I rejoiced—deeply, I say—that he was finding his way out. Now, I have brought him East and have enrolled him in a kindergarten where all the other children are white. But I have not yet been able to send him. What can be done to save my child from a plunge into utter confusion? What can be done to help my little black boy? What can the world of education do to alleviate his pain—and mine? Must he grow like Topsy: confused, angry, alienated, lighting chaotic fires from the burning bitterness within? By America's guilt ridden permissiveness, will he be ignored to become a black-helmeted, black-booted, black-bigoted replica of the swastika? Will my son see the necessity of asserting his blackness, his maleness, militantly and insensitively, riding roughshod over all who might in any manner oppose? Or, can the world of education, with all its demonstrated expertise, utilize the precociousness of my little black boy for the building of a better world for all people? How? When? **NOW** is the answer. (pp. 1–3)

This story highlights two important issues that must be faced in ensuring the inclusion of African-Americans in programs for the gifted. First, societal and educational resources and strategies must be inclusive in presentations to the general populations, and to students in particular. Secondly, bitterness about this lack of inclusion can undermine attempts to help students bridge the gap between maintaining cultural ties while developing skills and understandings that are appropriate for ability levels. This oversight by society and education has laid the foundation for some of the most vocal opposition to programs for the gifted by minority parents.

Curriculum Ideas and Teaching Strategies

Regardless of the identification strategies that are used, there is a need for curriculum principles that allow for differentiation as well as inclusion of historical and contemporary cultural content for *all* of the students. This concern is necessary for African-American students but is just as necessary for students of other ethnic and cultural backgrounds. Cultural inclusions provide opportunities for making connections with other cultures while making connections with ways in which the mind perceives its environment and assimilates knowledge. Each healthy human brain, irrespective of a person's age, sex, nationality, or cultural background, comes equipped with a set of exceptional features:

> the ability to detect patterns and to make approximations, phenomenal capacity for various types of memory, the ability to self-correct and learn from experience by way of analysis of external data and self-reflection, and an inexhaustible capacity to create. (Caine & Caine, 1991)

The learner is constantly searching for ways to connect on many levels; therefore, those who plan curriculum will need to plan experiences from which students can extract learning. As educators, we have joined the conglomerates who have thinking locked in. It prescribes inclusion of certain elements of thought and exclusion of others. As we become immersed in the plans and promises of the twenty-first century, a break from those conglomerates will require a concerted effort to provide the mechanism for opening the mind to new trajectories. These trajectories will of necessity involve the inclusion of contemporary and historical artifacts, and philosophies of different cultures. As Pritzkau (1970) stated, "the child pursues meanings, he puts them into relationships consistent with his [or her] view of things" (p. 21). It is therefore important that those meanings derive from content or experiences which broaden that view.

This author proposes that there are three important areas within which teachers and curriculum developers should facilitate these experiences. These areas are (1) Sensitivity Enhancement where all students begin to understand and appreciate the loneliness, pain disaffection, or isolation felt by those who might be different from the mainstreamed group; (2) Information Processing where oral and written dialogues and events are abundant for students to view knowledge and derive meanings; and (3) Concept Development where students manipulate various concepts within and across many disciplines and cultural content. Figure 1–3 gives a diagrammatic illustration of the infusion process that is described in the following section.

Infusion Process

Propositions. The curriculum design should begin with a set of propositions or beliefs, and from these beliefs, a set of goals should be

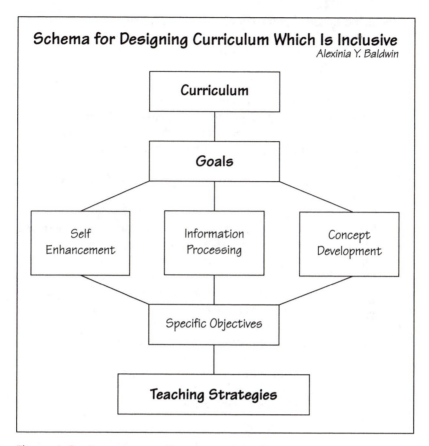

Figure 1–3 Diagrammatic illustration of the infusion process

generated. With a knowledge of the goals that have been set and the models through which these goals can be met, the teacher should design specific objectives that can be evaluated later.

There are many contextual factors affecting curriculum; therefore, a theory of curriculum that is responsive to the society and the complex changes in that society cannot be built around a singular concept. We can, then, define theory as a "set of propositions derived from data and creative thinking from which constructs are formed to describe interactions among variables and to generate hypotheses. Theory describes, explains, goes beyond the data; it predicts and leads to new knowledge" (Unruh & Unruh, p. 123). A proposition represents one's belief statement regarding the interaction of variables; it is a statement proposing something for development, testing, and verification. Propositions should include at least two variables and should formulate the theory to which one subscribes.

Inclusion means that the changes in attitudes come from the teacher who sees beyond the usual. An example of a reasonable set of propositions with inclusions in mind is as follows:

1. An expanded view of culture means that culture goes far beyond the textbook. It can include a rich environment of ideas, experience, beliefs, traditions, customs, institutions, sciences, arts, technologies, humanities, and commonsense ways of doing things that are part of the shared life of people.
2. Freedom to pursue ideas and concepts within the parameters of the environment is a basic right to be honored.
3. Good teaching promotes the development of a dynamic learning environment which leads to ongoing, lifelong learning.
4. The development of a positive concept for children of color unlocks potential ability heretofore sublimated.
5. Historical and contemporary events that recognize the contributions of a wide range of people broaden the scope of knowledge with which students can become involved.
6. Concept development that is enriched with a wide range of data from different cultural and ethnic experiences creates a learning environment where students can become more creative producers and effective consumers of information.
7. Insight into the world and environment of other cultures develops a wider sensitivity to those with whom students must interact.

Goals. From these propositions, a set of goals is derived. These goals represent the intent of the curriculum. They also help the teacher design the approach to be taken. Examples of such goals are as follows:

1. To help students of all ethnic groups become aware of hidden misconceptions about each group
2. To help students of all ethnic groups understand the bravery, the strength of character, and cleverness of various cultures, in spite of negative circumstances
3. To develop the self-concept of students of color through the development of trust and respect from students in all ethnic groups
4. To increase the knowledge of all students regarding the contributions of all ethnic groups
5. To provide for gifted students of color, an opportunity to experience differentiated curriculum experiences that draw upon their cultures
6. To guide students toward an understanding and respect of intercultural and intracultural traditions

Specific Objectives. The next steps in the process of designing appropriate pedagogical approaches include the design of specific objectives that are related to the content and the goals that have been designed. These objectives, which draw upon the three models mentioned earlier, represent only a sample of the parameters within which a teacher can work. The activities involved can be generated from students and teachers. Parents can also become a part of this framework of activity.

1. Students will be able to analyze and express inconsistencies in stereotypical behavior.
2. Students will be able to recognize and discuss the contributions of contemporary and modern achievers of various ethnic groups.
3. Students will be able to develop an appreciation of the interdependence for all ethnic groups.
4. Students will be able to acquire the concept of cause and effect through the analysis of events in history.

Sample Activities for Developing Inclusion Curriculum

Self-Enhancement Model—Role playing, game strategies, unfinished stories, debates

Information-Processing Model—Library research for original documents, local historians, field trips to historical landmarks, role assumption (historian or other significant personality in history)

Concept-Development Model—Use of poetry from various cultures to teach form or other concepts, rhetoric analysis, sociopolitical parallels; language structures, graphic and performing arts of the world, concept of family life, social concepts

SUMMARY

There are roles to be played by many in lifting the masks that inhibit the recognition of exceptional ability among African-Americans. The community can encourage academic striving and encourage a separation of the need to succeed academically from the need to preserve an ethnic reality. Teachers of all races play an important role by presenting an attitude of understanding, and acceptance of the potential quality of the minority student.

Resources such as the *Handbook of Research on Multicultural Education* (Banks & Banks, 1995), include extensive writings on the need to use new paradigms for the development of educational experiences that will help all students, with special emphasis on the African-American student, develop a broadened and comprehensive education. During the twenty-first century, our attention as educators must be turned to the *cultural challenges* involved in *lifting the kaleidoscopic masks* for African-Americans such as Shelley Goode (1994), a creative student who wrote this poem expressing her thoughts about her future.

WHO AM I

I am the first, I am the last.
I am the future, I am the past.
I have dreams, I have thoughts.
I am a thinker, I like being taught.
I have ten fingers and ten toes.
I have two eyes, and a big brown nose.
I have ears to listen, and a mouth to talk.
I have legs to run, and even to walk.
I have patience and determination.
I have the mind to dream, and win this whole nation.
My **determination** brings a force of control.
I have my steps ordered and things to behold.
This **force of control** causes the enthusiasm in me
To strive for the perfect gift that nobody else can see.
I have **stamina** to endure my hardest test.
When I put out my foot, I put out my best.
My mind can bring forth a pot of gold,
For I am an **unlimited thinker** with fortunes untold.
I am the only one, you see.
That know that there is a winner in me.
It is written, it is said.
My life is like a book with stories being read.
"The Little Engine Who Could," Oh, that was me.
I tried and said I know I can faithfully.
And one great day I drove through it all
Rode out to the horizon without a stall.
Now, if anybody ask you who I am.
Who is that girl who is always the best?
You just tell them I am **SUCCESS!!!!**

References

Baldwin, A.Y. (1977). Tests can underpredict: A case study. *Phi Delta Kappan, 58,* 620–621.

Baldwin, A.Y. (1984). *Baldwin identification matrix 2 for the identification of gifted and talented.* New York: Trillium Press.

Baldwin, A.Y., & Start, K. (1987). *Raven matrices scores and educational achievement of black underprivileged children*. Paper presented at the biennium meeting of the World Council for Gifted and Talented, Salt Lake City, UT.

Banks, J. (1989). Multicultural education: Characteristics and goals. In J. Banks & C. Banks (Eds.), *Multicultural education: Issues and perspectives* (pp. 2–26). Needham Heights, MA: Allyn & Bacon.

Banks, J. (1995). Multicultural education: Historical development, dimensions, and practice. In J. Banks & C. Banks (Eds.), *Handbook of research on multicultural education* (pp. 3–24). New York: Macmillan.

Banks, J., & Banks, C. (Eds.). (1995). *Handbook of research on multicultural education*. New York: Macmillan.

Borland, J., & Wright, L. (1994). Identifying young, potentially gifted, economically disadvantaged students. *Gifted Child Quarterly, 33*(4), 164–171.

Caine, R., & Caine, G. (1991). *Teaching and the human brain*. Alexandria, VA: Association for Supervision and Curriculum Development.

Cook, G., & Baldwin, A.Y. (1979). Unique needs of a special population. In *The gifted and talented NSSE yearbook* (pp. 388–394). Chicago, IL: University of Chicago Press.

Cornell, D., Delcourt, M., Goldberg, M., & Bland, L. (1995). Achievement & self-concept of minority students in elementary school gifted programs. *Journal for Education of the Gifted, 18*(2), 189–209.

Fordham, S. (1988). Racelessness as a factor in Black students' school success: Pragmatic strategy or pyrrhic victory? *Harvard Educational Review, 58*(1), 54–84.

Fordham, S., & Ogbu, J. U. (1986). African American students' school success: Coping with the "burden of acting white." *Urban Review 18*, 176–206.

Frasier, M. (1993). Eliminating the four persisting barriers to identifying gifted minority students. *Gifted International 7*(2), 60–65.

Gardner, H. (1983). *Frames of mind: The theory of multiple intelligences*. New York: Basic Books.

Golin, A., Moore, M., & Baker, C. (1992). Use of SOMPA in identification of gifted African-American children. *Journal for Education of the Gifted, 14*(4), 344–356.

Goode, S. (1994). *Who am I*. Class presentation, Storrs, CT.

Herrnstein, R., & Murray, C. (1994). *The bell curve: Intelligence and class structure in American life*. New York: The Free Press.

Hunsaker, S. (1995). The gifted metaphor from the perspective of traditional civilizations. *Journal for Education of the Gifted, 18*(3), 255–268.

Jensen, A., Schafer, E., & Crinella, F. (1981). Reaction time evoked brain potentials, and psychometric g in the severely retarded. *Intelligence, 5*, 179–197.

Kitano, M. (1991). A multicultural educational perspective serving the culturally diverse gifted. *Journal for Education of the Gifted, 15*(1), 4–19.

Mills, C., & Tissot, S. (1995). Identifying academic potential in students from underrepresented populations: Is using the Raven Progressive Matrices a good idea? *Gifted Child Quarterly, 39*(4), 209–217.

Ogbu, J. (1992). Understanding cultural diversity and learning. *Journal for Education of the Gifted, 17*(4), 355–383.

Pritzkau, P. (1970). *On education for the authentic*. Scranton, PA: International Textbook.

Shepard, C. (1972). The world through Mark's eyes. In J. Banks & J. Grambs (Eds.), *Black self-concept: Implications for education and social science* (pp. 1–3). New York: McGraw-Hill.

Sternberg, R. (1985). *Beyond IQ*. New York: Cambridge University Press.

Unruh, G., & Unruh, A. (1984). *Curriculum development: Problems, processes, and progress.* Berkeley, CA: McCutchan.

U.S. Department of Education Office of Planning, Budget & Evaluation. (1989). *No gift wasted: Effective strategies for educating highly able, disadvantaged students in mathematics and science* (Contract No. 300-87-0152). Washington, DC: Judith Alamprese & Wendy Erlanger.

CHAPTER

2

HISPANIC AMERICANS: USA

Yolanda is only nine years old; however, her bilingual fluency in Spanish and English is of crucial significance to her family. She is often asked by her Spanish speaking parents and grandparents to translate for them when they speak with English speaking individuals.

Vicente is eleven years old and in the initial stages of acquiring English as his second language. Vicente has an extraordinary ability for storytelling in Spanish, but when he tries to tell stories in English, his words seem distorted. Consequently, his teacher believes that he not only lacks linguistic skills but also has limited cognitive abilities. His outstanding storytelling abilities remained unnoticed.

Attempting to describe and discuss the wide range of concerns regarding gifted Hispanic students is both challenging and far-reaching. The combination of relevant cultural, linguistic, socioeconomic, political, personal, and other variables unique to each individual exacerbates any discussion of the issues. This chapter provides a brief introduction to the issues involved in identifying and nurturing talent among Hispanic students in the United States of America (USA). The current condition of Hispanics in the USA will be described; identification and programming concerns for this population will be discussed; and finally, suggestions for educational practice will be offered.

HISPANICS IN THE UNITED STATES

In order to gain a better understanding of gifted Hispanic students, we must understand the complexities of their lives. According to the United States Bureau of the Census (1995), there were about 26 million Hispanics in the USA in 1994, that is, 10% of the entire USA population. However, the Bureau of the Census cautions that these estimates may be incorrect due to the underestimation of working class and undocumented Hispanics. It is estimated that approximately 5.8% of the total Hispanic population, or 1.2 million people, and a sizable unknown number of undocumented Hispanic immigrants were not included in the 1990 census (Kanellos, 1993). Overall, the Hispanic population in the USA is increasing dramatically. The latest projections by the Census Bureau indicate that Hispanics will: (1) equal or surpass the Black population in the USA by the year 2005 and will become the nation's largest ethnic group by the year 2010; (2) double in size (52 million or 15.7% USA population) by the year 2020; and (3) comprise approximately 88 million, that is, 22.5% of the entire USA population by the year 2050 (almost one in four Americans will be Hispanic).

The terms *Hispanic* and *Latino* refer to Mexicans, Puerto Ricans, Cubans, Central and South Americans, and people with origins in other Spanish speaking countries, for example, those whose origins are in Spain (Jones-Correa & Leal, 1996; Kanellos, 1993). Today, Mexican Americans comprise the largest Hispanic group (64.3%), followed by Puerto Ricans (10.6%), and then Cubans (4.7%). Although Hispanics share a common origin and linguistic base, the groups that make up the Hispanic population are not monolithic, as they differ significantly in many important ways. According to Bean and Tienda (1987), Hispanics living in the USA come from twenty-three different countries. Therefore, major demographical, historical, cultural, political, and experiential differences exist between these groups. Their unique experiences have influenced them in different ways, both before and after immigration to the USA. These differences are crucial when we consider the identification and development of giftedness among Hispanic students.

Language
As Hispanics share a common linguistic base, Spanish, with group variations in language usage, several varieties of Spanish, determined by the country of ancestral origin, are spoken in the USA (Kanellos, 1993). Hispanics in the USA currently have a high retention rate of their ancestral language, making Spanish a strong home language in USA

Hispanic communities. In this regard, Meier and Stewart (1991) indicate that Puerto Ricans are very interested in having their children literate in Spanish. Yet, the majority of Hispanics born or raised in the USA also speak English, as a home language or a strong second language (Kanellos, 1993). Although Hispanics in the USA are shifting gradually from Spanish to English, bilingualism among Hispanics is prevalent. The range of language proficiency skills in Spanish and English among Hispanics varies widely, from fluent bilingualism to limited communication skills in either one of the two languages. It is important to acknowledge that there are many Hispanics who are not fluent in Spanish, especially because of their assimilation into the host society. Recently, research about bilingualism and cognitive development suggests that the development of a second language can have positive effects on cognitive skills (Cummins & Swain, 1986; Gonzalez, 1996; Hakuta, 1987; Hakuta & Gould, 1987). Bilingualism, therefore, should not be regarded as a handicap, but rather as an opportunity for cognitive growth and expansion.

Cultural and Family Values

Hispanic families often differ substantially not only from typical middle-class white families but also from other Hispanic groups' families. Although little has been written recently about Hispanic families, prior literature describes the traditional Hispanic family as an extended one in which members beyond the nuclear unit are considered an integral part of the family. This is a reflection of a cultural value called "familismo." This cultural norm tends to emphasize interdependence over independence, affiliation over confrontation, and cooperation over competition (Comas-Díaz, 1989; Falicov, 1982). Hispanic families are also characterized by their focus on the collective. In this sense, the needs of the family have priority over the needs of one person. Another cultural value deep-rooted in the traditional Hispanic family is "respeto" (respect). Comas-Díaz (1989) argues that "respeto" refers to appropriate differential behavior in interpersonal relationships according to age, socioeconomic level, sex, and authority status. For instance, older persons and parents are perceived to deserve "respeto" from younger people and children. In contrast, the North American society nurtures self-reliant, aggressive, competitive, and orally inquisitive behaviors among children. These traits run contrary to some Hispanic traditional values; and for Hispanic parents, these children are considered disrespectful (Figler, 1979).

Immigration

The heterogeneous migratory experiences of Hispanics comprise an extremely complex phenomenon that permeates their lives indefinitely.

Reasons for and patterns of migration are different for each Hispanic group. For example, Mexican incorporation to the USA took place by conquest and immigration. Unrestricted Mexican immigration until 1924 took place because of poor economic conditions in Mexico, a rapid increase in the size of the population, and the demand for labor in the USA (Meier & Stewart, 1991). Today, many Mexicans seeking illegal entry into the USA are apprehended by the Border patrol. The current reason for Mexican immigration still remains the economic difficulties in Mexico and the demand for cheap labor in the USA.

The integration of Puerto Ricans to the mainland has also taken place through conquest and immigration. In 1898, the USA invaded Puerto Rico and made it a USA territory. In 1917, Puerto Ricans were granted secondary USA citizenship enabling them to travel to the USA without restriction. Although Puerto Rican immigration existed since the nineteenth century, it was not until the 1940s that large numbers of Puerto Ricans immigrated to the USA for economic reasons.

Cuban immigration became more visible after 1959 when Fidel Castro declared Cuba a socialist state. At that time, many educated and wealthy supporters of the previous Cuban government immigrated to the USA. However, successive waves of Cuban exiles, especially in the 1980s, included persons who were less well educated and from low socioeconomic backgrounds. According to Meier and Stewart (1991):

> The immigration experience of Cuban Americans is unique among Hispanics in that they were accorded favored status. Federal funds were provided to help resettle Cuban refugees, and financial assistance was made available for education or to gain occupational certification for professionals (Pedraza-Bailey, 1985). Government policies assisted Cubans in attaining middle-class status, in direct contrast to the cheap labor policies that economically restricted Mexican Americans and Puerto Ricans. (pp. 39–40)

Central and South American immigration comprises mostly Salvadorans, Guatemalans, and Nicaraguans escaping the calamities of war and political persecution, and looking for a better future (Leslie & Leitch, 1989). During the 1980s, migration from Central and South American countries to the USA reached startling numbers.

Acculturation

Carrasquillo (1991) explains that "acculturation refers to a complex process whereby the behaviors and attitudes of the immigrant group change toward the dominant group as a result of contact and exposure to a cultural system that is significantly different" (pp. 55–56). During this process of adaptation, people usually take and incorporate traits from their own culture and the host society, creating unique cultural patterns. Accordingly, both subtle and obvious changes occur in their culture. Some clear intergenerational changes for Hispanics include: (1) the shift from Spanish to English dominance by the third generation, (2) the conflict between parents and children due to disparities in values, and (3) the assimilation of persons within the unique culture to the wider culture beyond. Hispanics demonstrate different degrees of acculturation. Some Hispanics have assimilated to the majority culture; this means that they have acquired traits from the majority culture to an extent that their Hispanic cultural traits have almost disappeared entirely.

Geographic Location
Hispanic groups are geographically concentrated in different regions of the USA. For instance, Mexican Americans are concentrated in the five southwestern states of California (34.1%), Colorado (1.9%), New Mexico (2.5%), Arizona (3.18%), and Texas (19.6%). Five states outside the Southwest account for 26% of the Hispanic population: New York (12.3%), Florida (8%), Illinois (4%), New Jersey, and Massachusetts (13.7%). Today, Puerto Ricans comprise the largest Hispanic group in the Northeast, and the majority of Cubans reside in Florida.

Income and Work Force
The average family income earnings for employed Hispanics were 36% less than for non-Hispanics in 1991. Hispanic families seem to be poorer than non-Hispanic families because of lower incomes from low-paying, semiskilled jobs, and higher unemployment rates. However, unemployment rates are higher for Mexicans and Puerto Ricans than for Cubans. Overall, Cuban Americans have incomes that are much higher than those for other Hispanic groups. In 1993, over 26% of all Hispanic families were below the official poverty level. There are more Puerto Rican families living in poverty than either Mexican American or Cuban families. In addition, Puerto Rican children are the poorest in the nation (National Puerto Rican Coalition, 1992).

Education
Different educational histories also exist for Hispanics in the USA. For instance, Mexican Americans have a longer educational history than Puerto Ricans, Cubans, and Central and South Americans. The educational histories of Mexican Americans and Puerto Ricans have been characterized by inequities or absence of access to equal educational opportunities. Suarez-Orozco (1991) argues that Mexican American students and Central and South American students follow different patterns of school performance and face different educational issues. Overall, researchers (Carrasquillo, 1991; García, 1992) believe that the

American educational system has failed to provide equitable educational services to Hispanic students. Hispanic students, especially those who are Puerto Rican, are considered educationally at risk. Educational data on Hispanic students consistently reflect a picture of low achievement levels, high dropout rates, poor school attendance rates, higher placements in special education and remedial tracks, higher enrollment in segregated schools, and underrepresentation in gifted programs (Alvarez, 1992; Meléndez, 1986; Passow, 1986; U.S. Bureau of the Census, 1995). Unfortunately, this low achievement has been a major barrier to the advancement of most Hispanics in the USA (Carrasquillo, 1991). Measures of educational attainment indicate that Hispanic students fall significantly behind the general population. Hispanic students in the USA also leave school at higher rates than non-Hispanic groups. A national report entitled "The Condition of Education in the Nation" (U.S. Department of Education, 1994) revealed that, in 1993, Hispanic students dropped out of school at a much higher rate (36%) than Blacks (17%) and whites (11%). In 1993, only 59% of Hispanic students aged 20–24 had a high school diploma or equivalent, as compared to 90% of whites and 83% of Blacks. In addition, among Hispanics 25–29 years old, only 30% had attended some college, and only 8% had attained a bachelor's degree.

A key element in the ongoing debate about the education of Hispanic students is the provision of bilingual education and other educational alternatives. According to Hakuta (1987), Hispanic students in the USA have demonstrated positive cognitive gains from bilingualism. Consequently, providing instruction and support in the students' first language and English is pivotal to success. Also, Ramírez (1992) argued that first language instruction not only facilitates higher levels of competence in the first language but also produces gains in mathematics and English achievement. Today, a variety of bilingual education program models are in place in the USA (Roberts, 1995). However, the most common type of bilingual program in the USA is the transitional model, where students are provided initial content instruction in the native language with increased instruction in English. Main purposes for transitional programming include student language shift from the native language to English and assimilation. In addition, students are frequently placed in English monolingual classrooms in less than three years. Unfortunately, subtractive bilingualism, or the loss of the first language, is a common outcome for students.

A more effective type of bilingual education is the two-way model, also known as bilingual immersion, developmental bilingual, enrichment bilingual, and dual language education. Two-way bilingual education is designed to develop dual language proficiency in students by providing them instruction in English and another language in a classroom that usually includes half native speakers of English and half native speakers of the target language. The pluralistic and additive bilingual environment of this program provides students with ample opportunities to: (1) develop two languages, (2) progress academically in both languages, and (3) gain an appreciation of another culture (National Center for Research on Cultural Diversity and Second Language Learning, 1994). The two-way curriculum is content-based and focuses on the development of strong academic achievement in both languages. However, although the goals of this type of bilingual program remain constant, the modes of instruction and the model of language development vary from program to program. Various reports (Collier, 1994; Lindhold & Gavlek, 1994) indicate that the two-way program model is effective in developing not only bilingualism but also academic excellence. Other instructional alternatives for Hispanic students involve English as a Second Language (ESL) services, Sheltered English classes, or "sink or swim" instruction in which students are placed in monolingual English classrooms without any language assistance.

To summarize, Hispanic groups in the USA possess great inter- and intradiversity. An awareness and sensitivity toward this diversity among Hispanic persons will enable educators, practitioners, and policy makers to be more responsive in creating educational opportunities for success, and nurturing giftedness in young people from all Hispanic groups.

GIFTED POTENTIAL AND DEVELOPMENT, ACADEMIC ACHIEVEMENT, AND LIFE SUCCESS

Our educational system often overlooks gifted Hispanic students who are acquiring English as their second language and/or are being raised with significantly different values and attitudes from those found in the dominant culture (Díaz, 1994; Maker & Schiever, 1988). Different cultures value, encourage, or inhibit the development of certain talents (Passow & Frasier, 1996). The American educational system is currently experiencing great difficulties in identifying and nurturing giftedness among Hispanic students. Research in gifted education and in bilingual education has indicated that, in general, the education system has focused its attention on the weaknesses rather than on the strengths of these students. Consequently, many gifted Hispanic students are denied learning experiences and educational services necessary to develop their potential. When that occurs, underachievement may result. This problem is even worse for those Hispanic students who are recent immigrants, due to linguistic differences and cross-cultural stress (Cohen, 1988). The limited educational research on this group further heightens the problem, as we do not understand the issues or some of the solutions.

Overall, Hispanic students, as well as other minority students, are underrepresented in programs for the gifted. Hispanic students account for 10% of the total school population, but they constitute only 5% of all students enrolled in gifted programs (Machado, 1987; Meier & Stewart, 1991). In other words, the number of Hispanic students in gifted classes is less than half of what would be expected from their number in the general population. In California, one-fifth of Hispanic students designated as gifted withdraw from school before graduation (Riddle, 1985). Main barriers to the participation and success of Hispanic students in such programs include the lack of identification; the scarcity of funding to develop, implement, improve, and maintain effective programs; the dearth of qualified personnel to work with these students; and inappropriate placement and services. Those who "make it" are usually placed in programs that focus on developing abilities valued by the majority culture. In this type of program, gifted Hispanic students must work twice as hard to succeed, overcoming obstacles of differing value systems and behavioral patterns, inadequate academic preparation, and differing language (Leung, 1981).

Some researchers (Frasier, 1991; Melesky, 1984) argue that this situation is due in part to discrimination, misunderstanding, and disinterest from the society at large. Several issues complicate the identification and proper service of gifted Hispanic students. These issues include educators' socioeconomic stereotypes, ethnic prejudice, and low expectations; differing manifestations of talent potential in comparison to widely accepted standards of giftedness imposed by the dominant white middle-class group; and inaccurate screening and identification methods including biased intelligence or achievement tests. For almost a century, most gifted programs have used a battery of standardized tests as a sole entrance criterion (Bailey & Harbin, 1980; Davis, 1978; Johnson, Starnes, Gregory, & Blaylock, 1985; Ortiz & Volloff, 1987). Today, many school districts still place a heavy emphasis on standardized test cutoff scores for student placement in gifted programs. For example, Patton, Prillaman, and VanTassel-Baska (1990) report that over 90% of the states and territories use norm-referenced tests and only 40% use some type of nontraditional measures to identify gifted students. These traditions are deeply rooted in a narrow, static, psychometric conception of giftedness as a high score on an IQ test.

Some researchers have reached a consensus about the detrimental impact of using IQ tests and other traditional methods as the sole measure for identifying giftedness among culturally and linguistically diverse children (de Bernard, 1985). It has been proven that such tests often underestimate the abilities of gifted Hispanic students, especially those who are in the process of developing English as their second language and experiencing acculturation (Bernal & Reyna,

1975; Zappia, 1988). Hartley (1987) claimed that most of the standardized tests used for the identification of gifted students are primarily dependent on English oral and written language. Minimal consideration, if any, is given to the procedural complexities of acquiring a second language and adapting to new contexts. These tests also neglect important psychosocial and cultural elements. Furthermore, some experts in the field consider standardized testing a tool that denies equal educational opportunity to these students by using test scores to demonstrate "that the students obtain lower scores compared with majority children due to internal factors, such as race" (Gonzalez & Yawkey, 1993, p. 43).

Considering the limited research literature, it has been found that several noncognitive factors (family, school, community, personal) influence the behavioral display of outstanding talents and academic achievement among gifted Hispanic students. For instance, parental and community involvement has been found to have a strong influence on the academic achievement of children, regardless of ethnic background (Delgado-Gaitan, 1988, 1990; Moll, 1992; Valencia, 1991). Yet, although some efforts have been made to integrate the community in the schooling experience of Hispanic students, many educational systems in the USA still exclude the personal and communal reality of these children.

Some research indicates that many Hispanic students attend schools that are considered poor, highly segregated, and with high dropout rates (Orum, 1986). Certainly, this type of school provides an environment that is far from conducive to learning. For example, Ortíz (1988) claims that Hispanic students are more likely to face school learning environments that foster poor academic performance, are dysfunctional regarding their type of learning style, and differ from the reward structure found in the home. Some teachers are likely to perceive Hispanic students as low achievers and, therefore, will set low expectations for them (Brown, 1986; Meléndez, 1986). In addition, the absence of relevant teacher preparation and professional development in areas pertaining to gifted Hispanic students such as culture-based characteristics and high potential, is likely to hinder seriously these students' educational opportunities and achievement. Other school factors that correlate with the low achievement of Hispanic students are unresponsiveness and inflexibility of schools (Nazario, 1980), poor teaching practices, negative interactions with school staff, tracking, inflexible or irrelevant curricula, and overreferrals to special education (Boston Public Schools, 1989; Weis, Farrar, & Petrie, 1989). These factors usually have a negative impact upon students, and may decrease students' sense of self-worth, which in turn increases the possibilities of students who develop negative attitudes toward the educational environment (Díaz, 1994).

OVERCOMING IDENTIFICATION AND PROGRAMMING CHALLENGES: SUGGESTIONS FOR PRACTICE

Identification

In order to overcome some of these barriers, researchers and practitioners have proposed various strategies and techniques. Some practitioners acknowledge the existence of talent potential among individuals from diverse cultural and socioeconomic groups. However, for significant change to take place in the current conditions, an attitudinal change must occur both with educators and with members of society at large.

Changes in Attitudes. There must be a development of respect for the different cultural values, personal traits, and behaviors of Hispanic students, and an ability to identify these students' cognitive strengths and talents. Acquisition of knowledge and sensitivity toward these students' traditions, values, and behaviors, as well as the reasons for these differences, is of foremost importance.

New Visions of Talent and Giftedness. New visions of talents and gifts must emerge, encompassing novel findings in the areas of creative potential, human intelligence as well as psycholinguistic and sociocultural elements such as cultural differences, acculturation processes, ethnic identity development, second language acquisition, and socioeconomic factors. These new visions should then be used to guide the design and implementation of responsive identification procedures and educational programs. Currently, a large body of theory and research exists on creativity (Clark, 1979; Guilford, 1959; Runco, 1993; Torrance, 1962). This body of knowledge, in light of recent advances in the fields of second language acquisition and psycholinguistics, provides instrumental insights on how to better identify and meet the needs of bilingual, gifted, Hispanic students. Ricciardelli (1992) reviews twenty-four research studies investigating the relationship between creativity and bilingualism. She concluded that "the majority of the reviewed studies show that there is a positive relationship between creativity and bilingualism. . . . The positive relationship between creativity and bilingualism has been interpreted as suggesting that bilingualism can both influence and be influenced by creativity" (p. 251). Researchers such as Sternberg (1985) and Gardner (1983, 1993) have proposed alternative views to the traditional definitions of intelligence. These new understandings will enable practitioners to examine talents and gifts as multifaceted, developmental, and process-oriented phenomena. The emphasis should be on performance, context, opportunities, and access to talent development. A definition of giftedness that already incorporates several of these understandings is Renzulli's three-ring conception. Renzulli (1978) defines giftedness as the "interaction among three clusters of traits—above-average but not necessarily superior general abilities, task commitment, and creativity" (p. 5). This definition takes into account not only intellective (that is, abstract thinking, verbal and numerical reasoning, and so on) and nonintellective (that is, perseverance, enthusiasm, hard work, self-confidence, and so on) factors but also environmental factors such as socioeconomic status and access to invigorating educational milieus. It also supports giftedness as "a condition that can be developed in some people if an appropriate interaction takes place between a person, his or her environment, and a particular area of human endeavor" (Renzulli, 1986, p. 60).

Adopting Comprehensive Assessment Models. The adoption of a comprehensive assessment model will also help us to identify and program for gifted Hispanic students. This model should reflect a multidimensional, developmental view of the students' abilities and be consistent with new conceptions of giftedness, assuring a more valid and reliable approach to identification. For this purpose, authentic and dynamic methods of identifying gifted Hispanic students must be developed. For instance, expanding the initial screening talent pool by integrating informal referral by parents, peers, community members, and self-nominations will facilitate the data-gathering process beyond the classroom. This strategy provides access to out-of-school resources that can provide invaluable information about the identification of unusual potential. Since some children participate in various programs outside the school, the people organizing these programs may provide helpful information about the child's performance in areas not included in the school experience. Parent and community involvement in the identification process must be strongly encouraged. Another strategy is the use of developmental curriculum (Richert, 1985) or enriched programs that enable gifted students to flourish and manifest their outstanding potential (Kitano & Espinosa, 1995; Passow & Frasier, 1996; Renzulli & Reis, 1985). Examples of such programs serving gifted Hispanic students include Project EXCEL in the San Diego Unified School District, California (Hermanson & Pérez, 1993); Project CUE in the Community School District #19, New York; and the program called "Multiple Intelligences: A Framework for Student and Teacher Change" at the Montgomery County Public Schools, Maryland (U.S. Department of Education, 1994).

A case study approach has also been suggested (Renzulli, Reis, & Smith, 1981; Renzulli & Smith, 1978) for the identification of culturally and linguistically diverse students. After the child is nominated as a high potential student, a case study involves assessment with a variety of data which are interpreted in the context of the student's individual characteristics. Psychologists, counselors, teachers, parents, and other persons collaborate in the process of collecting the data, which include: historical-developmental information, self-inventory, psychometric and academic data, student's work samples, parental input, and professional advice, among others. Decisions are made by an interdisciplinary team of qualified individuals or professionals who are committed to including a greater number of culturally and linguistically diverse students and accepting a multidimensional conception of giftedness (Thompson, 1987; Zappia, 1988). This team should include members who are knowledgeable in the areas of second language acquisition, bilingual education, cultural differences, and issues related to the assessment of the target population. When the data are analyzed, the professional team should summarize the results and recommend suitable programs for the child.

Another option is to develop student portfolios reflecting the student abilities to produce, to perceive, and to reflect. Portfolios may include many types of evidence such as observations of the students, videotapes, dialogue journals, writing samples, artwork, projects, samples from home, and so on. Therefore, portfolios have the advantage of expanding qualitative and quantitative evidence for performance assessment. Formal assessment tools can be integrated to further document student growth; however, standardized testing should be minimized. If standardized tests are going to be used, practitioners should make sure that psychometric instruments are appropriate based on the prior assessment of the child's language dominance and proficiency levels (Melesky, 1984). In addition, these tests must be consistent with the program conception of giftedness, program goals, and curriculum. The use of native-language instruments and nonverbal tools is possible. These instruments can be used in conjunction with verbal instruments or with more subjective measures involving expressive language. For instance, Ortiz and Gonzalez (1991) suggest that the WISC-R, a standardized intelligence test, may be used as part of multiple criteria to identify gifted Hispanic students. Other researchers such as Saccuzzo, Johnson, and Guertin (1994) recommend the use of the Raven Progressive Matrices (RPM) as an alternative nonverbal instrument with remarkable possibilities for identifying gifted Hispanic students. The Torrance Tests of Creative Thinking (Torrance, 1966, 1971) have also been found to be promising for the identification of creative Hispanic students (Meléndez, 1995). Again, a note of caution should be added to the administration of psychometric and educational instruments. Only trained professionals who have the necessary educational background in tests and measurement and are fluent in both the native language of the child and the language in which the test is being offered should administer the test and interpret the information (Melesky, 1984).

The assessment model used should stress the early identification of gifted Hispanic students. This is a priority for gifted Hispanic children if we want to increase their chances of optimal development and to prevent underachievement (Díaz, 1994). Finally, the assessment model that is selected must also relate to a conceptual framework that enlightens program design.

Awareness of Student Strengths, Talent Potential, and Performance. Teachers, administrators, and other personnel must be fully aware of the characteristics, strengths, and behaviors indicative of talent potential in Hispanic students. Teachers must be provided with opportunities to become familiar with not only typical but also culture-based characteristics. For instance, teachers' and observers' ability to identify giftedness in the target population can be improved by providing them with specific behavioral indicators of talent potential using checklists or nomination forms. This is the least that can be done as a starting point for developing an awareness of the characteristics of gifted Hispanic children. It is important to remember that potentially gifted Hispanic children are not a homogeneous group, and as a result, not every single gifted Hispanic student will display all or even most of the same characteristics. Inter- and intragroup differences must be expected; the different ways in which the students express their talents result from different values, attitudes, and opportunities as well as other factors.

Leung (1981) suggests two ways of characterizing giftedness using absolute aspects, or the underlying traits transcending historical time and cultural context, and specific aspects, or the behavioral manifestations of giftedness. Absolute traits are similar across cultural and socioeconomic groups. Absolute characteristics are common to most gifted children, while specific traits vary, often because of cultural issues. Table 2–1 shows several general characteristics of giftedness and the unique ways in which potentially gifted Hispanic students express them.

Bernal (1978), using interviews with members of three primarily Mexican American communities in Texas, characterized gifted Hispanic children also as exhibiting leadership in a sometimes unobtrusive manner, being street-wise, and accepting responsibilities generally reserved for older children. Other children showed ability to improvise with ordinary materials, use of rich imagery, skill in group activities, responsiveness to the concrete, a keen sense of humor, persistence in problem solving, understanding of others' feelings, and an ability to adapt quickly to change. Ruiz (1989) proposed that an unusual characteristic of gifted Hispanic students is the linguistic sophistication evidenced by code switching. For long time, code switching was perceived as evidence of linguistic interference. Today, much evidence suggests the opposite. Code switching, or the alternation of two or more languages, is a rule-governed and function-specific system serving both sociolinguistic and communicative strategies (Lindholm & Padilla, 1978). In addition, a recent study with bilingual Puerto Rican students (Hakuta, Gould, Malakoff, Rivera, & Rodríguez-Landsberg,

Table 2–1 Expressions of giftedness by Hispanic students

General Characteristics of Gifted Children	Manifestations in Hispanic Children
1. Precocious language and thought	1. Facility for learning a second language
	2. Fluent communication in native language with peers and within community
2. High capacity for processing information	3. Exceptional translation skills
3. Advanced mathematical, musical, and artistic abilities	4. Unusual ability to express feelings and emotions in storytelling, movement, and visual arts
4. Unusual imagination	5. Unusual ability to improvise with commonplace materials and design imaginative games from simple toys or household objects. Originality of ideas.

1988) found that these students display an exceptional ability for translation. Currently, several researchers at the National Research Center on the Gifted and Talented, University of Connecticut, are investigating translation and interpretation talents among Hispanic students. To summarize, no single profile of a gifted Hispanic child exists. Both Hispanic and non-Hispanic gifted students share similar cognitive, affective, and social characteristics. Yet, unquestionably, behavioral expressions of talent potential vary from student to student.

Programming

Witty (1978) called for the extension of services for culturally and linguistically diverse gifted students to prevent the loss of great talent and to provide equal opportunity for self-realization. He stated that for culturally and linguistically diverse students who are gifted, equal educational opportunity means

> early identification with attention to special needs; careful programming in light of their strengths, characteristics, and learning and living styles; intelligent and caring teaching free of limiting expectations; wide-range of releasing counseling programs; and parental and community support services interacting freely with the schools. (p. 344)

As mentioned previously, the development and use of relevant assessment procedures is critical to effective identification and program development. Careful development of programs is essential to enable gifted Hispanic students to participate in appropriate educational services. Programs for this population should include similar components and provisions as those designed for other gifted students as well as qualitatively different services, such as bilingual/antiracist educational experiences, that show respect for the unique needs of potentially gifted Hispanic children.

Solid Program Philosophy, Conceptual Framework, and Goals. A solid underlying philosophy and conceptual framework should support the program goals and components including instructional techniques, curriculum, teacher training, and parent-community support. This foundation should be based on relevant theoretical models and educational practices in the fields of gifted education, bilingual education, and Hispanic ethnic studies. Suggested goals for a program designed for gifted Hispanic students (Banda, 1988; Díaz, 1995) include: (1) developing student appreciation of their own talents and the abilities appreciated by the majority culture; (2) fostering student appreciation for the uniqueness, difficulty, and responsibility of being a gifted individual; (3) developing student sense of her/his individual and ethnic identities, and potential contributions to society; (4) assisting students in acquiring process skills necessary for the success in challenging classes, for example, research, independent study, computer use, listening, note taking, and class discussion; (5) developing in the student a strong system of coping skills that will aid her/him as a bicultural person; and (6) fostering in the student the development of bilingualism and helping the student value bilingualism as a strength. A program for gifted Hispanic students should celebrate cultural and linguistic diversity while simultaneously nurturing the ethnic identity of the individual child.

Alternative Program Options. Effective programming for gifted Hispanic students should also include alternative program options. In this regard, a clear management plan and flexible administrative arrangements for services must be available. Several program options such as cluster groups, pullout/resource rooms, cluster/pullout, special classes, special schools, acceleration, and enrichment should be considered. A cautious selection of an educational program that best meets the student needs, interests, and potentialities must be accomplished. The educational needs of gifted Hispanic students vary widely, depending on national origins, degree of acculturation, family socioeconomic levels, educational aspirations, fluency in English, and the form that talent potential takes in these students, among others. Programs for these groups must recognize and develop the abilities valued by the students' culture including areas such as bilingualism, traditional academics, leadership and organizational skills, divergent thinking, and other varied abilities that occur in bicultural individuals.

Programs should also provide opportunities to introduce and develop other abilities that will aid students to succeed as bicultural individuals. In other words, programs should emphasize the development of skills needed to succeed in the majority culture without sacrificing cultural values and talents. Integration of a specialist who is knowledgeable about the issues concerning the education of gifted Hispanic students is also a promising strategy.

Qualitatively Different, Pluralistic/Antiracist, Bilingual/Bicultural, High-End Learning Curriculum and Pedagogy. Curriculum and pedagogy constitute another extremely important dimension of gifted programs. The curriculum and instruction of the program must be aligned with the beliefs about the nature of giftedness, the methods of identification, and program goals. The curriculum and instruction should meet already established standards for a qualitatively different, pluralistic/antiracist, bilingual/bicultural, high-end learning curriculum. This means that challenging and enriching learning experiences based on an analysis of the children's interests, needs, and specific characteristics are provided. What these students bring to school in terms of cultural background, knowledge, experiences, and abilities is an essential starting point for the provision of a caring and meaningful education. Curricular and extracurricular provisions should be designed to evoke and develop potentialities in different areas including divergent thinking, creative thinking, languages, the arts, and others. Provisions that promote awareness and understanding of social issues such as racism, human relations, and peace are also necessary. Providing instruction in the native language, Spanish, is important, as language is a key component of culture. Learning the native language is learning about one's cultural heritage. First language instruction has been found to support the development of English proficiency. Therefore, the linguistic dimension of the program facilitates the students' exploration, interpretation, and construction of meanings, as well as the development of complex concepts.

Comprehensive Services. Other components of effective programs for gifted Hispanic students are comprehensive counseling services and parent and community education and involvement. Counseling services that provide affective, academic, and career support are extremely important for both students and parents. Students and parents would benefit from culturally and contextually relevant assistance in dealing with issues related to adaptation; biculturalism; conflict resolution; communication and acceptance, career exploration, and awareness; educational opportunities; and so on. In this regard, Grossman (1995) offers functional advice to those interested in making counseling services more suited to Hispanics. Strom, Johnson, Strom, and Strom (1992) state that gifted Hispanic students benefit from gifted programs that include parental education on giftedness. A strong parent and community component includes educational experiences and assistance to parents, family members, significant others, and community members. Educational experiences help parents and others to develop an understanding of the many aspects of giftedness, the uniqueness of their children, how to recognize and nurture their children's talent potential, cognitive strengths, and languages. Through systematic participation, parents and others will acquire the knowledge and skills necessary to foster talent development in their children. In addition, parent and community participation in the education of the children can help school officials to learn about and appreciate what the culture values as gifted behaviors.

Qualified Caring Teachers. Competent teachers are also needed. One of the most important characteristics of teachers for gifted Hispanic students is a willingness to see potential in these students and to work with parents, community, and other professionals in developing their potential. Teachers need the basic skills, knowledge, and joy of learning required to become effective with these young people. They also need to develop a high sense of cultural sensitivity, an ability to understand and respect differences, and the willingness and skills needed to translate these understandings into instructional practices. These are crucial variables in the success of the students, as is knowledge about second language acquisition. It is extremely important for these teachers to recognize that they play many different roles (maternal, therapeutic, and so on) in the lives of their students, since Hispanic students face great challenges during their lives which, in turn, affect negatively their road to success.

A Program Model for Gifted Hispanic Students

A proposed model for talent development in Hispanic students builds upon the previous discussion of crucial factors and two major milestones in bilingual education and gifted education: a two-way bilingual program design and the Schoolwide Enrichment Model (SEM) developed by Renzulli and Reis (1985). The pluralistic and additive bilingual environment of the two-way design provides both non-native English speaking and native English speaking students substantial opportunities to become biliterate, to excel academically in both languages, and to develop cross-cultural appreciation. The Schoolwide Enrichment Model (SEM) offers a pragmatic plan for the development of multiple potentials in young people. The SEM was originally created for gifted and talented students; nevertheless, it advocates broad, rich, advanced-level learning experiences for all students by using a variety of resources and implementing a continuity of services. The model focuses on students' strengths, interests, and learning styles, thereby enabling educators to develop a more challenging and meaningful curriculum. It embraces both excellence and equity in education by creating a school environment in which personal and cultural characteristics are valued and nurtured. The SEM also promotes the development of relevant partnerships among students, teachers, administrators, parents, and community members. (See Renzulli, 1994, for further details.) Independent research and practice in the two-way bilingual program design and the Schoolwide Enrichment Model suggest that the creative integration of these two exemplary, innovative programs has great potential in meeting successfully the needs of gifted Hispanic students.

Summary

The information provided in this chapter focuses on potentially gifted Hispanic students. Although the impact of the steady growth of Hispanics in the USA is evident in the nation's public schools, overwhelming evidence highlights the American educational system's failure to identify and provide appropriate education to gifted Hispanic students. One of the main premises of this chapter is that this absence of identification and nurturance of gifted Hispanic students is rooted in a considerable misunderstanding of this population's inter- and intradiversity and the complexities of Hispanic students' lives. This chapter highlights fundamental understandings in the areas of language, culture, immigration and acculturation, and education for Hispanic students; discusses main concerns about the identification of and program development for gifted Hispanic students; and offers suggestions for responsive educational practice including a two-way program model integrated with Renzulli's Schoolwide Enrichment Model to provide appropriate education to gifted Hispanic students.

References

Alvarez, M. D. (1992). Promoting the academic growth of Puerto Rican children. In A. N. Ambert & M. D. Alvarez (Eds.), *Puerto Rican children on the mainland: Interdisciplinary perspectives* (pp. 135–166). New York: Garland.

Bailey, D. B., & Harbin, G. (1980). Nondiscriminatory evaluation. *Exceptional Children,* 46(17), 590–596.

Banda, C. (1988). Promoting pluralism and power. In J. C. Maker & S. W. Schiever (Eds.), *Critical issues in gifted education: Vol. II. Defensible programs for cultural and ethnic minorities* (pp. 27–33). Austin, TX: PRO-ED.

Bean, F. D., & Tienda, M. (1987). *The Hispanic population of the United States.* New York: Russell Sage Foundation.

Bernal, E. (1978). The identification of gifted Chicano children. In A.Y. Baldwin, G. H. Gear, & L. J. Lucito, *Educational planning for the gifted.* Reston, VA: The Council for Exceptional Children.

Bernal, E. M., & Reyna, J. (1975). *Analysis and identification of giftedness in Mexican-American children: A pilot study* (ERIC Document Reproduction Service No. ED 117 885).

Boston Public Schools. (1989). *Hispanic dropout prevention program.* Boston, MA: Latino Parents Association.

Brown, T. (1986). *Teaching minorities more effectively.* Lanham, MD: University Press of America.

Carrasquillo, A. L. (1991). *Hispanic children & youth in the United States: A resource guide.* New York: Garland.

Clark, B. (1979). *Growing up gifted.* Columbus, OH: Merrill.

Cohen, L. M. (1988). *Meeting the needs of gifted and talented minority language students: Issues and practices* (ERIC Document Reproduction Service No. ED 309 592).

Collier, V. (1994). *Promising practices in public schools.* Paper presented at the annual meeting of the Teachers of English to Speakers of Other Languages, Baltimore, MD.

Comas-Díaz, L. (1989). Culturally relevant issues and treatment implications for Hispanics. In D. R. Koslow & E. P. Salett (Eds.), *Crossing cultures in mental health* (pp. 31–48). Washington, DC: International Counseling Center.

Cummins, J., & Swain, M. (1986). *Bilingualism in education.* New York: Longman.

Davis, P. I. (1978). *Community-based efforts to increase the identification of the number of gifted minority children* (ERIC Document Reproduction Service No. ED 176 487).

de Bernard, A. E. (1985). Why José can't get in the gifted class: The bilingual child and standardized reading tests. *Roeper Review, 8*(2), 80–82.

Delgado-Gaitan, C. (1988). The value of conformity: Learning to stay in school. *Anthropology and Education Quarterly, 19*(4), 354–381.

Delgado-Gaitan, C. (1990). *Literacy for empowerment: The role of parents in children's education.* London: Falmer Press.

Díaz, E. I. (1994). *Underachievement among high ability Puerto Rican high school students: Perceptions of their life experiences.* Unpublished doctoral dissertation, Pennsylvania State University, State College, PA.

Díaz, E. I. (1995). *Developing talent potential in culturally and linguistically diverse children.* Unpublished manuscript, University of Connecticut, Storrs, CT.

Falicov, C. J. (1982). Mexican families. In M. McGoldrick, J. K. Pearce, & J. Giordano (Eds.), *Ethnicity and family therapy* (pp. 134–163). New York: The Guildford Press.

Figler, C. S. (1979). *Puerto Rican families: Their migration and assimilation.* Unpublished manuscript, University of Massachusetts, Boston, MA.

Frasier, M. (1991). Disadvantaged and culturally diverse gifted students. *Journal for the Education of the Gifted, 14*(3), 234–245.

García, E. E. (1992). Hispanic children: Theoretical, empirical and related policy issues. *Educational Psychology Review, 4*(1), 69–93.

Gardner, H. (1983). *Frames of mind: The theory of multiple intelligences.* New York: Basic Books.

Gardner, H. (1993). *Multiple intelligences. The theory in practice.* New York: Basic Books.

Gonzalez, V. (1996). *Cognition, culture, and language in bilingual children: Conceptual and semantic development.* Bethesda, MD: Austin & Winfield.

Gonzalez, V., & Yawkey, T. (1993, Fall). The assessment of culturally and linguistically different students: Celebrating change. *Educational Horizons,* 41–49.

Grossman, H. (1995). *Educating Hispanic students: Implications for instruction, classroom management, counseling and assessment.* Springfield, IL: Thomas.

Guilford, J. P. (1959). Three faces of intellect. *American Psychologist, 14,* 469–479.

Hakuta, K. (1987). Degree of bilingualism and cognitive ability in mainland Puerto Rican children. *Child Development, 58,* 1372–1388.

Hakuta, K., & Gould, L. J. (1987). Synthesis of research on bilingual education. *Educational Leadership, 3,* 38–45.

Hakuta, K., Gould, L. J., Malakoff, M., Rivera, M., & Rodríguez-Landsberg, M. (1988, April). *Translation and interpretation in bilingual Puerto-Rican students.* Paper presented at AERA, New Orleans, MS.

Hartley, E. A. (1987). *How can we meet all their needs? Incorporating education for the gifted and talented into the multicultural classroom* (ERIC Document Reproduction Service No. ED 336 968).

Hermanson, D., & Pérez, R. I. (1993). *Project EXCEL.* San Diego, CA: San Diego City Schools, School Services Division, Exceptional Programs Development.

Johnson, S. T., Starnes, W. T., Gregory, D., & Blaylock, A. (1985). Program of assessment, diagnosis, and instruction (PADI): Identifying and nurturing potentially gifted and talented minority students. *The Journal of Negro Education, 54*(3), 416–430.

Jones-Correa, M., & Leal, D. L. (1996). Becoming "Hispanic": Secondary panethnic identification among Latin American–origin populations in the United States. *Hispanic Journal of Behavioral Sciences, 18*(2), 214–254.

Kanellos, N. (1993). *The Hispanic-American almanac: A reference work on Hispanics in the United States.* Detroit, MI: Gale Research.

Kitano, M. K., & Espinosa, R. (1995). Language diversity and giftedness: Working with gifted English language learners. *Journal for the Education of the Gifted, 18*(3), 234–254.

Leslie, L. A., & Leitch, M. L. (1989). A demographic profile of recent Central American immigrants: Clinical services and implications. *Hispanic Journal of Behavioral Sciences, 11*(4), 315–329.

Leung, E. (1981). *The identification and social problems of gifted bilingual-bicultural children* (ERIC Document Reproduction Service No. ED 203 653).

Lindhold, K. J., & Gavlek, K. (1994). *California DBE projects: Project-wide evaluation report, 1992–1993.* San Jose, CA: Author.

Lindholm, K., & Padilla, A. M. (1978). Child bilingualism: Report on language mixing, switching, and translation. *Linguistics, 211,* 23–44.

Machado, M. (1987). Gifted Hispanic underidentified in classrooms. *Hispanic Link Weekly Report, 5*(7), 1–2.

Maker, J., & Schiever, S. W. (1988). *Critical issues in gifted education: Vol. II. Defensible programs for cultural and ethnic minorities.* Austin, TX: PRO-ED.

Meier, K. J., & Stewart, J. (1991). *The politics of Hispanic education: Un paso pálante y dos pátras.* Albany, NY: State University of New York Press.

Meléndez, D. (1986). Hispanic students: Still not achieving. *Thrust, 15*(4), 14–16.

Meléndez, R. (1995). *The identification of creative and talented Puerto-Rican primary students.* Unpublished doctoral disseration, University of Connecticut, Storrs, CT.

Melesky, T. J. (1984). Identifying and providing for the Hispanic gifted child. *NABE Journal, 9*(3), 43–55.

Moll, L. C. (1992). Bilingual classroom studies and community analysis: Some recent trends. *Educational Researcher, 21*(2), 20–24.

National Center for Research on Cultural Diversity and Second Language Learning (1994). *Two-way bilingual education programs in practice: A national and local perspective.* Washington, DC: Author.

National Puerto Rican Coalition (1992). *Policy brief: Puerto Rican poverty.* Washington, DC: Author.

Nazario, I. (1980). *Intervention in the development of negative attitudes of fourth grade Puerto Rican children toward school.* Unpublished doctoral dissertation, Rutgers University, New Brunswick, NJ.

Ortíz, F. I. (1988). Hispanic American children's experiences in classrooms: A comparison between Hispanic and non-Hispanic children. In L. Weis (Ed.), *Class, race and gender in American education* (pp. 63–86). Albany, NY: State University of New York Press.

Ortiz, V. Z., & Gonzalez, A. (1991). Gifted Hispanic adolescents. In M. Bireley & J. Genshaft (Eds.), *Understanding the gifted adolescent: Educational, developmental, and multicultural issues* (pp. 240–247). New York: Teachers College Press.

Ortiz, V., & Volloff, W. (1987). Identification of gifted and accelerated Hispanic students. *Journal for Education of the Gifted, 11*(1), 45–55.

Orum, L. S. (1986). *The education of Hispanics: Status and implications.* Washington, DC: National Council of La Raza.

Passow, A. H. (1986). *Educating the disadvantaged: The task school districts face* (ERIC Document Reproduction Service No. ED 267 138).

Passow, A. H., & Frasier, M. M. (1996). Toward improving identification of talent potential among minority and disadvantaged students. *Roeper Review, 18*(3), 198–202.

Patton, J. M., Prillaman, D., & VanTassel-Baska, J. (1990). The nature and extent of programs for the disadvantaged gifted in the United States and territories. *Gifted Child Quarterly, 34*(3), 94–96.

Ramírez, J. D. (1992). Executive summary. *Bilingual Education Research Journal, 16*(1 & 2), 1–62.

Renzulli, J. S. (1978). What makes giftedness? Reexamining a definition. *Phi Delta Kappan, 60*(3), 180–184 & 261.

Renzulli, J. S. (1986). The three-ring conception of giftedness: A developmental model for creative productivity. In R. J. Sternberg & J. E. Davidson (Eds.), *Conceptions of giftedness* (pp. 53–92). London: Cambridge University Press.

Renzulli, J. S. (1994). *Schools for talent development: A practical plan for total school improvement.* Mansfield, CT: Creative Learning Press.

Renzulli, J. S., & Reis, S. M. (1985). *The schoolwide enrichment model: A comprehensive plan for educational excellence.* Mansfield, CT: Creative Learning Press.

Renzulli, J. S., Reis, S. M., & Smith, L. H. (1981). *The revolving door identification model.* Bureau of Educational Research, University of Connecticut, Storrs, CT.

Renzulli, J. S., & Smith, L. H. (1978). Developing defensible programs for the gifted and talented. *Journal of Creative Behavior, 12*(51), 21–29.

Ricciardelli, L. A. (1992). Creativity and bilingualism. *Journal of Creative Behavior, 26*(4), 242–254.

Richert, E. S. (1985). Identification of gifted children in the United States: The need for pluralistic assessment. *Roeper Review, 8*(2), 68–72.

Riddle, M. E. (1985, October). *California department of education report.* Sacramento, CA: The Council of Hispanic Affairs.

Roberts, C. A. (1995). Bilingual education program models: A framework for understanding. *Bilingual Research Journal, 19*(3 & 4), 369–378.

Ruiz, R. (1989). Considerations in the education of gifted Hispanic students. In J. C. Maker & S. W. Schiever (Eds.), *Critical issues in gifted education: Vol. II. Defensible programs for cultural and ethnic minorities* (pp. 60–65). Austin, TX: PRO-ED.

Runco, M. A. (1993). *Creativity as an educational objective for disadvantaged students* (RM 9306). Storrs, CT: The National Research Center on the Gifted and Talented.

Saccuzzo, D. P., Johnson, N. E., & Guertin, T. L. (1994). Use of the Raven Progressive Matrices Test in an ethnically diverse gifted population. In D. P. Saccuzzo, N. E. Johnson, & T. L. Guertin, *Identifying underrepresented disadvantaged gifted and talented children: A multifaceted approach* (pp. 29–42). San Diego, CA: San Diego State University.

Sternberg, R. J. (1985). *Beyond IQ: A triarchic theory of human intelligence.* Cambridge, MA: Cambridge University Press.

Strom, R., Johnson, A., Strom, S., & Strom, P. (1992). Educating gifted Hispanic children and their parents. *Hispanic Journal of Behavioral Sciences, 14*(3), 383–393.

Suarez-Orozco, M. M. (1991). Immigrant adaptation to schooling: A Hispanic case. In M. A. Gibson & J. U. Ogbu (Eds.), *Minority status and schooling: A comparative study of immigrant and involuntary minorities* (pp. 37–61). New York: Garland.

Thompson, G. B. (1987). An experimental program for highly gifted children in the early primary grades. *Gifted Child Quarterly, 31*(1), 34–36.

Torrance, E. P. (1962). *Guiding creative potential.* Englewoods Cliffs, NJ: Prentice-Hall.

Torrance, E. P. (1966). *Torrance tests of creative thinking.* Lexington, MA: Personnel Press.

Torrance, E. P. (1971). Are the Torrance tests of creative thinking biased against or in favor of "disadvantaged" groups? *Gifted Child Quarterly, 15*(2), 75–80.

U.S. Bureau of the Census (1995). *Statistical abstract of the United States: 1995* (115th ed.). Washington, DC: Goverment Printing Office.

U.S. Department of Education (1994). The condition of education in the nation. *Grants projects abstracts 1992–1993.* Office of Educational Research and Improvement, Washington, DC: Goverment Printing Office.

Valencia, R. R. (1991). *Chicano school failure and success: Research and policy agendas for the 1990s.* London: Falmer Press.

Weis, L., Farrar, E., & Petrie, H. G. (1989). *Dropouts from school: Issues, dilemmas, and solutions.* New York: State University of New York Press.

Witty, E. P. (1978). Equal educational opportunity for gifted minority group children: Promise or possibility? *The Gifted Child Quarterly, 22*(3), 344–351.

Zappia, I. (1988). Identification of gifted Hispanic students: A multidimensional view. In J. C. Maker & S. W. Schiever (Eds.), *Critical issues in gifted education: Vol. II. Defensible programs for cultural and ethnic minorities* (pp. 19–26). Austin, TX: PRO-ED.

CHAPTER

3

ABORIGINAL POPULATIONS: AUSTRALIA

A close analysis of the Australian situation indicates that the values espoused in most schools reflect and foster those of the majority culture and that, unless children exhibit particular forms of behaviour, they are not considered gifted and talented. It is frequently difficult for teachers to see beyond their own cultural values and to realise that other groups admire different talents and cultivate different values in their children. (Braggett, 1985, p. 3)

This chapter considers the problems associated with identifying and programming for gifted Aboriginal students in Australia due to the mask of cultural diversity. In the first section, a brief discussion of the term *culture* opens the chapter, followed by a historical description of Australian Aboriginal cultures. In the second section, factors that create problems in the recognition of and programming for gifted Aboriginal students are examined. Also in this section, relevant literature and research are considered in an attempt to further elaborate these factors. The third section reviews the factors that constitute the mask of cultural diversity and provides a summary of some actions that may assist in the removal of the mask. A case study of a gifted Aboriginal student concludes the chapter.

CULTURES OF AUSTRALIAN ABORIGINES

What Is Culture?

Currently, *culture* is a term used often in numerous contexts. As a result, the meaning of culture is often assumed to be understood. A definition of culture usually refers to the beliefs, traditions, and values of a group (Baldwin, 1991; Keats, 1988). Few would argue with this type of definition as far as it goes. However, such a definition does not acknowledge the aspect of change within a culture. In coming to an understanding of how cultural diversity is likely to affect behaviors indicative of giftedness, it is important that such a distinction is made when defining culture.

This omission is addressed in Bullivant's (1989) definition of culture, which he described as "a social group's design for surviving in and adapting to its environment. . . . The knowledge, ideas, and skills that enable a group to survive can be thought of as its culture or survival program" (pp. 27–28). In other words, a society or "social group" is maintained by its members through their adaptation to and modification of the society's given environments. This definition suggests that culture is unique to each social group and has an element of constant change. Therefore, the way in which a particular social group responds to events and specific aspects of the environment will vary over time within the group as well as between groups.

This change and variation of response apply to any given social group's perceptions of giftedness. That is, giftedness, as a psychological construct, will be whatever a particular social group perceives it to be, and therefore, "its conceptualization can change over time and place" (Sternberg, 1986, p. 4). The concept of giftedness is relative "to changes in our knowledge, and to changes in our social and political lives" (Coleman, 1985, p. 16). In fact, if a culturally based view of giftedness is accepted, it implies that there will never exist a single view of giftedness but rather that there will be many, and these views will change with respect to changes in a social group's culture. It follows, then, that behaviors that a culture deems to be indicators of giftedness will change to reflect the current view.

Australian Aborigines are classified as a minority group in Australia. Frasier (1997) noted that the term *minority* may be applied to a number of groups according to ethnic, political, economic, or cultural status that are different from a majority group. Australian Aborigines are a minority group with respect to this meaning of minority, as well as in terms of population size (Tonemah, 1987). However, in order to point out that the problems for gifted Aboriginal students arise largely from the aspect of cultural differences, the term *culturally diverse* will be used in this chapter.

Australian Aboriginal Cultures

The continent now known as Australia has been inhabited by Aboriginal people for at least 40,000 years. Prior to European contact, there were hundreds of Aboriginal groups living throughout Australia with a total population of about 300,000. These groups were culturally different from each other; they led various lifestyles and spoke over 500 different languages. Owing to this diversity, there has never been any single entity that could accurately be called "The Aboriginal Culture." However, there were some similarities across the large number of social groups. All operated within a hunting-gathering economy; they also shared similar beliefs about the creation and nature of the world that have been collectively titled the "Dreamtime" (Harker & McConnochie, 1985). The hunting and gathering way of life was dependent on cooperation and a strong sense of group identity.

Aboriginal cultures were based on laws associated with the Dreamtime and recognized as most knowledgeable and important, those persons who best knew "these laws, the religious mechanisms available to maintain them, and the strategies which enable intervention wherever possible to improve the chances of favourable outcomes" with respect to the laws (Harker & McConnochie, 1985, p. 45).

The arrival of Europeans brought contradiction to the Aboriginal cultures which had been reasonably stable and consistent. Viewing the Aborigines as a primitive culture with people inferior to their own white society, the Europeans set out to assimilate and in some cases to annihilate the Aboriginal people and their cultures (Harker & McConnochie, 1985). Laws and processes introduced to carry out these purposes led to a devastation of Aboriginal cultures. The Wastelands Act of 1842 brought "legality" to the seizure of Aboriginal lands resulting in the displacement of Aboriginal people from their lands, while the 1911 Aborigines Act allowed government seizure of reserved lands and empowered government officials to prohibit Aborigines from towns and municipalities (Passmore, 1985). Additionally, the 1911 act appointed protectors, usually the local constabulary, of all Aboriginal children under the age of twenty-one years. As the "protectors," they officially owned all possessions of an Aboriginal, could order Aborigines to move to different areas, and worked to ensure that Aboriginal children and, as much as possible, Aboriginal adults were confined to a designated reserve.

The 1923 Training of Aboriginal Children Act empowered protectors to commit Aboriginal children to an institution where they might be required to remain until either eighteen or twenty-one years of age with little or no family contact (Passmore, 1985). However, the traditions, beliefs and values of the society withstood this devastation, making necessary the use of an assimilation tactic by the government. The Aboriginal Act of 1934 contained a clause by which an Aboriginal person "by reason of his character and standard of development and intelligence, could be exempted forever of being an Aboriginal" (p. 26) and therefore exempted from the act. This part of the act, in particular, threatened the Aboriginal cultures and identities. Not until 1962 was the exemption clause replaced with the Aboriginal Affairs Act which instituted registration of Aborigines. Such assimilation attempts were destructive to the cultural identity of Aborigines and their communities.

Along with the attempts of assimilation and cultural annihilation through laws, the Aboriginal societies were subjected to an extensive program of Western education practices which largely supported an assimilation policy in terms of content and instructional methods (Folds, 1987; Harker & McConnochie, 1985; Woods, 1994). Governor Macquarie established the first Aboriginal schools with the view that the purpose of such schools would be to train Aboriginal children as a cheap labor force for the British colony (Woods, 1994). Colonial education authorities failed to appreciate the well-developed educational systems of the Aboriginal people. Traditional Aboriginal culture views of education did not include institutionalizing learning in the form of schools and classrooms. Rather, learning was viewed as a lifelong process incorporated in daily activities. Children learned from imitation and observation. Western education practices came into constant conflict with the Aboriginal culture's approach to learning (Folds, 1987). After more than one hundred years of experiencing culturally conflicting education practices and assimilation attempts, Aboriginal communities today are still struggling to achieve coherent cultures that are functional within Australia, yet still identifiably Aboriginal.

THE CULTURAL DIVERSITY MASK OF GIFTEDNESS

Though all Australian states and territories have policies concerning the education of gifted students, there has been a general reluctance by education systems to comprehensively support gifted students through effective identification practices and appropriate programming. As a result, large numbers of gifted students remain unrecognized and suffer inadequate educational provisions.

For gifted Aboriginal students, this problem is compounded by their cultural diversity which may not be taken into account in existing identification procedures, particularly when teachers, who are largely responsible for identification, are non-Aboriginal. Lack of understanding or misunderstandings about Aboriginal cultures and how giftedness may "look" when developed within an Aboriginal culture has led to low numbers of gifted Aboriginal children being recognized and appropriately catered for by the education system. The cultural diversity mask of giftedness is formed by a number of factors. The remainder of this section presents a discussion of five of these factors as they relate to the mask of cultural diversity worn by gifted Aboriginal students.

Traditional Views of Giftedness

To begin, the recognition of gifted Aboriginal children is made difficult by traditional views of giftedness. Historically, the most widely accepted conceptualization of giftedness related to a high intellectual quotient (IQ) score established through standardized intelligence tests. This view developed largely as a result of Terman's (1925) longitudinal studies of gifted children. High intelligence test scores and excellent academic performance were used as the criteria for determining participants in the study. Terman's work led to a view of giftedness that implied generalizability to all populations and was tied closely to abstract thinking skills associated with academic success. These perceptions still exist today and do little to acknowledge the cultural influences on giftedness.

Researchers (Bruch, 1975; Davis & Rimm, 1994; Frasier, 1989; Maker, 1989) maintain that standardized tests used to determine intelligence are based on mainstream, middle-class values ignoring even known minority cultural values. The use of IQ tests to identify gifted students does not adequately take into account cultural diversity nor Aboriginal students from non–English speaking backgrounds. It is important to investigate viable alternative methods of assessment to the standardized test approach that will more accurately assess the abilities of gifted Aboriginal children and reflect the conception of giftedness held by members of the Aboriginal community. Harslett (1992) found that Raven's (1962) "Coloured Progressive Matrices Sets" were useful as a nonverbal assessment tool for identifying gifted Aboriginal students from traditional backgrounds in Western Australia. Additionally, from his research findings, he modified the "Scales for Rating the Behavioral Characteristics of Superior Students" (Renzulli, Smith, White, Callahan, & Hartman, 1976) for use with this same population of Aboriginal students. Such instruments hold promise for assisting in the creation of a multisourced approach to identification that would be more sensitive to the cultural values and traditions of Aboriginal students.

It is heartening to note that the literature indicates that the last twenty years have witnessed a broadening of the concept of giftedness away from the view that giftedness is defined only in terms of a high IQ score or superior academic achievement (Braggett, 1985; Correll, 1978;

Richert, 1987). This broader concept recognizes that giftedness is influenced by environmental factors (Clark, 1992; Frasier, 1989; Gagné, 1985) and based on cultural values, beliefs, and traditions (Braggett, 1985; Frasier, 1989; Harslett, 1992; Keats, 1988; Maltby, 1986).

Recent models and definitions of giftedness (Frasier, 1989; Gagné, 1993; George, 1987; Harslett, 1992) that support the notion of cultural influences on giftedness have served to broaden the perceptions of giftedness to become more inclusive of culturally diverse gifted students. An increase in the general awareness and understanding of cultural conceptions of giftedness is essential to ensure more informed judgments by educators during identification procedures. Specifically, a heightened understanding of the cultural effects on manifestations of giftedness should be possessed by classroom teachers who are the most likely professional group to make initial identification (Gibson, 1991).

Other information for the identification process that takes into account the cultural diversity of the student can be gained from parents and community members familiar with the student and peers from the same culture. Subjective data of this nature should be considered on an equal level with the objective data gathered from standardized tests. However, according to Braggett (1985), giftedness is viewed largely from the majority culture perspective, which may place culturally diverse groups in a disadvantaged position. He asserted that the dominant view in Australia is

> that giftedness pertains basically to the academic domain viewed within a white, middle class, monocultural society, and that gifted children achieve outstanding success in virtually all academic areas with weaknesses in none. It is not usually expected that giftedness will be found in low income areas, among families with non-English speaking backgrounds, in children from different ethnic groups, or among people whose values differ from those of the school. Such stereotypes are deeply ingrained in Australian society and schools tend to reinforce them. (p. 3)

This view was supported by the Richardson Study (Cox, Daniel, & Boston, 1985) which pointed out that, despite the fact that conceptions of giftedness had broadened, operational definitions had not necessarily reflected these beliefs. Therefore, it is still the case that students who are high academic achievers are chosen for gifted programs and some students are not identified as gifted due to such circumstances as cultural diversity, poverty, and differences in language.

Related to the traditional view of giftedness is the view that only certain behaviors valued by the dominant culture indicate giftedness. Cultural diversity affects the way in which behaviors indicative of giftedness may be manifested (Baldwin, 1985; Braggett, 1985; Clark, 1992; Davis & Rimm, 1994; Kitano & Kirby, 1986). Thus, it is imperative that cultural influences on behaviors associated with giftedness are taken into account in identification practices. A greater array of culturally relevant abilities and behaviors should be recognized and considered as indicators of giftedness, thereby ensuring that the ability of a greater number of culturally diverse gifted students is identified.

Recent research conducted by Gibson (1995) in the state of Queensland revealed eleven attributes that were useful in the identification of gifted urban Aboriginal students. The attributes included communication, humor, interests, imagination/creativity, insight, inquiry, motivation, memory, reasoning, problem-solving skills, and intra/interpersonal skills. These are further elaborated at the end of the chapter. Such attributes established as culturally relevant for a particular social group of Aborigines should be included in any identification procedures conducted by schools that have populations of that social group. Teachers should become familiar with the attributes and examples of each, in order to more successfully identify gifted Aboriginal students. Further, assessment instruments should be chosen that will reveal exceptional ability related to these specific attributes.

The Deficit View of Cultural Diversity

Another factor that must be considered as part of the cultural diversity mask of giftedness is the view of the majority culture that there were mental deficiencies in culturally diverse students that needed to be remediated. For years, Australian Aboriginal education, conducted by the dominant Western culture, was based on a belief that Aborigines were innately less intelligent than non-Aborigines. This idea was supported by those espousing white racial supremacy, the failure of Aborigines to adopt work ethics of the European invaders, and the inability of schools to educate Aborigines (Kociumbas, 1988; McConnochie, 1982; Woods, 1994).

The idea of a hierarchy of cultures was developed in the nineteenth and twentieth centuries, and placed the cultures of Western Europe at the top (Groome, 1994). This hierarchical framework gave "scientific" legitimacy to the colonial invasion and suppression of "lesser cultures." Its strongest manifestation was in the policy of assimilation, whereby the majority culture, through its institutions such as schools, churches, and the legal system, sought to manipulate the lives of Aboriginal people in an attempt to destroy their original cultures and languages, substituting in their place a white servant class culture and the English language. These assimilation attempts were not successful and were followed by a dominant culture acceptance of a variety of cultural identities. However, the variety was seen as a problem and a positive valuing of cultural diversity by the majority culture was lacking. Rather, it was seen as something to be remedied through efforts to help the minority cultures "measure up" to the majority culture's standards.

As agents of the majority culture, Australian schools reflect and encourage that culture's values. Therefore, unless students display exceptional behaviors that are prized by the majority culture, they probably will not be recognized as gifted. "It is frequently difficult for teachers to see beyond their own cultural values and to realise that other groups admire different talents and cultivate different values in their children" (Braggett, 1985, p. 3). Schools, then, often view behavioral differences as deficiencies and seek to address the "problem" through remediation (Braggett, 1985; Forrest, 1985; Reid, 1992; Tonemah, 1991). This deficit-model approach displays little respect or value for the minority culture and creates cultural conflict between the Aboriginal social group and the school. Consequently, the effect of the deficit model that fails to value difference is one of discrimination and further disadvantage.

Perceptions of a deficit model exist with regard to Aboriginal education curriculum priorities (Braggett, 1985) and may be reinforced through the misinterpretation of recent research data. For example, in a study investigating the importance of school location as an influence on student performance in Western Australia government schools, Young (1994) reports a lower performance by Aboriginal and Torres Strait Islander students when compared to non-Aboriginal students in the areas of reading, writing, and mathematics. The danger exists that findings such as these become the central concern of educators, with a heavy emphasis on remediation needs, while little attention is given to the provision of opportunities in which gifted Aboriginal students can develop and display their potential.

Earlier Australian research (Kearins, 1981) found that the deficit-model approach had been fueled by lower test scores of Aboriginal students that resulted from test bias. Such test results are then misinterpreted by curriculum designers and serve to perpetuate the view that Aboriginal students are best served, educationally, in a remediation model.

The use of a deficit model focuses almost exclusively on a remediation approach to learning and teaching. With a heavy emphasis on remediation, then, the danger exists that little attention is given to the provision of learning opportunities in which gifted Aboriginal students can develop and display their potential (Braggett, 1985). Since Australian society views giftedness basically in an academic achievement sense and because definitions are generally reflective of the dominant culture's values (Day et al., 1991), it is likely that many gifted Aboriginal students are not recognized and identified for inclusion in programs and curriculum for the gifted.

Teacher Perceptions and Expectations

Teacher perceptions of student ability and their particular effect on culturally diverse students are closely tied to the deficit approach. Rhodes (1992) found that teacher perceptions of low achievement in culturally diverse students were a major contributor to the small numbers of these students in gifted programs. This perception is still evident today in the attitudes toward Aboriginal students of some teachers and educational administrators (Gibson, 1995).

Low expectations of students because of their Aboriginality continue to be a contributing factor to the underachievement of many Aboriginal students including those who are gifted (Green, 1982; Guider, 1991). This was made apparent by a seventeen-year-old Aboriginal girl's interview comment (Gibson, 1994) describing the difficulty she had in convincing her high school teachers that she was serious about her schoolwork even though she was Aboriginal. She said, "I had to prove myself so much when I went to school [pause] to prove to the teachers that I wanted to do something. And like first of all they didn't believe you. They just thought you were there just to muck around" [Interview 8, p. 2].

Low teacher expectations of Aboriginal students are also linked to the misinterpretation or misunderstanding of culturally diverse students' behaviors. In the past, groups of Aboriginal parents and their children have found that schools, as a cultural setting, reflect the dominant culture and offer them little if any control over educational outcomes (Folds, 1987; Guider, 1991; Harris, 1989). These feelings of helplessness and rejection lead to defensive behavior in the students who feel at odds with schools and school personnel.

Folds (1987) maintained that Aboriginal students' classroom behavior becomes a resistance against the school as an assimilation agent for the majority culture. He pointed out that this resistance takes the form of behaviors such as disrupting classes, absenteeism, failure to follow behavior rules, and noncompletion of school work. Consequently, these types of behaviors erroneously reinforce teachers' low expectations of Aboriginal students.

Lack of cultural understanding by non-Aboriginal teachers leading to misinterpretation of student behaviors can generate negative teacher expectations of Aboriginal students. For instance, an Aboriginal teacher noted that "an exceptional [gifted] Aboriginal child usually stands out from the rest of the class, by calling out to the teacher. To me, as an Aboriginal teacher, I see that this shows confidence, but to non-Aboriginal teachers the child is classified as disruptive" (Gibson, 1993, Survey 011).

Cultural diversity also influences the types of learning strategies that will prove productive with Aboriginal students and allow them to demonstrate gifted behaviors. For example, Aboriginal traditional cultures encourage acceptance of Dreamtime laws and customs without question. This learning strategy is directly opposed to a common strategy of the white teacher to employ questioning as a means to assess knowledge and understanding. The lack of response from Aboriginal students to this method of learning and teaching reinforces the ungrounded teacher beliefs about low achievement in Aboriginal students (Guider, 1991).

Teachers must become "students" of Aboriginal cultures and go beyond initial perceptions to look at Aboriginal cultural influences on learning and teaching in order to understand and uncover potential giftedness in Aboriginal students. It is important for teachers to undertake professional development to increase their awareness of the learning and teaching needs of Aboriginal students, to accept and positively value cultural diversity, and to actively search for gifted Aboriginal students in their classrooms. Professional development activities of this kind will enhance the success rate of identification efforts to recognize gifted, culturally diverse students.

The Misconception of One Aboriginal Culture

Another factor making up the cultural diversity mask of giftedness is involved with the misconception that a minority culture group is a homogeneous population (Frasier, 1989). Reference has been made earlier in the chapter to the existence of a number of Aboriginal cultures. Such differences in culture have resulted largely from geographical and social diversity (Forrest, 1985; Guider, 1991). Some Aboriginal groups observe a more traditional lifestyle as compared to Aboriginal groups who have adopted a lifestyle more typical of the dominant society. Some groups live in isolated regions while others make up a proportion of the population in large metropolitan areas. Some groups are best classified as rural while others exist in urban settings. Aboriginal cultures may be non–English speaking, speak only English, or be best categorized as a bilingual culture. Such diversity makes it impossible to speak of one Aboriginal culture. As a result, it cannot be expected that there will be one Aboriginal view of giftedness and one concise list of culturally relevant attributes by which giftedness can be identified across all Aboriginal social groups. This diversity of cultures within the Australian Aboriginal population serves to complicate the identification of and provision for gifted Aboriginal students (Forrest, 1985).

Lack of Culturally Relevant Learning Environments

The last factor that helps to create the cultural diversity mask of giftedness is the lack of opportunities presented by the classroom curriculum that would encourage and foster the gifted potential of Aboriginal students. As has been previously discussed in the chapter, it is important to articulate culturally relevant views of giftedness and culturally relevant attributes that may assist educators to recognize gifted Aboriginal students. However, little use can be made of this knowledge for identification and programming in an environment where such behaviors are not required or encouraged by the existing curriculum.

An appropriate classroom curriculum is essential to the emergence of students' gifted behaviors that can provide valuable information for the identification process (Hadaway & Marek-Schroer, 1992). It is essential that culturally diverse students should be given the opportunity to participate in learning experiences that evoke their exceptional potential and allow them to demonstrate their abilities (Richert, 1987). A nurturing and accepting environment is needed where children and their cultures are respected. Otherwise, students "from different ethnic groups will not reveal aspects of their own culture if they believe that the Anglo-Australian culture is the only one valued" (Braggett, 1985, p. 6).

Provisions that nurture culturally diverse gifted students will sometimes need unconventional settings outside of the school and need to involve nontraditional personnel such as community members (Reid, 1992). Teachers should be aware of these needs and be prepared to foster this type of learning environment.

The reduction of basic skills deficits in gifted culturally diverse and gifted disadvantaged children should also be a curriculum concern that is addressed before initiating identification procedures (Davis & Rimm, 1994; Passow, 1991). Often such deficits contribute to the under-identification of these students. According to Davis and Rimm, Frasier (1989) described the Program of Assessment, Diagnosis and Instruction (PADI). This technique was developed for African-American and Hispanic students who were not demonstrating their potential due to gaps in basic skills. PADI focused on increasing thinking skills and academic skills that were needed for success in gifted programs. Through student performance in the program, teachers were more successfully able to identify students for the gifted program.

However, these types of programs must be employed with caution and seen as a means, not an end. Callahan and McIntire (1994) urged that educators should think in terms of "a model of potential rather than deficiency" (p. vi). They argued that "a solid and challenging curriculum" (p. v) must be provided for culturally diverse students in order that their potential ability can be demonstrated and consequently recognized. Certainly, this should be the major goal in establishing culturally relevant learning environments.

Braggett (1985) described an environment that is conducive to the expression of gifts and talents as one that "is tolerant of difference, accepting of diversity, . . . free from value judgments about the worth of different cultures . . . [and] promotes self-esteem and pride in excellence regardless of the area of study" (p. 6). The classroom curriculum should reflect these same attributes in order to enhance students' feelings of worth and to confirm that their ideas, interests, and abilities are genuinely accepted and seen as valid. Braggett (1985) suggested that teaching strategies that foster the valuing of all cultures include the use of examples of excellence from a wide range of gifted and talented behavior, working in conjunction with parents, involving representatives from various cultures in the community, and providing suitable gifted and talented role models for culturally diverse students. Such a curriculum is not only educationally sound for all children but fosters potential outstanding ability as well.

Summary

Five factors contributing to the mask of cultural diversity worn by gifted Aboriginal students have been discussed in this chapter. These factors include traditional views of giftedness; the deficit-model approach to Aboriginal education; uninformed teacher perceptions and low teacher expectations; the myth that Australian Aborigines are a homogeneous social group; and the lack of culturally relevant learning environments and curriculum to encourage the gifted potential of Aboriginal students.

In order to remove the mask of cultural diversity, a number of suggested actions have been described. Following is a point summary of these suggestions.

- Definitions and conceptions of giftedness should be adopted that support the notion of cultural influences on manifestations of giftedness.
- As an alternative to culturally biased intelligence tests, assessment instruments and procedures should be utilized that reflect the conception of giftedness held by members of the Aboriginal community.
- The identification approach should be multisourced and incorporate objective, subjective, and nonverbal measures.
- It should be recognized that since the construct of giftedness is culturally based, attributes and behaviors indicative of giftedness will change from culture to culture.
- Assessment instruments should relate to the gifted attributes specific to the social group involved in the identification process.
- Educators should value cultural differences by viewing differences in behavior as just that—differences, not deficiencies, of a particular cultural group.
- Teachers should strive to increase their awareness of the educational needs of Aboriginal students, to accept and positively value cultural diversity, and to actively search for gifted Aboriginal students in their classrooms.

- Educators should recognize that there is cultural diversity within the Australian Aboriginal population, resulting in a variety of views of giftedness.

- A nurturing and accepting learning environment, where Aboriginal students and their cultures are respected, is necessary to encourage the expression of giftedness.

- Utilization by teachers of a culturally relevant curriculum demonstrates a valuing of Aboriginal cultures and fosters the expression of attributes and behaviors indicative of giftedness.

CASE STUDY

A Gifted Aboriginal Boy

The following case study of an Aboriginal boy illustrates just one way in which giftedness may be manifested in this population and the ways in which people have responded to his giftedness.

Kevin is fifteen years old and currently lives in a country town of over 10,000 people with his mother, stepfather, two stepbrothers and a baby stepsister. He has lived all his life in urban areas of this type. He is the oldest of the four children. Until the age of two, he lived solely with his mother and has never met his biological father. However, he was extremely close to his maternal grandfather until the age of 4. Kevin's mother is an Aboriginal health worker for the Community Health Service and completed high school. His father, who quit school at age fifteen, is employed by the city council in the maintenance department. Both parents have always lived in urban areas.

Kevin has never seemed to have any problems with his schoolwork, although his primary school teachers reported that he did not appear to make much of an effort with his work. Kevin's mother reports that he has always been fairly well behaved at school and his report cards have been consistently good. With Kevin now in high school, his mother reports that he rarely studies at home but still gets Distinctions in what she terms are the harder subjects such as mathematics and science. He has never been recommended by the school staff to participate in enrichment classes or interschool academic competitions. His current teachers describe him as a pleasant but average student who does not seem particularly interested in school. However, recently he joined the Aboriginal and Torres Strait Islander Tertiary Aspirations Program (AITAP) and competed at the state level, winning a trophy in Theatre Sports (these are competitive games that develop dramatic skills).

Kevin's mother reports that he has already mapped out plans for his future. He aspires to complete university and become either a scientific engineer or a mathematician. He has also decided that he wants to marry and have two children. His parents say he is very determined to achieve his goals.

According to his mother, Kevin has always seemed a bit more mature than others his age. He makes friends quickly but is not easily swayed by his peers. He looks down on others who smoke and drink. Other boys seem to respect him and often phone him for help with schoolwork. He is frequently invited to social events by his friends.

Kevin is quite an inquisitive person. His mother reports that as a young child he liked to find out how radios and televisions worked. He shows a great interest in problems faced by other people such as the famines in Africa and social injustices in Australia.

He is quick to defend his individual family members against racial comments by classmates which, in the past, has resulted in detention and reprimands at school. As well, he is sensitive to the circumstances of other people in the community. For example, he completes odd jobs for some neighbors free because they do not have enough money to pay. His mother reports that he seems to be especially attuned to other people's emotions.

Kevin is a talented sportsman and has always participated in a wide range of sports. He was asked to play men's reserve grade rugby league at the age of fourteen and was a highly respected tackler until a knee injury forced him to quit. During that time, he was leading in points for being the best and fairest player.

At present, most of Kevin's spare time is spent experimenting with the guitar which he has learned with amazing speed; he can play back any song he hears. In the past, he has shown an interest in art, learning about traditional art from an Aboriginal Elder. He is a self-taught woodcarver and recently completed carving the top of a large wooden table with flowers, swirls, and sayings such as "Never judge a book by its cover."

Kevin's parents are proud of his school achievement and point out that he continues to carry "with him the good Aboriginal traditions."

Suggestions for Classroom Practice

Classroom teachers play a major role in recognizing and providing for gifted urban Aboriginal students. It is important for teachers to have an understanding of the ways in which these Aboriginal students may demonstrate their exceptional abilities to increase teachers' abilities to effectively identify gifted Aboriginal students.

Eleven attributes were revealed in recent research conducted in Queensland (Gibson, 1995). The first ten attributes were originally described as indicators of giftedness in six minority groups in the United States, in research conducted by Frasier (1992). The Queensland research confirmed that these ten attributes were transferable to the Australian educational context and relevant to Australian Aboriginal cultures. Furthermore, the Queensland data suggested that an additional attribute, named Intra/Inter Personal Ability be included with Frasier's attributes for use with populations of urban Aboriginal children. The eleven attributes with definitions are presented below.

1. **Communication**—Highly expressive and effective use of words, numbers, symbols
    Examples:
    *   Have an unusual ability to communicate (verbally, nonverbally, physically, artistically, symbolically)
    *   Use particularly apt examples

2. **Humor**—Conveys and picks up on humor
    Examples:
    *   Have keen sense of humor
    *   Have a capacity for seeing unusual relationships
    *   Show an unusual emotional depth
    *   Unusually quick use of humor in response to a situation or person

3. **Imagination/Creativity**—Produces many ideas; highly original
    Examples:
    *   Be keenly observant
    *   Have wild, unusual, sometimes silly ideas
    *   Be highly curious
    *   Produce many different ideas
    *   Be exceptionally ingenious in using everyday materials

4. **Inquiry**—Questions, experiments, explores
    Examples:
    *   Ask unusual questions for his/her age
    *   Play or experiment with ideas
    *   Extensively explore materials, devices, situations to gain information
    *   Always asking questions, wanting to know about a wide variety of topics

5. **Insight**—Quickly grasps new concepts and makes connections; senses deeper meanings
    Examples:
    *   Be keenly observant
    *   Appear to be a good guesser
    *   Have exceptional ability to draw conclusions
    *   Intuitiveness

6. **Interests**—Intense (sometimes unusual) interests
   Examples:
   • Have unusual or advanced interest in a topic or activity
   • Be a self-starter
   • Pursue an activity unceasingly

7. **Memory**—Large storehouse of information on school or nonschool topics
   Examples:
   • Remember information easily
   • Pay attention to details
   • Already know many things
   • Have a wealth of knowledge about a topic(s)

8. **Motivation**—Evidence of desire to learn
   Examples:
   • Be persistent in pursuing/finishing self-chosen activities
   • Be an enthusiastic learner
   • Have aspirations to be somebody, to achieve

9. **Problem-solving Ability**—Effective, often inventive, strategies for recognizing and solving problems
   Examples:
   • Have exceptional ability in devising a systematic strategy for solving problems
   • Change strategy if it is not working
   • Create new designs
   • Be an inventor and innovator

10. **Reasoning**—Logical approaches to figuring out solutions
    Examples:
    • Demonstrate exceptional critical thinking skills
    • Have an unusual ability to make generalizations
    • Think things through in a logical manner and come up with a likely answer
    • Have an exceptional ability to use metaphors and analogies

11. **Intrapersonal/Interpersonal Ability**—An unusually heightened understanding of self and others
    Examples:
    • Knowledge of own strengths, emotions, and cognitive style
    • Leadership:
      —Persuade and influence people's behavior
      —Effectively organize people and events

—Independent thinker

—Be a leader in achievement

• Sensitive to the feelings and needs of others

• Self confident

• Mature behavior and thought

• Demonstrates a high degree of social responsibility, conscious moral behavior

Additionally, teachers should utilize their understanding of the eleven attributes and their knowledge of the students' background to design and develop culturally relevant curriculum. As Aboriginal students experience success in a culturally relevant curriculum, their self-esteem and confidence will increase, encouraging the expression of gifted behaviors.

Teachers should keep in mind strategies that could be included in the curriculum to heighten cultural relevance. Following are some suggestions that might be used to achieve greater cultural relevance in the curriculum for Aboriginal students.

• Choose syllabus content that has social relevance for Aboriginal students and that therefore can be contextualized for learning.

• Make use of a variety of learning and teaching strategies in order to take into account the learning styles of the Aboriginal students.

• Include the Aboriginal perspective of knowledge in the presentation content.

• Incorporate the students' real and current interests in classroom activities.

• Utilize Aboriginal guest speakers (community leaders, storytellers, athletes, musicians, poets, artists).

• Make frequent use of Aboriginal staff at the school for constructive feedback and suggestions about curriculum decisions as well as for direct teaching.

REFERENCES

Baldwin, A. Y. (1985). Programs for the gifted and talented: Issues concerning minority populations. In F. Horowitz & F. O'Brien (Eds.), *The gifted and talented: Developmental perspectives* (pp. 223–249). Washington, DC: American Psychological Association.

Baldwin, A. Y. (1991). Ethnic and cultural issues. In N. Colangelo & G. A. Davis (Eds.), *Handbook of gifted education* (pp. 416–427). Needham Heights, MA: Allyn & Bacon.

Braggett, E. J. (1985). *Education of gifted and talented children from populations with special needs: Discussion documents.* Canberra, Australia: Commonwealth Schools Commission.

Bruch, C. (1975). Assessment of creativity in culturally different children. *Gifted Child Quarterly, 19,* 164–174.

Bullivant, B. M. (1989). Culture: Its nature and meaning for educators. In J. A. Banks & C. A. Banks (Eds.), *Multicultural education: Issues and perspectives* (pp. 27–45). Needham Heights, MA: Allyn & Bacon.

Callahan, C. M., & McIntire, J. A. (1994). *Identifying outstanding talent in American Indian and Alaska Native students.* Washington, DC: Office of Educational Research and Improvement, U.S. Department of Education.

Clark, B. (1992). *Growing up gifted* (4th ed.). New York: Macmillan.

Coleman, L. J. (1985). *Schooling the gifted.* Menlo Park, CA: Addison-Wesley.

Correll, M. M. (1978). *Teaching the gifted and talented.* Bloomington, IN: The Phi Delta Kappa Educational Foundation.

Cox, J., Daniel, N., & Boston, B. O. (1985). *Educating able learners: Programs and promising practices.* Austin, TX: University of Texas Press.

Davis, G. A., & Rimm, S. B. (1994). *Education of the gifted and talented* (3rd ed.). Needham Heights, MA: Allyn & Bacon.

Day, A., Forbes-Harper, N., Houston, I., Langdale, O., Milne, H., Raboczi, C., & Watkin, E. (1991). Giftedness: A fair go for all Australians. In M. Goodall & B. Culhane (Eds.), *Teaching strategies for a clever country* (pp. 17–32). Melbourne, Australia: Barker & Company Pty.

Folds, R. (1987). *Whitefella school.* Sydney, Australia: Allen & Unwin.

Forrest, V. (1985). Providing for Aboriginal achievers. In E. J. Braggett (Ed.), *Education of gifted and talented children from populations with special needs: Discussion documents* (pp. 36–37). Canberra, Australia: Commonwealth Schools Commission.

Frasier, M. M. (1989). Identification of gifted Black students: Developing new perspectives. In C. J. Maker & S. W. Schiever (Eds.), *Critical issues in gifted education: Vol II. Defensible programs for cultural and ethnic minorities* (pp. 213–225). Austin, TX: PRO-ED.

Frasier, M. M. (1992). *Meeting the needs of gifted economically disadvantaged students: A long term plan.* A strand presented at Confratute '92, University of Connecticut, Storrs, CT.

Frasier, M. M. (1997). Gifted minority students: Reframing approaches to their identification and education. In N. Colangelo & G. A. Davis (Eds.), *Handbook of gifted education* (2nd ed., pp. 498–515). Needham Heights, MA: Allyn & Bacon.

Gagné, F. (1985). Giftedness and talent: Reexamining a reexamination of the definitions. *Gifted Child Quarterly, 29*(3), 103–112.

Gagné, F. (1993). Constructs and models pertaining to exceptional human abilities. In K. A. Heller, F. J. Monks, & A. H. Passow (Eds.), *International handbook of research and development of giftedness and talent* (pp. 69–87). Oxford: Pergamon Press.

George, K. R. (1987). *Identifying gifted and talented Indian students* (ERIC Document Reproduction Service No. ED 284 715). Las Cruces, NM: ERIC Clearinghouse on Rural Education and Small Schools.

Gibson, K. L. (1991, November). *The provision of defensible programs in Queensland schools.* Paper presented at the Australian Association for Research in Education Conference, Gold Coast, Australia.

Gibson, K. L. (1993). [Aboriginal teacher survey: What traits, aptitudes, and behaviors successfully identify Aboriginal primary school children with exceptional ability?]. Unpublished raw data.

Gibson, K. L. (1994). [Aboriginal parent and child interview]. Unpublished raw data.

Gibson, K. L. (1995, August). *A promising approach for identifying gifted Aboriginal students in Australia.* Paper presented at the 11th World Conference on Gifted and Talented Children, Hong Kong.

Green, N. (1982). The classroom teacher's influence on the academic performance of Aboriginal children. In J. Sherwood (Ed.), *Aboriginal education: Issues and innovations* (pp. 107–126). Perth, Australia: Creative Research.

Groome, H. (1994). *Teaching Aboriginal studies effectively.* Wentworth Falls, NSW: Social Science Press.

Guider, J. (1991). Why are so many Aboriginal children not achieving at school? *The Aboriginal Child at School, 19*(2), 42–53.

Hadaway, N. L., & Marek-Schroer, M. F. (1992). Multidimensional assessment of the gifted minority student. *Roeper Review, 15*(2), 73–77.

Harker, R. K., & McConnochie, K. R. (1985). *Education as cultural artifact: Studies in Maori and Aboriginal education.* Palmerston North, New Zealand: The Dunmore Press.

Harris, S. (1989). Culture boundaries, culture maintenance-in-charge, and two-way Aboriginal schools. *The Aboriginal Child at School, 17*(5), 3–19.

Harslett, M. G. (1992). *The identification of gifted Aboriginal children.* Unpublished doctoral thesis, University of Western Australia, Perth, Australia.

Kearins, J. (1981). Visual spatial memory in Australian Aboriginal children of desert regions. *Cognitive Psychology, 13,* 434–460.

Keats, D. M. (1988). Cultural concepts of intelligence. In G. Davidson (Ed.), *Ethnicity and cognitive assessment: Australian perspectives* (pp. 37–43). Darwin, Northern Territory, Australia: Darwin Institute of Technology Press.

Kitano, M. K., & Kirby, D. F. (1986). *Gifted education: A comprehensive view.* Boston: Little, Brown.

Kociumbas, J. (1988). The best years? In V. Burgmann & J. Lee (Eds.), *Making a life: A people's history of Australia since 1788* (pp. 147–151). Fitzroy, Victoria: McPhee Gribble.

Maker, C. J., & Schiever, S. W. (1989). *Critical issues in gifted education: Vol II. Defensible programs for cultural and ethnic minorities.* Austin, TX: PRO-ED.

Maltby, F. (1986). Teacher identification of gifted children in primary schools. In A. J. Cropley, K. K. Urban, H. Wagner, & W. Wieczerkowski (Eds.), *Giftedness: A continuing worldwide challenge* (pp. 427–433). New York: Trillium Press.

McConnochie, K. R. (1982). Aborigines and Australian education: Historical perspectives. In J. Sherwood (Ed.), *Aboriginal education: Issues and innovations* (pp. 17–32). Perth, Australia: Creative Research.

Passmore, T. (1985, September 24–26). A condensed history of Aboriginal people since the colonisation of Australia. *Wikaru.*

Passow, A. H. (1991). Educational programs for minority/disadvantaged gifted students. In R. Jenkins-Friedman, E. S. Richert, & J. F. Feldhusen (Eds.), *Special populations of gifted learners: A book of readings* (pp. 1–19). New York: Trillium Press.

Raven, J. C. (1962). *Coloured progressive matrices sets A, Ab, B.* London: H. K. Lewis.

Reid, N. (1992). *Correcting cultural myopia: The discovery and nurturance of the culturally different gifted and talented in New Zealand* (ERIC Document Reproduction Service No. ED 357 532). Paper presented at the Asian Conference on Giftedness, Taipei, Taiwan.

Renzulli, J. S., Smith, L. H., White, A. J., Callahan, C. M., & Hartman, R. K. (1976). *Scales for rating the behavioral characteristics of superior students.* Mansfield, CT: Creative Learning Press.

Rhodes, L. (1992). Focusing attention on the individual in identification of gifted Black students. *Roeper Review, 14*(3), 108–110.

Richert, E. S. (1987). Rampant problems and promising practices in the identification of disadvantaged gifted students. *Gifted Child Quarterly, 31*(4), 149–154.

Sternberg, R. J. (1986). A triarchic theory of intellectual giftedness. In R. J. Sternberg & J. E. Davidson (Eds.), *Conceptions of giftedness* (pp. 223–246). New York: Cambridge University Press.

Terman, L. (1925). *Genetic studies of genius: Vol. I. Mental and physical traits of a thousand gifted children.* Stanford, CA: Stanford University Press.

Tonemah, S. A. (1987). Assessing American Indian gifted and talented students' abilities. *Journal for the Education of the Gifted, 10*(3), 181–194.

Tonemah, S.A. (1991). *Gifted and talented American Indian students and Alaska Native students* (Eric Document Reproduction Service No. ED 343 769).

Woods, D. (1994). Discussion paper on Aboriginal and Torres Strait Islander education. *Curriculum Perspectives, 14*(4), 26–35.

Young, D. (1994). A comparison of student performance in Western Australian schools: Rural and urban differences. *The Australian Educational Researcher, 21*(2), 87–105.

CHAPTER

4

IMMIGRANT NON–ENGLISH SPEAKING POPULATIONS: AUSTRALIA

INTRODUCTION

As a result of the Carrick review (1990), the New South Wales (NSW) government in Australia released its Strategy for the Education of Gifted and Talented Students in 1991, expounding that "the aim of education is to assist in the development of each child's potential" and the "provision for helping children of exceptional ability is not a luxury but a necessity" (NSW Ministry of Education, 1991, p. 2).

During the next seven years, special programs for the gifted and talented students—ranging from full-time schools (known as Selective High Schools) and full-time classes at Years 5 and 6 (known as Opportunity C Classes), to a multitude of pull-out alternatives that may vary from one day or several hours per week to a one-off experience—were implemented throughout most school districts in

NSW. Where these programs were developed to focus on advanced academic skills, the overriding criterion for inclusion in the programs was the result of an intelligence test. A score in excess of 130 was usually required.

The development of research over the past twenty years has yielded a concept of intelligence that has taken on new dimensions. No longer is it necessary to rely on a very narrow, single-track idea of intelligence—that of a high IQ score—because the tools to determine the full scope of every individual are available if multiple procedures are implemented. Psychologists such as Vygotsky (1978) and Gardner (1983) propose that intelligence tests fail to yield any indication of a child's zone of potential development, and studies of intelligence and cognition have suggested the existence of a number of different intellectual strengths, or competencies, each of which may have its own developmental history. One of the main barriers to empowering every child to reach his or her full potential is teacher attitude (Carroll, 1982; Feldman, 1991; Gross, 1986; Renzulli, 1979; Resnick, 1976; Sternberg & Salter, 1982). Teachers and school counselors associate all concepts of intelligence with high-level thought patterns, informed decision making, ability to think laterally, and ability to use one's brain power—the resulting measure of an IQ test. As a result of these persisting attitudes, many students have been severely disadvantaged over the years.

Tests are encased in language, quite often a high level of sophisticated English, and thus children from a "deprived" background—for example, children from a non–English speaking background (NESB), Aboriginal children, and those from a low socioeconomic background—are at a distinct disadvantage when attempting these tests. As a result of the children's low scores, educational misplacements are frequently made. This barrier will be broken down only when the identification of children, both the gifted and those with learning problems, is administered at a very early age using a multiplicity of instruments. Appropriate and effective programs must then be implemented to assist the children in attaining their full potential. For far too many years, poverty, ethnicity, and Aboriginality have all been equated with a learning deficit, when what should be realized is that different cultures and social groups have different sets of values, not a deficit set of values.

Davis (1948) was among the first to draw attention to the cultural bias, including social class and race, that is inherent in IQ tests. More recent research (Baldwin, 1977, 1984; Black, 1963; Frasier, 1991; Hoffman, 1964; Passow, 1980; Richert, 1985; Richert, Alvino, & McDonnel, 1982) has focused on the importance of cultural differences in intelligence and the failure of IQ tests to identify an adequate proportion of children from outside the middle-class stream for gifted programs. Sternberg (1986) proposed that a greater emphasis had been placed on the role of knowledge and the interaction between this knowledge and mental processes and stressed that there was considerable emphasis of context and culture in defining intelligence. Many educators are concerned that children from certain races and lower socioeconomic groups continue to be underrepresented in programs for gifted students.

The notion that intelligence is fixed is closely related to the issue of heredity. If it is believed that intelligence is innate, then it is also believed that intelligence is fixed and that it is not possible to teach children to become smarter. Fortunately, there is an abundance of evidence that these conclusions are incorrect. Programs that indicate the inadequacy of these notions include Headstart Catalyst (Bringing Out Head Start Talents) Programs (Karnes, 1990) and Mary Meeker's (1963) "Structure of the Intellect (SOI) Techniques for Teaching Competency," both of which have had significant effects on the intellectual development of "disadvantaged" children in the United States.

There are many gifted children from economically disadvantaged backgrounds, but educators have to develop better ways of identifying them. Mitigating against such identification is the reality that many teachers still retain prejudices about poor children, NESB children, and Aboriginal children that result in low academic expectations for such children. Therefore, concerned educators need to instigate the use of alternative and reliable methods of identification that will not exclude these children from special programs.

Early identification of gifted students is imperative, and for middle-class Caucasian children, accurate identification is relatively easy. Alternatively, those children who come from homes where English is not used and early enriching experiences have been provided only by television programs, use of the same criteria found on checklists of characteristics of gifted children—for example, "has a large, enriched vocabulary," "is highly inquisitive, imaginative, and intellectually curious," "has mastery of foundation reading skills"—is not valid.

HOW MANY HAVE WE MISSED?

Silvana, Velice, Mohammed, Lupce, and Abdurrahman are gifted children from non–English speaking backgrounds. Through the encouragement of teachers, parents, and friends—combined with their powerful determination to prove their worth—these children have overcome all odds to demonstrate that high educational attainment can be a reality, even for children from an ethnic minority. A major barrier to such attainment, though, has been the utilization of narrowly based procedures to identify giftedness. Despite the wealth of available identification procedures for gifted children, particularly for those from a minority or underserved population within our society, we continue to rely almost completely on IQ and Achievement Test scores to place children in programs that will allow them to reach their full educational potential. This neglects the fact that cultural bias could be a factor, distorting the results of children who are not native speakers of English. Roedell and colleagues stated that

> [t]ests such as the Stanford-Binet or WPPSI which include measures of children's ability to deal with language in subtle and sophisticated ways may underestimate the abilities of children from bilingual backgrounds even if the children speak English fluently enough to communicate well in every day situations. (Roedell, Jackson, & Newman, 1980, p. 3)

The screening of Year 6 children for Selective High Schools in New South Wales is one example of this test-based procedure. Regardless of cultural diversity, degree of disadvantage, or proficiency in English language, all nominated children sit the same examinations in English, Mathematics, and General Ability (IQ) at exactly the same time on the same day. Their response sheets are posted directly to the Australian Council for Educational Research in Melbourne, where they are computer-scored and each child's level of attainment is assessed. The results are then forwarded to the respective elementary schools as Successful/Unsuccessful for each candidate. Placements for special programs in the upper elementary school classes are similarly assessed. Any candidate who does not achieve an IQ score of 135 or more is automatically eliminated from consideration.

Children whose results are close to the "successful group" (which is also determined by the set number of available places) are placed on a Prioritised Reserve List, and should any of the successful candidates decline their placement offer, this offer is then made, in order, to these children.

Doubtless this process of selection is both time- and cost-efficient—but is it candidate fair? More than test scores must be considered if we are going to sift out *all* children with a potential for academic success and placement in a high-ability learning track. To make the best informed decisions, we need to look for patterns emerging from behaviors as well as test results, and we need to be able to make these identifications much earlier, and thus plan elementary-level programs that will empower the students and facilitate our decision making.

Like most educational change or rethinking, a focus on giftedness occurs only when something within society is going wrong. By the mid-1980s, for example, Australia was experiencing one of its worst economic downturns in decades. The budget deficit was increasing and unemployment was steadily rising. The "lucky country" was very rapidly becoming the "worried country." The rebirth of emphasis on education of gifted children might prove to be one answer to this untimely predicament, some believed. However, the question remained as to what all consumers—administrators, staff, parents, community, students, and particularly the very strong teachers' union—would accept as politically and socially acceptable, as well as educationally sound. The concept finally became a reality in NSW when the State Policy for Gifted Education was released to schools in 1991, to be fully implemented in all state schools by the end of 1993. Training conferences for all regions were organized throughout 1991, and support personnel from all Department Clusters of Education were represented. For schools with high ethnic, Aboriginal, or low socioeconomic populations, the task of implementing the gifted policy was not going to be easy.

CASE STUDIES

Policy into Practice

The year 1989 saw the reestablishment in NSW of Selective High Schools (designed to cater to academically gifted children), with entrance to this specific track being based on the students' performance on computer-assessed tests in English, Mathematics, and General Ability (IQ). Children who were selected for this high-ability track were expected to learn more, faster, and thus they were taught more.

It was imperative that children like Silvana, Velice, Mohammed, Lupce, and Abdurrahman, all of whom demonstrated potential for academic giftedness in a short span of time, be immersed in an educational environment that would be conducive to their individual learning styles. I believed that they should be given every opportunity to take advantage of this special secondary school curriculum at the newly established selective high school. It would be a moral and social injustice to have such abilities overlooked because of one perceived deficit: a shortfall in their English language abilities.

In 1987, I was a new member of staff in a school whose student population consisted of children from twenty-seven different cultural backgrounds, predominantly Macedonian, Lebanese, Turkish, and Vietnamese, with only one Australian family in the school. The community was geographically isolated and housed on the perimeter of the local steelworks, which supplied employment for most of the fathers and many of the mothers.

Within a few months of working in the school and gradually getting to know members of the community, I became quite concerned about the number of young adolescents, "early school dropouts," who were aimlessly wandering the streets day after day. Many had brothers and sisters in our school who appeared to be good students, so I wondered why there would be so many who left secondary school just as soon as the leaving age was reached, usually without any formal qualification that would assist them with their search for employment. Could there be something that we could do better, or differently, that might make a difference? By October, I had made a decision that I knew would receive some staff opposition, but it was based on my own philosophy of education and the way I believed that children learn, as supported by Howes (1974) when he stated:

> As each child is born an individual, he develops as an individual in individual ways and all experiences are personal and individual in meaning. The task of schooling is to build upon a full recognition that the child, each child, is unique and individual. Considering individuality and uniqueness as basic building blocks is very different from building to foster or encourage individuality. The individual's uniqueness of experience, his perceptions and understandings, and his interests are the school's starting points from which to foster continued growth and development. These are the links to new experiences and extensions for further learning and patterning. (p. 132)

Children learn when they are active participants in the teaching-learning process. During the 1987 school year, it became obvious that my classroom strategies, where children worked in groups or individually—and only when necessary in a variety of classroom arrays—were not commonly practiced by other staff members. The majority of primary classes were very formally organized in rows, facing the main chalkboard. From discussions with staff, I learned that, to a large extent, this classroom organization was the result of parental expectations. Their memories of classrooms to which they had been exposed during their educative years had followed this format. The parents also believed that the school was the "sole domain" of the teachers and that they must not interfere. They would visit only if requested, and this usually meant "trouble." I have never taught guided by these environmental constraints. The children's classroom (not my classroom) is a busy (probably described by some as noisy) hive of activity. Parents, as many as I can coerce, come in to assist in a myriad of ways.

The children are encouraged to love learning and to recognize that how you go about any set project is entirely dependent upon the content, the resources available, and your own personal learning style. Therefore, within the classroom, rarely are any two people doing exactly the same thing at the same time. To establish such an environment for 1988 was not going to be an easy task, but it certainly was not impossible.

Throughout 1988 and into 1989, the children in my class, experiencing something "really different," seemed happy, even excited, about their "new educational environment" without realizing they had taken upon themselves, to a large degree, the responsibility of their own learning outcomes. It had also become obvious that among students so motivated and demonstrating high learning potential, there were some gifted students.

My responsibility was to address the following questions. What procedures could be employed to identify our gifted children, and at what stage of their schooling, if at all, would I be successful? How would I overcome the already ESL-laden curriculum to meet the needs of these special children? How would I identify these children early enough for them to compete equitably with their Anglo counterparts? They entered kindergarten without an enriched vocabulary or reading capabilities, and often without a word of English. Additionally, what could be done for the present unidentified upper-primary students, often still working on a program that was behind that of their English speaking peers in the economically advantaged areas? I felt strongly that the tests readily employed in the system often did not accurately measure the true abilities of minority group children.

Silvana

Silvana was in this class, and it was imperative that a child like Silvana, who had demonstrated potential for academic giftedness in just fourteen months, be immersed in an educational environment that was conducive to her learning style. Although there was a slight shortfall in English competency, she demonstated outstanding strengths in other areas. One of the highlights of her final year in elementary school was to gain a High Distinction for the National Mathematics Competition sponsored by the University of NSW (Sydney), which placed her in the top two percent of participating students from Year 6 throughout Australasia.

The concept of a Selective High School was viewed very unfavorably by the "upper-class areas" of Wollongong, in the early years. Many parents and school staff did not allow their children to compete for placement. So in 1989, five children from our school were successful in eventually gaining placement, although only Silvana was successful in the first round of offers for placement. For the five children accepted, it was the ideal opportunity to be immersed in a level of English that would empower them to attain the educational outcomes that they certainly had the potential to achieve.

During Year 7, in 1990, Silvana continued to work hard, and her performance in all curricular areas was well above average. By the end of the year, she had earned the honor of being named one of the five "Merit Placements" (the five children who had earned the highest total grades for the year). She had also attended a special Mathematics Enrichment Program for students from Years 7 to 9 conducted by the Faculty of Mathematics at Wollongong University, and had attained very pleasing results. I think that her most valued success during this first year at high school was gaining top place in English; she had listened to me say, probably a thousand times, "If only we could have worked together on a different English program a lot earlier." She was determined to succeed in this area, and she did.

In May, Silvana had been offered a scholarship from the Charles Sturt University, Bathurst Campus, to attend a Gifted and Talented Students' Weekend School for Years 5 to 10, but unfortunately the expense involved for the whole family to accompany her was beyond their means, and they (especially Dad) were not about to let a little twelve-year-old girl travel one hundred and fifty kilometers away and stay alone for the whole weekend.

Silvana's high level of performance and achievements continued in 1991 and through 1995. By the end of Year 9, she had gained the honor of top place in the year group, including top place in Mathematics, Science, Languages, Commerce, and English! She continued in the University Mathematics Enrichment Program and competed in the National Mathematics and Science

Competitions, gaining High Distinctions in both. She began public speaking and debating, representing the school at both regional and state levels.

Silvana still held strongly to her Macedonian origin and continued to attend Saturday School to maintain her oral language and develop her Macedonian reading and writing skills, as well as to gain insight into their literature. She belonged to the Macedonian Dance Group, which not only met on a local basis but also performed at special Cultural Festivals in many centers including Sydney. These activities were all accomplished with the same degree of enthusiasm and success as her regular schoolwork. Silvana eventually enrolled at the University of Wollongong to work on a Science-Law Degree.

Velice

Velice entered the Selective High School in 1992. Family commitments meant that he was away from Australia at the set time for the entry test, and to my surprise, I was granted special permission to submit results from standardized tests administered by our own school counselor, along with my own assessments, for placement consideration. He was successful! His mother spoke no English at all, and his father only a limited amount, but it was obvious that they would do everything in their power to give their son every opportunity in his educational pursuits.

Velice was an eager, self-motivated student. He was enthusiastic about everything he did. He was a perfectionist, and above all, he loved to learn. It would have been an impossible task to pinpoint his favorite subject or interest. He loved music, art, and drama. He delighted in reading and writing—be it stories, poems, or plays. The thought of problem-solving and mathematics made his eyes light up. He was anxious to know more about the world and its people, and to be asked to make a speech or thank visiting guests just "made his day."

In 1995, Velice was in Year 10, and in several of his subjects (Mathematics, Science, and English), he was grade-accelerated, enabling him to undertake some university units as part of his Year 12 studies. During that year, he also returned to our primary school to assist me in a mentor capacity for the after-school-hours "Mathematics for Gifted Children" class I had established. Children in Years 5 to 7 from all schools in our district attended. Not only were Velice's mathematical skills highly valued, but his outstanding leadership skills also began to emerge.

Eventually Velice could speak six languages fluently. He was also artistically talented and became involved with outside-school art competitions and activities. He was interested in doing some kind of engineering work someday.

Mohammed

In 1992, I felt that the Year 6 candidates sitting the Selective High School Entrance Examination were the most promising group we had ever put forward for placement consideration at the Selective High School, but the only successful student was not Mohammed but our one Anglo-Australian! I could not believe the results of this testing and immediately lodged a lengthy, detailed appeal, but with no success. Mohammed, although an Arabic Muslim, enrolled in our local Catholic Boys' College where he did very well academically. He sat the Year 9 Entry Examination for the Selective High School in 1994, and this time he was successful. All he needed was the extra exposure to English—the sophisticated English of IQ and standardized tests.

Lupce

Another student involved in my failed appeal, Lupce, enrolled at the local Technology High School and became a "computer whiz," working on programs with Wollongong University professors and local business personnel. His skills were featured in an article from the local newspaper:

High-Tech Master of the World

Lupce, 15, knows his way around a computer keyboard. His parents, by contrast, admit they know nothing about the high-tech world which has seduced their son and so many of his peers. The only screen they watch is the television, but Lupce spends most of his free time at home gazing at the computer screen.

Despite their lack of know-how, Drage and Ruza are bursting with pride at their youngest child's mastery of virtual reality programming and robotical engineering.

The Year 10 Keira Technology High School student, who last year lectured Canberra education experts on his pet subject, is planning a career in software programming.

He recently completed a special Wollongong University course designed to help him master the computer language needed to help him hook his school into the Internet. (Carty, 1996, p. 3)

Lupce was very disappointed at missing selection for the Selective High School, but he still excelled academically, as I knew he could and would.

Abdurrahman

Abdurrahman was the eldest of three children, born of Turkish parents. Turkish was spoken exclusively in the home. Although the parents had excellent understanding of English, they were embarrassed by, and lacked confidence in, their skills of spoken English. The grandparents were unable to communicate in English. Both of Abdurrahman's parents were well educated in Turkey. Abdurrahman, therefore, received many enriching experiences in Turkish as a preschooler, and it was obvious to his parents that he was a "bright child," keenly interested in all kinds of things, particularly in the world around him.

By Year 3, when Abdurrahman was in a composite Year 3/4 class, he was coping with ease at the Year 4 level of activities, so in Year 4 we were able to include him in a Language Enrichment Group (for senior primary children) as well as the After-School Enrichment Program in Mathematics that was initiated in conjunction with the Wollongong University (Mathematics Education Faculty) for "mathematically gifted" children from Years 5 to 7 in our cluster of schools.

As the teacher of both of these groups, I was able to form a close relationship with Abdurrahman, and from the many conversations that we had, it was obvious that he was indeed a bright child. After one vacation, I had the Language Group list at least three books that they had read during the vacation. He asked if it would be all right to include Turkish books, and when I later checked the references, I found that they were writings of Turkish philosophy. During the vacation, he had accompanied his parents to Monash University (Melbourne, Australia), where the Turkish community was conducting a "Retreat," and he had been included in the discussion times with the men. His areas of interest and knowledge were not narrow. He loved Mathematics and Science equally as much as Literature, Art, and Music. He held firmly to a very strong Muslim faith, but could discuss openly with me the similarities and differences of his religion and my Christian beliefs. He had a keen sense of humor (our shared lunchtimes, which is a school policy, were spent joke-telling). He loved acting and role play and never minded being the recipient of a joke. He spoke, read, and wrote Turkish as fluently and as well as he did English.

During 1992, Abdurrahman was nominated by the school (his class teacher, the principal, and the school counselor) and his parents to sit for the Opportunity C (OC) Class Entrance Examination. These classes were established as "District Classes" for academically gifted students, situated within the grounds of appointed schools and drawing successful students from all regional schools to commence Year 5. Students were chosen on the results of a battery of tests—English, Mathematics, and General Ability (IQ > 130). To his great delight, Abdurrahman was notified in writing of his success and excitedly looked forward to the following year. However, this excitement was short-lived, as the school received a phone call late in November, just prior to the summer vacation and the end of our academic year, advising that the class had been disbanded "due to lack of acceptances."

You can imagine my dilemma on seeing his reaction to the cancellation of the OC Class. Abdurrahman's disappointment was obvious, and I felt strongly that, as an educator, I owed this child some sort of "compensation." I was angry on my own behalf, without trying to think of reasons that I could give this child for the bureaucratic decision that had been made without any form of consumer consultation. However, with all the administrative requirements of the end of a year, I did not have the time to do all that I would have liked to do at that time.

Upon returning to school for the 1993 school year, I decided that one possible option that would meet Abdurrahman's educational needs was planned acceleration. If the identification procedures are adequate, and the transition is professionally supported, the chances are ninety-five percent or better that the advanced placement will be of great benefit to the educational development of the child, especially when ability to adapt socially, emotionally, and academically in a peer group that is older in chronological age is obvious (Roebeck, 1983).

Why did I feel that it was necessary for this child to be promoted to a higher stage ahead of peers? Why not consider an enrichment program? Southern, Jones, and Stanley (1993) state:

Acceleration and enrichment may be regarded as legs that support the same chair. . . . Whatever the appearances, the rationales for acceleration and enrichment are based on different assumptions about four basic issues: the nature of intellectual giftedness, affective characteristics of giftedness, the goals of regular and gifted education, and the adequacy of regular education curricula. (p. 387)

A wide range of options is available to cater adequately for the gifted student. Accelerated progression is one of many strategies that schools may employ to respond to the academic and social needs of some gifted students—only those students who would benefit from such a program. It must provide a challenging and satisfying educational environment without disadvantaging the student educationally, emotionally, or socially (Daurio, 1979). "While enrichment or lateral extension might be appropriate for most of our highly able students, for the gifted—rather than highly able—acceleration matched with enrichment might be the most appropriate action" (NSW Board of Studies, 1991, p. 5).

It is unfortunate, however, that in New South Wales we find that there exists widespread skepticism toward "grade-skipping acceleration":

Attitudes to acceleration vary widely from state to state. In the sense of grade skipping, acceleration is practised in all states and in virtually all systems when the need is acute and when other forms of provision have been exhausted. In general, however, lock-step methods of promotion and adherence to the concept of age-cohorts still prevail in most schools, grade acceleration being viewed with suspicion or opposition. Nevertheless there are notable exceptions and evidence of change in some states. (Braggett, 1993, p. 821)

Brody and Benbow (1987) proposed that acceleration offered students an opportunity to select a program of work that they would find both challenging and interesting, while at the same time proving time- and cost-effective to the school, as a special program does not have to be developed and implemented for some carefully selected gifted students. This certainly sufficed for the case of Abdurrahman at the beginning of 1993.

To assume that gifted students have high self-esteem can be erroneous. Social and general self-esteem can be extremely low in gifted children who have little or no access to other gifted young people who share their abilities and interests. Boredom is also a danger that can occur when a student is stimulated only by horizontal enrichment, and unfortunately, boredom can manifest itself in the gifted child falling into the underachiever category. For highly precocious young students, and as far as we were able to ascertain, Abdurrahman could be classified as highly precocious, acceleration seems to be vastly preferable to most types of enrichment, as these students will be appropriately challenged and will continue to gain enthusiasm for work (Daurio, 1979). Accelerants do not suffer academic harm. "The accelerated students remained highly productive and maintained their academic advantage even in new, more demanding settings" (Kulik & Kulik, 1984, p. 87).

Another consideration was that acceleration not be used in isolation but, rather, be coupled with well-planned enrichment. It is not enough to allow students accelerated progression and then leave them alone to cope, according to Davis and Rimm (1985):

> A program for gifted students should provide a comprehensively planned curriculum that utilises within discipline and/or across-disciplinary studies. These studies should allow for both vertical (acceleration) and horizontal (breadth and depth in a topic) movement that is educationally relevant. The program should stress higher-level thinking skills such as inquiry skills, problem-solving, and creative thinking. In addition, development of self-direction, risk-taking, curiosity, imagination and interpersonal relations should be emphasised. The program framework will allow for individual projects and peer group interactions. The long-range goals of this program are self-actualisation for the gifted person and the development of a sense of responsibility to self, school and society. (p. 108)

The final consideration, and the one that took the greatest amount of thought and discussion, was that of the needs of the "whole" child. Accelerated students must be able to handle anxiety and perseverance at reasonably accelerated levels without evidence of stress or obsessional behavior. There must be a readiness by the student to separate from friendship groups, although only partial separation time, that of classroom hours, may be required. At this point, the whole concept of acceleration was put to the child for consideration and family discussion.

> A crucial consideration is the extent to which the child is encouraged to take an active part in the educational decision-making process . . . eg How eager is the child to skip a grade? . . . Also how effectively are the child's parents facilitating their offspring's social, emotional, athletic and cultural development? (Southern et al., 1993, p. 389)

After lengthy discussions among all involved in Abdurrahman's education, past and present, all comments and suggestions were carefully weighed and debated before a decision was finally reached that we all agreed would be in the best interests of the child—that of "trial acceleration" in the form of grade-skipping. He would move from Year 4 directly to Year 6, and he was delighted with this move.

My Year 6 class into which Abdurrahman moved was a heterogeneous group—abilities within the group ranging from very high ability to moderate learning disabilities—so within the class I had already established a differentiated curriculum of work, constructed much in accordance with Bloom's Taxonomy. It was a relatively easy task to include Abdurrahman in the existing program of instruction. Our senior primary classes also operated on an "ungraded" morning program for Reading/Language and Mathematics, and

Abdurrahman had previously been placed in the top levels for both these curricular areas, which made the acceleration less of an ordeal. According to Davis and Rimm (1985):

> There are at least two major concerns regarding grade-skipping. The first is the problem of missing critical basic skills. Many teachers feel that if a child is not taught an important math or reading skill, he or she will be at a great disadvantage in later grades. They frequently predict that the child (1) will not be able to maintain good grades, (2) will see him or herself as less capable, and therefore (3) will lose school motivation. It is true that some skills are absolutely critical to the learning of later skills, and their absence could place stress on the student. . . . As a precaution, a series of diagnostic tests for the grade to be skipped can identify missing skills, and the motivated gifted child typically can learn these quickly, either working independently or with the help of interested adults. (p. 105)

This concern had already been addressed. To place our senior students in their academically appropriate groups for Reading/Language and Mathematics, we had administered a standardized mathematics test and the Australian Council for Educational Research Reading Comprehension Test (followed by the Neale Analysis of Reading Ability, an individual test where we felt there was a particular need) to all Year 5 and Year 6 students. Abdurrahman's results were extremely high in both, so I felt that where the "basics" were concerned, there would be no anxiety. My only real worry was that the differentiated classroom program would be extensive enough to meet his needs, as he was obviously a gifted child.

An in-depth "running record" was kept on Abdurrahman's academic performance, social and emotional development, and health and personal development. Within a few weeks of entering the group, he was faced with the statewide Year 6 Basic Skills Testing in Literacy and Numeracy. His results in these tests further verified that there was no concern that he might have omitted some essential skills by skipping Year 5. His scores were well in advance of the state mean and school results in all categories.

My classroom strategies incorporate both cooperative learning and individualized or small homogeneous group activities. The classroom program is also a literature-based or whole language format, be it Science, Social Studies, or Language lessons, which automatically allows for extensive choice and ability range. Abdurrahman was able to work equally well as a group member as when he was formulating his own problems and the strategies he would employ to solve them. His ability to analyze, synthesize, and evaluate materials and to formulate an action plan for his research also demonstrated his very high level of thinking skills. He was articulate, both orally and in written work, often posing hypotheses or questioning the status quo.

His ultimate ambition for Year 6 was to be successful at the Selective High School Entrance Examination. During the latter part of 1992, his parents had planned a holiday to Turkey for May to September of 1993, thinking at the time it would be a year that would not interfere too drastically with their children's school progress, and giving them the opportunity to meet their maternal grandparents for the first time. Their dilemma now was should they go? Could they leave Abdurrahman in Australia while the rest of the family continued with the arrangements as planned? Ultimately, this was the decision made. Abdurrahman would remain in Australia with his paternal grandparents, while his immediate family visited, for an extended time, the rest of the family in Turkey. This caused me concern. How would this child, who had just left his grade friends and entered a new cohort, now cope with the added trauma of Mum, Dad, sister, and brother leaving him behind, many thousands of miles away, for a period of at least four months? We had regular "counseling" sessions, and although it must have been very difficult for him at times, he always talked positively about their experiences and was able to call them with any special news. Once again, he came through the situation with flying colors! He was successful in gaining his placement at the Selective High School for 1994. Acceleration, in the form of grade-skipping, is not for everyone. For Abdurrahman, however, it appears the choice was correct, but only time will tell.

LESSONS LEARNED

These brief recounts of children's educational experiences raise for me two very important issues that are of universal concern. The first is that of classroom instruction, particularly instruction for gifted students. Research continually expounds that children with high ability and special talents thrive in a child-centered environment, where motivational level is high and continuous progress is supported. Narrow learning tasks and objectives are replaced by opportunities to choose open-ended pursuits based on individual choice of preferences and interests, encouraging the indicators of high-ability skills and talents to emerge. These indicators are thus used by the astute teacher to further design individual goals that will become the foundations for lifetime learning. The process of ongoing assessment allows the child the opportunity to build his or her own construct of knowledge and understanding of the world, while capitalizing on individual learning rates and styles (Eggen & Kauchak, 1988; Roedell et al., 1980; Wang & Walberg, 1985).

The child-centered classroom provides a security based on successes, so that the child comes to view himself or herself with self-confidence as a competent learner and a worthwhile human being. For the gifted child, in particular, it removes all grade barriers, presenting opportunities for self-evaluation—an essential tool for continued success. Nevertheless, we find daily instruction given to the whole class, usually in an expository mode, pitched at the middle ability range, and requiring the same activities and responses by all children.

How can such a classroom be based on child successes, ongoing progress, or even student interests? In this kind of repeated performance, year after year, the gifted child is at risk of quickly becoming a behavioral problem or even an underachiever.

For the gifted child from a non–English speaking background, the "risk" is much greater, where much of the curriculum for these children has been based on a deficit model, focusing almost exclusively on a remedial approach to education, and English in particular. This problem may be eradicated when our teachers and administrators are better equipped to identify giftedness, regardless of race, color, or gender, and are able to overcome their obsession with the IQ score. Vialle (1993) reinforces this premise when she states:

> The most critical problem that the field of gifted education has to confront is the reified view of giftedness that it has inherited from the IQ testing movement. Despite decades of evidence questioning its basic assumptions, the IQ test still looms large in the identification of gifted children. Additionally, as many of the studies in gifted education are based on a view that equates giftedness with performance on IQ tests, many of our working assumptions must also be in some doubt. I contend that the marriage of convenience between IQ testing and giftedness is no longer fertile and a formal separation is long overdue. (p. 1)

My greatest concern, however, is that it is highly probable that in our educational system, many children with potential similar to that of Silvana, Velice, Mohammed, Lupce, and Abdurrahman have failed to be recognized. How many of these gifted minority students have we overlooked? According to Baldwin (1973):

> It is sad when a "pint" is expected to yield a "quart" and fails to do so, but it is a tragic loss to society when a "quart" produces only a "pint" or much less for lack of societal effort and programs. (p. 1)

Because these minority group children (children from a variety of ethnic backgrounds, Aboriginal children, as well as children from low socioeconomic backgrounds) enter school not only with a deficit in English skills, or no English at all, but also with a lack of early educational experiences, identification of giftedness has been completely neglected.

When we do finally realize that children from these minority groups are "different" from the norm, it is often late in primary school or, worse, in the secondary school years. Their upper- and middle-class counterparts have been immersed in special programs of varying kinds and degrees for the past five or more years. Educational "equity," however you might define or describe it, is fantasy, not fact. If we are truly committed to the premise of an equal chance for all children, then we must put into place a structure that will include all of our children, remembering that the process of this identification, because of the nature of the group, will of necessity be different. Cooke (1974) proposes:

> Early identification of the gifted disadvantaged and appraisal of the seeming range (intellectual, talented and creative socially gifted) and quality of their giftedness is of importance to the individual and our nation; the individual—because he is afforded an opportunity to develop his personal talents to the utmost—the nation benefits because he is afforded an opportunity to develop his personal talents to the utmost. (p. 86)

To ensure that no child is excluded from a special program for the gifted, whether it be a full-time class, a pull-out program for a specified time, or simply differentiated instruction within the regular classroom, it is essential that multiple criteria be employed over time. These identification procedures may include both "nontraditional" assessment and standardized assessment measures. One method for combining these elements was developed and validated in a recent doctoral dissertation (Carnellor, 1997) and is summarized in Figure 4–1.

If teachers hold firm to the ideal that it is our responsibility to educate all children to their full potential, after identifying these culturally different, gifted students, we must follow up this process with well-planned, qualitatively differentiated programs. To ensure that there is a whole-school commitment to the notion of gifted education, it is essential that a school policy is developed from the outset (see Figure 4–2). This policy development process must include the parents working in partnership with the school at all levels of decision making if the greatest benefits for all students are to be attained.

Effective ongoing staff development programs that will provide training—at both a preservice and inservice level—and ongoing support for teachers, for systematic procedures of identification, curriculum differentiation, and appropriate classroom strategies, are also essential components of the whole school policy. This is endorsed by McClelland (1958), who stated:

> As students from impoverished backgrounds and from racial and ethnic minorities have "achieved" when provided with appropriate educational opportunities, they have demonstrated that the "right kinds of education" can indeed transform potential into "actually talented performance." (p. 8)

For decades the notion of giftedness has been equated with test scores and, more specifically, IQ scores. The tradition of relying on IQ scores to define one's ability was prevalent with psychologists and educators at the beginning of the century when the technology of measurement took hold. Numbers became the determinants of what we believed students could accomplish in schools. There was a special

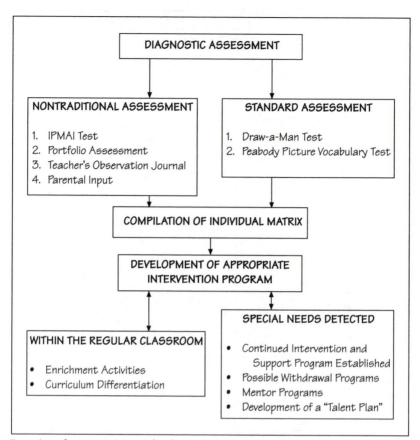

Records such as a portfolio of the child's work samples in conjunction with a teacher's observation journal will enhance accurate identification of children's abilities.

Figure 4–1   Identification of potential giftedness

comfort with this "solid objective" approach to assessment, even when this comfort was challenged when there appeared dramatic differences between the actual academic accomplishments of students and what the numbers had predicted the accomplishments should be.

However, given insight, along with new theories of intelligence by Gardner (1983) and Sternberg (1985), it is necessary to look much further afield, to seek guidance from practitioners and policy makers, in the identification process of gifted students. Braggett (1992) reinforces this premise by suggesting:

> Nor will the traditional range of standardised test be of very much use as they have been standardised on specific populations with different outlooks. The whole issue of identification challenges educators to broaden their concept of giftedness and talent

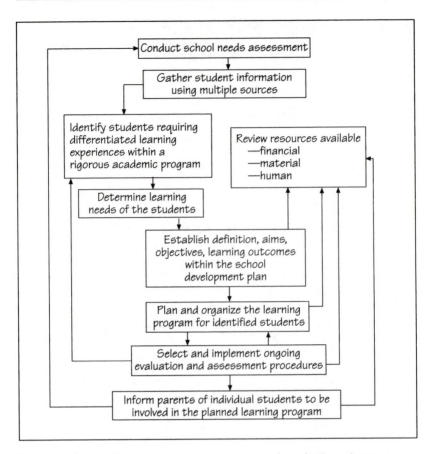

Figure 4–2 Developing a school-based program for gifted students

to embrace other ethnic groups, to accept varied social customs, to tolerate a range of attitudes and to acknowledge pluralistic values. (p. 11)

How many have we missed? Too many!

REFERENCES

Baldwin, A. Y. (1973, September). *Instructional planning for gifted disadvantaged children.* Technical paper. Storrs, CT: National Leadership Institute—Teacher Education/Early Childhood.

Baldwin, A. Y. (1977). Tests do underpredict: A case study. *Phi Delta Kappan, 58*(8), 620–621.

Baldwin, A. Y. (1984). *The Baldwin identification matrix 2 for the identification of the gifted and talented: A handbook for its use.* New York: Trillium Press.

Black, H. (1963). *They shall not pass.* New York: Morrow.

Braggett, E. J. (1992). Where will the gifted movement be in the year 2000? Major issues. *Australian Journal of Gifted Education, 1*(2), 5–13.

Braggett, E. J. (1993). Programs and practices for identifying and nurturing giftedness and talent in Australia and New Zealand. In K. A. Heller, F. J. Mönks, & A. H. Passow (Eds.), *International handbook of research development of giftedness and talent* (pp. 815–832). Oxford: Pergamon Press.

Brody, L. E., & Benbow, C. P. (1987). Accelerative strategies: How effective are they for the gifted? *Gifted Child Quarterly, 31*(3), 105–110.

Carnellor, Y. (1997). *An examination of the characteristics of young, potentially gifted children from culturally diverse backgrounds, as the basis for the development of appropriate educational programs.* Unpublished doctoral dissertation, University of Wollongong, New South Wales, Australia.

Carrick, J. (1990). *Education reform act.* Report of the Committee of Review of New South Wales Schools. Sydney, New South Wales, Australia: NSW Ministry of Education.

Carroll, J. B. (1982). The measurement of intelligence. In R. J. Sternberg (Ed.), *Handbook of human intelligence* (pp. 29–120). Cambridge, UK: Cambridge University Press.

Carty, L. (1996, February 8). High-tech master of the world. *Illawarra Mercury,* 3.

Cooke, G. J. (1974). *Guidance services for gifted disadvantaged children and youth.* Storrs, CT: National Leadership Institute.

Daurio, S. P. (1979). Educational enrichment versus acceleration: A review of the literature. In W. C. George, S. J. Cohn, & J. C. Stanley (Eds.), *Educating the gifted: Acceleration and enrichment* (pp. 13–63). Baltimore, MD: John Hopkins University Press.

Davis, A. (1948/1965). *Social-class influences upon learning.* The Inglis Lecture. Cambridge, MA: Harvard University Press.

Davis, G. A., & Rimm, S. B. (1985). *Education of the gifted and talented.* Englewood Cliffs, NJ: Prentice-Hall.

Eggen, P. D., & Kauchak, D. P. (1988). *Strategies for teachers: Teaching content and thinking skills.* Englewood Cliffs, NJ: Prentice-Hall.

Feldman, D. (1991). *Nature's gambit.* New York: Teachers' College Press.

Frasier, M. (1991). Disadvantaged and culturally diverse gifted students. *Journal for the Education of the Gifted, 14*(3), 234–245.

Gardner, H. (1983). *Frames of mind.* New York: Basic Books.

Gross, M. U. M. (1986). Dispelling the myths. *Gifted International, 4*(2), 65–66.

Hoffman, B. (1964). *The tyranny of testing.* New York: Collier Books.

Howes, V. M. (1974). *Informal teaching in the open classroom.* New York: Macmillan.

Karnes, M. B. (1990). *BOHST (Bringing Out Head Start Talents).* Urbana-Champaign, IL: University of Illinois, Institute for Child Behavior and Development.

Kulik, J., & Kulik, C. (1984). Synthesis of research on effects of accelerated instruction. *Educational Leadership, 42,* 84–89.

McClelland, D. C. (1958). Methods of measuring human motivation. In J. Atkinson (Ed.), *Motives in fantasy, action and society* (pp. 7–42). New York: Van Nostrand Co.

Meeker, M. (1963). *SOI techniques for teaching competency.* El Segundo, CA: SOI Institute.

NSW Board of Studies. (1991). *Guidelines for accelerated progression.* Sydney, New South Wales, Australia: Government Printing Office.

NSW Ministry of Education. (1991). *Policy for the education of gifted and talented students.* Sydney, New South Wales, Australia: Author.

Passow, A. H. (1980). The nature of giftedness and talent. *Gifted Child Quarterly, 25*(1), 5–10.

Renzulli, J. S. (1979). *What makes giftedness? A re-examination of the gifted and talented.* Ventura, CA: Ventura County Superintendent of Schools Office.

Resnick, L. B. (1976). Changing conceptions of intelligence. In L. Resnick (Ed.), *The nature of intelligence* (pp. 1–10). New York: Wiley.

Richert, E. S. (1985). Identification of gifted students: An update. *Roeper Review, 8,* 197–204.

Richert, E. S., Alvino, J. J., & McDonnel, R. C. (1982). *National report on identification: Assessment and recommendation for comprehensive identification of gifted and talented youth.* Sewell, NJ: Educational Information Resource Centre.

Roebeck, M. C. (1983, July). *Identification and intervention in early childhood.* Paper presented at Education for the Gifted: Patterns for the Future Conference, University of Oregon, Eugene, OR.

Roedell, W. C., Jackson, N. E., & Newman, E. (1980). *Gifted young children.* New York: Teachers College Press.

Southern, W. T., Jones, E. D., & Stanley, J. C. (1993). Acceleration and enrichment: The context and development of program options. In K. A. Heller, F. J. Mönks, & A. H. Passow (Eds.), *International handbook of research and development of giftedness and talent* (pp. 387–409). Oxford: Pergamon Press.

Sternberg, R. J. (1985). *Beyond IQ.* Cambridge, UK: Cambridge University Press.

Sternberg, R. J. (1986). A triarchic theory of intellectual giftedness. In R. J. Sternberg & J. E. Davidson (Eds.), *Conceptions of giftedness* (pp. 223–243). Cambridge, UK: Cambridge University Press.

Sternberg, R. J., & Salter, W. (1982). Conceptions of intelligence. In R. J. Sternberg (Ed.), *Handbook of human intelligence* (pp. 3–28). Cambridge, UK: Cambridge University Press.

Vialle, W. (1993, September). *The challenge of giftedness.* Paper presented at the Canada-Australia conference, University of Wollongong, New South Wales, Australia.

Vygotsky, L. (1978). *Mind in society: The development of higher psychological processes.* Cambridge, MA: Harvard University Press.

Wang, M. C., & Walberg, H. G. (Eds.) (1985). *Adapting instruction to individual differences.* Berkeley, CA: McCutchan.

CHAPTER

5

TOTALITARIAN SOCIETIES: UKRAINE

INTRODUCTION

In trying to understand the many faces of giftedness, different authors in the West (Feldhusen, 1992; Gardner, 1983; Renzulli, 1978; Sternberg, 1988) have challenged the traditional view of giftedness as the only personal feature that is done "by birth" to someone and that remains unchanged for a person's whole life. By describing a wide variety of human abilities and, most importantly, the possibilities of nurturing them, they have looked at giftedness as a multifactorial phenomenon that can be understood only if one takes into account a great complex of different factors.

It is important to show that the totalitarian mask (totalitarian consciousness) is the functional system that has been created by the tools of the totalitarian society in order to "fit" the person into the system. It is also important to consider psychological interventions that can be powerful enough to overcome the mask and to break it. The author has chosen an educational, pedagogical method of "error analysis" (Luria's method is also used in neuropsychology) in order to attempt to revitalize the mask, to open possibilities to the development of greater levels of excellence in social and leadership skills. Different age groups have been investigated, assuming that the level of "burden" of the totalitarian mask is harder on adults and lesser on teens. The author has tried to answer the question: "How can an individual stop the deadly influence of totalitarian society on his or her development as a gifted person?"

Scholars from the former Soviet Union have traditionally used another approach to and view of giftedness and gifted development. For them, Vygotsky's idea about "holistic view, holistic theory" should be applied every time one wants to study human development. Vygotsky's theory can help us understand how cultural variables can be transformed into individual psychological processes and abilities, because of his main idea that development as a whole is a process of acquiring culture through interactive activity. According to Vygotsky's theory, the social situation of development of a person is determined by whether tools exist that can help develop giftedness or whether such tools are absent. (For a discussion of Vygotsky's ideas in English, see Kozulin, 1990; Wertsch, 1985).

The basic idea of Vygotsky's theory is what he called the "general law of cultural development." Vygotsky (1991) wrote:

> Each higher psychological function in child development appears on the stage twice: First as a social collective activity, an inter psychological function; second as an individual activity, which is the inner manner of a child's thinking, an intra psychological function. (p. 387)

According to the theory, a high level of development can occur only where there is a high quality of cultural interactions during which one can acquire the cultural tools. Where such interactions are absent, a child will not have a chance to develop his or her abilities. This situation is described in Vygotsky's essay "Difficult Child," which presents the case of a bilingual girl from the Tatar Republic (a nation within the Russian Federation) who was diagnosed as being mentally retarded. In fact, her poor performance on the cognitive test was due to her limited proficiency in both Russian and her native language; as a result, her development was frustrated and even blocked, and she appeared to be mentally retarded (Gindis, 1995, p. 80).

Vygotsky's work should be viewed within the context of important events. Vygotsky was encouraged by the Great October Social Revolution and was enthusiastic about testing how great social changes influence the development of psyche. One effort to research this topic produced a famous story about how Luria (his colleague and student) and Vygotsky studied the impact of cultural changes in the lives of people from the rural area of Uzbekistan on their abilities. For Vygotsky, two major factors were involved in the changes of the lifestyle of Uzbeki peasants following the revolution—collectivization (creating collective farms) and the mandatory literacy program, which was intended to teach everybody how to read and write. Luria demonstrated, in a series of clinical interviews and tests, that Uzbekis who lived in new socialist circumstances had changed their responses to classification and reasoning tasks. On the other hand, Uzbekis who retained the traditional patterns of their culture (outside collective farms and illiterate) responded to such problems using concrete examples based on their own experience (Luria, 1979, pp. 58–81).

Luria's research showed that many psychological characteristics, contrary to previous understanding, are influenced by cultural circumstances. For example, the Uzbekis who had become collectivized (some of them had learned to read and write) responded to tasks differently. In their classification of objects, they switched from functional criteria, that is, how they would use the named object—which common functions this object could fulfill in their everyday lives, to the more abstract level of classification of the object based on taxonomic relations. Even more striking, the "new" Uzbekis perceived Gestalt figures, as expected, with illusions, but the traditional Uzbekis did not. This result demonstrated an unexpected cultural variation in perception, which had been viewed as a universal, biologically coded process (leading to Luria's famous telegram to Vygotsky with the news that "Uzbekis have no illusions").

This and some others' research proved the main idea of Vygotsky's theory. According to his theory, unique modes of thoughts are associated with unique modes of social interaction. Thus, whenever a person's cultural environment changes and he or she experiences a new type of social interaction, this change will have a crucial impact on the development of all his or her abilities. By analyzing the special patterns of interactions and (what is for Vygotsky even more important) the *history* of interactions, the nature of one's exceptionalities can be understood.

The author believed, therefore, that the post-totalitarian society in Ukraine was an absolutely intriguing laboratory for cross-cultural research in many fields, but especially in the field of gifted education. It provided an opportunity to examine how a major change in society affected the development of gifted people.

According to Vygotsky's historical-cultural theory of human development, the social changes cannot be neutral to the development of the psyche. In every case of every individual's development, Vygotsky began with an analysis of what he called the social situation of development. Through the analysis of the social situation of development of the child, it is possible to continue, for example, the analysis of that child's cognitive development or emotional development. If the scholar forgets to start with analyzing the social situation of development, he or she can misunderstand the whole situation.

The period following the revolution was a very good time for Vygotsky and his followers, since society was changing rapidly, and those changes enabled them to make contemporary "field" experiments about the influence of the changes on the psyches of persons experiencing the changes.

The task in this chapter is to look at a society during the "opposite" revolution, since communism has collapsed and, at least nominally, a switch has been made to a capitalistic, free-market economy and a democratic society. This change, it is believed, makes the post-totalitarian society in Ukraine an absolutely unique laboratory for cross-cultural research in the field of gifted education. It presents a unique opportunity to investigate how a totalitarian society forced its "totalitarian mask" on children who were not totalitarian by birth but who were forced during the process of socialization and development to fit into the system. It is very interesting to investigate this issue from the point of view of the developmental aspect of creativity, leadership skills, and other social skills that recently have begun to be discussed in the literature as special gifted skills (Gardner, 1983; Sisk, 1993).

To develop a better understanding of the effect of the totalitarian mask on the development of education of the gifted in Ukraine and the former Soviet Union, it is important to view this effect through the lens of Vygotsky's theories on the approach to diagnostics and teaching. Before the case study is presented, however, some background on Vygotsky's approach to diagnostics and teaching and the history of gifted education in the former Soviet Union will be discussed.

THE VYGOTSKIAN APPROACH TO DIAGNOSTICS AND TEACHING

This now-world-famous psychologist and his followers have had little, if any, impact on the system of gifted education in practical, applied terms, but they have contributed a great methodological and theoretical treasure for the field. As Davidov (1994) wrote: "it is clear to us why Vygotsky's general ideas could not be used for such a long time in the education system of a totalitarian society—they simply contradict all of its principles" (p. 13).

In analyzing any kind of child development, including the development of gifted children, Vygotsky would start with analyzing what he called the social situation of development. Vygotsky's famous "zone of proximal development" concept was drawn from his understanding of the crucial role of the social and cultural situation for the development of any child, and particularly for the development of gifted children.

Much of the conceptualization of assessment in school psychology and pedagogy, including the identification strategy for gifted children in the former Soviet nations, stems from the seminal work of Vygotsky. Vygotsky's approach to assessment involved dynamic probing of the process by which children perform learning acts. By interacting with and observing a child performing tasks and by exploring the child's learning history, the psychologist is able to determine the child's "zone of proximal development" and to estimate his or her potential for moving to another level of psychic processing. In this way, instruction may be tailored to the child's personal abilities. The Vygotskian model is an analytical and highly useful approach for diagnosing specific individual cognitive processing abilities and their development. This model of assessment came from Vygotsky's understanding of the whole process of schooling, which, according to the general ideas of this theoretical framework, is the historically institutionalized acquisition of cultural tools with the help of more knowledgeable adults. And this process depends heavily on two major elements: development and teaching. Vygotsky believed that understanding the relationship between those two elements in schooling can take us beyond the controversy of nature or culture, because humans are products of the dialectical play between the two.

With Vygotsky's general law of cultural development, every attempt to analyze children's development starts with an analysis of the "social situation of development" of the particular child because, by default, none of the individual abilities can appear by themselves without first existing as *social collective activity."* In other words, Vygotsky believed that an individual's abilities begin in the social environment, inside of the social situation, and only through internalization of the process of acquiring what one observes outside can the abilities be transformed to the inside, to become a part of one's psyche.

Vygotsky's approach to the diagnosis and assessment of giftedness is very different from the traditional psychometric approach in Western psychology. The usual American question of how much the child knows at present was not very interesting for Vygotsky. He was much more interested in predicting the future of the particular child's development. He believed that every child has a high potential for development if certain, appropriate teaching gives him or her tools with which to develop. In this context, Vygotky believed that a lot of gifted children exist but can develop their potential only through the appropriate cooperation of adults.

The question of "how much" a child knows "now" was not so important to Vygotsky, as it was much more interesting to look at the process of how different functions of a child develop—to research strategies for a child's development that achieve results, to notice how and to what extent a child can benefit from the help of adults, and more generally to determine how wide a child's "zone of proximal development" is (that is, to what extent the development of different functions can be enhanced "tomorrow"). A diagnostician has to concentrate on assessment using some qualitative criteria of the developmental stages of different functions, their interactive relationships, and individual profiles of processing capabilities. Thus, according to Vygotsky, the appropriate assessment of the development of psychological functions can be made only by assessing at least two levels of child development: the "actual level of development" and the child's "zone of proximal development." This approach does not compare an individual's test score with that of other test takers to determine his or her standing in the national scheme of things, as is traditional in American assessments, but rather predicts an individual's future (proximal) development. The typical American concept of assessment distances us from an understanding of how the process of teaching can influence the child's development. For Vygotsky, the process of school learning has crucial importance on one's development abilities and can have a direct impact on the "tomorrow" of the child.

In Ukraine, this "individualized" approach has been seen as the most appropriate approach for nurturing gifted children. Hany (1993), in his discussion about methodological problems and issues concerning identification, wrote in support of this approach, explaining it from the Western cultural view.

HISTORICAL TOTALITARIAN MASKS OF THE FORMER SOVIET UNION

Although the former Soviet Union boasted of its programs for the gifted, the context within which these programs existed provided a totalitarian mask that began to be lifted when the Union was separated. The political, economic, and social changes that followed the transformation period in the territory of the former Soviet Union have had a tremendous influence on the development of the field of gifted education.

Historically, during the Soviet period, within the ideological framework of egalitarianism, there was "equal for everybody" education, although many special programs existed for children with high abilities in the fields of math and physics, music, arts, sports and circus, and foreign languages. A special statewide network was created with a lot of attention devoted to the identification of highly talented children. For example, special extracurricular activities and olympiads were held on all subjects nationwide, and those with special talents were tracked through the system of highly specialized schools, which had different curricula than the mass, general schools. That system of gifted education worked quite effectively, since many qualified experts were involved in the procedures of identifying, assessing, and educating gifted children. That system was effective because of state support for all kinds of special schools that belonged to the "ideologically" correct kinds of schools (Dunstan, 1978).

Some lessons can be drawn from the success of that system for gifted education and from the story about how it broke down during the transformation period. The main lesson is about the great conflict between the personal development of gifted children and pressure from a totalitarian society. This story provides an excellent example of the importance of social/cultural implications of giftedness, demonstrating that giftedness and creativity require not only challenge of new ideas, but also acceptance of these ideas by society. That is what Vygotsky would call "ecological validity" of the gifted programs (Gindis, 1995, p. 80). The case of gifted education in the former Soviet Union illustrates the fact that a great gap can be created in society between the individual's potential abilities ("zone of proximal development") and the societal, economic, and political needs at the particular historical period of time.

This case has even more illustrative power when one looks at what has happened to the gifted education during the transformation period, when society was trying as a whole to create a new way of development. The many changes in traditional attitudes, ideological views, and political beliefs, together with the tremendous changes in the economic and social life of society, created new "demands" for leadership in new emerging fields of professional knowledge. Society was changing its priorities in everyday life, which immediately had an impact on gifted education by changing its priorities. New types of schools for gifted children emerged, and although the traditional gifted schools continued to operate, the new schools became more popular among the youth. What were the leadership roles needed in the new fields? Those in which society felt it had a tremendous shortage, including, for example, economists, businesspersons, lawyers, public relations specialists, and bankers. In general, leaders were needed in all the professional fields that are required to make a switch from a totalitarian, totally planned economy and totally controlled society to a free-market economy and democratic society.

In other words, society felt the need to create a new type of leadership, and it attracted talented individuals who could develop the needed leadership characteristics such as risk taking, responsibility, democracy, creativity, and flexibility. This was the opposite of the old type of leadership in a totalitarian society, which focused on power and control, and the suppression of individual initiative. This was a spontaneous turning point in the gifted field. Suddenly, the criteria for who was gifted (talented, successful, expert, and so on) was changed in society. According to Vygotsky's logic, this situation can be understood as follows:

1. In the past, society provided tools for developing mathematical, technological, and all other traditional types of giftedness among children through appropriate schooling and the involvement of highly qualified experts directly in the gifted education.
2. All other kinds of talents were suppressed. The previous society did not support the development of children with the creative social type of talents, like leadership and management.
3. As a result, when the new situation came, a great gap existed between the needs of society for the new type of leadership and the ability to provide needed education. Although many young people were eager to develop these new talents, there was a shortage of "high-level" experts who could provide desirable education for them.

This situation describes the context for the case study that follows. This study concerns the Carpathian Branch of the International Management Institute (IMI), which was created in Uzhgorod, Ukraine, in 1993. The creation of the Institute was a response to a great need in society for special leadership skills, mainly managerial skills, necessary to the switch from a monopolistic, state-owned economy to the declared free-market economy and democratic state.

This transformation period was an interesting one for gifted education in Ukraine and the whole former Soviet Union, and it exemplified theories of "societal appropriate gift." Before that time, gifted education (the priority for which was determined by the Communist Party) was concentrated in the fields of math, science, music, and foreign languages; topics like leadership and social skills were never mentioned. During the "perestroika," however, literally thousands of new schools suddenly were created for the purpose of training gifted children and adults in the fields of leadership, business, and public management.

CASE STUDY

The author was involved in the gifted education field during this "new era," working as a school psychologist and consultant for different types of schools (lyceums, colleges, and so on) as well as traditional types of schools for the gifted in Ukraine.

During 1990 to 1995, the author was directly involved in a special educational program for gifted teenagers offered by the Carpathian Branch of the International Management Institute (IMI–KIEV) in Ukraine. The IMI was created primarily to educate people for leadership in emerging professions, and its emphasis was on training managers. The "business" manager was a new figure in the society, which was trying to create a new organizational culture in the workplaces, replacing the culture of "red managers" in the planned economy. Together with postgraduate adult education, the Institute decided to create a school for gifted children who were interested in developing their leadership talents and receiving preparation for entering business and economic schools on the university level. The students of the school were selected on a competitive basis by comparing their achievements in regular public schools. The students, however, were not required to have only Bs and As in their regular school records. Some students were nominated for participation in the program by teachers through the questionnaire, and some students nominated themselves after seeing the program advertised in the local newspaper.

Special Educational Program

One element of the training was the stimulation of managerial creativity. This training was part of the education for both groups of students: adult managers and teenagers. Since the situation was new for everybody, it was interesting to compare the results of this type of intervention and its different impact on different age groups.

According to logic of the Vygotsky theory, all psychological abilities, including problem-solving capacities and creative thinking, are borrowed from social practices. Vygotsky formulated the main law about any education as a movement inside of the "zone of proximal development" to the higher level of functioning: the movement between an "actual developmental level as determined by independent problem solving to the higher level of potential development as determined through problem solving under adult guidance or in collaboration with a more capable peer" (Vygotsky, 1978, p. 96).

The program was created on the basis of such understanding of the logic of developing creativity and problem-solving abilities. Since the situation was new for everybody in society, and there was no one to provide "guidance," it was decided that it would be useful to create a program that would take advantage of group problem solving, and through the group problem solving, each individual's ability to become creative could be enhanced.

The training program included theoretical training and extensive use of game simulations with different scenarios, which were designed to be as close as possible to hypothetical situations in a "free-market economy." Special instruction was given to all groups of students. They were encouraged to be as creative as possible during the program, and they were told that the game simulations would allow them to "take a look" at their "tomorrow" and try to develop special skills of creative thinking and behavior.

As usual, because it was a group type of intervention, the students were informed about the rules of group training and encouraged to learn from each other as well as from the group behavior as a whole. They were told that no one (including the authors of the program) knew the wrong or right decisions in solving all the problems, which were described in scenarios. Every group was to try to make a group decision and then evaluate that decision from the point of view of how innovative it was. Was it really creative, or did it just repeat their usual behavior in that type of situation?

Since every activity in the class was organized in the form of a simulation game, all class activities were videotaped, and the videotapes were used in the second part of the lesson, which involved feedback and an opportunity to analyze the situations that occurred in the class. Therefore, all the sessions consisted of two different parts. The first part was a simulation game, and the second part was analysis of the simulation game using videotapes of the session. For the second part of the session, a special structure of group-analyzing procedure was established, mainly trying to direct the analysis of the "errors and mistakes" made by every member of the group. Behavior was examined in terms of attempts to behave creatively and to find an innovative solution in every situation. Again, it was up to the group (not the instructor) to decide during the "self-analyzing" session whether or not the particular behavior or strategy of thinking was creative.

Since the "young managers" were young people without any practical management experience in the previous system, they could serve as the control group to account for general cultural attitudes. The "young managers" did not have the burden of totalitarian system experience and attitudes, and therefore, the strategies they applied to solving a scenario were very different from the strategies of the adult managers who were observed.

Every situation described in the scenarios had two dimensions. First, the scenarios described real situations that needed technical decisions to be resolved; in other words, the group was required to come up with a real decision about the real problem after discussion. The second dimension was the social dimension: every situation involved consideration of the social relationships, values, and social roles of all participants in the situation. It was observed that often both age groups had no problem with finding the "technical" solution to the problem, but the adult groups had a lot of difficulty dealing with the social side of the situation. As a result, even a very easy technical task seemed to be difficult for adult managers to solve, and sometimes problems became unsolvable because some groups could not overcome the social barrier. To illustrate the kind of problems, or barriers, that were labeled as social, consider the following group situation.

Every member of the group was asked to come up with ideas about how he or she would deal with this hypothetical situation: assume that you are the principal of the school, and about midnight, you receive a personal call at your home from one of the students from the school. The student informs you that he has decided to commit suicide by jumping from the seventeenth floor of an apartment building, but before doing that, he has decided to call to talk to you at the very last moment.

Everybody was asked to think about this situation and to decide what kind of answer they would give to this student. Long before any group was ready to give an answer, one of the members of a group asked the instructor, "How do you want me to think and to answer—as a person, or as a principal of the school?" In response to an inquiry about what would be the difference between his answer in both of the considered cases (person versus principal), he said that as a principal, that is, an official, he would have to have an official version of an answer, but as a person, he would express sympathetic attitudes toward the student who was trying to commit suicide. After group discussion on this issue, the group of adult managers agreed on this point—that if you are an official, you cannot bring any personal attitudes or views to the way in which you deal with problems. This was the typical socially appropriate behavior of totalitarian educators, whom Davidov (1994) described as Communist Party bureaucrats: "teachers and *vospitateli* (upbringers) worked only as bureaucrats carrying out Communist Party and government dictates but basic human moral, aesthetic, and religious values were foreign to these dictates" (p. 12). This type of group decision was labeled as a decision with "social" problems and barriers for creative group decision making.

By comparing the behavior of the teenage groups with the adult groups, an interesting phenomenon was observed. None of the teenage groups had difficulty in dealing with the social side of the problem-solving situation. For them, it seemed there were no barriers in terms of their attempts to come up with creative problem solving. This was unlike the adult groups, which had problems formulating creative solutions. The type of social barrier that always existed in the adult groups appeared to be the result of their experience of behaving within the totalitarian society—the special "totalitarian mask," which consists of very rigid, noncreative attitudes acquired during socialization within the totalitarian society.

Since additional proof was needed, a closer look was taken at this phenomenon by using Q-methodology for a comparative study to analyze the managerial attitudes of Ukrainian and American managers. The main purpose for using Q-methodology was that it could contribute significantly to an understanding of the nature of transformation in Ukraine, and its influence on the attitudes and behavior of citizens. In broader terms, the investigators wanted, through the comparative empirical study, to take a look at how the changes that occurred recently in society influenced the culture in Ukraine, especially the role and value orientations of managers. Not less interesting was the comparative aspect of the study, which contributed to an understanding of the attitudes of American managers and Ukrainian managers concerning their jobs.

One of the hypotheses was that changing the organizational culture, according to the Vygotsky's theory, would influence the views and attitudes of the managers in Ukraine toward their jobs, but that this process could not occur immediately. To test this hypothesis, Q-sorts were administered to managers at different stages of their careers. A variety of managers were invited to participate in the study, including experienced managers and administrators in the United States and Ukraine along with less experienced young managers, which group included students studying management and related subjects in both countries. The Ukrainian and American students had little or no practical experience with managerial activity. Thus, by definition, Ukrainian "young" managers did not carry the burden of having worked as professional administrators in the past totalitarian society, and they could serve as the control group for testing the general cultural differences in attitudes about roles and values of leaders in both countries.

The results of the study showed that significantly different factors predominated in the attitudes of experienced managers from Ukraine and the United States. Experienced managers in the United States had very different views of their jobs and their role within society than experienced managers in Ukraine. Also, American managers tended to have similar views of their jobs (an analysis of the Q-sorts showed that most clustered together in one factor), but Ukrainian managers had more diverse views (an analysis of their Q-sorts showed they were distributed across three factors). The attitudes of "younger" managers from Ukraine and America, however, were similar; thus, many American and Ukrainian students clustered together in the same Q-factor.

Because it was found that different age groups in Ukraine had different attitudes toward their social role as managers within society, this study helped to explain why adult managerial groups have had so many problems from the point of view of creative behavior.

Intervention

As noted earlier, during the sessions, all group activities in the classroom were videotaped, and intervention was created as a form of self-analysis of the group from the point of view of their mistakes and errors. This special type of feedback using videotapes of all group activity during the problem-solving situation proved to be an effective intervention. Also, the groups could compare their performance with the performance of other groups on the same task.

The structure of self-analyzing was not very rigid; however, the groups were encouraged to try to identify and explain those social barriers in their interactions during the group problem solving that prevented them from coming up with an effective and creative decision. During this intervention, the group could judge the members of the group by pointing out what kinds of errors they made in terms of being noncreative, rigid, or sometimes simply not having enough sense of humor or playfulness to join the group problem solving. The assumption behind this kind of intervention was that through this type of procedure, an intervention could be built based upon Vygotsky's beliefs that the meaning of one's own activity is formed by mediation through another individual. Vygotsky believed that this principle applies to each psychological function, and also holds for the whole personality as well: "One may say that only through the other do we become ourselves, this rule applies to each psychological function as well as to the personality as a whole" (Vygotsky, 1983, p. 144).

Some of the results of the intervention proved that the right approach was chosen. First of all, using an analysis of the videotaped group activities, a higher level of playfulness was achieved in the adult groups. In working with groups of gifted teens, it was not difficult to involve groups in different kinds of activities. With adult groups, however, it was a different picture—a lot of members of the groups rejected even the idea to play; for some of them, the situation looked like a threat, even after they had a chance to observe the members of the group "playing" with the situation during the group problem-solving activities. These nonparticipants rationalized and explained their actions in a very typical way, saying something like: "I am a serious professional; I possess a high-level position in society; I am a serious (man/woman), and I do not see any sense in participating in your play." Such cases were treated as another "social type of barrier" (totalitarian mask) that these group members had acquired during their interaction within the totalitarian past.

This phenomenon (the lack of spontaneity and creativity) was observed in all groups of adult managers, but no problem with playfulness appeared in the groups of young managers. This difference can be explained as a consequence of patterns of behavior in special situations that are different for the adults and teens (since young managers had no practical experience in the totalitarian society). By using videotapes and analyzing the situation every time it occurred (typically members of the adult groups objected to playing if the situation became too complicated and unusual for them), the investigators tried to break these barriers. As a result of such efforts, by the end of the program, almost all of the participants had improved their playfulness.

Another interesting phenomenon observed in adult groups but never in the teen groups is what the researchers called the "collectivism-individualism" contrivers dilemma. Even though it was always stressed that all the exercises were "group" problem-solving activities, not individual ones, many groups did not accept this instruction, leading to a lot of errors and obstacles for adult group work. The more influential factors (which the groups themselves observed on video and recognized) were:

1. the general threat posed by examinations, which deeply impacted the adults' behavior during decision making. (We assumed that because for teenagers, "examinations" are so usual in everyday school life, they never showed any sign of a negative emotional reaction to our situations.)

2. the factor that we called the "status-in-real-life" factor. In many situations, when a collective group decision was called for, those members of the adult groups who possessed a higher position in the work hierarchy in real life tried to avoid the consensus of the group and tried to persuade the group to follow his or her own decision, sometimes even if it was a totally wrong decision.

A brilliant example of the influence of the second factor is the following. During a group problem-solving game, every participant was assigned a number to be used to send anonymous letters to other participants. It happened that the most important person (the highest official) was assigned the number 2, but he subsequently signed all of his letters as "Participant Number 1." The group failed its assigned task because its members received different and conflicting information from the persons signing letters as "Participant Number 1" (both the participant assigned the number, and the important person erroneously signing with this number). During a video analysis of the exercise, the group discovered the problem and asked the participant who wrongly signed his letters as "Participant Number 1" to explain what had happened. His explanation was very simple; he told the group that he was so used to being "Number 1" in real life, he had made this mistake unconsciously.

The two factors described in the preceding paragraph were typical "social type" errors that interfered with the "collective" decision making of the adult groups, but which very rarely appeared in groups of gifted teenagers. Again, the case showed a very special type of mask of giftedness—a totalitarian mask—that appears to be a very influential factor that can frustrate, or even block, the development of creativity and giftedness. The mask appears in somebody's life as a result of developing in a very restrictive, rigid, totalitarian society with a shortage of tools that one can acquire to develop creativity, and with a very low level of acceptance of any novelty, innovation, and spontaneity within the society.

The most optimistic conclusion of the research comes out of comparing the attitudes and behavior of adult and teenage groups in the program. Young people from Ukraine did not appear to wear the totalitarian mask, due to the positive changes that had occurred recently in society—democratization and more openness of society. It was a pleasure to learn that young Ukrainians were more likely to have the attitudes of their American peers in the same situations and that they had not inherited the burden of the totalitarian past. A logical question can follow. Where did Ukrainian teenagers get the tools to develop their creativity, since in their own environment, a shortage of them existed (as seen in the case of "adult" managers)? It is possible that Ukrainian youngsters are trying to emulate a Western model of personal initiative and leadership in circumstances of a more "open" society.

CONCLUSION

Usually the discussion about giftedness within a different culture concentrates on the issue of intercultural problems during the movement of the child from one country to another (problems of gifted immigrant children), or from one socioeconomic strata to another within one country with a generally stable situation, or from one ethnic or racial group to another. This chapter has described the situation in a country that is moving from one culture to another (in this case from a totalitarian to a democratic society). This shift is very painful for all the members of society: for its older members, who have great difficulty in changing their personalities and ways of thinking, and for its younger members, for whom the way of socialization is not clear. In terms of Vygotsky's theory, this means that the members of society do not have enough tools in their cultural environment for the full development of their talents. At this point in Ukrainian society, there is a shortage of "more knowledgeable adults" who can help children develop their abilities through cooperation and interaction with them. The logic of Vygotsky's methodology leads us to conclude that some cultures may not have enough tools for the development of the gifted children: these cultures can inhibit the development of gifted children (as in the example of a totalitarian society) if they treat different talents and abilities, especially exceptional abilities, as a danger to society.

The hypothesis has led to a provocative conclusion: a totalitarian society with a noncreative social situation for the development of a child eliminates that child's ability to become gifted. The main harm of the totalitarian society is naturally included in its main characteristics: (1) to be as restricted and rigid as possible (which means a shortage of and no diversity of cultural tools at the children's disposal, which, as Vygotsky has pointed out, leads to the elimination of possibilities for development, especially the development of the creativity); and (2) to offer no possibilities for members of society to acquire "outside" tools from others countries and cultures, which would enable children to communicate with the outside world and maybe to overcome the shortage of tools in their own culture.

This conclusion, though provocative, provides hope for resolving this problem. The approach that has recently emerged holds hope: the tendency toward global cooperation and improvement of international relationships. This tendency of "global openness" in terms of sharing information means that children may be able to find the tools for their development within the broader culture, the broader social situation of development, that is now more worldwide. It also means that adults need to understand their responsibilities to help every child to develop, by means of creating enough tools for their development.

When we talk about totalitarian society, it is useful to remember that in broader terms, from the point of view of child development, the danger of a totalitarian mask may exist also in a totalitarian family or totalitarian school or totalitarian organization, each of which can create an unacceptable situation for the development of a gifted child, preventing the child from developing a creative approach to the world. Adults are creating the culture that may or may not help children develop their potential talents.

In regard to developmental aspects of giftedness and creativity and the "social situation of development" of the child, a lot of questions remain unanswered and call for further investigation. They include:

1. What are social and technical parts of creativity?
2. Which society is creative (versus noncreative)?
3. What are the psychological characteristics of a totalitarian society?
4. How can we measure creativeness of society?
5. What is a totalitarian society, a totalitarian school or family, a totalitarian relationship?

But the most important question is: What kinds of interventions can we apply to help?

REFERENCES

Davidov, V. V. (1994). The influence of L. S. Vygotsky on education theory, research, and practice. *Educational Researcher*, 24(3), 12–21.

Dunstan, J. (1978). Paths to excellence and the Soviet school. Windsor, UK: NFER Publishing Co.

Feldhusen, J. F. (1992). Talent identification and development in education (TIDE). Sarasota, FL: Center for Creative Learning.

Gardner, H. (1983). *Frames of mind.* New York: Basic Books.

Gindis, B. (1995). The social/cultural implication of disability: Vygotsky's paradigm for special education. *Educational Psychologist, 30*(2), 77–81.

Guthke, J., & Wingenfeld, S. (1992). The learning test concept: Origins, state of the art and trends. In H. C. Haywood & D. Tzuriel (Eds.), *Interactive assessment* (pp. 64–93). New York: Springer-Verlag.

Hany, E. A. (1993). Methodological problems and issues concerning identification. In K. A. Heller, F. J. Mönks, & A. H. Passow (Eds.) *International handbook of research and development of giftedness and talent* (pp. 209–232). Oxford: Pergamon Press.

Kozulin, A. (1990). *Vygotsky's psychology: A biography of ideas.* Cambridge, MA: Harvard University Press.

Luria, A. R. (1979). Cultural differences in thinking. In M. Cole & S. Cole (Eds.), *The making of mind: A personal account of Soviet psychology* (pp. 58–81). Boston: Harvard University Press.

Renzulli, J. S. (1978). What makes giftedness? Reexamining a definition. *Phi Delta Kappan, 60*, 180–184.

Sisk, D. A. (1993). Leadership education for the gifted. In K. A. Heller, F. J. Mönks, & A. H. Passow (Eds.), *International handbook of research and development of giftedness and talent* (pp. 491–506). Oxford: Pergamon Press.

Sternberg, R. J. (1988). *The nature of creativity.* New York: Cambridge University Press.

Vygotsky, L. S. (1978). *Mind in society: The development of higher mental processes.* Cambridge, MA: Harvard University Press.

Vygotsky, L. S. (1983). *Collected papers* (Vol. 3), Moscow: Pedagogika.

Vygotsky, L. S. (1991). O pedologicheskom analize pedagogicheskogo processa [About pedological analysis of pedagogical process]. *Pedagogicheskaya Psychologiya* [Pedagogical Psychology]. Moscow: Pedagogika, pp. 430–449.

Vygotsky, L. S. (1991). Problemu obucheniya i unstvennogo razvitiya v shkolnom vozraste [Problems of teaching and mental development in school ages]. *Pedagogicheskaya Psychologiya* [Pedagogical Psychology]. Moscow: Pedagogika, pp. 374–390.

Wertsch, J. V. (1985). *Vygotsky and the social formation of the mind.* Cambridge, MA: Harvard University Press.

OTHER RESOURCES

Bauer, R. (1959). *The new man in Soviet psychology.* Cambridge, MA: Harvard University Press.

Das, J. P., & Gindis, B. (1995, Spring). Lev S. Vygotsky and contemporary educational psychology. *Educational Psychologist, Special Issue 30*(2).

Learning Disability: The Mysterious Mask

P
A
R
T

2

....

CHAPTER

6

USA PERSPECTIVE

Giftedness may mask a learning disability, and a learning disability can and often does hide a child's giftedness. This leads to much confusion and misunderstanding. To the general public, as well as to many educators, the concept of a gifted/learning-disabled (GLD) student appears to be a contradiction in terms. The most common understanding of the term *giftedness* is that gifted children have superior intelligence, are well-adjusted, and demonstrate excellent academic achievement and abilities in all areas. The stereotype of learning-disabled children is that, while they may have average intelligence, they do poorly in all school-related tasks. Therefore, the terms *gifted* and *learning disabled* appear to be contrasting terms, making it difficult for people to believe that one individual could be both at the same time. However, the combination of learning disabilities and giftedness is not a new phenomenon—only a relatively new and steadily growing concern (Udall & Maker, 1983). In fact, Hollingworth (1923) described the needs of this special population over sixty years ago.

Approximately sixty years after Hollingworth expressed concerned for these special students, researchers, and educators (e.g., Baum, 1988;

Daniels, 1983; Fox, Brody, & Tobin, 1983; Whitmore, 1980) began to demonstrate, through research and classroom activities, that individuals can be both gifted and learning disabled. Biographies of such exceptional people as Thomas Alva Edison, Woodrow Wilson, Hans Christian Anderson, and Leonardo da Vinci indicate that they had significant learning problems. Aaron and colleagues (1988) evaluated biographical data for the cognitive, neurological, and biological characteristics of these famous men and determined that they had a number of the characteristics that are associated with a reading disability. The authors concluded that these individuals most likely would be labeled learning disabled in our current educational systems. Whether their giftedness would have been identified and nurtured is the crucial issue. Goertzel and Goertzel (1962) studied the lives of four hundred eminent people and found that one-fourth had handicaps and learning problems. This indicates that the depth and breadth of the problem is great and there is a need for the educational system to acknowledge and address the issue of these special children.

Students who are identified as gifted/learning disabled (GLD) demonstrate many of the characteristics and potential associated with gifted students who do not have learning problems (Baum & Owen, 1988; Tannenbaum & Baldwin, 1983). They may exhibit advanced verbal ability with complex language structure and sophisticated problem-solving skills; a high level of creative, productive thinking; and markedly advanced interests combined with impressive knowledge.

The GLD student also exhibits some of the characteristics associated with learning disabilities that can become obstacles to school success and usually mask the child's giftedness (Silverman, 1989; Tannenbaum & Baldwin, 1983; Whitmore, 1980). The student may have difficulty with fine and gross motor activities, organizational skills, and visual and auditory perception. The child may also be easily distracted, hyperactive, inattentive, manipulative, and either actively or passively withdrawn from the classroom.

PROBLEMS OF IDENTIFICATION

Unfortunately, the majority of GLD individuals are not identified as either gifted or learning disabled while they are in school. Some become underachievers and drop out of the educational system, either by withdrawing or refusing to produce the work required at an adequate level. Others demonstrate negative behaviors that get them into trouble with teachers. There are other GLD students who continue to struggle, producing average work, and blaming themselves for their apparent inadequacies. Biographies and case studies of gifted adolescents and adults often reflect the personal pain, lack of self-esteem, and confusion suffered by individuals because their learning disability was undetected (Mindell, 1982; Reis & Neu, 1994; West, 1991; Whitmore & Maker, 1985). They were told by teachers to try harder, to pay attention, and to stop wasting time. And yet, even with these obstacles, it has been documented that with proper assistance or through their own persistence, motivation, and creativity, they were able to utilize their talents and gifts in highly productive ways as adults (West, 1991; Whitmore & Maker, 1985).

Why do gifted students who have learning disabilities go undetected by the educational community? There are a number of reasons why the identification process is difficult. One reason is the lack of teacher training and knowledge about gifted and GLD students (Boodoo et al., 1989; Hemmings, 1985). Most teachers do not receive training in gifted education in either undergraduate or graduate school. As noted before, the typical educational and societal view of giftedness is one in which the gifted child is well-adjusted, behaves appropriately, and does exceptionally well academically in all areas. This view, largely based on the results of the longitudinal study done by Terman (1925), is frequently used when establishing gifted programs within school systems. Therefore, students who meet the local gifted program criteria score high on intellectual assessments and above grade level on group-administered achievement tests. These gifted students also perform well on the academic tasks required in the classroom and tend to excel in a variety of areas such as leadership and creative endeavors.

The GLD child, on the other hand, tends to demonstrate very uneven academic development that appears to be paradoxical and, therefore, is confusing. The GLD child may be reading several years above his or her expected grade level but at the same time struggling with learning basic math facts and handwriting skills. There are other GLD students who struggle to learn how to read and yet have exceptional abilities to conceptualize advanced math concepts. Many GLD students have difficulty with organizational skills as well as processing information. Because of these problems, classwork and homework can be incomplete, disheveled, or lost. If the problem is due to an eye-hand coordination immaturity, handwriting may be almost impossible to decipher or the child may hesitate to do more than the minimum required during any writing assignment. At the same time, the child may be able to conceptualize as well as the top-functioning student but may be struggling academically and emotionally, watching other students succeed and wondering why he is unable to read, write, or compute like his peers.

Although the child may demonstrate some of the characteristics and behaviors attributed to gifted children, such as a keen sense of humor and the ability to consume and understand large volumes of information and to think creatively (Clark, 1979), the student may be demonstrating them in a manner that is considered negative in the school environment. For example, the keen sense of humor can be used to demean others or to be the class clown. Even though a child may be a voracious consumer of knowledge, he or she may try to compensate for his or her inability to do written work by avoiding the task, complaining that it is too easy or boring, or trying to digress from the topic during class discussions (Tannenbaum & Baldwin, 1983). Some GLD students have difficulty with rote and drill exercises and are not able to memorize the multiplication tables or spelling words. They also may try to perform the task in a new or creative way that differs from the teacher's directions (Baum et al., 1991). Thus, unless the teacher is aware of the child's strengths, even when they are misused as defense mechanisms, it becomes more difficult to identify the gifts. Daniels (1983) states:

> The frustration of children in trying to understand and deal with both abilities and disabilities might well lead to a fight or flight reaction. For a child to know that in the areas of knowledge, concepts, and interests, he or she is superior to most other classmates but lags seriously behind them in processing abilities must lead to confusion and self-doubt. (p. 154)

Whitmore (1980) also identified some of the problems of screening and identifying young gifted children with learning problems:

> Most of these unrecognized gifted pupils had been somewhat shy or nonassertive in the classroom, doing what was expected but no more, and not volunteering information about their interests or abilities. Some had been "cutups" or children the teachers tended to describe as socially immature, tending to dominate or to be in frequent conflict with classmates. The disruptive child usually had consumed a lot of teacher attention but had not evidenced exceptional academic achievement or potential. (p. 77)

Students who demonstrate negative school behaviors or whose learning deficits severely affect academic achievement are more likely to be referred to the school's child study team for evaluation. The school psychologist and the resource teacher, in evaluating the student, have the opportunity to note the weaknesses as well as the child's strengths. These same strengths and weaknesses can also be identified by a well-trained classroom teacher before the child experiences serious failure. Unfortunately, most GLD students experience some type of failure either academically or socially before they are referred to experts for evaluation in order to be identified as gifted and learning disabled. Those GLD students who "act out" are the ones most likely to be identified, whereas the majority who struggle quietly go unidentified, often with tragic consequences. The lack of identification, or a diagnosis after failure has occurred, can lead to negative results for the child, the family, and society.

CASE STUDY

In order to better understand the dilemma of identification and programming for GLD students, the life of a "typical" GLD student will be explored. The following case study of Gary is a poignant example of a young man whose giftedness and learning disabilities were evident very early, and yet they went unrecognized until his frustration and confusion led to behavior that could not be tolerated in the classroom. Gary's educational journey demonstrates many of the issues, problems, and concerns that GLD students, their parents, and their teachers and school personnel encounter and try to solve. Gary's story is an opportunity to understand on a personal level and in greater depth what worked and what did not work as he experienced more than twelve years of struggle, confusion, and successes.

Sensitivity, confusion, pain, and embarrassment are the words that Gary uses to describe his feelings about being both gifted and learning disabled. With the exception of two years in elementary school and his last two years in high school, his experiences were mostly negative. Even many of his experiences in college would be characterized as challenging and stressful. Gary illustrates the constant emotional "battle" that rages within an intellectually gifted child to understand, accept, and overcome the negative aspects of a learning problem. His case study also demonstrates the struggle to realize and utilize his gifts, particularly in the school setting. We can learn a great deal from exploring the successes and the hindrances to success that Gary experienced.

Gary is the older of two children in an intact family living in a small suburban community just north of New York City. Gary's father has an associate degree and works as a project engineer, focusing on electronics. His mother has worked full-time as a nurse since Gary was in the third grade. His sister, who is four years younger, suffers from juvenile diabetes, but her physical disability does not interfere with either her academic or social success in school. Gary worries a great deal about his sister, feels protective of her, and views her as a close friend.

Gary's mother was aware of his brightness as well as his problems at a very early age, and she tried to advocate for him from the beginning of his schooling, frequently with very little success. Gary was speaking in full sentences at eighteen months, and by the time he was three, he had a very large and impressive vocabulary. He learned the alphabet by age two independently by watching Sesame Street and playing with the Creative Playthings Alphabet Blocks. Not only was he precocious and curious, he was also a very loving and affectionate infant. Gary's mother appreciated and was amazed by his abilities but was also concerned by his high level of activity and clumsiness. According to his mother, he would go nonstop from the time he woke up in the morning. He was her first child, so she spent the time following him, never taking her eyes off him. When she consulted the pediatrician, he told her that he was not hyperactive and that she should not worry. When her daughter was born, however, the contrast between their activity levels was dramatic. The daughter was calm and content, able to sit in her infant seat and watch her brother moving actively around the room.

Gary's mother was very aware of his clumsiness, which became even more evident when his sister was born. His sister did not learn to walk until she was thirteen months, but when she learned, there were no problems. Gary, on the other hand, was trying to stand up and walk from the time he was eight months old. His mother notes that he fell constantly and that he frequently had bumps and bruises. His clumsiness and difficulty with gross motor activities also resulted in having two broken elbows, once in elementary school and again in middle school.

Gary's mother trusted the professionals, the pediatrician, and the school personnel to give her the right advice even though she instinctively disagreed with their assessments of her son's needs. She had listened to Gary complain about his difficulties making friends, following the teacher's directions, and completing tasks required in kindergarten. Although she felt that he needed another year in kindergarten, when confronted with the principal's evaluation that he was ready for first grade, she complied. The principal felt that Gary's testing indicated that he was academically ready for first grade work and that he was too big to be left behind.

According to Gary's mother, first grade was very difficult. Even though his reading skills were excellent, his handwriting and math were serious problems. Because his mother had trouble with math in school, she understood what he was going through but also realized that his problems were much more severe than her own. She would try to get basic concepts across with hands-on, concrete materials such as pieces of candy and coins, but with little or no success. Although her husband, who was good in math, felt that Gary was not trying hard enough, his mother was aware that he was trying but was unable to grasp the concepts even on a one-to-one basis.

Second grade was equally as difficult academically, but now students were beginning to tease him because of his large size, his clumsiness, and his learning problems. The teacher downplayed his joy at learning how to tie his shoelaces because it gave other students more ammunition to tease him.

Gary's memories of first and second grade are very similar to his mother's recollections. He refers to himself as a Golden Retriever, friendly and innocent, trying to make people happy. However, whether it was due to his trying too hard or his learning problems, he did not feel like he fit in. Instead, he became the brunt of the other students' teasing.

Gary was painfully aware that he was having a much more difficult time than his classmates learning math. Looking back on that time, he states:

> I don't think the teachers had any concept of learning disabilities or how to go about helping someone with a math problem. They looked at it, I would say, as some type of affliction—something that maybe I didn't want to learn or that I didn't spend as much time as someone else

so, therefore, maybe I was a wiseguy. Maybe that image was reinforced because I was hyperactive, but their way of dealing with it definitely wasn't conducive to overcoming the problem. Some of my earliest memories were being in the classroom, reviewing math and having this incredible dread of being called on. I would put my head down and almost will myself to disappear so I wouldn't be called on. I knew that I didn't have any idea what the answer was. I would try to study it. I would look at the numbers at night and go over and over and over it. It took me years to grasp the times tables. It seemed like the teachers were into public humiliation more than anything else.

During third grade, the gap between Gary's abilities and his academic results began to widen. He was becoming more and more frustrated. His mother went to the principal to request an evaluation, but she was told to wait because it was not needed. His mother chose to believe the professionals were correct even though she continued to be very concerned. In the meantime, Gary's frustration about his math and written work and his poor peer relationships turned to anger. He had several fights in school and had run out of the classroom. On one particularly difficult day, his mother received an emergency phone call from the school telling her that he had overturned a desk and was trying to run away. When she got to the school, she was horrified to see them restraining her terrified and angry son. He was immediately suspended from school and put on homebound instruction. This traumatic incident led to a complete psychological and educational evaluation and to a program that would address both his giftedness and his disabilities.

The psychoeducational evaluation determined that Gary was both gifted and learning disabled. The administration of the Wechsler Intelligence Scale for Children–Revised (WISC-R) indicated very superior verbal abilities and average nonverbal abilities overall, but also a specific learning disability related to attentional and visual-motor integration factors. There was a twenty-seven-point discrepancy between his Verbal and Performance scores. The discrepancies between subtests were very dramatic. On the Verbal Subtests of Similarities, Vocabulary, and Comprehension, he scored in the 99th percentile, and on Information, he scored in the 91st percentile. However, he scored in the 16th percentile on Arithmetic, Digit Span, and Mazes. His lowest score was on Coding, which bottomed out at the 9th percentile. The psychologist's report noted that Gary's nonverbal problem-solving skills on the WISC-R declined as the motor component increased. She noted that his anxiety increased noticeably as he completed the perceptual-motor items. Although he was able to persist, he became visibly anxious, complained loudly, and often ran his fingers through his hair and tugged at his clothing.

Gary's grapho-motor difficulties were confirmed by his performance on the Bender Visual Motor Gestalt Test. He made errors in distortion, angulation, and rotation that were reflective of a child two years younger. The psychologist's report stated that the lack of organization and planning were typical of a learning-disabled child.

The administration of academic assessments also confirmed the discrepancies between Gary's strengths and weaknesses. As a third grader, he was scoring at the end of sixth grade on the reading evaluation. However, the evaluator noted that his visual tracking was a problem, since he skipped entire lines of print. His math demonstrated numerous problems and deficiencies, with most of his scores being a year below grade level.

With the psychoeducational evaluation having been completed, the Committee for Special Education (CSE) classified Gary as learning disabled. After much investigation and advocacy by Gary's mother, it was decided that sending Gary to the Gifted Special Education (GSE) Program would best meet his needs.

The GSE Program is a self-contained classroom program for gifted students who have learning and emotional problems. It consists of elementary, middle, and high school classes, all housed in different public school facilities in southern Westchester County, New York. Each GSE class has a multiage and multigrade organization, with at least a three-year age and grade range. There is one teacher, one teacher aide, and a maximum of twelve students per class. The teacher is responsible for the academic portion of the student's day, providing state-mandated curriculum, remediation, and creative projects, acceleration, and enrichment. The students are mainstreamed with their age-appropriate peers for electives such as art, gym, and music. A psychologist meets with the students once a week as part of a group and again individually to discuss school issues that are interfering with their progress.

Gary entered the GSE Program at the end of third grade and remained there until the end of sixth grade. Gary and his mother acknowledged both the positive and negative feelings that Gary experienced by being in the GSE Program. The creative projects, the individual attention, the focus on his cognitive strengths, and the remediation of his learning problems were considered to be positive and helpful.

There were many aspects of the program that Gary identified as being particularly positive toward his development. He developed a love of reading and an interest in research, history, and current events. He participated in research projects that required that he utilize his strong cognitive abilities to develop multimedia or other creative products.

As part of the program, he also participated on a weekly basis in the "train room." A retired teacher from the school had set up a model railroad in the room across the hall from the GSE elementary class. The retired teacher was so excited by the challenge of working with dually exceptional students that he agreed to team-teach several days each week and to collaborate with the GSE teacher in order to develop an integrated, hands-on curriculum, and real-life experience utilizing the model railroad. Not only did Gary study transportation, government, politics, interdependence, future travel, inventions, geography, and physics, he also had the opportunity to learn math and utilize it in a practical way as he assisted in building the physical structure for the model railroad community—which eventually became the size of the entire classroom. Gary was exceptionally proud of his contribution to the project, particularly since he was aware of his math and eye-hand coordination problems.

Gary calmed down emotionally and became a productive student. He learned how to study, how to take responsibility for his own behavior, and how to control his impulsiveness. He also made friends for the first time in his life. The friendships he made with other GLD students were positive and lasted several years beyond the time they spent together.

However, Gary was very sensitive to appearing different from his peers. He felt that he was not accepted by his mainstream peers. The positive peer interactions that occurred within the GSE classroom did not eliminate or offset his emotional reaction to the perception that others in the school viewed him as different or, in some way, defective. It was important to him to be accepted by the general population and he felt that he was not.

When his family moved at the end of sixth grade, it was determined by the CSE in his new school district that they had an educational program that would meet his needs. Gary thought that in seventh grade, when he left the GSE Program to return full-time to public school, he would be viewed by his peers as "one of the guys," especially since all of the students were new to the middle school environment—they were coming from different elementary schools across the district, and this was a new school district for Gary where none of the students knew him or his special education background. What he experienced, instead, were the same feelings of being different. He felt that he was ostracized because he still had the learning disability label and attended special classes for math and English.

Gary had academic, social, and behavioral problems during middle school. Both he and his mother noted that this was a very rough period. He resented being in the special education classes and felt that his disability defined who he was, what he could accomplish, and how others viewed him. He limped along with barely passing grades and questionable behavior. In fact, he was running through the hallways between classes when he tripped over another student's foot and fell, breaking his elbow. There was no acknowledgment by school personnel during this period of time of Gary's giftedness even though he spent the previous three years in a program for gifted students.

It was not until his junior year that this downward trend began to change. Gary voluntarily decided to take an entrance exam for a college English course given by the high school. He passed the exam and was accepted into the course. He was delighted to finally have an opportunity again to prove that he had abilities beyond those that caused him to be labeled. The course challenged him and excited his intellect. Gary talks about the feelings of relief he experienced when the English teacher gave him the opportunity to take the entrance exam for the advanced placement class even though he was still in the special education English class:

> Well, he accepted me into the college English class without prejudging me like with the resource room or the math classes. He gave me a real shot. I took the entrance exam and I did very well on it. That was all that mattered to him, as it should be. He welcomed me in there.

During his senior year, Gary also took a social studies elective that he viewed as positive. It focused on his verbal strengths, challenged him to produce a real-life product, and demanded a rigorous adherence to academic excellence. Gary acknowledged that he enjoyed this challenge and that he did well. There were two parts to the course—one in which he was involved with the Senior Senate, and the other in which they participated in a mock trial. The teacher was both inspirational and influential in Gary's development of positive self-esteem. His greatest accomplishment in school, however, was winning Law Day, an event in which teams of students from all over the county competed. He and his student partners were given a law case to defend and prosecute in front of a panel of local lawyers and judges. His superior analytical and verbal skills were tapped, and he was able to display his strengths in a meaningful way.

When Gary graduated from high school, he received five commendations, scholarships, and honors for such things as outstanding citizenship, exceptional ability in history, and most improved student. The positive experiences of the last two years helped him to see that his strengths and verbal gifts could be tapped in the school environment and gave him encouragement that he could move forward to realize his dreams of becoming a lawyer or a college professor.

Gary chose to attend the local community college after graduation because of his mediocre high school grade point average and financial constraints. Even though he began school with a positive attitude, it quickly changed when he realized that in order to receive an associate degree, he had to acquire six math credits. He had to take a remedial math course before he could take the first three-credit math course; according to Gary, it was an unmitigated disaster. He talked about the efforts to assist him but how that did not change the requirement:

> I had a professor who went to the Dean of Students and the President to try to get an exemption for me in math. He made the case. They had all the documentation about my learning disability. The professor went there and said, "This isn't someone who doesn't feel like doing the work. He is doing well in all other classes. It would serve a good purpose to let him not take math—to take some science classes instead." But, it didn't materialize. What the professor told me was that different departments guard their territory furiously and they are afraid of a slippery slope—justification allowing one, then another, to have exemptions until they are allowing people to take reading or basket weaving classes because they are not good in this or that.

His learning disability has not been Gary's only obstacle. His father never believed that Gary's problems were due to a learning disability but, instead, verbalized that if Gary just tried harder and weren't so lazy, he could do better. This view of Gary's difficulties led to bitter disagreements between his parents. It also resulted in Gary's resentment toward his father as well as feelings of guilt and inadequacy. Numerous professionals tried to explain to

Gary's father that the difficulties that his son experienced in school were not purposeful or willful misbehavior; however, even with his son in college, Gary's father still did not acknowledge his son's learning problems as a diagnosed disability. On the other hand, through his involvement in counseling, Gary became comfortable enough to discuss and even tease his father about his lack of understanding.

And so, with his math disability still haunting him, Gary transferred to another university. He learned to cope with his poor handwriting by utilizing a computer and with his disorganization by incorporating a variety of study skills. He developed some solid friendships, particularly with the students in his high school social studies class and extracurricular activities. But his math disability continued to be his overriding concern. The difference, however, was that he could discuss it, and he developed unique problem-solving techniques to overcome the obstacles. Gary was anxious to move on with his life and to begin realizing his dream of becoming a professor or a lawyer.

DISCUSSION AND IMPLICATIONS

A great deal can be learned from exploring the successes and the hindrances to success that occurred in this case study. Utilizing what has been learned from research and gleaned from Gary's experience, the rest of this chapter covers the issues of early identification, teacher training, programming options, and teaching strategies. It concludes with a review of social and emotional issues and parent involvement.

Early Identification and Screening

Emotional conflict and nonachieving behavior can occur at a very early age. Gary was having problems as early as kindergarten and first grade that were obvious to his teachers. Although he tried to comply with teacher requests and the demands of the classroom, as much as he struggled, he could not fulfill the teacher's desires or his own perfectionist tendencies. Frustration, confusion, and anger were the feelings that he experienced. The negative and self-deprecating feelings that resulted from failing were strong and long-lasting. Whitmore (1980), in her work with underachieving and GLD students, states:

> With students who are highly sensitive, the effects of being in a classroom environment that is incompatible with their needs can be disastrous and produce severe emotional problems as well as a lack of academic achievement as early as ages 7 to 9. (p. 395)

It is, therefore, crucial to identify the GLD child as early as possible. Like all students, the GLD child is an individual with a variety of strengths and weaknesses, but there are some dissimilarities that can assist teachers in screening for giftedness. Parents of young gifted children frequently report that their child exhibited advanced language skills and problem-solving abilities. Excellent memory and a curiosity for investigating and learning is another frequent descriptor of young gifted children. Because the child has not started school yet, the indicators of a learning disability are not as obvious. When the GLD student starts school, the severity and type of learning disability frequently determines whether the child is identified as gifted, learning disabled, or simply as an average child who could be doing better with proper effort. There appear to be three patterns of identification (Baum, 1994; Olenchak, 1994) that can assist when screening for the GLD child.

The first pattern is the identification of the child as learning disabled. The child who is having significant difficulty learning basic skills or is having social and behavioral problems, particularly in the first few years of school, is tested and frequently identified for remedial assistance. Gary is an example of a student who came to school already reading but was unable to master holding and using the pencil correctly, could not grasp basic math facts or concepts, and had difficulty establishing friendships with his classmates. His learning problems coupled with his behavior problems forced the issue, and he was tested and subsequently identified as learning disabled. One of the problems that occurs once the child has been identified as learning disabled is the emphasis on remediation and trying to "fix" the child. There are several problems with this approach. First, there is rarely any recognition or attention to the child's strengths or giftedness. Gary was fortunate that his mother advocated for him to be placed in the GSE Program where both his strengths and weaknesses were addressed. However, when he left that program in middle school, the emphasis again returned to remediation with no acknowledgment of his giftedness. He became frustrated, angry, and nonproductive. He appeared to be an average or disabled student, but certainly not gifted.

The second problem with the fix-it, remedial approach is that the materials that are frequently used are cognitively below the child and are, therefore, frequently boring and sometimes degrading. If the child is pulled out of the classroom for remedial help during social studies and science group discussions, he or she may miss an opportunity to expand his or her knowledge and contribute to the classroom.

And third, the GLD child feels inadequate and different from his or her peers. No one has to tell the child that he or she is not keeping up with classroom assignments or reading as well as his or her classmates. The GLD child is very sensitive to the differences. The emphasis on only the disability reinforces the child's view of himself or herself that says he or she is defective or dumb because otherwise he or she would be able to compete academically with the rest of the students. Meisgeier, Meisgeier, and Werblo (1978) also expressed concern for these special students, noting that studies conducted at the University of Houston showed that "gifted children with some kind of learning problem or other handicap have disengaged to such a degree that they are discovered in special education classes limping along with very little evidence of the giftedness being manifested" (p. 85).

Another group of students are those who have been identified as gifted but who have subtle learning disabilities (Baum, 1994). Because there is an assumption that gifted students excel in all areas and do not have academic difficulties, their learning problems are rarely identified, and if they are, it is not until late elementary school or middle school when they have difficulty with assignments that have become longer and requirements that are more involved. At this point, even the verbally and academically capable child begins to struggle. The reading assignments have become more complicated so that they can no longer compensate for their reading difficulties by listening to others read orally in class. Greater independence is required, and so if the child's organizational skills are weak, the task may begin to look overwhelming. Written assignments may be lost or never completed, or they may be too sloppy to decipher. The child also may be doing particularly well in certain subject areas but beginning to slip noticeably in other areas. Teachers and parents become exasperated that the child is so bright and capable and, yet, is doing minimum or inadequate work. They are perplexed as to why the child appears to be underachieving. The child, too, becomes frustrated, confused, and sometimes angry, particularly if he or she had been receiving good grades and accolades in the earlier years. The child's parents may seek the school's assistance in understanding their child's problems but are frequently told that the child is scoring too high or is too bright to qualify as learning disabled. They may also be told that the child is lazy and simply needs to try harder. It is not unusual for the parents to seek an outside evaluation in order to have confirmation that a problem truly does exist.

The third group are the GLD children who are never identified as either learning disabled or gifted and who struggle along through the system as average students (Baum, 1994; Olenchak, 1994; Whitmore & Maker, 1985). They are able to compensate or cope with the school system, although poorly, and rarely call attention to or distinguish themselves in any significant way. They work very hard, usually achieving grade level competencies, and follow teacher directions, thus appearing to be run-of-the-mill students. In college, or once they graduate, they may read or hear about learning disabilities and begin to realize that the struggle they had in school may have had a neurological basis.

Training Educators

Teachers, psychologists, and administrators can be trained to recognize the characteristics of GLD children in the classroom. In order to do so, they must first understand the characteristics of gifted children with or without a learning problem. They also must be aware of the impact that a learning problem will have on the children's functioning. Minner (1990) found that both classroom teachers and teachers of the gifted hold stereotypical notions about learning disabled and gifted children that interfere with their ability to identify atypical gifted children, especially GLD students, and to recommend them for gifted programs. Whitmore (1989) addressed the same issue and stated that one of the obstacles to identification is that teachers of the gifted receive no training in handicapping conditions and so are unfamiliar with how the handicap can mask the gift. Likewise, the typical learning disability specialist rarely takes a course in gifted education. Inservice and pre-service programs need to be provided to sensitize, inform, and train teachers about the special needs of this population.

There are a few informal checklists and lists of characteristics that have been compiled that can be used to assist teachers in understanding, identifying, and learning about the behavioral and learning characteristics of GLD and underachieving gifted students (Tannenbaum & Baldwin, 1983; Udall & Maker, 1983; Whitmore, 1980). They can assist teachers during the initial screening. Table 6–1, developed by Tannenbaum and Baldwin (1983), is a list comparing some of the characteristics of gifted students to characteristics and behaviors of GLD students.

Teachers can utilize their curriculum activities to screen for potentially gifted students. When the classroom focus is on paper and pencil tasks with a strict adherence to a textbook and workbook orientation, GLD children will have more difficulty demonstrating their gifts, thus making it more difficult for teachers to identify them as gifted. Many GLD students have their greatest problems with aspects of traditional school environments that emphasize sitting quietly, listening attentively, and reading textbooks and answering workbook questions without discussion or student participation. However, teachers who provide a stimulating and enriching curriculum that encourages active participation and different types of presentations and products will have far more opportunity to see potential in students where it was not noticed previously. When teachers expose students to a variety of domains of learning and activities, they can begin to assess which student shows strong abilities in poetry writing, scientific inquiry, or computer programming. For instance, Gardner's (1993) theory of multiple intelligences, which encourages teachers to utilize an active, multisensory approach to teaching and learning, provides a solid basis for uncovering giftedness and talents beyond the typical linguistic emphasis.

Formalized Testing

The federal government defined learning disabilities in Public Law 101-476, the Individuals with Disabilities Education Act (IDEA, 1990),

Table 6–1 Characteristics of high-IQ, highly motivated versus high-IQ, learning-disabled children

The child with high tested intelligence and strong motivation	The learning-disabled child with high tested intelligence
Perfectionist—high expectations of self and others.	Frustrated with inability to master high priority, scholastic skills.
	The need to avoid failure leads to a refusal to perform required tasks.
	Unhappiness over failure to live up to own expectations often leads to frustration and anger.
	Denies learning problem by stating that school activity is *dumb* or too easy.
	Deceives by doing work so sloppily that it is impossible to evaluate.
Voracious consumer of knowledge—retains extraordinary quantities of information; desires to explore, to know, to discover.	Bored with regular curriculum, particularly if it is textbook- and workbook-oriented.
	Has large knowledge base, which may have been acquired through intact sensory processes, but often suffers from *verbal diarrhea* to compensate for perceived failures in various school subjects.
	Bores classmates with long-winded or pompous disquisitions that reveal more information than anybody wants to know.
	May feel comfortable in revealing solid knowledge only in the safety of a one-to-one situation with challenging subjects.
Able to generate creative ideas about new problems and innovative solutions to old ones.	May be performing a task in a new or creative way, but seems not to be following directions.
	Dislikes rote and drill exercises, such as reciting arithmetic facts.
Is unusually sensitive to the feelings of self and others.	Sensitive to criticism by others, and highly critical of self and others, including teachers.

Table 6–1 (Continued)

	Can understand and express concern about the feelings of others even while engaging in antisocial behavior.
	Able to size up situations and utilize them to own advantage; may become skillful at manipulating others, including parents and teachers.
	Is sensitive to inconsistencies in teachers' disciplinary procedures and will complain about such unfairness.
Possesses a keen sense of humor.	May use a sense of humor to clown and divert attention from failure in school activities. May use humor to demean or make fun of other students.
Possesses extraordinary critical thinking skills and sees unusual relationships in objects, events, and ideas.	May combine ideas or express solutions that peers and teachers find bizarre.
	May be regarded as disrespectful because of tendency to question teacher's facts or conclusions.
Possesses a variety of special abilities.	May also have a wide variety of interests, but is handicapped in pursuing them because of process and learning difficulties.
	Parents often report many interests at home, but child seems dull, uninterested in activities at school.
	Is capable of self-entertainment for long periods of time when there is not required work to do.
Language skills are highly developed.	May use verbal skills to avoid specific language and behavior disorders.
	May not use a large vocabulary when speaking, but can explain meaning of words far beyond age expectancy.
Enjoys playing with words and their diverse meanings, even at inappropriate times and in inappropriate ways.	May use verbal skills to avoid specific language and behavior disorders.
	May not use a large vocabulary when speaking, but can explain meaning of words far beyond age expectancy.

Table 6–1 (Continued)

	Enjoys playing with words and their diverse meanings, even at inappropriate times and in inappropriate ways.
Shows alertness, high energy level and pace of thinking.	May be viewed as hyperactive accelerated because of need to be actively involved.
	Frustrated by inactivity or too much emphasis on deficient skills in the classroom.
	Impatient during social studies and science lessons that are textbook-oriented.
	Asks thought-provoking questions that may be misinterpreted; may also try to divert class discussions to current events.
	Easily distracted by activities and conversations going on in other parts of the classroom.
	Has difficulty focusing attention on written tasks or workbook pages.

and the earlier version, Public Law 94-142, Education for All Handicapped Children Act (1975). There are two parts to the law. The first part defines learning disabilities:

> The term "children with specific learning disabilities" means those children who have a disorder in one or more of the basic psychological processes involved in understanding or in using language, spoken or written, which disorder may manifest itself in imperfect ability to listen, think, speak, read, write, spell, or to do mathematical calculations. Such disorders include such conditions as perceptual handicaps, brain injury, minimal brain dysfunction, dyslexia, and developmental aphasia. Such term does not include children who have learning problems which are primarily the result of visual, hearing, or motor handicaps, of mental retardation, of emotional disturbance, or of environmental, cultural, or economic disadvantage.

The second part is operational and states that a student has a specific learning disability if (1) the student does not achieve at the proper age and ability levels in one or more of several specific areas when provided with appropriate learning experiences, and (2) the student has a severe discrepancy between achievement and intellectual ability in one or more of the following areas—oral expression, listening comprehension, written expression, basic reading skill, reading comprehension, mathematics calculation, and mathematics reasoning.

Schools and states vary in their criteria and guidelines regarding what qualifies as a severe gap between performance and potential in order to be identified as learning disabled, but most use a quantitative measure to determine eligibility (Lerner, 1993). Unfortunately, GLD students who are struggling to keep up with their classmates rarely meet the criteria for classification as learning disabled even if they are screened and tested. In fact, when Fox (1983) studied the number of gifted cases at the Temple University Clinic who had reading problems:

> only 10% performed 2 or more years below grade placement on a standardized reading test, a discrepancy most likely used for school screenings. Thus, a far larger percentage scored at or above grade level making it unlikely that schools would refer students for evaluation. (p. 135)

There are a number of tests used to determine a student's intelligence or cognitive ability, which are administered individually or in groups. Because of reading and language processing problems and difficulty completing written tasks within time constraints, many GLD students do not score well on group-administered IQ tests (Fox, Brody, & Tobin, 1983). For example, Whitmore (1980) described one of her learning-disabled students who scored an 89 on a group intelligence test but raised that score to 163 when tested on an individually administered intelligence test.

The Wechsler Intellegence Scale for Children–Revised (WISC-R) and the newer version, WISC-III, are individually administered tests that are frequently used when evaluating a student for learning disabilities. A number of researchers (Baum et al., 1991; Fox, Brody, & Tobin, 1983; Schiff et al., 1981; Silverman, 1989) have focused their attention on the WISC-R as a diagnostic tool for obtaining valuable information regarding a student's giftedness and weaknesses and for identifying GLD students. Because the WISC-R is made up of two distinct areas—the Verbal and Performance—with subtests that assess specific abilities, it provides the evaluator with detailed information in which to determine a child's strengths and weaknesses. A number of patterns have emerged from the studies focusing on the GLD student's WISC-R or WISC-III results.

(1) Educators should be aware of the discrepancy patterns that GLD students seem to demonstrate on the WISC and other testing instruments. The GLD population is heterogeneous. The patterns of discrepancies vary, but in most cases, there is much subtest scatter. In fact, it is not unusual for the GLD student to have some subtest scores that fall one or more standard deviations below the mean while also having some scores that are one or more standard deviations above the mean. When Schiff, Kaufman, and Kaufman (1981) analyzed WISC-R subtest

scores of learning-disabled children with superior intelligence, they found that the subscale scatter on both the Verbal and Performance subtests was substantially greater for the GLD student than for the learning-disabled child with normal intelligence. They also found that the GLD group scored significantly higher than the learning-disabled child in the following areas: Information, Similarities, Vocabulary, and Comprehension. High scores in these areas are consistent with parent and teacher reports that these students grasp concepts readily and are able to solve problems and think abstractly. This same type of pattern was identified by Silverman (1989) when evaluating test protocols of the gifted students at the Gifted Child Development Center, with the addition of significantly higher scores in Block Design as well.

These researchers also noted that the scores on Arithmetic, Digit Span, and Coding, were consistently much lower. This pattern of low scores in the Freedom from Distractibility Scale indicates weaknesses in attention and memory, and possibly sequencing problems.

Another comprehensive method for looking at the subtest scores has been presented by Baum, Owen, and Dixon (1991). This method incorporates the WISC research done on both LD and GLD students. The data is broken into two distinct areas, Integrative Intelligence and Dispersive Intelligence. The first area, Integrative Intelligence, groups together subtests that have as their connection the "capacity to discern broad patterns and connections in visual or verbal information" (p. 45). The subtest categories and the WISC subtests that make up the categories are Spatial Manipulation (Block Design, Object Assembly), Patterned Sequencing (Picture Arrangement, Mazes), and Abstract Conceptualization (Similarities, Comprehension). "High scores on subtests included in Integrative Intelligence provide evidence that such students can think abstractly, see patterns, and make connections among ideas—all pieces of creative productivity" (p. 46).

The second area, Dispersive Intelligence, focuses on conventional knowledge and meaningless sequences. According to the authors, Dispersive Intelligence is equally as important as Integrative Intelligence because it allows the individual to memorize spelling words, times tables, and phone numbers without concentrating on or being distracted by the broader patterns. Many of the daily activities in school, such as reading, spelling, and basic math, use primarily Dispersive Intelligence. The following subtest categories and the WISC subtest are considered as Dispersive Intelligence—Detailed Memory (Arithmetic, Picture Completion), Quick Detailed Processing (Coding), and Meaningless Sequencing (Digit Span).

Gary's WISC-R subtest results showed a pattern in which he scored in the 99th percentile on the Similarities, Vocabulary, and Comprehension subtests and the 91st percentile on Information. His next highest scores were on Picture Completion and Picture Arrangement, both in the 75th percentile. This was in direct contrast to Arithmetic, Digit Span, and Mazes, on which he scored in the 16th percentile. His lowest score, in the 9th percentile, was on Coding. The importance of these scores is to understand Gary's thinking and learning strengths as well as weaknesses in order to assist him in the classroom. His verbal reasoning and vocabulary knowledge are exceptionally strong, but his nonverbal problem-solving skills are very weak, and they become even weaker when a motor component is introduced. Although he has strong cognitive abilities with which to deal with concepts and abstract ideas, and excellent verbal skills, he has difficulty with putting his ideas or concepts on paper.

(2) A significant discrepancy can occur between Verbal and Performance scores (Schiff, Kaufman, & Kaufman, 1981; Udall & Maker, 1983). As noted before, the importance of this information is to identify the child's specific areas of strength and weakness in order to facilitate meeting the child's educational needs.

Gary's WISC-R results demonstrated the substantial discrepancy between the Verbal and Performance areas. His Verbal Score of 138 was 27 points higher than his Performance score of 101. His Full Scale score was 123, a score that would not have qualified him for most schools' gifted programs.

(3) It is recommended (Daniels, 1983; Fox, 1983; Wolf & Gygi, 1981) that a Full-Scale IQ cut-off score of 120 or 125 be utilized for screening purposes or identification into gifted programs rather than the traditional 130. As noted previously, there is much variability in the GLD student's subtest scores, which tends to pull the Full-Scale score down below the level considered as gifted.

Rather than being concerned about the total score or simply the final result, the importance of the WISC is the interpretation of the subtest scores and the types of patterns that they indicate. When being evaluated for the determination of services, this measurement becomes important in helping to determine a student's potential, particularly when it is being hidden by behaviors that the school considers to be negative and unlike the "typical gifted child." Higher scores tend to reflect the child's abilities and lower scores and discrepancies indicate the possibility of a disability.

Although the WISC is the most widely and consistently used assessment tool in the identification of learning disabilities and giftedness, other tests must be given to complete the total picture of the student's abilities and disabilities. When evaluating a student, a battery of tests as well as interviews with the child's parents, teachers, and the student are important. Tests such as the Detroit Test of Learning Aptitude and the Bender Visual Motor Gestalt Test are administered to determine or confirm the psychological processing abilities and weaknesses. Achievement tests that are individually given, like the Key Math and the Brigance Diagnostic Comprehensive Inventory of Basic Skills, provide the examiner with information regarding the academic skills the student has acquired as well as some of the strategies the student uses to answer the questions. When trained evaluators compare the results of the academic achievement and psychological processing tests used to determine a learning disability, the evaluator can begin to piece together important patterns that will assist in planning for the type of teaching strategies and programming options that will best accommodate the child's uneven educational patterns and needs.

Programming

Once a student has been identified as GLD, the next concern is how to provide an educational program that best addresses the student's needs. Because the GLD population is heterogeneous, there is no one solution or program option that will meet the needs of this diverse group of individuals. Just as there is a continuum of services for learning-disabled and gifted students, likewise, there must be a variety of alternatives for the GLD population. There are GLD students whose needs can be accommodated in the regular classroom with compensatory strategies. Whether or not other programming options are considered, the utilization of compensatory strategies is extremely important to the GLD child's ability to succeed in the regular classroom or any other educational setting. A number of compensatory strategies are discussed in the next section.

There are GLD students who can function effectively by attending a resource room program for the learning disabled. In order for this to be an effective strategy, however, the child's giftedness must then be nurtured in the regular classroom or other school environment. The learning-disability specialist must be aware of the child's strengths and utilize techniques and materials that emphasize and nurture the child's strong cognitive abilities. As has been noted previously, GLD students become very frustrated by teachers who focus on remedial skills and the deficit areas to the exclusion of the gift. They are willing to receive help in these areas but do not want to be held back from learning more important concepts and ideas because of their disability. They are very curious about the world around them and want to learn. Gary felt that too much time was spent in special education classes, particularly in middle and high school, that focused on the same skills over and over again. He felt that the remedial emphasis was counterproductive and that no matter how hard the teachers tried, he would never be able to meet their goals and standards in math. Even though research (Baum, 1985; Nielson & Mortorff-Albert, 1989; Whitmore & Maker, 1985) has indicated that the focus on remediation with GLD students is ineffective and frequently leads to poor self-esteem, lack of motivation, and depression, there is still a tendency to provide only remediation once the student has been identified as learning disabled.

There are GLD students who function effectively in gifted pull-out programs, but this is usually because the gifted coordinator is prepared and willing to accommodate for the child's reading and writing problems and poor organizational skills. However, there are potential problems with this approach also. If the child is being pulled out for both remediation in the resource room and for enrichment in the gifted class, this may be problematic because the child may have even greater difficulty keeping up with the work in the regular classroom (Daniels, 1983). This approach also requires a great deal of coordination between all of the teachers involved.

Research has demonstrated that placing GLD students in a gifted program without adequate support can be detrimental to their self-esteem. Waldron, Saphire, and Rosenblum (1987) found that GLD students who participated in an enrichment program had lower self-concepts than did their age-appropriate gifted peers, with the lowest factor rating being their own feelings of intelligence and school status. The authors noted that the same asocial tendencies existed in that environment as in the regular classroom.

There are GLD students whose educational needs are best met within a specialized special-contained class for dual-diagnosed students (Baldwin & Garguilo, 1983; Daniels, 1983; Hishinuma, 1991; Nielsen et al., 1989; Udall & Maker, 1983; Whitmore, 1980). This programming alternative, although usually very effective, is offered by very few school districts nationwide. The advantage of this option is that GLD students are educated with students who have similar needs so the teacher can emphasize aspects of the child's giftedness while also paying attention to the learning disability and the emotional/social issues. One such specialized and beneficial program is the Gifted Special Education (GSE) Program offered by the Southern Westchester Board of Cooperative Educational Services (BOCES) in New York that was described in Gary's case study.

Although the various self-contained programs have elements that are unique to the individual school districts, there are some commonalties that make them an effective programming choice. Enrichment, acceleration, and remediation can be provided in the same environment with a teacher and staff trained to work with the diversity of needs presented by this special group of students. The teacher usually has been certified in either learning disabilities or gifted education and has sought extra training in the other areas that are needed to teach this complex population. The teacher tends to be highly creative, energetic, and student-centered. Most programs have a small teacher-student ratio, with a range of as few as six students to a maximum of fifteen students, and most provide a paraprofessional to assist with the classroom activities. The classes are housed in public school buildings with students frequently being bussed to the school from other parts of the city or county. Most of the students participate in the activities offered by the school and are mainstreamed with their age-appropriate peers in either academics or electives, depending on the student's needs.

Frequently, the programs have a psychologist assigned to meet with students to discuss social/emotional issues or to consult with the teachers regarding specific strategies to assist with the behavioral and emotional concerns.

The decision as to the type of programming option offered should be determined by the Committee for Special Education or a team of professionals that understands the complexities of the GLD child. The decision-making process should also include the GLD student's parents and the student, if appropriate. This team must review all of the testing and assessment data and carefully evaluate the student's educational and emotional needs.

Regardless of the type of programming option chosen, there are some important teaching elements that research and interviews with GLD students have noted are important to their success (Baldwin, 1994; Baum, Owen, & Dixon, 1991; Bireley, Languis, & Williamson, 1992; Silverman, 1989). Teaching strategies such as focusing on student strengths, teaching and utilizing compensatory strategies and technology, and emphasizing critical thinking, problem-solving abilities and organizational skills are recommended. Hands-on and independent projects and an interdisciplinary curriculum are also very effective with this special population. The following is a description of some of these strategies and elements.

Focusing on Student's Strengths

When Gary was in the GSE Program, he was exposed to curriculum and enrichment activities that were geared to the highly verbal and cognitively gifted students in the class. He had opportunities to utilize his areas of strength and interest. Both Gary and his mother acknowledged that this emphasis made a positive difference in the way he felt about himself and the way he functioned as a student. It was not until he was in his junior year of high school that this type of opportunity occurred again. He was accepted into a college-level English class and the mock trial club, which he found challenging as well as intellectually stimulating. When he felt that his intellectual abilities were respected, his self-esteem increased, his negative behavior decreased, and he became very productive.

Another example is Stuart, an artistically and verbally talented elementary GSE student who was working on an American Indian research project as part of the social studies curriculum. All of the students were using various sources for gathering information including the Internet and videodisc. The final project was to be a written research paper. However, because the teacher allowed the students to utilize other methods for presenting their ideas, Stuart requested to complete his research project in a comic book format. He and the teacher developed a contract that stipulated the time lines and the specific expectations. Stuart agreed to hand in all of his note cards as scheduled and to include all of the required information into this more creative and unique presentation. As the teacher had predicted, it was far more work than the traditional term paper, but because it was his idea, demonstrated his talent, and allowed him to utilize his area of strength, he persisted. Both the teacher and Stuart were proud of the final product.

Educators should use caution, however, when planning to use a student's strength, particularly as it relates to remediation. It is important not to take the student's area of interest and use it only during remediation as a means of motivating the student. This approach has been known to "kill" students' enthusiasm because the area that they have been excited about exploring has now been attached to the subject or skill area that they hate. For example, a dyslexic GLD student who is struggling to learn how to read will begin to avoid learning and reading about the Civil War, even if it is that student's favorite subject, if the only time the student is presented with the material is during remedial reading lessons.

Compensatory Strategies and Technology

One of the reasons students are identified by the CSE as learning disabled is to ensure that they receive the extra help they need. Although remediation is important, the learning-disability specialist or other specialist working with the GLD child on the area of weakness, when cognizant of the child's positive attributes, such as strong cognitive abilities, can tap the child's strength. For example, there are many methods for teaching reading, but many dyslexic GLD students respond positively to the Orton-Gillingham approach because it is a cognitive approach and it focuses on the patterns and rules that govern eighty percent of the words in the English language. It is a multisensory, systematic approach that teaches students to see and understand the patterns within words.

There is a point in which continuing to focus on remediation becomes counterproductive. For example, elementary students should be taught cursive handwriting, but when it becomes obvious that only minimal progress will be made, then emphasis should be taken off the task and more energy focused on compensatory strategies, such as teaching the child to use the word processor.

Because many GLD students have difficulty with rote memory, particularly of nonmeaningful material (Silverman, 1989), teaching them to use compensatory strategies is absolutely vital. One of the frustrating problems for GLD students is that they are frequently held back from more advanced ideas and classes because they have not mastered the times tables or memorized spelling words and certain important facts and dates. Technology is available that can assist GLD students, and they must be taught and encouraged to use it (Silverman, 1989; Tobin & Schiffman, 1983; West, 1991). Many GLD students find that they are able to "write" lengthy and creative compositions utilizing the computer, whereas they produce minimal written products when they must do the same assignment with paper and pencil. Gary and his teachers recognized early that if he was going to fulfill his desire to write and create stories that others could read, he was going to have to use a word processor. Knowing that many GLD students have difficulty memorizing the math times tables or their weekly spelling words, it is extremely helpful to teach them how to use a calculator and a computer spell check function. Although there are those individuals who regard these tools as unnecessary crutches, for many GLD students these technological advances allow the students to function competitively in the classroom. As noted by Baum (1994), "Preventing an LD student from using a word processing program to complete all written assignments is like prohibiting a blind child from using texts printed in Braille" (p. 14).

It appears to be a paradox that the GLD student will frequently miss the simple or rote memorization problems on tests and classroom worksheets but is able to tackle the more elaborate and thought-provoking questions asked orally in class. They are not satisfied by just learning facts, especially if the facts are in isolation and do not accompany a more in-depth understanding of the material. They report that they enjoy abstract thinking and the give-and-take of a stimulating conversation that deals with ideas or has application to the real world. They can become bored or even irritated by discussions that remain at the lower end of Bloom's taxonomy and will sometimes challenge the teacher or the textbook. Gary responded positively to teachers who challenged his thinking and who were willing to take the time to answer his questions at a deeper, more introspective level. In fact, Gary stayed after school to have more in-depth conversations and debates about the books that his English teacher had assigned.

Organizational and Study Skills

GLD students need to be taught study and organizational skills. Many GLD students are disorganized, losing papers and assignments or not utilizing their time correctly. Although they are bright and there is an assumption that they should be able to complete tasks in a timely manner, they need to be taught how to break tasks down into segments that they can accomplish without being overwhelmed. This does not mean that the assignment should be watered down because that, too, can be demeaning. Instead, they need assistance in analyzing a task and learning how to establish workable timelines and expectations for themselves.

For example, Jake wanted to participate in the Science Fair but was afraid to undertake the task of planning a project. Although he had a strong interest in physical science, he had never succeeded in completing a long-term assignment or task in previous years. He had a wonderful idea for building an electromagnetic engine; however, Jake's dyslexia and poor organizational skills were great hindrances to his starting and completing projects. He felt defeated before he even started. Because so many GLD students are like Jake, they need assistance in planning the various steps of the project. With the end product in mind, Jake had to be helped with planning the steps in very concrete terms—what materials did he need, where would he get these materials, who would assist him with the research, and what was the time frame for completion. This was written in a contract and reviewed on a weekly or, in some cases, a daily basis. In Jake's case, he knew that some of his information would come from Books on Tape; he would meet with the resource teacher on a daily basis to work on the notes, outlines, and spelling for the written presentation; and he would request his father's assistance for acquiring the material. With this type of structure and plan, he was able to complete his project successfully.

Because GLD students have a tendency to lose their homework assignments and, sometimes, even their books, systems can be put in place to assist them. A second set of books that are left at home can be very helpful. Teachers have also established buddy systems so that students have someone to call to verify their assignments or someone to help take class notes. Sah and Borland (1989) also found that when the teacher worked with the parents to develop an organizational plan, structuring the GLD child's time at home, both the school and home saw positive changes in the child's organizational abilities and school behaviors.

Social and Emotional Considerations

GLD students have unique social and emotional needs. The research indicates that GLD students demonstrate poor self-concept and self-esteem, and have a negative outlook toward the school environment (Baldwin, 1994; Baum et al., 1991; Daniels, 1983; Schiff et al., 1981; Supplee, 1990; Tannenbaum & Baldwin, 1983; Vail, 1987). As noted earlier, they suffer from the confusion that occurs by being both disabled and very able. The knowledge that there is a discrepancy between one's advanced comprehension and one's ability to perform relatively simple school tasks appears to seriously threaten the GLD child's self-concept (Gerken, 1979; Whitmore, 1980; Whitmore & Maker, 1985). Several researchers (Baum, 1985; Schiff et al., 1981) have noted that the emotional reactions and behaviors of the GLD child appear to be more severe and pronounced than those of the more typical learning-disabled or gifted child. Schiff et al. (1981) states, "The emotional complications of the group as a whole include inadequate impulse control, defective self-concept, narcissistic hypersensitivity, and poorly developed integrative functions" (p. 403). GLD students have stated that they feel different, defective, and inadequate. These feelings were confirmed by Gary's comments that he felt lonely, different, and "like a pariah." It is imperative that professionals who work with GLD students are aware of the intensity of these students' emotional needs and feelings and utilize strategies that will allow them to gain a better understanding of themselves and their strengths and weaknesses. Counseling, class placement, focusing on their strengths, and collaborating with their parents have been recommended strategies that have been effective.

Group and individual counseling is important. If possible, the group counseling should include other GLD students who are at risk and who have many of the same issues. The students must have an opportunity to discuss their feelings of frustration, sadness, fear, and anger with other students who are experiencing many of the same problems. With the help of a psychologist who is cognizant of the GLD emotional issues, the students can develop problem-solving techniques to take more responsibility for their behavior and progress and to cope with their feelings.

Gary was involved in school-related counseling when he was in the GSE Program to help him with his anger and negative peer relationships. Not only did the psychologist meet with Gary, but he also collaborated with the teacher and Gary's parents so that all of the individuals working with Gary were consistent with their approach. When Gary continued to have difficulty in college, he sought out a private psychologist who helped him to continue to look at his issues with academics, his sense of frustration, and his difficulty with his father's lack of acceptance.

Utilizing Parents as Part of the Educational Team

Parents have considerable knowledge about their child that can be tapped in order to facilitate the identification and classroom progress. When parents are viewed as part of the team, they can assist in supporting the school's efforts. However, researchers (Baldwin, 1994; Bricklin, 1983; Vail, 1987; Whitmore, 1980) have noted that parents are often as confused, angry, and frustrated as their children. Many of their children were curious, active toddlers who appeared to be happy until they started school. When their children began to have difficulty in school, the parents attempted to work with the school but soon found it to be a frustrating experience. As previously pointed out, Gary's mother tried to discuss her concerns with the school personnel before and during the time he was having his initial difficulties. But like many parents, she was told not to worry because the professionals were taking care of the problem or that the child would simply mature and the problems would go away.

Sometimes the school is totally unaware of the difficulty that the child is having, but the parents see the effect when the child returns home frustrated and defeated. Such was the case of Samantha Abeel, a gifted young poet who wrote the book *Reach for the Moon* (1994). Although Samantha's mother had discussed her concerns with personnel in Samantha's elementary school, she was told not to worry because Samantha would outgrow the problem. By the time Samantha was in middle school, she was working hard, but was barely passing math, was struggling with grammar and writing, and was arriving home on a daily basis feeling defeated and overwhelmed. Her mother approached the school personnel again and demanded a more thorough evaluation, and this time, she did not give in to the pressure that she should not worry or that the problem would be solved with the use of a calculator. She succeeded in having Samantha diagnosed as learning disabled and having her receive the remedial help she needed in math, but she noted that it was "not without controversy." She also had Samantha placed in an advanced creative writing class where she successfully sought the assistance of the teacher to nurture Samantha's area of strength and giftedness. Her mother's advocacy efforts and the balanced approach to Samantha's strengths and weaknesses led to the beautiful and sensitive poetry book that was published while she was still in middle school.

When a child's learning problems begin to affect his or her ability to behave in the classroom, it is not unusual for school personnel to notify parents that they need to take more responsibility and to indicate that this may be a home problem. Parents have reported that the school has requested that they monitor homework more closely, acquire a tutor, or seek family counseling. Whitmore (1980) and Baldwin (1994) found that school personnel became defensive with parents when questioned about the child's classroom activities and experiences. These parents reported that the total responsibility for their child's school difficulties was shifted from the issues at school to the home, and the difficulties were attributed, by the school personnel, to a poor home situation or a lack of adequate discipline. The cycle of blame in which teachers focus on what the parents are doing wrong and the child's parents become disillusioned, frustrated, and sometimes accusatory, because the school is not solving their child's learning problem, becomes nonproductive and can block the child's progress. In the middle is the GLD child who is negatively affected by the lack of consistency.

Parent support and advocacy is very important. Most GLD students who receive help for either their disability or their giftedness note that their parents' active support and involvement made a significant difference in their lives (Baldwin, 1994; Reis & Neu, 1994). In almost all cases, the mother is very visible and active, providing not only constant encouragement and love but also specific strategies and advocacy activities such as asking for information, seeking testing, interacting with the school personnel and outside agencies, and monitoring homework and assignments. The father, too, is frequently involved, but, as in Gary's case, it is not always positive. Silverman (1989) found that many of the parents, particularly fathers, exhibited the same pattern of strengths and weaknesses in childhood as their children do now. Many of the fathers reported doing better as they got older and became successful adults. Both Silverman (1989) and West (1991) recommend working with the father-son dyad therapeutically, since the father can be hostile toward the child because the child may prompt unpleasant memories of the father's childhood. Reis & Neu (1994) also found that a number of the fathers in their study were too busy working to be involved at all in their children's education.

It is imperative that a level of trust be established between the parents and the school in order to be successful with these special students. In order to do that, parents must be viewed positively as the ultimate educators of their children, and school personnel must listen and respond to their needs and concerns. Numerous researchers (Bricklin, 1983; Mendaglio, 1993; Pehrson & Robinson, 1990; Sah & Borland, 1989; Supplee, 1990; Whitmore, 1980) have suggested that parent meetings are an effective way to build that trust. When parents are included in the decision making or are consulted for their opinions, as they were when the child was part of the GSE Program (Baldwin, 1994) or the Underachieving Gifted Program (Supplee, 1990), the parents begin to trust the school. They work with the school personnel to reinforce many of the strategies and school activities. Because they are feeling more positive, they communicate this attitude to their child. The IEP meeting is another time in which the parents should be working collaboratively with the school to develop the goals and objectives for their child's total school experience.

Conclusion

The terms *frustration* and *conflict* have been used numerous times throughout this chapter because they are themes that run through the lives of the GLD students and those who touch their lives—parents and educators. It is imperative that if we are going to help these special students, we identify them early, provide them with appropriate programs and compensatory strategies, and nurture their giftedness. Without these considerations, the positive contributions these exceptional students can give to society may never come to full bloom. When Gary was asked what advice he would give to other GLD students, he said:

Well, I'd say don't let your disability get you down. You have to look at things that are positive and try to do well in those areas.

Don't let yourself get down to a point where you don't do well in what you excel in or let yourself not care about what you are capable of doing.

REFERENCES

Aaron, P. G., Phillips, S., & Larsen, S. (1988). Specific reading disabilities in historically famous persons. *Journal of Learning Disabilities, 21*(9), 523–528.

Abeel, S. (1994). *Reach for the moon.* Duluth, MN: Pfeiffer-Hamilton.

Baldwin, L. J. (1994). *Portraits of gifted learning disabled students.* Unpublished doctoral dissertation, Columbia University Teacher's College, New York City, NY.

Baldwin, L. J., & Garguilo, D. A. (1983). A model program for elementary age learning disabled/gifted youngsters. In L. H. Fox, L. Brody, & D. Tobin (Eds.), *Learning disabled/gifted children* (pp. 207–222). Baltimore, MD: University Park Press.

Baum, S. (1985). *Learning disabled students with superior cognitive abilities: A validation study of descriptive behaviors.* Unpublished doctoral dissertation, University of Connecticut, Storrs, CT.

Baum, S. (1988). An enrichment program for gifted/learning disabled students. *Gifted Child Quarterly, 32,* 226–230.

Baum, S. (1994, Spring). Meeting the needs of gifted/learning disabled students: How far have we come? *The Journal of Secondary Gifted Education,* 6–16.

Baum, S., & Owen, S. (1988). High ability/learning disabled students: How are they different? *Gifted Child Quarterly, 32*(3), 321–326.

Baum, S., Owen, S., & Dixon, J. (1991). *To be gifted and learning disabled: From identification to practical strategies.* Mansfield Center, CT: Creative Learning Press.

Bireley, M., Languis, M., & Williamson, T. (1992). Physiological uniqueness: A new perspective on the learning disabled/gifted child. *Roeper Review, 15*(2), 101–107.

Boodoo, G., Bradley, C. L., Frontera, R. L., Pitts, J. R., & Wright, L. B. (1989). A survey of procedures used for identifying gifted/learning disabled children. *Gifted Child Quarterly, 33*(3), 110–114.

Bricklin, P. M. (1983). Working with parents of learning disabled gifted children. In L. H. Fox, L. Brody, & D. Tobin (Eds.), *Learning disabled/gifted children* (pp. 243–260). Baltimore, MD: University Park Press.

Clark, B. (1979). *Growing up gifted.* Columbus, OH: Merrill.

Daniels, P. R. (1983). *Teaching the gifted/learning disabled child.* Rockville, MD: Aspen Systems Corp.

Fox, L. H. (1983). Gifted students with reading problems: An empirical study. In L. H. Fox, L. Brody, & D. Tobin (Eds.), *Learning disabled/gifted children* (pp. 117–140). Baltimore, MD: University Park Press.

Fox, L. H., Brody, L., & Tobin, D. (Eds.). (1983). *Learning disabled/gifted children.* Baltimore, MD: University Park Press.

Gardner, H. (1993). *Creating minds: An anatomy of creativity seen through the lives of Freud, Einstein, Picasso, Stravinsky, Eliot, Graham and Gandhi.* New York: Basic Books.

Gerken, K. C. (1979). An unseen minority: Handicapped individuals who are gifted and talented. In N. Colangelo & R. T. Zaffran (Eds.), *New voices in counseling the gifted* (pp. 321–326). Dubuque, IA: Kendall/Hunt.

Goertzel, V., & Goertzel, M. (1962). *Cradles of eminence.* Boston, MA: Little, Brown.

Hannah, C. L., & Shore, B. M. (1995). Metacognition and high intellectual ability: Insights from the study of learning disabled gifted students. *Gifted Child Quarterly, 39*(2), 95–109.

Hemmings, B. (1985). The gifted/handicapped: Some basic issues. *Exceptional Child, 32*(1), 57–62.

Hishinuma, E. S. (1991). Serving the needs of the gifted/learning disabled. *Gifted Child Today, 14*(5), 36–38.

Hollingworth, L. S. (1923). *Special talents and defects: Their significance for education.* New York: Macmillan.

Lerner, J. W. (1993). *Learning disabilities: Theories, diagnosis, and teaching strategies.* Boston, MA: Houghton Mifflin.

Meisgeier, C., Meisgeier, C., & Werblo, D. (1978). Factors compounding the correct handicapping of some gifted children. *Gifted Child Quarterly, 22*(3), 83–87.

Mendaglio, S. (1993). Counseling gifted learning disabled: Individual and group counseling techniques. In L. K. Silverman (Ed.), *Counseling the gifted and talented* (pp. 131–149). Denver, CO: Love Publishing Co.

Mindel, P. (1982). The gifted dyslexic: A case study with theoretical and educational implications. *Roeper Review, 4*(3), 22–23.

Minner, S. (1990). Teacher evaluation of case description of learning disabled gifted children. *Gifted Child Quarterly, 34*(1), 37–39.

Nielsen, M. E., & Mortorff-Albert, S. (1989). The effects of special education service on the self-concept and school attitude of learning disabled/gifted students. *Roeper Review, 12*(1), 29–36.

Olenchak, R. F. (1994, Spring). Talent development: Accommodating the social and emotional needs of secondary gifted/learning disabled students. *The Journal of Secondary Gifted Education,* 40–52.

Pehrson, K. L., & Robinson, C. C. (1990). Parent education: Does it make a difference? *Child Study Journal, 20*(4), 221–226.

Reis, S., & Neu, T. (1994, Spring). Factors involved in the academic success of high ability university students with learning disabilities. *The Journal of Secondary Gifted Education,* 60–74.

Sah, A., & Borland, J. H. (1989). The effects of a structured home plan on the home and school behaviors of gifted learning disabled students with deficits in organization skills. *Roeper Review, 12*(1), 54–57.

Schiff, M. M., Kaufman, A. S., & Kaufman, N. L. (1981). Scatter analysis of WISC-R profiles for learning disabled children with superior intelligence. *Journal of Learning Disabilities, 14,* 400–404.

Silverman, L. K. (1989). Invisible gifts, invisible handicaps. *Roeper Review, 12*(1), 37–42.

Supplee, P. L. (1990). *Reaching the gifted underachiever.* New York: Teachers College Press.

Tannenbaum, A. J., & Baldwin, L. J. (1983). Giftedness and learning disability: A paradoxical combination. In L. H. Fox, L. Brody, & D. Tobin (Eds.), *Learning disabled/gifted children* (pp. 11–36). Baltimore, MD: University Park Press.

Terman, L. (1925). *Genetic studies of genius.* Stanford, CA: Stanford University Press.

Tobin, D., & Schiffman, G. (1983). Computer technology for learning disabled/gifted students. In L. H. Fox, L. Brody, & D. Tobin (Eds.), *Learning disabled/gifted children* (pp. 195–206). Baltimore, MD: University Park Press.

Udall, A. J., & Maker, C. J. (1983). A pilot program for elementary age learning disabled/gifted students. In L. H. Fox, L. Brody, D. Tobin (Eds.), *Learning disabled/gifted children* (pp. 223–242). Baltimore, MD: University Park Press.

Vail, P. (1987). *Smart kids with school problems.* New York: Dutton.

Waldron, K. A., & Saphire, D. G. (1990). An analysis of WISC-R factors for gifted students with learning disabilities. *Journal of Learning Disbilities, 23,* 491–498.

Waldron, K. A., Saphire, D. G., & Rosenblum, S. A. (1987). Learning disabilities and gifted: Identification based on self-concept, behavior and academic patterns. *Journal of Learning Disabilities, 20*(7), 422–427.

West, T. G. (1991). *In the mind's eye: Visual thinkers, gifted people with learning difficulties, computer images, and the ironies of creativity.* Buffalo, NY: Prometheus Books.

Whitmore, J. R. (1980). *Giftedness, conflict, and underachievement.* Needham Heights, MA: Allyn & Bacon.

Whitmore, J. R. (1989). Voices of experience: Four leading advocates for gifted students with disabilities. *Roeper Review, 12*(1), 5–13.

Whitmore, J. R., & Maker, C. J. (1985). *Intellectual giftedness in disabled persons.* Rockville, MD: Aspen Systems Corp.

Wolf, J., & Gygi, J. (1981). Learning disabled and the gifted: Success or failure? *Journal for the Education of the Gifted, 4,* 119–206.

AN AUSTRALIAN CASE STUDY

Steven's mother's eyes filled with tears as she spoke about the difficulties that her youngest son was experiencing. Now in his fourth year at school, he was constantly in trouble with his teacher and was struggling with most academic tasks. He was becoming increasingly angry and frustrated, and frequently described himself as "dumb" or "stupid." He was reluctant to participate in many class activities, and homework sessions were becoming battlegrounds as Steven tried to do the tasks that had been set for his class. When asked what, as parents, they were especially concerned about, his mother replied, "We're afraid that he's losing his smile. His self-esteem is so low, we are desperately worried about him."

What was happening to change this formerly happy, mischievous child into an angry, sullen, and fearful student? A brief look at his history provides many clues. Steven's developmental milestones were within the normal range, except for one critically important factor. At three years of age, he was barely speaking, and his articulation was very difficult to understand. An assessment by a speech pathologist confirmed that he had significant delays in both receptive and expressive language development and severe articulation problems. Subsequent auditory testing indicated that he was experiencing mild fluctuating conductive hearing loss and that this was a major contributing factor to his language difficulties. Intensive therapy helped Steven catch up with his peers by the time he started school at the age of five years and five months. However, he continued to have mild articulation difficulties that needed ongoing attention.

Steven loved school from day one. He participated in every activity with his customary exuberance and was a successful learner and popular with his classmates. In year one, he began to experience difficulty with learning to read and write and started to fall behind his peers. Assessment at the end of this year indicated that he had severe problems with phonemic segmentation skills and lacked the ability to decode and encode words. At this stage, he was skilled at mathematics, since minimal reading was required in the subject. His general knowledge was exceptional, his vocabulary was advanced for his age, and his sense of humor was quite sophisticated. He loved creating and constructing with Lego blocks, and his motor skills were excellent. His teacher described him as a "bright little boy who is a very capable student who is steadily developing reading skills."

At the completion of year two (chronological age 7.6), Steven's reading tests showed minimal improvement had been made in the previous twelve months of instruction, and in fact, he had slipped even further behind his peers in spite of a remedial reading program that he participated in throughout the year. His teacher noted that he seemed to prefer oral activities rather than written ones. This was especially noticeable in mathematics where he could do complicated procedures "in his head" if the teacher read out the problems, but he was unable to complete many simple mathematics exercises if he had to read the work for himself.

Midway through year three, Steven was experiencing great difficulty with much of his schoolwork. Because at this stage, reading skills are absolutely essential, he found that he was not able to access information from texts in every subject that had a reading component. At this time, research skills were introduced and much learning was completed from private projects and information gathering. Steven began to flounder, with his confidence plummeting at every level. He was genuinely confused by his lack of reading ability, as he could obviously understand everything that other people read to him. He could plan projects and discuss them in detail, but he could not read or write well enough to do any of the projects on his own.

Throughout year three, Steven was placed in remedial groups for reading and mathematics. All of the students in these groups were academically low-functioning, and some of them were integrated special education students. They were often teased by their classmates and were generally labeled as "dummies." Steven's behavior started to change, both at home and at school, and he continuously referred to himself as being "stupid" or "retarded." His parents were in constant contact with the school, expressing their concern and discussing options that might lead to improvement in both his skills and attitude. They were advised that their expectations were too high and that they had to try to accept the fact that he was a "slow learner."

Fortunately, his parents rejected the notion that he was "slow" and stressed that literacy skills were the problem, not a general lack of intelligence. They were able to cite many instances of Steven's successes, for example, his skill at soccer where he was able to "read" the game and organize the team effectively; his interest in science activities and his understanding of many topics; his ability to recall most of the information someone read to him; and his interest in current events such as Aboriginal Land Rights and his ability to discuss these ideas with adults. When discussing this latter interest, they mentioned that Steven was quite insulted to be given pictures of boomerangs to color as his assignment for the class social studies topic on Aboriginal culture. He really wanted to research the Mabo decision. His parents were told that he was "only up to coloring in yet." At this point, Steven's father insisted that his son be given a full battery of psychometric tests to get a better understanding of his cognitive abilities. Much to the surprise of the school personnel, the results on the WISC-R were as follows: Performance, 132; Verbal, 112; Full-Scale, 123. Steven was definitely not a "slow learner." A reassessment of his reading skills indicated that he was then in excess of two years below his chronological age on every subtest. His problems were definitely in the area of literacy, and since reading impacts every other area, this had serious implications.

Steven was placed on an intensive reading program throughout year four, and the results indicated improvement in all areas, although the scores were still up to two years below his chronological age. His parents reported that the school did nothing other than this to help him that year. They were concerned that the emphasis was still exclusively on his problems and that no special attention was placed on his abilities and talents. In fact, he was still treated as a "remedial" student, and he still regarded himself as "stupid" because he could not read as well as his peers.

Susan Winebrenner (1996) warned that giftedness in children with learning difficulties will go unnoticed because the deficit label usually takes precedence over other learning exceptionalities. She could have been writing about Steven.

REFERENCES

Winebrenner, S. (1996). *Teaching kids with learning difficulties in the regular classroom.* Minneapolis, MN: Free Spirit.

Sensory and Physical Challenges: The Hidden Mask

....

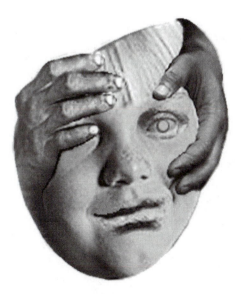

CHAPTER

7

THE DEAF

INTRODUCTION

The mask of deafness has traditionally concealed the gifted potential of students, primarily because of assumptions that deaf children are without language—or, at least, are retarded in language development. As language is often equated in practice with intellectual ability, the abilities of deaf children have been called into question. Indeed, the history of deaf education is replete with examples of a deficit approach, with teachers holding lower expectations of the academic potential of their deaf students. In recent years, the medical model utilized with people who are deaf has been challenged by an increasingly vocal Deaf[1] community. An essential element in the reconstruction of deafness is the recognition of the diverse abilities of deaf people.

---

[1] The term *Deaf* is capitalized when it is used to refer to the specific cultural group; it is lowercased when the word is used generally.

Research by the authors of this chapter (Paterson & Vialle, 1995; Vialle & Paterson, 1996, 1997) with gifted people who are deaf has indicated that many of them are not comfortable with being labeled as "gifted"; they report that their identity with the Deaf community is vital to their lives and they do not seek to be set apart again by such a label as "gifted." As with the other cultural minority groups described earlier in this book, then, it is necessary for giftedness to be defined, understood, and operationalized in terms that are sensitive to those who are deaf. Educators need to consider how those who are deaf regard giftedness rather than accepting a modified version of the dominant, hearing culture's definition. This chapter, therefore, explores the ways in which education can be structured in order to maximize the intellectual potential of people who are deaf. In other words, it seeks to reveal the giftedness that may have been concealed by the mask of deafness.

The chapter begins with an exploration of the mask of deafness, which includes a brief historical view of the way in which educational services have assumed an intellectual deficit among those who are deaf. This is followed by a review of the research into giftedness in Deaf populations, an extremely small body of literature. Case studies of two gifted deaf women are presented in order to demonstrate the common educational experiences of many deaf students while also highlighting the diversity among those who are deaf. These case studies provide the basis for a discussion of the implications for the education of gifted students who are deaf. The chapter concludes with some suggested activities for teachers to raise awareness of the issues presented in this chapter.

It is important, at this stage, to clarify the views of the authors on deafness and intelligence. People who are deaf are as diverse in their beliefs and attitudes as those who are hearing. There are those who strongly identify with the Deaf community and see themselves as constituting a cultural and linguistic minority. Such people prefer the label "Deaf" to "hearing impaired." There are also people who are able to use speech but have a significant hearing loss, many of whom prefer to be regarded as people with hearing impairment. This chapter is written from the perspective of the former group because the majority of the authors' work has been with those from the Deaf community. The authors define *intelligence* in its broadest sense to encapsulate a wide range of human capabilities, and not just those that may be measured by an IQ test.

THE IMPACT OF THE DEAFNESS MASK

As indicated, the prevalent attitude toward people who are deaf is essentially a negative model that emphasizes disability rather than ability. At the basis of the deficit approach to education of deaf students has been a disturbing association between deafness and pathology. For example, Harry and Deitz (1985) refer to literature in which the deaf are described as being more inclined to passionate anger, crimes of violence, and even sex delinquency. They conclude that there is no evidence to link prelingual deafness to criminality, but note that the prelingually deaf are overrepresented in civil and security mental hospitals. This association of deafness with pathology has an interesting parallel with the nineteenth century attitude toward giftedness in which genius was linked with insanity and dire predictions of "early ripe, early rot" were prevalent. Although the deaf "delinquency" descriptors have been discounted, there are nevertheless faint echoes of persisting negative attitudes when the educational attainments of deaf students are examined. In fact, the major barrier to those who are deaf attaining their potential lies squarely in the "audiocentrism" of the wider society. *Audiocentrism* is a term the authors have devised to encapsulate the majority (hearing) culture's imposition of its values, attitudes, and beliefs on those who are deaf.

Studies conducted in the 1960s in the United States and Canada, for example, demonstrated that the vast majority of persons who were born deaf did not acquire functional language competence even after many years of schooling (Furth, 1966). It was found that deaf students, on average, did not advance even one full grade in reading ability between the ages of ten and sixteen. Such statistics were not limited to the North American continent, as research in Britain (Conrad, 1979) showed that less than ten percent of deaf school-leavers could read at an age-appropriate level.

More recent examinations of the academic achievement scores of deaf students have shown that this disadvantage has not changed (Lane, 1988). This situation was highlighted in a report by the United States Commission on Education of the Deaf (1988) that unequivocally determined that the status of education of the Deaf was unacceptable and characterized by inappropriate priorities and inadequate resources as thousands of lower-functioning adults were leaving high schools yearly. The report stated that the educational system has not been successful in assisting the majority of deaf students to achieve reading skills that are on a level equal to their hearing peers.

It is interesting to compare the educational attainments of deaf students and other minority groups whose "depressed" academic performances have been more visible to the general populace. According to McLoughlin (1982), only one-third of the hearing impaired population in the United States had high school diplomas compared to three-quarters of all African-American students. Although these data are somewhat dated, this finding indicates that the deaf, because of their lack of visibility, were lagging behind other minorities in educational attainment levels.

The Deaf community, however, does not view deafness as a condition to be pitied and cured, as is the view held by the "medical condition" construct that has characterized much of deaf education in the past. According to Butow (1994), it is no longer appropriate to use the terminology that has been used historically now that there is a change away from the welfare focus to a human rights focus. However, Deaf people have a continuing struggle with changing the public perception of their abilities. While Deaf people are arguing for support systems that will give them access to mainstream education and society, such as interpreters and TTY (telephone typewriter) machines, the main types of support still tend to be within the health and disability sectors.

One dilemma for the Deaf community is the fact that people who have experienced some form of acquired hearing loss do tend to view deafness as a disability and are comfortable with the deficiency terminology that describes their experience of deafness. In this respect, their experiences are different from the experiences of those who were born deaf. As a result of their "acquired deafness," this group does tend to seek remedies that are within a health and disability context. Again, this emphasizes that, like the gifted, deaf people cannot be regarded as a homogeneous group.

Education continues to be largely constrained by intolerance of student diversity beyond very narrow prescribed limits (Christensen, 1992). It has been this lack of flexibility in recognizing and accommodating student diversity that creates disabled students. There is no questioning of the school's inflexible approach and intolerant attitudes; the difficulty or disability remains focused on the student rather than on the school's limitations. Solutions to the education of gifted students and deaf students, then, lies in educators being cognizant of the diversity within the group and responding accordingly.

Power (1992) asserts that members of the Deaf community, in defining themselves as a cultural-linguistic minority, accept that deafness cannot be cured and in this acceptance find an ease, stability, independence, and personal identity. Thus, according to Power, deafness can no longer be viewed as a deficit requiring medical intervention but, rather, should be viewed as a defining quality of a minority group that has had its rights ignored and infringed in terms of access to the various systems of society.

In response to the politicization of deafness occasioned by this shift, educational institutions are increasingly being challenged to consider the provision of bilingual/bicultural programs that reflect a perspective of deaf people as a linguistically diverse group. Programs that adopt a bilingual/bicultural perspective are scattered across the world but notably in North America, Scandinavia, Britain, France, and Australia. These programs vary greatly in the time that they have been established, but the majority are still within the first few years of operation. Indeed, the longest existing programs are only of approximately ten years' standing. Programs that have been significant in influencing bilingual/bicultural models in North America and Australia are the Swedish and Danish models that emphasize the first language of the Deaf community as a basis for teaching and acquiring the second language. This is in accord with the growing evidence in cognitive sciences that stresses the importance of the child's first language in the development of cognitive structures (Minami & Ovando, 1995; Ramirez, Yuen, & Ramey, 1991; Sacks, 1989; Willig, 1985).

RESEARCH INTO GIFTEDNESS IN DEAF POPULATIONS

Although there is a substantial body of research in the separate fields of gifted children and the education of deaf populations, there is a decided lack of research that looks at the education of students who are both gifted and deaf. Nevertheless, the limited studies that are available, combined with the more general literature on gifted minorities and education of the Deaf, have provided an important background for the authors' research efforts into this area. It is the authors' hope that publications such as this one will provide an impetus for educators to recognize and nurture the giftedness in their deaf students.

The majority of studies that have examined gifted deaf children have been descriptive, with the emphasis on identification issues (e.g., Baker, 1985; Timms, 1982; Yewchuk & Bibby, 1989). Other research has explored the effects of deafness on achievement or described gifted programs for the Deaf. In his national survey of programs for gifted deaf students, for example, Gamble (1985) concluded that only fifteen percent of gifted deaf students are enrolled in gifted programs. Interestingly, students whose parents are also deaf are far more likely to be enrolled than those whose parents are hearing. Vernon and LaFalce-Landers (1993) conducted a longitudinal study to examine the adult achievements of gifted deaf people and concluded that they did not attain the levels of achievement that would be expected of their potential. Vernon and LaFalce-Landers attributed this situation to inadequate challenge and support in their schooling. For example, one gifted deaf girl was denied interpreter services because she was achieving at near grade level. Vernon and LaFalce-Landers (1993) also determined that people who experienced hearing loss later in life were more prone to requiring mental health treatment.

Gifted Traits

As indicated previously, the history of the education of deaf students has been replete with a preoccupation with language and speech. As deaf students have been regarded in deficiency terms—their language and communication skills being described as delayed, impaired, and so on—it has been difficult for teachers to recognize giftedness in such students. Indeed, this is often as true of specialist teachers of the deaf as it is of teachers without such training. Labov stated that "[t]he educators' prejudice is akin to the ethnocentrism shown by numerous teachers of English who claim that only standard English is correct, while nonstandard dialects are ungrammatical corruptions of the 'pure' language. In the process of teaching 'correct' English, they make the speakers of nonstandard English feel that their dialect is inferior" (cited in Markowicz, 1980, pp. 278–279). The discourse of the deaf as deficient language users is not compatible with a view of their being gifted when giftedness is narrowly defined and when conventional language use operates as a de facto measure of intelligence. Further, there is every chance that students who develop competence in English, particularly oral English, may be regarded as being more gifted than their counterparts because of such facility. As with the other "masked" populations in this book, the deaf person who is gifted will be disadvantaged by narrow definitions of giftedness and associated identification procedures.

In seeking giftedness in deaf students, educators need to be aware of the falsity of the notion of "compensation" skills. While students with a sensory impairment may utilize their other senses to a greater degree, outstanding traits are more likely to represent individual cognitive functioning than a compensatory talent. Statistically, there is no reason to believe that deaf students are any more or less gifted than their hearing peers.

Assessment of the abilities of culturally Deaf children remains a task for research development. Even instruments that purport to be designed specifically for use with the Deaf have built-in biases of the hearing culture. An example of this is the Meadow-Kendall Socioemotional Inventory Scale (in Meadow-Orlans, 1983) developed at Gallaudet. One item in the scale judges the socioemotional development of Deaf children according to their wearing and acceptance or rejection of hearing aids as a measure of their adjustment. This is a clear example of the intrusion of the medical, deficit model of deafness that does not allow for the cultural orientation where some Deaf people reject the wearing of hearing aids. It remains, then, for culturally sensitive assessment instruments to be developed that can be delivered as well as assessed in the preferred communication of the Deaf person. This implies the input of Deaf people in their development and the training of personnel in Sign languages to be able to deliver the assessment as well as understand the responses of the recipients.

In order to combat the limitations of traditional IQ testing, some researchers have attempted to adopt alternative identification measures. These have included nonverbal IQ measures (Baker, 1985); nominations by parents, teachers, peers, and self (Yewchuk & Bibby, 1989); and the use of characteristics lists (Timms, 1982). The major problem with these approaches is also true of approaches with many other cultural minority groups: there is a sense in which the alternatives selected are still defined by the dominant culture's views of the nature of giftedness. Thus, the attempts to "detect" giftedness in deaf students in the research cited here, while noble in intent, still operate from the base of the hearing culture. The authors' research is focused on the development of flexible identification procedures that are culturally sensitive to the way the Deaf community views itself and linguistically sensitive to the special language situation created by the primary orientation of the Deaf community toward signed communication.

In 1983, Howard Gardner theorized the existence of seven, relatively discrete intelligences to challenge traditional views of intelligence. The seven intelligences capture the diverse ways in which people know and understand their world and include linguistic, logical-mathematical, spatial, musical, bodily-kinesthetic, interpersonal, and intrapersonal intelligences. More recently, Gardner (1997) has added an eighth intelligence to this list, which he has termed naturalist intelligence. Gardner's theory of multiple intelligences is a framework that may offer a more promising and broader approach to giftedness that recognizes diverse abilities rather than judgments based on language facility. Further, the theory allows for diversity in the expression of the different intelligences. For example, a more veridical picture of a deaf person's language ability would be their ability in their first language—and often this is a native sign language—rather than spoken English. It is important to recognize that neuroscience has confirmed that sign languages utilize similar parts of the brain's structure to spoken languages (Sacks, 1989).

CASE STUDIES

The following two case studies represent the diversity to be found within gifted deaf students. Despite the differences between Alice and Trudy, their experiences highlight critical issues for educators in ensuring that deaf students attain their potential for giftedness.

Alice

As referred to by Vialle and Paterson (1997, pp. 554–555), Alice is a young woman who describes herself as third-generation Deaf. She attended a school for the Deaf from the age of three to sixteen. She describes her home life as being extremely warm and supportive, with both parents supporting her intellectual development through discussion, reading, and so on. On completing school, Alice worked briefly at a bank and, for the first time, experienced the prejudice of hearing people. She resolved her crisis of confidence by leaving that position and attending a university in addition to working with the Deaf community.

In describing her school experiences, Alice felt very positive about the socialization that she found in a school for the Deaf. She reported that she and the other Deaf students developed their own signs, and the camaraderie was welcome. There were the usual frictions that occur among people everywhere, but as one member of a Deaf school community, Alice had a strong sense of identity with her peers.

However, Alice was less positive about the quality of the education she received and commented on the repetitive and boring nature of the work that left her unchallenged and unextended. In essence, she stated, the teachers expected less of Deaf students, despite the fact that the school catered specifically to Deaf students. She emphasized that many of the students were disadvantaged by the lower expectations that many of the teachers had of their ability:

> We didn't really learn how to think or to criticize or to do things like that. It's unfortunate because I started with some good teachers and then I got hopeless teachers again so it sort of went up and down. So that meant that it blocked out education and development. If we had had good teachers all the way through we would have done brilliantly. I would have been far better than what I'm doing now I feel.

Alice also commented on the poor communication skills of her teachers, the variation in the teachers' interest levels in their students, and their laxity in discipline. However, it appears that Alice's potential was recognized by at least one teacher, as she was accelerated from Year 5 to Year 6 and later to Year 7.

When asked about education for Deaf children, Alice suggested that more Deaf people should be involved. She also commented on what she thought would be a preferable model for educating Deaf students:

> I think bilingual schools are excellent because they teach children in a natural environment using a natural language, AUSLAN, and at the same time they can teach them English, change things to English so that the child can sign things and then you can say, "This is how you say it in English" and sometimes you might get stuck and think, "How do I write this in English?" so I think that it's excellent to have both so you're not putting down sign language, you're encouraging that as a natural language. But at English time you get to do the writing and teaching what that means and you can change that so that children understand this is what it means in English so that you can interpret between the two. For me it became a natural thing for me. I would sign things in AUSLAN but then when it came to writing I would make the change into English. It's an automatic process. . . . When I'm writing I never think in sign language, I always think in English when I'm writing.

When asked whether she thought of herself as a gifted Deaf person, Alice expressed a certain discomfort with the label "gifted." However, she admitted that she had always known that her abilities were superior to most of her peers, particularly in the area of English literacy. Alice clearly associates gift-edness with opportunities received rather than an innate potential. Thus, in describing her own accomplishments, she emphasizes the support and encouragement that she had received compared to the limited opportunities of her Deaf peers:

> I never think of myself as a gifted person or being gifted; I don't think of myself like that. I would see myself as a normal Deaf person. When I look at myself I feel that I'm just more fortunate than other Deaf people because of my background, my family background was excellent. Growing up we had lots of conversation, open discussions. I learnt a lot from my parents . . . compared with others who had a difficult life or a sad life. I've just been more fortunate and that's how I see myself.

Trudy

Trudy was born profoundly deaf as a result of her mother contracting rubella during pregnancy. Both of her parents and her siblings are hearing. At the age of one, Trudy was sent to the Shepherd Centre, which offered an intensive oral approach, training children to use their residual hearing. She was also fitted with hearing aids to both ears. In addition to the time at the Shepherd Centre, Trudy spent ten hours per week being taught by her parents, a specialist teacher who worked with Trudy at home, and a speech therapist. Desiring a "normal" education for her, Trudy's parents enrolled her in regular schools, although the high school had a reputation for offering specialized facilities for deaf children. Following her completion of high school, Trudy continued her education at the tertiary level and then engaged in postgraduate studies.

Trudy was generally positive about her educational experiences, commenting that her academic needs were met because the school she attended was aware of her needs. Her schooling was supplemented by extra itinerant teacher support and the efforts of her own parents. Teachers varied in quality, ranging from those that Trudy regarded as excellent to those who were poor. Characteristics of the latter included ignoring her in class when she raised her hand to answer a teacher's question to the class, being "too soft," or making her feel uncomfortable:

> If I went up to them after the class they would be mouthing their words and maybe sometimes, I remember, like I would hand in some assignments and they were absolutely shocking; I didn't even deserve to get an A and sometimes they would give a really good mark and you knew that you didn't deserve that mark but sometimes you wonder whether you got it because they thought, "Oh, you know, she's deaf, so this is not her fault that this work is poor, so we'll just give her a good mark."

The better teachers were those who treated her no differently from other students and wore a phonic ear—a device that amplifies sound, enabling the deaf person to hear more easily—without creating any "drama." Trudy comments that she excelled in the classes taught by these teachers. Other teachers refused to wear the phonic ear or treated her differently.

A common experience of the gifted deaf people in the authors' research has been the experience of a personal crisis of identity related to their deafness, particularly as it impacted on their social relationships. Trudy experienced such a crisis in the transition from primary school to secondary school. She described her feelings in the following manner:

> [S]uddenly it just dawned on me suddenly when I was in Year Seven that there was a problem here, like I was deaf and suddenly I noticed the change in how people treat you and it was something which hadn't happened to me before. And suddenly I had to start explaining to people that I was deaf and these are the things that you've got to do to help me, all those sorts of things, and suddenly I realized it was a little bit harder to make friends, because they were a bit hesi-tant about you and all those things happened when I was in Year Seven, and every teenager goes through problems when you're about thirteen or fourteen and it was just that little bit harder for me because I had all those problems. Suddenly the issue of being deaf became an issue and it was something I found hard to deal with.

Most of the interviewees solved their crises by identifying with the Deaf community. However, Trudy knew only one other deaf person and so identified primarily with the hearing culture. Her approach, therefore, involved drawing on her own resources and developing personal determination. She stated that being deaf meant that she had to work ten percent harder than hearing people to achieve similar results. In fact, Trudy consciously rejected the stereotypes of deaf people that she was encouraged to follow. She recounted her worst experience at school:

> [W]e had to organize our work experience when we were in Year Eleven, and my Drama teacher for some reason decided that I should go and do work experience at the Theatre of the Deaf, because I was really into drama at that stage and I thought I would make a career out of it and all that sort of thing. So she decided that I should go to the Theatre of the Deaf. Looking back I probably took it too strongly but I was absolutely against going to the Theatre of the Deaf to do work experience there. Now all the teachers were all in the staffroom and they were all having little debates about it and they were all very distressed about the fact that I didn't want to go there and they all thought that I was not coping with being deaf and I had people coming to me and saying, "Look, what's your problem," that sort of thing. . . . I didn't want to have a career where I was working with disabled people all the time and I think that is the direction that people thought I should take, because that would be the natural thing for me to do; and I didn't want to do that; and that was kind of the way that they were pushing me like I wouldn't be good enough for any other career. . . . It's the stereotype making your career for you.

When asked to describe the kind of education that deaf students should receive, Trudy endorsed her own experience in arguing for education in an integrated setting where her needs were understood and met. At the same time, though, she acknowledged that not all students coped with that setting as well as she did. Social acceptance and the degree of familial support were vital ingredients in Trudy's success in the integrated setting compared to other deaf students in her experience who did not fare as well. It must also be recognized that Trudy's primary orientation was to the hearing community, and her high level of oral skills ensured that people often were not aware of her deafness.

Like the other deaf adults in this study, Trudy declined to accept the label of giftedness for herself. Whereas the other interviewees rejected the label because they did not wish to be set apart from the Deaf community with which they had established their sense of personal identity, Trudy viewed her achievements as the result of effort and opportunity. She initially defined giftedness in terms of genius or prodigious attainment but then later attributed sporting giftedness to personal effort.

> My definition of giftedness is someone who's got an IQ of 200 and I think of those kids that you read about who are twelve years old and are already at university. . . . That's what I class as gifted. And also somebody who can excel, like I think of an Olympic athlete being gifted as well; it takes so much to become an Olympic athlete and to win that gold medal, I think they are fantastic; to dedicate their life to it and finally they got there with not much support; you know they had to get there themselves.

Case Study Conclusions

Alice and Trudy represent the diversity to be found among gifted deaf students. Alice was born deaf into a deaf family, and her primary orientation throughout her life was to the Deaf community; Trudy was born deaf into a hearing family, and her primary orientation throughout her life was with the hearing community. Alice attended schools for the Deaf where she was instructed in Sign language, while Trudy was given an intensive oral English education at an early age and sent to mainstream schools. Despite their vastly different backgrounds, experiences, and orientations, there are several points on which Alice and Trudy agreed. A comparison of these case studies will highlight the elements the authors consider essential in ensuring that the mask of deafness is lifted so that deaf individuals can attain their true potential.

Alice and Trudy illustrate the range of factors that contribute to giftedness. Both were born with gifted potential, and in each case, similar factors influenced their academic success. First and foremost was the parental support that both received. From an early age, their parents explicitly educated them, although the form of that education differed. In Alice's case, her parents communicated through AUSLAN—Australian sign language—and focused on developing Alice's critical thinking skills through constant challenges and lively debates on a wide range of issues. She was taught to read English as a second language and became proficient in both languages, switching easily between them according to the demands of the situation. Trudy's parents intensively educated her to recognize and produce intelligible English through the use of hearing aids and tactile sensations. Trudy's mother also created special picture books to capture Trudy's direct experiences of the world. Although the nature of the education differed, what was critical was the amount of time devoted to the child and the appropriateness of the level of instruction that allowed them to develop their cognitive skills.

Another critical factor for Alice and Trudy was that their intensive early education with their parents occurred in their first language so that their cognitive skills could develop naturally alongside their language development. Alice was born into a deaf family, and the first language of the home was AUSLAN; Trudy was born into a hearing family whose first language was English. Thus, both were able to learn in the language of their homes.

Although Alice reports frustration at the lack of challenge that she was often provided in the school setting, she still recognizes that the educational opportunities she received were an important factor in her academic success. Trudy's schooling experiences were highly positive. Schooling becomes an important element for the gifted deaf student on two levels. The first relates to teacher expectations. The teachers who were able to get the highest levels of attainment from both Trudy and Alice were those who recognized their abilities and appropriately challenged them rather than focusing on language and speech production. The second element relates to appropriate support to ensure that communication was maximized. Again, the type of support differed because of their different educational environments, highlighting that the appropriateness rather than the precise nature of the support is the key issue. Thus, in the school for the Deaf, the use of Sign may be sufficient, while in mainstream settings, the provision of hearing loops, FM systems, interpreters, or note-takers may be necessary.

The development of a personal identity with which they felt comfortable was also a crucial element for Alice and Trudy. Alice's identity was strongly oriented to the Deaf community and involved her developing a sense of competence within a structure where she saw herself as no different in her potential from other Deaf people. She attributed her superior attainments to the opportunities she had received rather than innate ability. Trudy, by contrast, identified with the hearing community and developed a sense of personal determination in order to succeed. She developed a competitive instinct whereby she was determined to prove that she was as good, if not better, than the hearing people around her; she stated that this meant she had to work harder than everybody else. Despite their differing orientations, both women felt comfortable with their identities. They both indicated that social acceptance was an important factor in their senses of self for both academic accomplishment and personal well-being. This is a theme that was consistent for the people throughout the study.

Alice and Trudy also brought to bear a number of personal qualities that were important in their attainments. Their determination to succeed has already been indicated. Related to this element is that both women had high levels of intrinsic motivation and a willingness to persist in the face of difficulties. Both set themselves clear goals and were willing to work in a focused manner toward the attainment of those goals.

The factors that related to the academic success of Alice and Trudy reinforce the conceptualization that Gagné (1985) provides of giftedness and talent. They both had the gifted potential to succeed and received the appropriate catalysts of a nurturing home environment, positive school experiences (although not uniformly so), and a combination of personal factors related to personality, motivation, and attitudes that enabled them to translate their giftedness into talent.

IMPLICATIONS FOR EDUCATION

This chapter has discussed the poor record of the educational establishment in terms of outcomes for deaf students, particularly those who are gifted. This situation exists regardless of whether the student is in a school for the Deaf or in a mainstream setting. As educational policy currently favors integration and the Deaf community increasingly favors separation, the debates regarding the ideal education for deaf students generally—and gifted students particularly—will continue unabated. As bilingual/bicultural classrooms for deaf students are still in their infancy, it remains to be seen whether the achievements of Deaf people will be positively impacted from such an approach, although the authors' evidence to date supports this stance.

Holliday (1976) has suggested the theory of cultural-educational continuity where new educational strategies are brought into play to reinforce values such as cultural heritage. Such a theory may be of relevance to the educational aspirations of the Deaf community.

Residential schools for the Deaf once served as the vehicle to perpetuate Deaf culture. As these have largely been replaced by a variety of educational options based mainly on the mainstreaming principle, Deaf people may be looking for other means of communicating aspects of Deaf culture to successive generations of Deaf children. A concept of cultural-educational continuity that provides for the Deaf cultural experience to be incorporated into the curriculum offering for deaf students may be an idea that the Deaf community will want to embrace.

Educators need to recognize that Deaf people are finding a pride in their separate identity and that other groups, too, are embracing what has been described as the "culture of disability" (Hallahan & Kauffman, 1994). This separatist identity is a way of coming to terms with past oppression, affirming a new identity, and rejecting the role of victim and oppressed minority. Glickman (1986) asserts that hearing people need to accept a level of anger expressed toward them by Deaf people, and through this acceptance, hearing people can establish themselves as advocates of Deaf people. By allowing a separatist stage, Glickman believes that Deaf people can move toward a healthier and less threatening bicultural identity. The end point of a bilingual/bicultural education program hopefully will be to see the Deaf individual defining himself or herself through finding an identity in Deaf culture and an identity in the hearing culture of the wider society with a realistic understanding and appreciation of both of these cultures.

The reality, though, is that for some time into the future, many deaf students who are gifted will continue to be placed in mainstream settings. As many teachers do not fully understand the nature of giftedness, the likelihood of gifted students who are also deaf receiving appropriate challenges in mainstream settings will undoubtedly remain questionable. There is an urgent need, therefore, for teacher-training institutions and school systems to ensure that teacher training and professional development address the issues of giftedness in special populations.

The teacher who is faced with deaf students in the class must commence with the awareness that deafness affects their communication, not cognition. The starting premise should always be to seek the intellectual strengths in the students, not to focus on remediation of supposed deficits. In determining the potential strengths of the students, teachers should determine whether the deaf student's primary orientation is to the Deaf community or the hearing culture. In the case of the former, the teacher should ensure that assessment of abilities occurs in the student's first language in order to gain a more accurate and culturally sensitive view of the student's potential. The provision of appropriately challenging work across a wide spectrum of content areas is essential. Gardner's theory of multiple intelligences is a useful framework for the teacher to ensure that the child's abilities and skills across all intelligences are being developed. Assessment in natural contexts, again, is more likely to provide the educator with useful knowledge about the student's potential.

Teachers need to be wary of any tendencies to compensate for the student's deafness by lowering their expectations of what the student can achieve. Accommodations that allow for enhanced communication should occur within a context of high expectations of cognitive output.

Regardless of whether the student's primary orientation is to a Deaf or a hearing culture, the teacher should value the Deaf culture through the curriculum provisions and the attitudes that are inculcated in the classroom. Examples of such approaches are included in the suggested activities at the end of this chapter. The development of identity is important for all students, but it seems to be even more important for students who belong to minority cultures. To enhance deaf students' sense of personal worth and pride in their Deaf heritage may be one of the most positive steps that can be made in assisting such students to realize their potential. The use of positive role models in the classroom will help enormously in this process. Finally, teachers should encourage the deaf student in developing and maintaining positive social relationships with their peers.

The challenge of celebrating diversity and ensuring that all children attain their potential remains a vital one for educators to embrace. This chapter has outlined the way in which deafness has masked giftedness. It remains for educators to lift this mask and ensure that the gifts of these students are not lost for themselves and for society. The activities that follow are some suggested starting points that teachers may wish to employ in their classrooms to raise awareness of the richness of the Deaf experience. By honoring this diversity, teachers will be better placed to enhance the educational experiences of all students and, in so doing, create a classroom environment that is more likely to reveal the giftedness of those who are deaf.

ACTIVITIES

- Interview some successful Deaf people. How do they describe themselves?
- Debate the issue "Is there a Deaf Culture?"
- Collect newspaper and magazine articles about Deaf people. How are they portrayed? Classify the articles according to the stance they take toward Deaf people.
- Argue the case for and against the use of hearing actors portraying Deaf people in film and theater.

- Create a family tree for your family and trace the appearance of Deaf members in various generations.
- Describe a Utopia for Deaf people. Would there be a role for hearing people?
- Research the origins of the Deaf Community in your area. Are there similarities to other cultural groups and their experiences?
- Draw a mind map that anticipates the needs of Deaf persons to carry out their daily life (for example, TTYs, interpreters, and so on).
- How do Deaf people describe themselves? (Personal identity exercise—for example, Black Deaf, Native American Deaf, feminist Deaf.)
- What are the barriers to Deaf people that still need to be conquered?
- Create an autobiographical video using sign, speech, mime, music.
- Compare Deaf and Hearing humor. Why is something funny in one culture but not in another? Tell the funniest visual joke.
- Plan a Deaf Festival—you are the guide for a visiting hearing person.
- Design a poster to break down myths about deafness.

REFERENCES

Baker, R. (1985). *A description of gifted deaf children.* Doctoral dissertation, University of Denver, Denver, CO.

Butow, H. (1994). Concepts of impairments, disability and handicap. *Interaction, 7*(5), 12–14.

Christensen, C. (1992). Deviant, disabled or different: The politics of labelling. *Australian Disability Review, 3,* 5–12.

Conrad, R. (1979). *The deaf schoolchild: Language and cognitive function.* London: Harper & Row.

Furth, H. (1966). *Thinking without language.* New York: Collier Macmillan.

Gagné, F. (1985). Giftedness and talent: Reexamining a reexamination of the definitions. *Gifted Child Quarterly, 29*(3), 103–112.

Gamble, H. (1985). A national survey of programs for intellectually and academically gifted hearing-impaired students. *American Annals of the Deaf, 130*(6), 508–513.

Gardner, H. (1983). *Frames of mind.* New York: Basic Books.

Gardner, H. (1997, January). *Multiple intelligences and education for understanding.* An address delivered to the "Using Your Brain" conference, Melbourne, Australia.

Glickman, N. (1986). Cultural identity, deafness and mental health. *Journal of Rehabilitation of the Deaf, 20*(2), 1–10.

Hallahan, D. P., & Kauffman, J. M. (1994). Toward a culture of disability in the aftermath of Deno and Dunn. *The Journal of Special Education, 27,* 496–508.

Harry, B., & Deitz, P. E. (1985). Offenders in a silent world: Hearing impairment and deafness in relation to criminality, incompetence and insanity. *Bulletin of the American Academy of Psychiatry and Law, 13*(1), 85–95.

Holliday, F. (1976). Towards a prospective of cultural-educational continuity. *Documentation and Technical Assistance in Urban Schools* (Eric Document Reproduction Service No. ED 228 365).

Kosslyn, S. M. & Koenig, O. (1995). *Wet mind: The new cognitive neuroscience.* New York: The Free Press.

Lane, H. (1988). Paternalism and deaf people: An open letter to Mme Umuvyeyi. *Sign Language Studies, 60,* 251–270.

Markowicz, H. (1980). Some sociolinguistic considerations of American Sign Language. In W. Stokoe (Ed.), *Sign and culture* (pp. 266–294). Silver Spring, MD: Linstok Press.

McLoughlin, W. (1982). The deaf, the law and higher education. *The Volta Review, 84*(6), 275–283.

Meadow-Orlans. (1983). *The Meadow-Kendall social-emotional inventory for deaf and hearing impaired students.* Washington, DC: Outreach Pre-College Program, Gallaudet University.

Minami, M., & Ovando, C. J. (1995). Language issues in multicultural contexts. In J. A. Banks & C. A. M. Banks (Eds.), *Handbook of research on multicultural education* (pp. 427–444). New York: Macmillan.

Paterson, J., & Vialle, W. (1995, July 16–20). *Issues in the education of gifted deaf people.* A paper presented at the 18th International Congress on Education for the Deaf, Tel Aviv, Israel.

Power, D. (1992). Deaf people: A linguistic and cultural minority community or a disability group. *Australian Disability Review, 4,* 43–47.

Ramirez, J. D., Yuen, S. D., & Ramey, D. R. (1991). *Longitudinal study of structured English immersion strategy, early-exit and late-exit transitional bilingual education programs for language-minority children.* Final report to the U.S. Department of Education. San Mateo, CA: Aguirre International.

Sacks, O. (1989). *Seeing voices.* Berkeley, CA: University of California Press.

Timms, M. (1982). *Freedom unmasked: The identification of giftedness/talent in deaf children.* Unpublished dissertation.

U.S. Commission on the Education of the Deaf. (1988). *Toward equality: Education of the Deaf. A report to the President and the Congress of the United States* (Eric Document Reproduction Service No. ED 303 932). Washington, DC: U.S. Government Printing Office.

Vernon, M., & LaFalce-Landers, E. (1993). A longitudinal study of intellectually gifted deaf and hard of hearing people. *American Annals of the Deaf, 138*(5), 427–34.

Vialle, W., & Paterson, J. (1996). A sign of the future: Recognising the intellectual strengths of the Deaf. *Australian Journal of Education of the Deaf, 2*(2), 32–37.

Vialle, W., & Paterson, J. (1997). Deafening silence: The educational experiences of gifted deaf people. In J. Chan, R. Li, & J. Spinks (Eds.), *Maximizing potential: Lengthening and strengthening our stride* (pp. 553–559). Proceedings of the 11th Conference of the World Council for Gifted and Talented Children. Hong Kong: The University of Hong Kong Social Sciences Research Centre.

Willig, A. C. (1985). A meta-analysis of selected studies on the effectiveness of bilingual education. *Review of Educational Research, 55,* 269–317.

Yewchuk, C., & Bibby, M. (1989). Identification of giftedness in severely and profoundly hearing impaired students. *Roeper Review, 12*(1), 42–48.

CHAPTER 8

VISION IMPAIRMENT

Bryan was given an IQ test in primary school. He did not remember the name of the test and was not told his score. He was told that he scored in the top one percent. Bryan went on to make the top score in the state on the Higher School Certificate Examination (HSC) in three subjects and to score in the top five percent in the state in his remaining subjects. Bryan had been totally blind since birth. By the time he was in his late thirties, he was married, had two small children, and worked in a mid-management position in a medium-sized organization.

Bryan's education did not begin until the age of five. He received no early intervention and did not attend preschool. He attended a central school for the blind as a day student for grades one through ten. Bryan entered a local high school for years eleven and twelve. He had no itinerant support; although there was a unit for the partially sighted at the school, they did not address the needs of a student who was totally blind. He continued his education with a three-year bachelor's degree from a local university.

Bryan was read to by his parents from an early age. His parents encouraged him to explore his environment and did not prevent him from doing things that may have challenged him. At the central school for the blind that he attended, the students were encouraged to read as much and whatever they liked. The library was full of books in braille. Students were encouraged to find answers to their questions and were provided a variety of activities and concrete experiences. There was an emphasis on books and real experiences.

When asked if he felt he missed anything or if anything could have been added to his education, Bryan had a few complaints. The school did not have science facilities, so he could not study any science. He would have liked to have had more choice in studying foreign languages. When he went to university, he wanted to study psychology but was told that the practical work would be too difficult for him, and he was sent to another department. He does feel that if the technology that is available today was available when he went to school, he would have had access to more information.

Bryan's major complaint was that when he went to the local school and university, he felt socially isolated. He felt he was experiencing a cultural change and was very lonely. He did not really feel a part of his peer group. The social activities of the school for the blind had been varied, but they were very structured and did not allow for spontaneous movement and expression as happened in the local school.

WHAT IS A VISION IMPAIRMENT?

A vision impairment may be defined legally or educationally (Scholl, 1986). The definition of legal blindness is used primarily for qualification for government assistance. The definition varies from country to country but generally includes: vision of 6/60 (20/200) in the best eye with correction or field of view of 20 degrees or less (Pagliano, 1994; Scholl, 1986). Educationally, a vision impairment may be interpreted more broadly. Children whose vision impairment impacts on their ability to learn can be considered to have an educationally significant vision impairment. Eligibility for support services from local education agencies (LEAs) varies from state to state and country to country. The definition in New South Wales, Australia, is: "Students who have been identified as having a significant visual disability, that is, 6/24 or less in the better eye, or 6/18 or less with nystagmus or reduced fields of vision" (NSW Department of School Education, 1991, p. 25).

Students with vision impairment may be tactual learners, visual learners, auditory learners, or a combination of these. Some students have no vision or only light perception, while others may be considered to have low vision. "A person with low vision is one who has impairment of visual function, even after treatment and/or standard refractive correction, and has a visual acuity of less than 6/18 to light perception or a visual field of less than 10 degrees from the point of fixation, but who uses or is potentially able to use, vision for the planning and/or execution of a task" (Best & Corn, 1993, p. 309). Individuals with the same visual acuity level may functionally use their vision quite differently. The population of individuals with a vision impairment is a heterogeneous group that crosses all cultures and ethnic groups. Visual abilities in this population range from difficulty reading small print or negotiating the environment, to total blindness, while other abilities cover the entire spectrum.

Vision impairment is a low-incidence disability. The prevalence rates of vision impairment in the general population in developed countries are generally considered to be .1% or 1 per 1000 (Scholl, 1986). Reports on school-age children indicate prevalence rates between 1 per 1000 in North America and Europe for students with low vision (Best & Corn, 1993) and 1.5 per 1000 in the United States for those with a vision-related print disability (Nelson & Dimitrova, 1993).

An estimated percentage of children who have both a vision impairment and superior ability is not available. Anecdotal information suggests that the cognitive abilities of children with vision impairment do not follow the normal bell curve but, instead, group more at either end of the spectrum (Chorniak, 1984). It has been estimated that between 49 and 60% of children with a vision impairment also have additional disabilities (Gates & Kappan, 1985; Kirchner, 1990; Rogow, 1988). This high proportion of students with additional disabilities may, in part, be attributed to developmental delays due to the impact of vision loss on learning.

HISTORICAL PERCEPTIONS OF INDIVIDUALS WITH VISION IMPAIRMENT

Lowenfeld (1975) divides the history of the status of individuals with vision impairment in western civilization into four phases: separation, ward status, self-emancipation, and integration. The separation phase is divided into two stages, prehistory and antiquity. Reports on conditions in prehistoric time are based on the generalized treatment of the aged, sick, and infirm by primitive tribes in various parts of the world. Negative treatment of individuals with disabilities was the prevalent practice. Much of the negative treatment, usually separation by elimination, can be attributed to the harshness of living conditions and the social need for the survival of the group through sacrifice of weak individuals.

The roots of western civilization are generally traced back to the antiquity era of ancient Greece and Rome. These civilizations, including the great philosophers Plato and Aristotle, supported the notion of separation or elimination of individuals who were weak or deformed. Based on the frequency of blindness in Greek mythology, it is possible that blindness was common at that time, with a large population blinded by force as punishment for defeat in war or as a result of disease. There are also many stories in Greek and Roman lore that support the theory of separation by veneration, as those who were blinded late in life became famous philosophers, poets, lawyers, politicians, and teachers (for example, Homer, Tiresias, Appius Claudius Caecus). This era also first gave rise to the notion of individuals without sight possessing extraordinary abilities (for example, blind soothsayers).

The ward status phase begins with the introduction of Christianity and continues through the eighteenth century. The western religions fostered the attitude of "my brother's keeper," and individuals with disabilities were to be protected, pitied, and given special concern. The first centers for individuals with vision impairment were established during this era (beginning in 1254) to care for individuals, but they did not provide for educational or vocational opportunities.

"The 17th and 18th centuries may, so far as the blind are concerned, be called the era of self-emancipation" (Lowenfeld, 1975, p. 44). It was during this era that the philosophy of individual independence for all people was spreading through the western world. Until the mid-eighteenth century, there were only scattered attempts to educate children with vision impairment, none of which provided for the development of systematic programs (Roberts, 1986). The establishment of educational facilities was profoundly influenced by the examples and achievements of numerous individuals who were blind (for example, Thomas Blacklock, Carolan, Francois Huber, John Metcalf, Nicholas Saunderson, Melanie de Salignac, Lenitre). The philosophical groundwork for the education of children with vision impairment has been attributed to Diderot's "Letter on the Blind for the Use of Those Who See" in 1749, which Diderot based on encounters with three individuals who were blind and which set forth the philosophy that individuals who are blind can lead normal lives and are intellectually competent (Roberts, 1986).

The first residential school for children who were blind was opened in Paris in 1784 by Valentin Haüy. The curriculum focused on the study of music, vocational skills, reading, writing, and daily living skills. The concept of the residential school spread throughout Europe in the late 1700s and spread to the United States in 1829 with the establishment of what is now the Perkins School for the Blind. Residential schools were established across the United States throughout the nineteenth century, with most states (forty-one) eventually either establishing schools exclusively for children with vision impairment or, as in states with smaller populations or less financial ability, adding a section for these students to schools for the deaf (ten of forty-nine schools for the deaf are schools for the deaf *and* blind, mostly in southern and western states of the United States).

In Australia, the establishment of residential schools differed slightly from the pattern in the United States. The majority of the schools in the United States were established by the state as part of the educational system. In Australia, the residential schools were established as charities, beginning in 1866 in Victoria, through the efforts of community leaders and outside the state system of education. In Australia, probably due to the sparse population and financial constraints, four of the six residential schools were established either in addition to, or as adjuncts of, schools for the deaf. Many of the administrators, curricula, and teachers in schools for the deaf and blind came from, and still come from, the field of deafness. The higher incidence of deafness in dual schools, in both Australia and the United States, effectively overwhelms the smaller numbers of children with vision impairment, thereby adding to their difficulties.

Curricula in residential schools for children with vision impairment varied, but had some similarities. Much of the education focused on instruction in various forms of mechanical arts (for example, basket weaving, chair caning), music, and some form of primary education (reading, writing, simple computation). As students graduated from the residential schools, they had difficulty finding employment. This led to the building of vocational workshops attached to the schools or the development of separate adult vocational services.

Students who were blind and those with low vision were educated in the same manner, as people believed that using vision caused further deterioration in vision capacities. Separate education for children with partial sight began in 1908 in London, and then spread to Massachusetts in the United States in 1913, and to Australia, in Hobart, Tasmania, in 1940. These students were still educated in a manner designed to save their sight. In the 1930s, the approach of "protecting" vision through nonuse began to change as ophthalmologists began to suggest that using vision did not reduce that capacity. It was not until the 1960s, when a study by Natalie Barraga indicated that children with low vision could improve their visual functioning through training, that the methods for instructing children with low vision changed.

In the early years, education for children with vision impairment involved oral instruction, memorization, and reading with a variety of embossed linear types. It was not until Louis Braille published details of his system in 1829 that a system of communication that could be both read and written without sight was available. Braille was not internationally accepted until 1882, and not fully accepted in the United States until the 1930s. The Perkins brailler was not developed until 1951; it was introduced in Australia in the 1960s. Currently, there remain some differences in the codes of English Braille among England, the United States, and Australia. Discussions are underway for the adoption of a unified code for English speaking countries. Separate codes are used for literary works, mathematics, music, and computer notation.

The age of integration is difficult to document and follow because separate records were not kept. Two early leaders in the education of children with vision impairment, Samuel Gridley Howe in the United States and Johann Wilhelm Klein in Austria, advocated for education with sighted peers; however, neither accomplished that goal. The first system for teaching children with vision impairment in local schools was established in London in 1873, but this system did not last. In the United States, integration began in 1900, with the establishment of an itinerant teacher service, resource room, and support services for students with vision impairment in the public school system in Chicago. This model was copied widely in the United States. In 1933, Thomas Cutsforth published *The Blind in School and Society*, which pointed out many of the problems of the residential school programs and created much discussion on the efficacy of such programs. This book gradually effected a change in the practice of separately educating children with vision impairment. In the United States, during the late 1940s and early 1950s, there was a sudden increase in the numbers of children with congenital vision impairment, due to retinopathy of prematurity. There was a further increase in the numbers of children with multiple disabilities due to rubella epidemics in the late 1960s in the United States and in the early 1970s in Australia.

Beginning in the mid-1950s, changes in the population of students with vision impairment caused the residential schools to redefine and expand their services to include children with additional disabilities and to develop day school services. As the demand for education of students with vision impairment began to outstrip the services available and as parents began demanding that they be able to keep their children at home, many residential schools expanded their services further to include a support service system within the public schools. In Australia, Queensland was the first state to partially integrate students into the public schools, in 1956. The itinerant model of support to students in public schools in Australia was developed in the various states between 1973 and 1981.

Currently, in both Australia and the United States, the majority of residential schools serve children with both vision and additional impairments. Students with only a vision impairment are generally educated in local schools and provided support through the services of a Vision Support Teacher (VST) on an itinerant basis.

The transition phase, the 1950s to the 1970s, of the education of students with vision impairment from a central residential school concept to integrated education in the public school created difficulties for numerous students. As students, like Bryan, were allowed into public schools, the support systems were not in place. Many had to arrange for their own transcription services, were not socially prepared for the new school culture, and had no access to much of the instructional material used in the schools.

Throughout the residential school era, most of the schools had "stars"—those students who were paraded out for public view to show "what the blind can do." Were these "stars" truly possessed of superior abilities, or were they average students whose capabilities were encouraged through the individualized, disability-specific systems of education provided by the centralized school? We shall never know. The "stars" of today with vision impairment are likely to possess some form of musical talent (for example, Stevie Wonder, Ray Charles, Jeff Healey). All too often, the literature, film, and television of today depict characters who can do it all (for example, the blind character played by Al Pacino driving the streets of New York in "Scent of a Woman"). What models of vision impairment are the media presenting to children? Can even those with exceptional abilities live up to these stereotypes?

THE IMPACT OF VISION ON LEARNING: WHAT HELPS TO CREATE THE MASK?

Vision is the primary integrating sense (Hatlen & Curry, 1987). It plays a vital part in learning. It has been estimated that eighty percent of education is presented through the visual sense (Pagliano, 1994). Vision allows for immediate preview and appreciation of the layout of an object or environment at a distance. Vision constantly updates and unifies this information. Vision allows for the whole, or gestalt, to be absorbed almost in an instant. Tactual exploration, aided by other senses, takes more time and is only available in sequential pieces that need to be organized mentally into the whole.

The education of children with vision impairment is often based on the concepts expressed by Lowenfeld (1948/1981). He states, "Blindness imposes three basic limitations on the individual: 1) In the range and variety of experiences. 2) In the ability to get about. 3) In the control of the environment and the self in relation to it" (Lowenfeld, 1948/1981, p. 68).

Children with vision impairment are often identified by sighted norms to have delays in concept development, social skills, daily living skills, and travel skills. In his review of research on the early development of children with vision impairment, Warren (1984) addressed the areas of perceptual-motor, cognitive, language, social, and personality development. Areas of difficulty identified included: (1) the complex and integrative categories of perception, and (2) specific and general cognitive abilities. Developmental lags were noted in the area of social skills. In all of these areas, the children were compared to sighted norms; thus, Warren recommends using the optimal development of the children themselves as the appropriate frame of reference.

Children with a vision impairment are unable to imitate visual information and, therefore, have difficulties in social situations. Facial expressions and gestures are learned through visual imitation and are difficult to reproduce without these models. The result may be a mask of indifference projected to the world. The limited ability to give and receive nonverbal communication often results in social isolation (Hackney, 1986).

Education needs to include opportunities for critical thinking, concrete experiences, problem solving, independent living, and orientation and mobility. Educators should provide opportunities to succeed in varied situations and help to create support systems (Hackney, 1986).

IDENTIFICATION OF STUDENTS WITH SUPERIOR ABILITIES

The Division on Visual Handicaps (DVH) of the Council for Exceptional Children (CEC) has adopted the following position:

> Students with visual handicaps should be assessed for and included in programs for students who are gifted. Once identified, decisions regarding educational options and settings, curriculum, and counseling services should address the student's giftedness, visual handicap, and the needs of individuals who have the dual exceptionalities. (Corn & Scholl, 1992, p. 19)

Identification of students with a vision impairment who also have superior abilities is difficult, as there are several obstacles to overcome (Whitmore & Maker, 1985). One such obstacle is stereotypic expectations. A student with a vision impairment who completes high school may be perceived by some as gifted, yet the expectation should be that the average student would complete high school. The lack of opportunity to exhibit superior abilities may also serve as a mask, making it difficult to identify a child with a vision impairment as being gifted. For example, if Bryan had been afforded the opportunity to study science, his choices of careers would have been greater, and he might have demonstrated a talent in that field. Another obstacle to identification of giftedness is developmental delays in children due to their lack of experience. For example, young children with a vision impairment will not be able to develop concepts of conservation unless they have had the experience of filling and emptying different containers and exploring the contents and properties during play.

Children with a vision impairment should be considered in relation to the ability levels of other children with similar impairments. If they are compared to sighted peers, there are no guidelines as to what extent equal performance or above identifies them as gifted (Corn, 1986).

Intelligence tests are primarily visually based, with many tests relying on visual discrimination abilities and containing visual references. Often children with a vision impairment are given only the verbal portion of a test, usually the WISC (Lin & Sikka, 1992). However, this test is not normed on the population of students with vision impairment, and administration of only a portion of the test, while providing some useful information, destroys the validity of the test.

It has been suggested that certain segments of the population of individuals with a vision impairment are more likely to be gifted. For example, students whose vision loss is due to retinoblastoma may show above average intelligence (Chase, 1970; Chorniak, 1984; Levitt, Rosenbaum, Willerman, & Levitt, 1972; Williams, 1968). Williams (1968), in a study of students with retinoblastoma in England and Wales, found an intellectual superiority in the group with retinoblastoma (mean IQ 119, range 97–152) over a sample of peers with a vision impairment not caused by retinoblastoma (mean IQ 102, range 62–142) and a peer group with sight (mean IQ 102, range 72–147) on the Williams Intelligence Test Scale (1956). However, Levitt et al. (1972) indicated that "while retinoblastoma per se is not associated with intellectual superiority or inferiority, retinoblastoma associated with blindness may result in selective cognitive superiority" (p. 939).

Specific identification procedures have not been developed for the population of individuals with vision impairment who are gifted. Checklists and other criteria should be examined to determine their appropriateness (Corn, 1986). One such checklist of observable characteristics of giftedness in children with disabilities, including those with vision impairment has been provided by Day and colleagues (1992). The characteristics suggesting above average ability, creativity, and task commitment are addressed in this checklist. Another checklist that is more specific to children with vision impairment has been provided by Johnson (1987). For example, orientation and spatial organization may be predictive of future academic success (Johnsen & Corn, 1989).

The suggested process for identifying giftedness in students with vision impairment involves three stages: nomination, identification, and selection (Johnsen & Corn, 1989). Nominations can come from parents, school counselors, teachers, and vision support teachers (Hackney, 1986; Johnsen & Corn, 1989). The identification stage can include information gathered from intelligence and achievement tests, informal data, checklists, observations, and class grades. The selection process should include a personal interview (Hackney, 1986). Gifted programs that follow this identification phase should accept students based on both academic ability and creative potential.

Educational Options

Several educational setting options are available to students with vision impairment. Most students with a vision impairment are included in their local schools, with central and residential schools primarily providing education for students with additional disabilities. For the student with a vision impairment and superior ability, there are several options for programming (Corn, 1986). Within the school, an adaptation of the traditional curricula for students with vision impairment (for example, orientation and mobility skills, social skills, daily living skills, braille) can be provided. Another option is the adaptation of traditional programs for gifted students. For example, extension work can be provided along with specific skill development (such as grade III braille, optacon).

One model that appears to be successful is that of offering a summer enrichment program such as that provided by the Texas School for the Blind and Visually Impaired (TSBVI) (Hackney, 1986) or the music camp program in Australia. Some students with vision impairment may attend school in the model programs for gifted children that involve attendance at a magnet school for students with interests and gifts in particular areas, along with the support of itinerant teachers. Unfortunately, though, special programs for individuals with vision impairment tend to focus on remediation and compensatory skills, while gifted programs tend to ignore the adaptations needed by this population (Johnsen & Corn, 1989).

Issues Related to Vision Impairment

There is no "Blind Culture" per se as there is a "Deaf Culture." Individuals with vision impairment neither practice nor are the victims of cultural isolationism such as described in the previous chapter on deafness. The low incidence of vision impairment may result in the individual rarely coming into contact with others with a similar impairment. Individuals with low vision may have problems identifying with either the sighted or blind population, as they fall between the two. Individuals with vision impairment and superior abilities may have difficulty establishing an identity with a group, not quite fitting in with the gifted, and possibly having greater perception of the stereotypes applied to them by sighted individuals (Corn, 1986). Contact with consumer organizations, such as the American Council of the Blind, the National Federation of the Blind, the National Association of Parents of the Visually Impaired, and the National Federation of Blind Citizens of Australia, may be helpful. There are also groups interested in specific conditions (for example, the Retinitis Pigmentosa Association) that may also be of assistance.

Two of the most serious problems encountered by individuals with vision impairment are unemployment and underemployment (Wolffe, Roessler, & Schriner, 1992). There are indications that only about one-third of individuals with vision impairment of working age are actually employed. Yet, surveys in the United States have indicated that students with vision impairment have higher rates of participation in postsecondary education and training (forty-three percent) compared to students with other disabilities, and this rate is similar to that of students without disabilities (fifty-six percent) (DeMario, 1992). Students with superior academic abilities are often guided toward higher degrees (many earning doctorates) because they excel at study, yet they find it difficult to gain employment commensurate with their qualifications. There is often an emphasis on academics with no specific career or goal in mind. In the urgency to maintain academic standards, skills in less academic areas are often overlooked (DeMario, 1992). Career development needs should be addressed, including a wide range of independence behaviors such as daily living skills, orientation and mobility, integrating into the community, verbal and nonverbal communication skills, developing social networks, job interviewing skills, and knowledge of access and rehabilitation laws. A mentorship program would provide opportunities to explore career options. The student with a vision impairment needs to be aware that options exist outside some of the more traditional choices of education, rehabilitation, social work, music, radio, and law. There is a need for students with vision impairment to be more "well-rounded" and to realize that higher education is not the only option open to them.

There is currently some concern about a decline in braille literacy. There is a feeling that technology that provides auditory output (for example, tape recorders, Kurzweil readers, speech access computers) interferes with the braille skills of students. For example, Bryan was not allowed talking books in school because it was feared that he would not practice reading braille if he could access books auditorially. Yet, as an adult, he accesses material in braille and auditorially with equal facility. In spite of her use of a variety of technological devices, Susie, another case study described later in this chapter, prefers braille. In reality, current technology (for example, scanners, embossers, computers with refreshable braille) has provided greater access to print materials in braille than ever before. Students should be encouraged to use specific technology aimed at increasing access to computers (for example, Eureka, Mountbatten, Keynote). Schools can provide materials in braille on the spot, without the need for special training. Material can be put into a computer through the use of scanners or regular keyboards, translated into the braille code through Duxbury or a Ransley interface, and embossed in braille (for example, Mountbatten, Versapoint).

Of increasing concern to individuals with vision impairment is the move in technology toward graphical user interface (GUI). The emphasis on the more "user friendly" and increasingly visual software and hardware (use of icons and mice) has the potential to exclude people who rely on auditory or tactile output. Nosenko (1994) states that there is concern from individuals with vision impairment that manufacturers "cannot make data which is inherently visual presentable in tactile or verbal format" or "present a viable means of getting around visual ways of working in graphical applications when there are no keyboard alternatives" (p. 5). People with vision impairment are concerned that unless GUI can be adapted for their use, they will be cut out of the technological revolution and be unable to use the technology for communication and employment that is available. Consumer organizations are challenging manufacturers to address this inequity.

CASE STUDY

Susie is fifteen and attends her local high school in Year 10. She has been totally blind from the age of two when she had both her eyes removed due to retinoblastoma. She was born, and has always lived, in a small, remote mining town. Susie's family migrated from a middle European country before she was born. The family speaks its native language at home, and her parents have difficulty reading English. Susie speaks her second language fluently and is highly articulate. From an early age, she has had a thirst for literature, with an intense interest in words and their meaning.

Susie's parents were adamant that she should live at home, and she has always attended the local neighborhood school. She quickly learned to read and write braille in her first year at school, and all her braille work and books are provided by the resource center. Susie uses the latest electronic adaptive technology with ease to produce her work in braille for herself and print for her teachers. A Vision Support Teacher visits the school once a term to provide assistance and advice, and a teacher aide is employed twenty hours a week to assist Susie.

Toward the end of primary school, the results of testing on the verbal items of the WISC-R showed that Susie was in the above average range. The testing psychologist felt her disability masked her true potential. School reports and anecdotal evidence from the staff yielded the information that Susie was quick to grasp new concepts, her work was of a consistently high standard, she was a great asset in class discussion and debate, and she was well-liked and respected by both students and staff.

Although there are no specific programs for gifted children in Susie's local school, she has always been included in any extension work offered, and she is not excluded from activities because of her blindness.

Initially, Susie was reluctant to agree that she was gifted. However, she did volunteer that she had "always had straight As" and was in "at least the top two to three students in all classes." She felt that there were benefits in being good at her school work because, "being blind, if I wasn't as bright as I am, I'd be in a lot of trouble." When asked, she was unable to select a favorite school subject, saying she enjoyed and looked forward to them all. She was perceptive about the staff's different teaching and management styles and described the different ways in which she was able to accommodate these styles.

Susie is a successful runner; she trains daily, and her sport is an important part of her life. As a member of her state team, she participates in the National Multi-Disability Sports and has set Australian records. Her frustration in this endeavor is that, due to the remoteness of the area in which she lives, there is a lack of appropriate coaching expertise and a consistent guide runner with whom she can build a rapport.

Early in life, it was evident that Susie had musical abilities. She plays the piano by ear and has had private piano lessons as well as some instruction in basic braille music. She has chosen not to pursue her music studies but feels she has the option to resume this interest at a later stage in her life.

Susie is looking forward to going to university. Presently, her plans are to study law, but she also wants to explore the possibilities of sociology, social work, and physiotherapy. She may be able to have work experience in at least some of these areas, but her regret is that she will not have the opportunity to work with professionals who are blind. Independently, Susie has raised the question of access to equipment at university. Already she is formulating a plan to ensure she starts her university career with everything she needs.

In response to a question about her perceptions of difficulties at school, Susie said her main anxiety was not being fully accepted by her friends. She felt the problem stemmed from her blindness rather than being gifted. "They seem to think I'm such a perfect little girl, because I'm always doing my work. They think I'm a bit of a square. They don't realize it takes longer if you're blind. One girl swore and then apologized, just to me! I told her blind people swear the same as sighted people." Susie said the times she enjoyed most were when her friends fully accepted her as a member of the group—"like when they jokingly hit each other in play and include me in the 'kidding around'—it makes me feel really accepted and one of them."

Susie identified two other major disadvantages of being blind, both of which appear to be exacerbated because she is also gifted. The first was not having ready access to a library. She would love to be able, like her sighted friends, to "have the choice to browse and flip through books, read a little, just to see if they were really what I wanted, then take them home and read them straight away. Being blind, I have to look through a catalogue and wait perhaps two weeks before they arrive, by which time I'm probably interested in something else." Susie does have access to an optical scanner that reads print texts to her, but she feels this is second best. From choice, she prefers her books in braille, so she can independently read and reread them without relying on the scanner.

The other disadvantage Susie identified was her lack of independent mobility. She commented wistfully on how she would love to be able to "look at a map, take in the whole, and set off exploring on my own."

Despite these disadvantages, Susie said she feels lucky to be living in Australia. On a recent visit to her parents' native country, she noticed, particularly in the small villages, how people appeared to be frightened of her. They spoke to her mother, and not directly to her; they found it difficult to believe she was succeeding so well at school, and they appeared to be disbelieving that she was planning to attend university. Susie, her parents, and the high school are very happy with the human and material support they receive to help Susie overcome her disability of blindness. However, it is uncertain whether suitable programs are being provided for Susie's dual exceptionalities of blindness combined with giftedness.

SOME SUGGESTED ACTIVITIES FOR STUDENTS WITH A VISION IMPAIRMENT

The following activities are some suggestions that teachers can provide and encourage their students to complete.

- Create a dictionary of slang terms used by peer group.
- Contact organizations for individuals with a vision impairment (NFBCA, NFB, ACB).
- Evaluate three similar pieces of technology that you might find useful to determine which would be best for your use.
- Contact or read books on professionals with a vision impairment.
- Research outstanding people with a vision impairment in history (Homer, Tiresius).
- Take a class in dance or a sport, join a club, try mime.
- Identify your personal learning style.
- Research ways to manage stress and relaxation.
- Research how to manage others' attitudes.
- Learn positive communication skills.
- Study vocal and facial expressions, and appropriate gestures to accompany speech.
- Take a course in fluid movement (ballet, yoga, tai chi).

REFERENCES

Best, A., & Corn, A. (1993). The management of low vision in children: Report of the 1992 World Health Organization Consultation. *Journal of Visual Impairment and Blindness, 87*, 307–309.

Chase, J. B. (1970). Cognitive patterns in subjects blinded by retinoblastoma. In *Proceedings of the 50th biennial meeting of the Association for Education of the Visually Handicapped* (pp. 166–172), New Orleans, LA.

Chorniak, E. J. (1984). Conceptualizing the gifted blind child. In A. Sykanda et al. (Eds.), *Insight in sight: Proceedings of the Canadian interdisciplinary conference on the visually impaired child* (ERIC Document Reproduction Service No. ED 260 566, pp. 175–190). Vancouver, BC: Canadian National Institute for the Blind.

Corn, A. L. (1986). Gifted students who have a visual handicap: Can we meet their educational needs? *Education of the Visually Handicapped, 18*, 71–84.

Corn, A. L., & Scholl, G. (1992). Education of students with visual handicaps who are also gifted. *DVH Quarterly, 39*(3), 18–19.

Day, A., Forbes-Harper, N., Houston, I., Langdale, O., Milne, H., Raboczi, C., & Watkin, E. (1992). *Giftedness: A fair go for all Australians.* Sydney, Australia: AAEGT.

DeMario, N. (1992). Skills needed for successful employment: A review of the literature. *Review, 24*, 115–125.

Gates, C., & Kappan, D. (1985). Teacher preparation in the education of visually impaired children: A multi-competency approach. *Journal of Visual Impairment and Blindness, 79*(7), 306–307.

Hackney, P. W. (1986). Education of the visually handicapped gifted: A program description. *Education of the Visually Handicapped, 18*, 85–95.

Hatlen, P., & Curry, S. (1987). In support of specialized programs for blind and visually impaired children: The impact of vision loss on learning. *Journal of Visual Impairment and Blindness, 81*, 7–13.

Johnsen, S. K., & Corn, A. L. (1989). The past, present, and future of education for gifted children with sensory and/or physical disabilities. *Roeper Review, 12*(1), 13–23.

Johnson, L. (1987). Teaching the visually impaired gifted youngster. *Journal of Visual Impairment and Blindness, 81*, 51–52.

Kirchner, C. (1990). Trends in the prevalence rates and numbers of blind and visually impaired schoolchildren. *Journal of Visual Impairment and Blindness, 84*(9), 478–479.

Levitt, E., Rosenbaum, A., Willerman, L., & Levitt, M. (1972). Intelligence of retinoblastoma patients and their siblings. *Child Development, 43*(4), 939–948.

Lin, S., & Sikka, A. (1992, November). *The gifted–visually handicapped child: A review of literature* (ERIC Document Reproduction Service No. ED 355 698). Presented at the Mid-South Education Research Association Conference, Knoxville, TN.

Lowenfeld, B. (1975). *The changing status of the blind.* Springfield, IL: Thomas.

Lowenfeld, B. (1981). Effects of blindness on the cognitive functions of children. In B. Lowenfeld, *Berthold Lowenfeld on blindness and blind people: Selected papers.* New York: American Foundation for the Blind. (Original work published 1948)

Nelson, K. A., & Dimitrova, E. (1993). Severe visual impairment in the United States and in each state, 1990. *Journal of Visual Impairment and Blindness, 87*, 80–82.

Nosenko, G. (1994, September 15). *Nightmares realized: If communications work exclusively by the graphical-user-interface or how technology can bypass the blind.* Paper presented at the Negotiating the Information Superhighway with a Print Disability Conference, Sydney, Australia.

New South Wales Department of School Education. (1991). *Who's going to teach my child?* Parramatta, New South Wales, Australia: Author.

Pagliano, P. (1994). Students with a vision impairment. In A. Ashman & J. Elkins (Eds.), *Educating children with special needs* (pp. 345–385). Sydney, Australia: Prentice-Hall of Australia.

Roberts, F. K. (1986). Education for the visually handicapped: A social and educational history. In G. Scholl (Ed.), *Foundations of education for blind and visually handicapped children and youth* (pp. 1–18). New York: American Foundation for the Blind.

Rogow, S. (1988). *Helping the visually impaired child with developmental problems: Effective practice in home school and community.* New York: Teachers' College Press.

Scholl, G. (1986). What does it mean to be blind? In G. Scholl (Ed.), *Foundations of education for blind and visually handicapped children and youth* (pp. 23–34). New York: American Foundation for the Blind.

Warren, D. H. (1984). *Blindness and early childhood development.* New York: American Foundation for the Blind.

Whitmore, J. R., & Maker, C. J. (1985). *Intellectual giftedness in disabled persons.* Rockville, MD: Aspen Systems Corp.

Williams, M. (1956). *Williams intelligence test for children with defective vision.* Birmingham, UK: University of Birmingham, Institute of Education.

Williams, M. (1968). Superior intelligence of children blinded from retinoblastoma. *Archives of Diseases of Childhood, 43,* 204–210.

Wolffe, K., Roessler, R., & Schriner, K. (1992). Employment concerns of people with blindness or visual impairments. *Journal of Visual Impairment and Blindness, 86,* 185–187.

CHAPTER

9

CEREBRAL PALSY

THE CONDITION OF CEREBRAL PALSY

One can argue that cerebral palsy (CP) creates some of the most difficult barriers to the recognition and development of giftedness. Cerebral palsy is a multihandicapping condition that can be manifested in many ways. The range of disabilities and the range of resulting impairments mean that it is impossible to talk of a homogeneous group. There are children who are gifted and either severely or mildly impaired with cerebral palsy.

Cerebral palsy has been defined as follows:

> The term cerebral palsy (CP) is used to describe a group of chronic nonprogressive conditions characterised by abnormalities in motor function involving strength, tone, posture or coordination. There are three main types of CP: spastic, athetoid, and ataxic. Spastic CP (the most frequent) is characterised by stiff or difficult movement. Athetoid CP involves involuntary and uncontrolled movements, and ataxic CP is characterised by unsteadiness and difficulty with rapid or fine movements. Some

175

individuals have a mixture of all three types of CP (United Cerebral Palsy Associations, 1993).

Most recent studies have estimated the prevalence of CP to be 2 per 1000 live births (Shapiro & Capute, 1994). The risk of CP is increased in low birth weight babies (less than 2500 g) (Cummins, Nelson, & Cummins, 1993). With increases in survival rates of premature infants and increased numbers of multiple births, educators are likely to be providing services for a growing number of children with CP. (Tyler & Colson, 1994, p. 4)

Further, the associated complications with CP have been delineated by Tyler and Colson (1994):

CP rarely occurs without associated deficits (Shapiro & Capute, 1994). In addition to movement and posture disorders, children with CP may have other disabilities associated with damage to the CNS *(Central Nervous System)*. For example, approximately two thirds of the children with CP have mental retardation, and among those with normal intelligence, many have some degree of perceptual impairment and learning disability (Kurtz, 1992). Other common associated deficits include seizures, sensory deficits, communication disorders, feeding problems, and behavioral/emotional disturbances (e.g., attentional deficits and impulsivity). (p. 4)

NEUROLOGICAL IMPAIRMENTS

Hallahan and Kauffman (1986) describe the impairment as follows:

One of the most common causes of physical disability in children is damage to or deterioration of the central nervous system—the brain or the spinal cord. Damage to a brain may be so mild as to be undetectable as far as the child's functioning is concerned or so profound as to reduce the child to a very low level of functioning. There may be focal brain damage (involving a very specific and delimited area, often with specific effects on the child's behavior), or diffuse brain damage (involving a large or poorly defined area, often with generalised behavioral effects). (p. 336)

Hallahan and Kauffman (1986) further describe the effects of cerebral palsy as follows:

When the brain is damaged, sensory abilities, cognitive functions and emotional responsiveness as well as a motor performance is usually affected. A very high proportion of children with cerebral palsy are found to have hearing impairments, visual impairments, perceptual disorders, speech defects, behavior disorders, mental retardation, or some combination of these several handicapping conditions in addition to motor disability. (p. 339)

Although this chapter discusses children with cerebral palsy, some description of those children suffering from traumatic brain injury has been included. Some of the resulting physical and learning impairments are similar to those caused by CP, with the difference that the brain-injured child's needs may change if, and as, the brain recovers. Some long-term impairments, for example, physical and perceptual impairments, may be similar to those of a child with CP, and the children may well be placed in an educational setting with children who have CP.

Traumatic Brain Injury

Hallahan and Kauffman (1986) note that children "whose brains are damaged after they are 6 or 8 years old are not usually thought of as having cerebral palsy, even though they may have the same behavioral and physical characteristics" (p. 337).

Tyler and Colson (1994) describe traumatic brain injury as follows:

The term *brain injury* is medically defined as trauma to the head with evidence of brain involvement (Rivara, 1994). Traumatic brain injury (TBI) is also educationally defined. The U.S. Department of Education (1992) provides the following definition:

Traumatic brain injury means an acquired injury to the brain caused by an external force, resulting in total or partial functional disability or psychosocial impairment, or both, that adversely affects a child's educational performance. The term applies to open or closed head injuries resulting in impairments in one or more areas, such as cognition; language; memory; attention; reasoning; abstract thinking; judgement; problem solving; sensory, perceptual and motor abilities; psychosocial behavior; physical functions; information processing; and speech. The term does not apply to brain injuries that are congenital or degenerative; or brain injuries induced by birth trauma. (p. 33802)

It has been estimated that 1 per 500 children is hospitalised *(in the USA)* annually for traumatic brain injury (Center for Disease Control, 1990). However, the incidence of brain injury is significantly underreported because not all children who receive brain injuries are taken to hospital. (p. 5)

The Incidence of Children with CP Who Are Gifted

Hallahan and Kauffman (1986) note that:

Some individuals with cerebral palsy have normal or above-average intellectual capacity, and a few test within the gifted range. The average tested intelligence of children who are victims of cerebral palsy, however, is clearly lower than the average for normal children (Cruickshank, Hallahan, and Bice, 1976; Nelson and Ellenberg, 1978; Thompson et al., 1983). As Cruickshank et al. point out, proper testing of these children requires a great deal of clinical sophistication, since many intelligence tests or specific items are inappropriate for children with multiple handicaps. Consequently, one must be cautious in interpreting test results for such children. (p. 339)

However, the fact that CP affects the central nervous system must inevitably lead to the belief that the incidence of gifted children with CP must be less than the incidence of gifted children in the nonaffected population.

We can question the use of traditional intelligence tests and ask whether assessment with other tools would detect a greater number of children with talents. It is a fair assumption that there are many gifted children in this population who are not identified. Nevertheless, it appears logical to accept that the incidence of gifted children would be lower than that of the total population. It is also logical that the incidence of giftedness decreases as the severity of impairment increases. Mildly impaired children would comprise the majority of children with CP who are also gifted. Nevertheless, there are striking exceptions to this rule, for example, the Irish artist Christy Brown, whose story was the subject of the film "My Left Foot." Children with CP who are severely physically impaired and gifted pose extraordinary challenges to educators and families as they seek to maximize their achievement.

IDENTIFICATION

It is clear that many gifted children with CP are not identified because of the rarity of special programs for gifted children in special education institutions (Davis & Rimm, 1989). Willard-Holt (1994) notes that only "sixteen (USA) states have special provisions for disabled gifted students" (p. 1). Davis and Rimm (1989) argue that there are 7.5% children in United States programs for students with disabilities of which a realistic 5% would be gifted. Willard-Holt (1994) cites research "by the U.S. Office for Handicapped Individuals (1976) concerning children with various types of disabilities which found that 12% of the disabled children involved in the study were gifted, three times as many in the general school population" (p. 1).

Informal identification measures, such as observational checklists of gifted characteristics, are freely available. Such checklists, while not designed for children with motor disabilities, may offer more than formal ability testing because the former allow the assessor to accept the modified behaviors of such children. If gifted children with CP develop compensatory skills (Willard-Holt, 1994), then observational checklists modified, or specially developed, for the range of disabilities evident with CP offer greater identification validity.

Robinson and Fieber (1988) point out that children with significant motor disabilities have been excluded when populations were "recruited for the standardisation of instruments" (p. 130). They argue that this violates the validity of standardized tests when used with children with motor disabilities. They also argue that the extreme variability of children with CP and their different learning histories need to be taken into account. They argue strongly against the use of standardized tests for predictive and placement purposes.

As the means of assessing gifted children with CP are still being refined (Robinson & Fieber, 1988), it is only right to use an inclusive approach when identifying gifted children rather than exclude children who may be gifted but difficult to identify. In the context of children with CP, theories that broaden the notion of intelligence (Gardner, 1983; Sternberg, 1985) are more appealing than the more traditional beliefs that intelligence is finite, global, and immutable. More recent intelligence theories, because of their inclusive nature, allow us to approach all learners with an educational program that expects differences in learning styles, rates, and expressiveness. Gardner's multiple intelligences theory and Sternberg's triarchic theory allow an approach that respects all learners and all people, searching for the strengths of each learner rather than categorizing learners according to a global continuum of high to low intelligence.

Gardner believes that gifted children need to be selected for specialist programs using "intelligence-fair" assessment that takes place in the natural setting and is based on "context rich" activities (Vialle, 1993). This accords well with Robinson and Fieber's process-oriented approach described in the following text.

If intelligence were a global ability, then it would be possible to argue that the global intelligence of a child with associated central nervous system deficits was impaired. If intelligence is considered to be comprised of a number of strengths, however, it can be argued that it is quite possible for a child to have central nervous system deficits, for example, a perceptual deficit that affects the ease and rate of learning, and yet be considered to be gifted.

One of the barriers to the identification of gifted children with CP is that teachers trained to work with children with disabilities rarely have training in the specific area of giftedness (Miller & Terry-Godtip, 1991). In regular classrooms, teachers untrained in identifying giftedness have been shown to have difficulty in identifying giftedness (Clark, 1983; Davis & Rimm, 1989). This failing appears far more frequently in the special education setting. The disruptive child with a disability may well be an unchallenged gifted child. Disruptiveness has been shown to be a good indicator of giftedness with children with disabilities (Davis & Rimm, 1989).

If gifted children with disabilities, in the mainstream classroom, function at an average level because their handicap prevents them from showing their true giftedness, they may not be identified as gifted and may not receive specialist teaching appropriate to their giftedness. Mares (1993) notes that Australian school counselors may not have been trained in identifying gifted underachievers, this being a new demand upon their skills.

The mask of CP impairment may decrease test scores in a subject in which the child is otherwise talented. For example, a learner may be talented in computer programming but have difficulty with the movement of hardware or typing. A child may be skilled in reading and writing and in analyzing aspects of geography but be limited by the graphing and modeling aspects of the syllabus because of perceptual impairment. A child may be talented in music composition but be limited by the performance side of music because of poor muscle tone. To teachers and assessors, the child's total performance may present as average. It is essential, therefore, that a policy of inclusiveness is followed with regard to identifying giftedness.

Colangelo and Davis (1991) would argue that "stereotypically, we think of a gifted child as having advanced language skills" (p. 431). Children with language difficulties may be gifted in nonverbal areas of intelligence such as the creative arts. We can search for talent in various intelligences when attempting to identify gifted children with CP. Obviously, children with CP will not be physically talented, but they may well be talented in art, music, sensitivity, writing, mathematics, computers—and still be assessed on various global assessment tools as having average or lower total ability. While this applies to all children, it is perhaps even more relevant to children with CP because of their specific impairments and the effect of these impairments on test measurements of global ability.

Psychologists and educators in institutional settings may ask themselves, "Am I exaggerating the giftedness of this child? Is this child presenting as a big fish in a small pond?" This dilemma is somewhat resolved by Colangelo and Davis (1991), who argue that a "barrier to the identification of many handicapped gifted children is expecting these children to demonstrate the same characteristics and at the same level as the nonhandicapped gifted. It should be recognized that handicapping conditions may obscure or suppress their gifts" (p. 430). They argue that gifted children with disabilities should be compared with each other. This is somewhat more difficult with the child with CP because the range of impairment is so great. It is, nevertheless, good advice.

When discussing the identification of gifted children with CP, we are talking about an array of identification instruments because of the multiple handicaps involved. For example, a child with CP who is profoundly deaf would need to be assessed using an instrument appropriate for those who are deaf. If the child also has difficulty in pointing, then other modifications may need to be made, such as cutting and pasting pictures onto a larger piece of card to allow better discrimination of eye gaze direction. A child with vision impairment would require instruments suitable for those who are vision-impaired. The reader should refer to other chapters in this book to seek appropriate identification procedures if vision or hearing impairment is the dominant disability.

However, a standardized identification test, such as a picture vocabulary test, will only form part of an identification process. Hallahan and Kauffman (1986) note the need for "careful and continuous assessment of the individual child's capabilities" (p. 399). Often, a whole range of data needs to be collected from a range of professionals working with the child. The responsiveness of the child when being fed may be as important a clue to a child's ability as is test recognition of a cat or car. Parental information is an important source of data, particularly as the child may have made a correct response to a stimulus similar to that required by a test item, yet the response may not be elicited in the assessment situation for a variety of reasons (for example, a lack of known relationship with an assessor; the assessor's ignorance of a particular communication signal the child may give; the tiredness or lethargy of the child; the child's age; or the background of the assessor). For children with CP, assessment using pointing or eye gaze can be even more difficult because the child's "emotional state and general activity level may affect his or her movements, the disorder becoming more apparent when the child is under stress or moving about than when he or she is at ease" (Hallahan & Kauffman, 1986, p. 338).

For example, in the case study of Katerina that follows, during a preschool occupational therapy assessment, Katerina quickly became bored and tired by the assessment session. As with all young children, she had no awareness of the need to perform and to provide the answers that the therapist, more used to working with students who had CP and were intellectually impaired, desired. Her lateral thinking sometimes naturally led her to give more complex answers than were required by the simplistic assessment response requirements of the standardized test. The therapist failed to consider that giftedness could have been the cause for the lateral nature of Katerina's responses. Consequently, the assessment erred on the side of caution, and her ability was underestimated.

Whitmore and Maker (1985) recommend the use of indicators that are particular to those with physical impairments. For example, an unusual ability to compensate for, or to cope with, disability is an excellent indicator of giftedness. Their case study of Herb noted his ability to set long-range goals for himself and to develop plans to achieve these goals, and his persistence and motivation to succeed. Whitmore and Maker recommend: the adaptation of tasks on standardized tests; the recognition of the possible effects of experience upon performance; the use of tests that can be easily adapted; and the extensive use of observational methods or informal procedures in a variety of settings. All data collected should be compared with the data on performance of other children with similar disabilities. Whitmore and Maker suggest weighting the nonimpaired characteristics of the gifted child with a disability to compensate for the handicap.

Robinson and Fieber (1988) state that standardized assessment tools often violate the assumption that children with motor impairments have equal opportunities for acculturation with test items. If this is correct, it is logical to argue that one measure of assessment of giftedness in a child with CP attending a special class or school is the child's understanding of the institutional culture. The institutional culture often has characteristics related to a medical model. The day is divided into routines of feeding, toileting, therapy, and transport. Within this culture, the child is dependent on caregivers (teachers, therapists, aides, doctors) for many of the necessities of life. If we assess children without CP through their understanding of their world of regular school, busy playgrounds, shopping expeditions, and play in the park, then we should, in fairness, be examining the understanding of children with CP regarding their particular institutionalized culture.

Robinson and Fieber (1988) believe that when assessing the child with motor impairments, a process approach should be used, rather than the modification of test tasks. They argue that "the limitation that lack of motoric input and output may have on typical developmental pathways" is unknown (p. 134). They also believe that the process-oriented approach advocated by Dubose and colleagues, which views the child as an active agent, measures the learning process used by the child, and observes the child in a learning situation with corrective feedback, is the only meaningful approach to the assessment of such individuals.

The RAPYHT model (cited in Willard-Holt, 1994) is a useful process-oriented identification model in which those identifying preschool children are encouraged to observe them during structured thinking activities. Parents are involved in the assessment process, and individual talents are fostered.

One positive factor in the early identification of gifted children is the early contact children with CP have with a range of professionals. Therapists are often quick to recognize the child's strengths. Gifted children often demonstrate their responsiveness through their anticipation and their use of eye gaze to communicate. The gifted child who is severely physically disabled and has low muscle tone, however, may be more difficult to identify. For child who has difficulty with supporting the head, communication, eye gaze, and an alert awareness of the world around them is that much more difficult to determine.

To facilitate the identification data collection process, it is advisable for a nominated person to be the collator of all information and for files and data to be centralized within the school or facility so that all professionals can view the total data on the child. Unfortunately, this sharing of data and excellent communication is not always present.

BARRIERS TO ACHIEVEMENT

The child with severe CP: The child who is severely impaired faces obvious speech and language communication difficulties. Communication devices and communication systems will reduce the quality and quantity of expressive communication. Nevertheless, quality communication is produced by gifted individuals, although requiring prodigious amounts of physical labor and intense concentration. Such concentration and dedication to a task must be a measure of the giftedness of these individuals.

The child with mild CP: The child who is mildly impaired can face a completely different set of problems from the child who is severely impaired. If the physical manifestations of the impairment are mild and the child's mobility is not grossly affected, if the child can talk without obvious difficulty and if learning appears to be easy, many educators find it hard to accept that there is indeed a disability. There may be a lack of recognition of how the impairment can affect learning. Balance problems, difficulty in performing certain movements, and perceptual problems that affect learning are often overlooked by those without a special education background (especially teachers in a regular school setting), yet the effect of these impairments is significant. The effect upon the child's general growth, development, and socialization can also be significant, and this socialization effect has compounding effects on learning and cognitive development.

Placement
The number of gifted children with CP placed in classes for the gifted in New South Wales, Australia, is small, yet there is strong evidence that gifted children learn better in specialist classes (Kulik & Kulik, 1984).

Concrete Experience Versus Observation
Robinson and Fieber (1988) discuss recent theories that suggest that children can develop perceptual and conceptual structures through observation, in the absence of the actual manipulation of material.

They also note the increasing evidence of the integrated nature of development. Although some children may developmentally progress utilizing observation when physical impairment prevents adequate exposure to concrete experience, it is reasonable to assume that such development of stages may be delayed with some children and that the pathways utilized will differ from those used by children without CP.

It is not uncommon for children with CP to have gaps in understandings and skills either related to their specific impairments or related to their limited experiences.

Poor Concentration

Attention deficit disorders are a frequent result of CP. The resulting poor learning behaviors are an immense barrier to the child's achievement of potential.

Low Expectations

It has long been recognized that high expectations of a learner are an important factor in encouraging learners to reach their potential. With a multihandicapping condition such as CP, where children may be placed in an institutionalized setting with teachers inexperienced with gifted children, it not surprising that high expectations of a child's ability greatly vary. Educators, therapists, and family members may well expect less than the child's true potential.

Motivation

Also recognized as a key to the achievement of potential is motivation. Yet the child with CP, whether severely or mildly impaired, may well lack motivation because of any of the following:

- the lack of high expectations by others, as already described;
- frustration in communicating;
- frustration with the demonstration of skill;
- the lack of ability to present skills; and
- the lack of healthy competition with other children.

A child's CP impairment and potential is usually so singular that another same-age child with the same level of difficulty may not be nearby, and therefore, performance may never be compared by the educators *or the child*. Interaction between children in a special education class may be difficult because of mobility problems and because of the small numbers in the class. Yet interaction between children is a vital element in motivating children through games, shared activities, and cooperative learning.

Learning Dependency

The natural desire to protect children with CP from falls, pain, and discomfort, along with the extreme level of physical care often required for these children, frequently develops an extreme state of dependency in the children. From the earliest age, children with CP must trust caregivers to anticipate their needs and, if the impairment is severe, to lift, move, feed, and assist with the toilet. The child is reliant on others to maintain a feeling of both safety and dignity. It is very understandable that the child develops a habit of dependency.

It is difficult for those who are not impaired to understand the level of dependency created by even mild physical disabilities. Even children mildly affected with CP are exposed from their earliest moments to protective caregivers and professionals who manipulate their bodies, often without asking, anticipate their needs, and generally manage their lives at a more intense level than that of children without CP.

The following real life example illustrates this point. Three-year-old Katerina (the author's case study) was receiving physiotherapy. Her therapist continued holding her leg during a long dialogue with Katerina's mother. Katerina, growing tired of being held, asked, "Have you finished with my leg now?" Katerina had the verbal skill to be able to call attention to the fact that she owned her body, but many children with CP cannot do this or may have much less understanding therapists.

When a child's learning experiences occur almost totally through the medium or aid of caregivers and communication is partly, or wholly, dependent on the understanding and specialist communication skills of caregivers, it is not surprising that children with CP do not internalize their role as active learners who need to strive for knowledge, skills, and understandings.

The desire to protect the child will also be evident in social situations, particularly in the limited interaction children with CP may be encouraged to have with children who do not have such impairments. Children with limited social interactions have limited social understanding that not only affects social skills but also affects their understanding of the social world, whether the social world exists in real life or whether it is described in a poem, a story, or even a mathematics problem. Some children may never have come across a "bully" or a "nasty" person. They may never have gone shopping, showered at a public swimming pool, or engaged in energetic conflict with another child during sport. Children with limited understanding of the social world achieve skills and understanding in a limited way.

Dependent learners may range from children who never communicate at all, to children who communicate only when a response is required, to children who depend on their teachers to make that little extra effort rather than make the effort themselves.

Successful caregivers will naturally encourage children to accept responsibility for their own learning and the achievement of new skills. Only the most determined children overcome this dependency barrier by themselves. Encouraging dependent learners to perform to their true ability requires the teacher or parent or caregiver to step back and expect more from the child, as painful as this may be sometimes. Constant encouragement for student-initiated learning is required.

Sometimes the educator needs to manipulate the situation to elicit more response and responsibility from the child. This could involve any of the following:

- exposing the child to a change in routine (such as forgetting the daily NEWS session or serving the eggs unboiled);
- naming objects or animals incorrectly;
- making deliberate mistakes in mathematics or music; and
- not "knowing" the answer or where to find information.

Encouraging dependent learners to express their ability is yet another challenge. Although students may seek information and skills, they may still not communicate these skills and their understanding in situations in which they are being assessed. Dependent learners may naturally think that the assessor will understand that:

- the learner has the information or skill;
- the answer is obvious; or
- they are bored and would rather be examining the red pencil with the funny top.

Dependent learners may have difficulty in relating to an assessment situation and tests, and may not strive to perform to their best, in much the same way that very young children will see no point in winning a race. Dependent habits not only reduce learning, but also reduce the expression of learning and the ability of assessors to identify giftedness and talent.

Frustration with Nonrecognition of Ability
Children with CP must often think, "Not again!" as they are asked to demonstrate their level of ability and knowledge to each new teacher or therapist. The gifted student with a severe physical disability may well appear, at first contact, to be intellectually impaired because of the child's difficulty in communicating a high level of knowledge and skills.

Isolation
Those who argue for "inclusion," the complete integration of the child into the regular classroom and school no matter how severe the

impairment, argue for the moral imperative of the child to receive the same experiences and services as other children without impairments. In Australia, during the late seventies and early eighties, the "normalization" movement, which aimed at providing the best possible "normal" environment for children with CP, grew strongly. Large centralized institutions were broken up into a number of smaller units, with children integrated or placed in support classes alongside regular mainstream classes. The rationale behind these smaller units and support classes was that resources could economically be gathered and utilized while the child was placed in a more normal educational setting. In the 1990s, the development of the "inclusive" movement has sought to integrate all children into regular classroom settings, no matter how severe the impairment or how uneconomical the utilization of resources may be.

Isolation from the learning and social world of the mainstream classroom must inevitably affect the learning of the gifted child with CP. It is hard to disagree with the argument that a child, supported by professionals and resources, will achieve more in the mainstream classroom. On the other hand, if the child is integrated or "included" without adequate support, the integration or inclusion may negatively affect the child's learning.

Integration

Integration, while exposing the child to mainstream school culture, can have its own specific problems, such as the following:

- If the child's comfort in the regular classroom is not maintained at a high level, the child's learning will suffer. The maintenance of comfort in the regular classroom may be difficult given the lack of space for specialist equipment, distance from facilities, and sufficient aide time.

- Perceptual difficulties may not be recognized by teachers inexperienced in special education and, therefore, may remain uncompensated. Mild difficulties with handwriting, caused by hand tremors, may earn low assessments. Children with CP often tire quickly, as they constantly use energy to compensate for such difficulties as poor hand control and mild mobility difficulties. This may lead to unrealistic expectations of a child as inexperienced teachers compare the work completed when the child is fresh with the work completed when the child was tired. The child's work may appear carelessly completed.

- The effort in moving through a crowded classroom littered with resources and children working in groups may tire a child with CP or lead to a fall. All this effort detracts from the concentration a child can bring to learning.

- To other children, mild disabilities often appear bizarre. Children with motor disabilities, for example, those who are in wheelchairs, are obviously physically impaired. In such situations, it is often easier for children without impairments to understand the impairment and relate to the child with CP. The child who is mildly impaired and mobile may appear to be simply strange, awkward, or different. If the child is also gifted intellectually, it is even more difficult for children to understand the physical impairment. Students without impairments will therefore find it hard to understand that the child cannot catch a ball with ease, play hand tennis, or run with speed. Thus, the gifted child with CP may become a social isolate and social skills may also be affected. As the gifted child may be confident around adults and older students, this social isolation may not be recognized by teachers or parents. When it is recognized, inexperienced teachers may be reluctant to intervene for fear of drawing further attention to the physical impairment. Nevertheless, in such situations, it is vital for adults to intervene—to emphasize to the classmates that the child is physically impaired, and to develop better pupil understanding about the nature of the disability.

- Tannenbaum has drawn attention to the fact that gifted children are much better accepted by their nongifted peers when they are skilled at sport and other physical pursuits (Gross, 1989). Many gifted children are skilled in these areas, but the gifted child with CP is certainly not. The giftedness and the CP impairment may combine to create a dual social impairment.

It is now well accepted that underperformance by gifted children is often the result of gifted children masking their abilities because they seek acceptance from age peers (Cross, Coleman, & Stewart, 1993). Integrated children with mild CP may mask their achievements and also seek to conceal the disability that seems to draw attention to their "difference." Davis and Rimm (1989) state that "[i]t is virtually common knowledge that handicapped students have poor self-concepts, due to some amount of rejection by other students" (p. 370). The resulting effects on self-esteem will affect the child's achievement, or at least performance, in competitive situations. As children with CP become adolescents, and peer acceptance becomes even more vital to them, the children may well become depressed as they see no end to a cycle of "difference" and nonacceptance by peers. It is worth noting that the peers may be well disposed toward the child, willing to go more than "halfway" toward the child in social situations. However, the adolescent gifted child with CP may feel, rightly or wrongly, that peer acceptance is not on equal terms but because of sympathy for the impairment. This cycle can be extremely difficult to break and may remain until the child with CP is able to mix with older students or adults of similar ability.

The mandatory curriculum may also present difficulties, particularly in the secondary setting. Students in the nonintegrated setting may only be able to work toward a modified qualification. Integrated students may well have to complete mandatory hours of physical education, food science, or design and technology to meet various standard qualifications. Meeting the needs of children with CP in these settings is often difficult. Unless teachers are alert to modifying the syllabus where the syllabus allows, or in seeking exemptions or alternatives from certifying authorities where this is not possible, then the child may be disadvantaged by being required to work and compete in areas where the child is patently unskilled or even becomes a danger to self or others. Hot water, hockey sticks, chisels, and machinery become lethal to the child and bystanders in the hands of even a slightly clumsy child with CP. Unless the curriculum is modified, the gifted child with CP is obviously discriminated against by such curriculum requirements. Certifying authorities need to be more flexible in their expectations of integrated students attempting to qualify for standard qualifications.

Technology

It is not unknown for technology to be poorly utilized because demands from other students mean that the regular class teacher has little time to devote to the time-consuming task of setting up and maintaining equipment and instructing the child in the successful use of the technology. Integration may also mean that the child lacks easy access to technology support. Computers are still unreliable technology and often fail. The most suitable technology may not be known to the staff in the integrated setting. Children in some nonintegrated settings often have specialist support in the same building, or at least nearby. Technology is therefore often managed better in such a setting.

If the child with CP is dependent upon technology, such as a computer, to perform at the same level as peers, this also brings problems, as indicated below:

- Peers may envy the child's access to a word processor.

- The technology may take up scarce space in the classroom, or its noise may disturb other students.

- The secondary student may have difficulty accessing power points in each classroom, or the school may have difficulty in ensuring the correct furniture or learning aid is available in each learning situation, particularly the specialist rooms such as the science laboratory, the workshop, or the kitchen.

New communication devices are constantly becoming available, and old ones are being refined. A combination of laptop computer technology and dedicated communication device technology is allowing more robust (but still expensive) communication devices to become more commonly available. Dual keyboards allow those who are profoundly hearing impaired to communicate directly with people without knowledge of the communication language. Synthesized speech devices are benefiting many children with CP who are unable to communicate using speech. The difficulty of using two switches (one to operate a communication device and one to drive a wheelchair) is being overcome by the development of integrated systems (*Technotalk*, 1996). Software, especially developed for the child who is severely physically impaired, is becoming more readily available and will do much to overcome the experiential deficit of young children in particular.

The technology in use is at the "cutting edge" of development. The equipment is still frail and prone to faults. To view technology as the "cure" to communication problems is naive. Katerina (see case study) was often without her laptop computer, essential for writing, for lengthy periods because of faults in the hardware or software. The delicate nature of the hardware combined with the sometimes rough treatment a child with CP will administer and the constant movement of the hardware with the child means that a high rate of breakdowns often occurs.

Not only must the hardware and software be appropriate to the child's needs, but the supporting teachers or therapists must also be familiar with the software and able to support and train the child in its use in a variety of situations: classrooms (a number of these in the integrated secondary situation), at home, and in the wider society. As a result of the rapidly changing nature of the technology, it is difficult for parents and therapists to maintain a current knowledge. Teachers and therapists who are unskilled in current technology inevitably resort to simpler technologies that are less effective in supporting a child's communication and learning.

The use of technology in some curriculum areas is still fraught with difficulties. Mathematics software is often demanding to use and well beyond the skill of the early learner. Students may have difficulty, for example, in the use of the computer's calculator, which may not be accessible while other programs are operative.

Children with CP, after experiencing the failure of numerous technologies that were promised by teachers and therapists as the answer to their difficulties, may develop a resistance to attempting new technologies, fearing another technology failure. This lack of motivation is easy to understand.

Technology is not at first easily accessible to the child with CP. Learning to access a computer and mastering word processing are difficult enough for a child without CP. A child with a severe motoric disability must overcome further difficulties. Even children with mild disabilities must be aware of the need for good posture and the need to rest.

While students with vision and hearing impairments in New South Wales have itinerant teachers to support them in regular classrooms, this is not the case for those with physical disabilities. There is a need for such teachers who would be accessible to support the teacher of the class with the integrated child, particularly in the use and mastery of the technology.

With any discussion of technology, it is important to state that technology is only useful if it is the correct technology for the task. Expensive technology can sit in the corner of the classroom because it does not meet the educational or communication needs of the child or because it is difficult to operate in the classroom setting. Specialist educators, especially speech pathologists, have developed assessment processes that allow the best technology to be chosen for the individual user and the task. Processes such as the Physical Characteristics Checklist (Stone, 1996, p. 3) guide the assessment of body parts and movement that might be used to access computer technology, assistive technology, and seating and postural considerations. Specialist services such as those provided by the Assistive Technology Service of the Cerebral Palsy Association in New South Wales are well worth utilizing to ensure that the child makes the best use of the latest technology. Such specialist services consider cost-effectiveness and the criteria for success. Such services also consider the consumer's acceptance by the community and the consumer's right to make life choices (*Technotalk*, 1996). Use of equipment for a trial period before buying it is recommended to ensure that the equipment is appropriate and useful.

It should be recognized that not all speech pathologists are experienced in the latest technology available for the child who is severely physically impaired (Barnes-Hughes, 1996), and there may be a need to liaise directly with specialist services. There is an obvious need for speech pathologists and teachers to work closely together when a child has communication difficulties.

Integrating the child's skills in technology into the curriculum requires some thought by teachers. Interviewing, for example, may require that a child with CP have technology that is mobile. Map making can also present difficulties. Setting another task of equal value that can be managed using the child's technology needs to be perceived not as diluting the curriculum but as varying it. Again, the child's strengths need to be used.

In spite of the difficulties discussed here, gifted children with CP can make excellent use of available technology, and the technology may allow them to more fully achieve their potential giftedness.

SOME STRATEGIES TO ASSIST THE GIFTED CHILD WITH CP

The learning discussed here may be learning in any field, regular classroom syllabuses, social skills, and occupational and physiotherapy activities.

Placement

It is essential that the child be placed in the setting that provides the best service after consideration of all factors. All aspects of learning and all the physical needs of the child should be considered. Such a setting may be mainstream, a support class, or a special unit. It is also essential that placements are frequently reviewed, as the needs of the child change and as technology advances, to ensure that the child is placed in the most "normal" and advantageous setting where the child's academic self-esteem is maintained.

If the child has been affected by the dual effects of CP and giftedness—both factors in isolating the child from peers—then high academic self-esteem offers one avenue for the child to succeed. Making the child aware of academic talents is of value in explaining the child's intellectual isolation from age peers. Contact with other gifted children will do much to extend the child while encouraging a realistic perception of personal academic performance. More importantly, the child will relate better to peers of similar interests and tastes and may not suffer as much from the feeling of being "different" intellectually from age peers. This has implications for a child's placement in learning settings designed to cater to gifted children. The integration of children with CP into gifted classes may be a new concept for many educators and may require strong advocacy from parents and other professionals. As Willard-Holt (1994) notes, "A mainstream setting with opportunities to interact with nondisabled gifted children has been widely recommended" (p. 5).

Teaching to the Child's Strengths

Thorough assessment and recording of the total picture of the child by all professionals will result in a picture of the child's intelligence strengths and weaknesses. As with all learners, the learner will achieve more if the strengths are used to compensate and to remediate the weaknesses.

Katerina, the subject of the author's case study, was able to use her excellent verbal skills to assist her with standing, walking, and sitting. When her physiotherapist verbalized the necessary movements for various limbs, Katerina was able to channel her verbal ability to self-instruct and to carry out the movements. Showing or manipulating Katerina was not as successful because one of her intelligence weaknesses was her perception of her body in space. Similarly, Katerina used her verbal ability as a major learning strategy. Visual cues were not as effective for her as verbal cues.

Children with CP may make better progress when the intelligence weaknesses are bypassed. A child may make more progress in geography if map-making skills are replaced with map reading or other activities in which the child has talent, such as conducting surveys. Another child may make more progress in music if writing musical notation is ignored until the child is able to use software for this purpose.

Peer tutoring may assist in raising self-esteem. The contact with other children of similar interests through this medium can be especially valuable and useful if the child is not placed in a specialist gifted learning situation. The use of individual learning programs using the communication means of the child is also appropriate.

Cooperative learning techniques allow valuable interaction with other children. They encourage problem solving, the development of individual learning habits, and the acceptance of responsibility for one's own learning that a learning-dependent student may not have. As noted, the dependency habit of the child with CP is certainly an area requiring attention.

The development of independent learning and study skills, such as personal timetabling, keeping a learning journal, and filing skills, is important to combat dependency habits and to assist the child who may have intelligence weaknesses in the areas of space, materials, or time management. This is especially important with a child who has CP, as these are common areas of weakness. Of interest is the involvement of the child in the personal constructive evaluation of abilities. The use of feedback, self-assessment, and peer review is also recommended.

Activities, generic to all gifted programs, are recommended. Activities that extend the child into the higher-level thinking skills of hypothesizing, synthesizing, and evaluating are valuable, as opposed to lower-level thinking activities such as the collection, classification, and retention of data. Lateral-thinking activities, as advocated by de Bono (1986, 1991a, 1991b) in his thinking programs will do much to stimulate the child to higher levels of thinking, retaining the child's interest and enthusiasm and encouraging creative thinking and further imaginative leaps.

Reis (1992) recommends opportunities for autonomy and individual pursuits. The difficulty of providing such activities in a regular classroom setting, although highly skilled practitioners may well be able to do so, further encourages the placement of the child in a specialist setting for the gifted. It is also worth noting that placement in a specialist setting will be of little use to the child unless the curriculum is well differentiated. In the regular classroom, grouping children according to individual strengths is recommended.

A team approach to the child's curriculum is recommended. The utilization of all parental and specialist skills in an agreed program requires communication and planning time.

The use of mentors, a well-proven strategy for assisting the gifted, is recommended even more so for the gifted child with CP. Contact with a mentor can overcome some of the lack of experiential learning the child may have been denied and also serve to motivate the child. Where mentors are unavailable, paid tutors (for example, in music or art) will do much to stimulate the child. Such tutors should be chosen for their ability to relate to the child with CP and their willingness to capitalize on the strengths of the child rather than attempt to concentrate on deficits. For example, it may be better to extend a music student's skills in composition rather than continue to work on poor performance posture. Many professionals are trained to identify and remedy deficits, not identify and extend talents.

Excursions and field trips are useful in overcoming experiential deprivation.

Parenting

Opportunities for early intervention abound when a provision exists, as in New South Wales (NSW), for children to commence at a special education school before the age of five. However, the mildly impaired child may not have this opportunity. In NSW, an early enrollment provision exists for any gifted child, and parents, suspecting giftedness in their child with CP, are urged to take up this opportunity.

Parents need to advocate for extension activities while advocating for compensation for disability. This is not easy for parents, especially parents of the child with mild impairment who is in the regular school setting. The need exists because some teachers may believe they are providing for the child by providing for either giftedness or the CP condition, although they may not be providing for both conditions. Indeed, some educators may balk at the concept that a child can be gifted as well as have CP. Establishing a comfortable relationship with the child's teachers and therapists will assist communication. Strategies to achieve this provision include making full use of review meetings. Regular review meetings are often part of the integration policy, as, for example, in NSW. It is essential that parents attend review meetings and put forward their opinion and intimate knowledge of the child when future goals and strategies are discussed. Parents know their child best and know what he or she can achieve at home. This knowledge is important to the professionals involved who may only see the child for a short time each day. Professionals may be better able to compare the child's performance with other disabled children when they have intimate parental knowledge of a child's functioning skills.

Parents need to advocate for modified assessment procedures, such as extra time, the use of computers, and test breaks. Qualifying boards can be very helpful and will be able to provide information on this topic.

Explanation of a child's disability to fellow students will do much to foster acceptance by classmates. This is especially essential if the condition is mild and the child appears awkward and clumsy but not necessarily very disabled. The teacher or another professional may be best at providing this explanation.

Parents also have a role in gathering evidence of the child's achievements and performance and making sure these data are passed on to all involved professionals. Reports from various professionals are not always freely available to other professionals, but parents have the right to share this information with all professionals so that all are fully informed and better decision making occurs. In the secondary school where a number of teachers, including casual teachers, may teach the child, this is essential.

Rimm (1987) recommends that both parents be consistent in their expectations and goal setting for their gifted child.

Providing for the gifted child with CP at home is, of course, a challenge. The parent must cater not only to the CP condition but also to the child's giftedness. The gifted child with CP is more likely to be frustrated by lack of stimulation and, therefore, may become more demanding. Sometimes outside support agencies can be of assistance, as can mentors and tutors. Support groups for parents of children with disabilities, as well as those for parents of gifted children, may be of great assistance. For example, regular camping programs exist for those who are disabled as well as for gifted children.

Parents have an important role in assisting the child to socialize and develop social and independence skills. The fine line between protection and overprotection will be familiar to many parents. Parents also have difficulty in knowing whether they are encouraging the child to be more independent or whether they are demanding too much and adding stress to the child. Discussion with professionals and other parents will prove helpful.

Parents have an essential role in exposing the child with CP, limited experientially, to as many varied learning situations as possible. At home, reading to the child, discussing educational television programs or music, and having the child help in the kitchen or garage or with shopping, are all valuable. Visits to different environments, such as community parks, national parks, sporting events, and different homes with varied cultures, are also valuable.

Parents may need to seek additional support in managing a child's inappropriate behaviors. "Acting out" is a sign of frustrated intelligence. Seeking support from appropriate professionals for children isolated from peers because of the dual factors of CP and giftedness may be necessary. Bibliotherapy (where the main character must overcome disabilities) may be a useful tool.

Finally, Davis and Rimm (1989) remind us that it is more important to view the child "primarily as a gifted child" rather than as a child with a disability (p. 377).

CASE STUDY

Katerina: A Case Study of a Gifted Child with Cerebral Palsy

Children who are gifted with intellectual brilliance, have, like other children, areas of strength and weakness. (Martin, 1993, p. 13)

Katerina was born after thirty-three weeks and four days of gestation. At birth, she weighed 2.048 kilograms. During the birth, Katerina suffered oxygen loss, and she was immediately placed in an oxygen crib. Her breathing failed at times, and she could not maintain her body temperature. Despite this, her doctors assured her parents that Katerina had suffered no ill effects.

Katerina failed to feed strongly. All her physical milestones were delayed. It was not until Katerina was two years, seven months, that her parents finally received the diagnosis they had long suspected: that Katerina had suffered a degree ("moderate to mild") of cerebral palsy, specifically spastic diplegia. Katerina had poor control of all her muscles (high tone combined with low tone), but suffered a greater loss of control on her right side. The damage appeared confined to the parts of the brain controlling motor areas. Katerina had very poor balance control.

While Katerina required physiotherapy to eventually reach most of her physical milestones, her academic milestones were advanced. Katerina had a rich vocabulary at an early age—over six hundred words at sixteen months. At eighteen months, she was completing eighty-piece puzzles. This interest was used as an aid to maintaining her concentration during her physiotherapy sessions.

Katerina would ask her physiotherapist to tell her what she did when she walked so that Katerina could do it. When her physiotherapist finally verbalized the movements, instead of just manipulating Katerina's limbs, her progress rapidly increased. Katerina appeared to be using her good language pathways to compensate for her poor motor pathways. The physiotherapist would verbalize, "Get your leg up, Katerina. Put your weight over your hip, Katerina." Once, Katerina was standing but unable to sit down. "Nobody told Katerina how to sit down," she complained.

Katerina's physiotherapist explained that Katerina had to use an incredible amount of thought and, therefore, mental energy to physically perform as well as she did and that she was really overperforming, given her limited physical abilities, because of her excellent intellectual ability.

When Katerina was twenty-six months, her grandparents thought her parents were coaching her to read when they discovered Katerina recognized and discussed the frequency of all the letters on the pages of a book that they were reading to her. Katerina had been watching the television program "Sesame Street." Upon enrollment at school at age four years, eight months, Katerina still could not walk for any distance unaided, but she was a fluent reader and was writing stories, despite her difficulty in grasping a pencil.

Although she frequently fell, could not control a pencil easily, tired easily, and limped because of the tightness of her tendons, Katerina's teachers found it difficult to accept that Katerina had suffered a degree of brain damage, because of her exceptional performance at school.

As time went on, it became apparent that Katerina had suffered a degree of perceptual damage as well. Being gifted and learning disabled are not "mutually exclusive" (Toll, 1993, p. 34). Katerina's orientation in space was poor; she became easily lost because of her poor sense of direction. Her weaker academic areas—handwriting, organization of materials, layout of projects, and some areas of spatial mathematics, art, and craft—reflected her weak awareness of herself and objects in space. These areas constitute a significant disability when Katerina's performance is compared with other gifted children. Katerina's use of language in stories and conversation was excellent.

Some teachers and counselors remarked that Katerina's major difficulty with her peer friendships was not her physical impairment, but her giftedness. However, both Katerina and her mother believed that Katerina's physical impairment and her giftedness distinguished her as "different" from her peers.

In Year 4, Katerina's ability was assessed on the WISC-R at around 148 to 158 in the Language area, with some scores at the top of the scale, and at around 135 to 145 in the Performance area, with lower scores in some areas depressing her performance average.

Year 7 was a difficult year for Katerina. Her parents had thought that perhaps she needed to attend a selective school, for which she easily qualified, but were happy that her chosen school provided better pastoral care, care which Katerina required. Her last two years in primary education had not been easy. Katerina had transferred to a new primary school in fifth class where a new group of students, unfamiliar with Katerina, had created some difficulties for her. She was harassed by larger and smaller pupils. This rejection of gifted students by peers has been well documented, for example, Tannenbaum noted in 1962:

> American high school students actively reject those of their peers who demonstrate high level academic or intellectual prowess without the ameliorating effect of sporting or athletic interests. (Gross, 1989, p. 190)

Katerina was also isolated because of her physical disability. Her poor balance made her an easy target for any student because she was easily pushed over. A tacit school policy of minimal intervention in this harassment was explained by staff as a desire not to intervene too much on Katerina's behalf, with the hope of preventing her from being singled out more in the eyes of other students. Her parents believed that this policy was seen by students as a signal that Katerina was "fair game" in the eyes of her teachers. The constant mental and physical harassment led to counseling. This assistance only followed intervention by her parents.

According to the principal and the counselor of Katerina's chosen non-selective secondary school, she would have some intellectual peers. Katerina had some difficulties with secondary mathematics classes. She was slower to complete written work than her peers but was not given extra time for tests. She objected to repeating numerous examples of the same algorithm. Toward the end of Year 7, Katerina announced that she was having difficulty keeping her eyes in focus. Investigation led to a diagnosis that Katerina had sustained damage to her retinas at birth, affecting her lower field of vision. This explained some of her falls but did not explain the extent of her apparent loss of focus. Another later medical opinion was that Katerina's eye muscles tired with the effort of focusing. For a time, this problem was a significant disability when reading. Her doctors recommended to her school that she have at least a third more time than her peers to complete tasks. This removed some of the pressures on Katerina. Movement between classes that delayed her arrival at classes and buses, stairs, sighting the chalkboard, and sport and physical education were also difficulties. Compulsory hockey was a dangerous activity for all concerned. Her physical education teachers knew that Katerina required special programs, that she had a significant degree of disability, and that, indeed, she could not sit up from a prone position without needing support; nevertheless, some staff were still skeptical about whether Katerina had a significant disability.

When Katerina was thirteen, she was placed in the highest Year 8 graded class at her school. She was Dux (top student in the year group) of Year 7, based on marks in mathematics, science, and English. She won a public speaking award in a regional competition. She was allowed to explore individually and at a much higher level in computer education classes. Her interest in and understanding of computers were vast. She instigated a computer club at school attended by students from Years 7 to 12 who were interested in programming. She programmed in quite a few computer languages. In English, she had the opportunity to perform at her best, although the novels studied probably did not extend her. In mathematics, she appeared to have to work to achieve at the top of the class, to which she aspired. In the sciences and social sciences, she had much to gain from the new material with which she was presented. She was bored with music, having achieved Grade 3 theory certification in Year 7. She played piano, but not very well because of the poor muscle tone in her fingers. Katerina was composing at an early age. In sport and physical education, her teachers appeared to try to consider her particular physical needs, although sometimes this was difficult given the school program. She was not accelerated because her parents were unsure that she was achieving well enough in mathematics, and because her physical and visual difficulties placed pressure on her. She was, however, already young for her grade level. She used a laptop computer to record most of her written work and typed at almost the speed of speech. Her laptop computer, although a nuisance to carry and manage, and prone to failures, allowed her to compete on her own terms. Her ability to present work using a word processor was sometimes looked upon as an unfair advantage by other students. Her interest in mathematical problem solving led to awards in statewide mathematics competitions. Katerina had good relationships with her teachers and older students. She found it much easier to relate to adults and older students than to her age peers.

Toward the end of Year 9, Katerina's posture became more affected, and more physiotherapy was required. Once again, she required plastering of her leg to stretch her tendon. Medical advice recommended rest when fingers and wrists became painful, but she was still allowed to type, use a keyboard, and play the piano. This was a great relief to Katerina because she would have had great difficulty functioning in secondary school at the level she wished without typing. School furniture had to be organized to meet her posture needs. A teacher threatened (jokingly?) to fail Katerina for the year because of incomplete attendance at physical education lessons. Other staff supported Katerina during this stressful time.

During Year 9, Katerina's laptop computer frequently broke down. She had to take very scribbled notes and then transcribe these on her computer at home. Some of her teachers assessed her by taking into consideration this difficulty and the necessary time delays in assignments. Others gave her lower marks for overdue assignments. She often lost assignment marks because she had not produced beautifully illustrated title pages for assignments. Producing this type of work required lettering and drawing skills beyond Katerina.

At the commencement of Year 10, Katerina required permission from the NSW Board of Studies for special conditions when sitting for the School Certificate examinations conducted at the end of Year 10. She required assessment of her writing speed and her typing speed over short and long test conditions. Her occupational therapy report recommended extra time for tests that required writing (typing), plus extra time to compensate for fatigue (in the wrists and neck in particular) that would set in on longer tests.

During Year 10, Katerina believed that fellow students were pleasant to her because of her impairment but did not want to be in her company because it would not be "cool" to be seen in the company of a student with an impairment. This concern greatly affected Katerina's self-esteem.

The need for further physiotherapy treatment requiring plaster splints also affected Katerina's movement around the school. Throughout secondary school she was late to classes because of the need to travel carefully and slowly. She often missed the start or conclusion of lessons.

Katerina required special test conditions for her major examinations in which she achieved excellent results. Following secondary school, she began studying information technology at a university.

The following excerpt from one interview with Katerina is included to give readers greater insight into the thoughts of this young woman.

An Interview with Katerina, Aged 14

I: What areas of school do you enjoy the most? Why?

K: Oh, mainly computing studies because it's really easy, and Music for the same reasons but also because you're allowed, you can create a lot, things of your own. English is all right because I like fiddling around with words. I don't like Maths. Design and Technology is all right in the design stages but as soon as I get into the practical room, I end up stuffing everything up. I generally like designing things and creating things and being really good at things.

Katerina's difficulty in manipulating objects in space and her poor motor control made the manipulation of materials, tools, and machinery very difficult. Her persistence with these activities was probably related to her giftedness.

I: How would you rate your achievement/performance in school work?

K: Well, I'd say in subjects where there is no definite right answer and wrong answer, I'm especially good at. I would say I'm above the level of most of the kids in my classes in even things like Maths. But some subjects like Maths and Design and Technology, I'll always lack because it targets on areas, especially Design and Technology that I'm not very good at. I mean subjects that require a large amount of using motor skills with precision, and tests, sometimes where I have to do diagrams and draw by hand, I think I sometimes score a bit lower than I would. I'm a bit lower than what I would if I didn't have screwed up hands, things which make me use areas where I am especially disabled.

I: How does your physical impairment create problems for you at school?

K: Lots of many different ways actually. My school, although all the buildings are linked very intricately and you can get from one building to the other without too much trouble. There's still an awful lot of stairs. There are two and three story buildings all over the place and it takes me a while to get up and down stairs, some days especially with the computer and that in my bag, and although kids are fairly tolerant, they, everybody knows that's its me and they wait behind me.

Katerina was further handicapped by her poor general mobility. She was aware not only that it made class punctuality difficult but that her fellow students knew she was slow and uncertain (mainly because of her poor balance and poor eyesight) on stairs. She had a very bad fall on the stairs at school. This poor general mobility further distinguished Katerina from her peers.

I: Is that the only problem? Getting around stairs?

K: Sometimes having the lap top computer will create problems because normal kids don't have lap top computers at school and the same thing with the general fact that I'm disabled. Everybody wants to have a look at the computer and everybody wants to know why I'm disabled and how, and everybody wants to have a go at the computer, and everybody wants to see my leg splint, and everybody wants to ask what happened and why I'm disabled and how I'm disabled. Everybody wants to know everything. Just general slowness is a problem sometimes, but usually people are fairly tolerant of that.

I: How do you think you relate to kids of your own age?

K: I try to blend in with the other kids of my age without going outside my own boundaries but I often find that many kids of my own age are very different from me and do very different things, dress very differently, think very differently, even talk very differently but generally I try to be friendly and try to blend in.

Katerina's comment reinforces the observations by Cross et al. (1993) that "gifted adolescents would not try to blend-in with others unless they believed that standing-out . . . would preclude their ability to maintain normal relationships" (p. 38).

I: Do you think that you're more different because you're physically impaired or because you're gifted, or both, or one more than the other?

K: I would say that both make a big difference but especially because I'm physically impaired. Whereas most people can cope with having a very bright person around but a lot can't even understand half the things about my impairment and half the things I can't do, and don't understand that because of my physical impairment, I do things a lot differently and some things better and some things a lot worse than other kids.

I: How do you think you relate to older kids? Which age group do you relate to the best?

K: I would definitely say kids a good four or five years older than me. They seem to be into things in the same depth as me, and want to do the same things. . . . My learning needs are very different from other kids. I would rather I had a higher level in some subjects, like Drama, Geography, English. I think that without a lap top computer, school would become more of a hassle. My work, the amount of work I could complete would become unbearably small. And, um, I think that teachers need to consider sometimes that I will be late to class sometimes because I'm slow and I'll need larger print books or need to sit closer to the board than some kids because I have bad eyes and that sometimes I will need to do much more advanced work than some kids.

I: You haven't said much about your eyes. Tell us about those.

K: Just the fact that one day they'll be really sharp and good and the next day my vision will be pretty yuck. One day I'll go to school and I'll be able to see things okay but then that afternoon or the next morning I'll be unable to read a fine print book. That often tires me out a lot. And I'll sometimes slow down work that involves reading or close work, which is most of school really.

Katerina is a gifted child according to the traditional standardized ability testing criteria. According to multiple intelligences theory, she could be described as gifted in the areas of language, logical thinking, and music. She displays many of the qualities of gifted children, such as perseverance with tasks in which she is interested, high achievement in some areas, unusually high vocabulary at a young age, "quick mastery and excellent recall of factual information," "reads a great deal on her own," "is easily bored with routine tasks," "needs little external motivation," and "is often self-assertive (sometimes even aggressive), stubborn in beliefs" (Davis & Rimm, 1989, pp. 198–201).

How CP Masked Katerina's True Ability

1. At an early age, Katerina's occupational therapy assessment did not pick up Katerina's ability. Katerina wanted to provide lateral answers to questions that required specific answers. She was bored by many of the tasks she was set, and her attention wandered.

2. Katerina's difficulty in writing was to some extent offset by her typing ability. However, the necessity to process most of her writing to maintain speed and legibility created a lot of extra work for her, especially when the technology failed, as it frequently did. The delay in gaining the technology at an early age also disadvantaged her at the time.

3. Katerina had to concentrate on simple physical tasks, such as walking, at all times. She often had bone-jarring falls. This amount of concentration was tiring and detracted from energy she would have had for mental activity.

4. Katerina's perceptual problems, related to fine and gross motor planning, made high achievement in some areas difficult. Her music achievement was affected by weaknesses in performance, although she composed well beyond her age peers. Her performance in mathematics and geography was affected by difficulties with creating graphs and maps. Her mobility difficulties affected travel on excursions. Some of these activities were necessary for her studies. Her poor physical education performance was seen by some teachers as sufficient excuse to detract from her overall performance. Some of her teachers commented negatively on her writing and setting out of written work (not processed work), and this earned her lower marks than she would otherwise have been given. Her parents constantly needed to represent her giftedness to educators and to argue for consideration of her impairment when assessing her achievements.

5. Katerina was encouraged by her parents to be as independent as possible. Therefore, her work was not greatly affected by a dependency upon her learning facilitators. Katerina's level of impairment, however, was mild compared to many children with CP.

6. Katerina's level of disability was a barrier to developing a broader personal circle of friends. When other girls were playing physical games, Katerina was isolated, sitting by herself or sometimes talking to a friend. This isolating factor was significant in affecting Katerina's social confidence.

7. Katerina had two differences to manage. Her giftedness and her cerebral palsy both set her apart from her peers.

....

CONCLUSION

[F]ailing to actualise one's potential creates a breeding ground for frustration and poor mental health. (Colangelo & Davis, 1991, p. 428)

In some cases, it may not be possible to assist the gifted child with CP to achieve her or his full potential, but we must utilize every tool, skill, agency, and educator available in the attempt to do so.

ACTIVITIES FOR EDUCATION STUDENTS

The following activities may be useful for raising teachers' awareness of this special population of children.

1. Read the case study. In what ways are the needs of the gifted child who is mildly impaired with CP different from the needs of the gifted child who is severely impaired with CP?
2. Develop a relationship with a child who has CP. Investigate the complexity of the multiple impairments.
3. Visit a technology center that specializes in meeting the needs of people with disabilities. Such centers usually can be found through contact with a major institution or government agency. Pay special attention to the communication technology. Visit a classroom where this technology is utilized and judge how well the technology meets the needs of the child in the learning situation.
4. Talk with a professional either integrating a child with CP or working in a specialist institution. Ask how profiles of students or children are maintained and made accessible to all concerned so that those in contact with the child are utilizing the strengths of the child in learning situations.
5. Ask educators how they review the needs of the child and review the placement so that the child is placed in the most advantageous setting.
6. Ask to sit in on a child's review meeting. Parental and professional agreement will be required.
7. Discuss with the parent of a gifted child with CP how they meet the needs of the child as well as meet the needs of their other children. Are the needs of the gifted child with CP greater

than those of other children, or are all gifted children demanding of parents?

8. Compile a list of successful adults with CP.

9. Compile a list of educational excursion experiences within the local area at sites that are accessible to a child with CP.

10. Investigate the relative merits and disadvantages of the support class setting versus the fully integrated setting for a student who is severely impaired with CP. Visit each setting with this purpose in mind.

11. Investigate the services for gifted children with CP available in an isolated country area. Compare these with the services available in a large regional center. What advantages exist in each area? How can the limitations of an area be overcome?

12. One of the aspects of CP is learning disability. Investigate ways in which compensation for learning disability through curriculum modifications may assist children with CP.

REFERENCES

Barnes-Hughes, T. (1966). *Technotalk*. Allambie Heights, New South Wales, Australia: The Spastic Centre of NSW.

Clark, B. (1983). *Growing up gifted: Developing the potential of children at home and at school.* (2nd ed.) Columbus, OH: Merrill.

Colangelo, N., & Davis, G. (1991). *A handbook of gifted education.* Needham Heights, MA: Allyn & Bacon.

Cross, T. L., Coleman, L. J., & Stewart, R. A. (1993). The social cognition of gifted adolescents: The exploration of the stigma of giftedness paradigm. *Roeper Review, 16*(1), 37–40.

Davis, G. A., & Rimm, S. B. (1989). *Education of the gifted and talented* (2nd ed.). Needham Heights, MA: Allyn & Bacon.

de Bono, E. (1986). *CoRT thinking: Teachers' notes* (Vols. 1–6) (2nd ed.). New York: Pergamon Press.

de Bono, E. (1991a). *Six thinking hats for schools: Adult educators' resource book.* Logan, IA: Perfection Learning.

de Bono, E. (1991b). *Six thinking hats for schools: 3–5 resource book.* Logan, IA: Perfection Learning.

Gardner, H. (1983). *Frames of mind.* New York: Basic Books.

Gross, M. (1989). The pursuit of excellence or the search for intimacy? The forced-choice dilemma of gifted youth. *Roeper Review, 11*(4), 189–194.

Hallahan, D. P., & Kauffman, J. M. (1986). *Exceptional children: Introduction to special education* (3rd ed.) Englewood Cliffs, NJ: Prentice-Hall.

Kulik, J., & Kulik, C. (1984). Synthesis of research on effects of accelerated instruction. *Educational Leadership, 42*, 84–89.

Mares, L. (1993). School counsellors and gifted and talented education. *Gifted, 76*, 15 & 24.

Martin, C. (1993). Sources of self-esteem for gifted children. *Gifted, 75*, 13–14.

Miller, M., & Terry-Godtip. (1991). The handicapped gifted. In R. Jenkins-Friedman, S. Richert, & J. Feldhusen (Eds.), *Special populations of gifted learners* (pp. 85–91). Melbourne, Australia: Hawker Brownlow Education.

Reis, S. M. (1992). Advocacy: The grouping issue. *Roeper Review, 14*(4), 225–227.

Rimm, S. (1987). Why do bright children underachieve? *GCT, 10*(6), 30–37.

Robinson, C., & Fieber, N. (1988). Cognitive assessment of motorically impaired infants and preschoolers. In T. D. Wachs & R. Sheehan (Eds.), *Assessment of young developmentally disabled children.* New York: Plenum Press.

Sternberg, R. J. (1985). *Beyond IQ.* London: Cambridge University Press.

Stone, H. (1996, February). Review of McGregor, G., Arange, G. A., Fraser, B. A., & Kangas, K., *Physical Characteristics Assessment: Computer Access for Individuals with Cerebral Palsy* (Don Johnston Inc.) in *Technotalk,* 4(2), newsletter of the Assistive Technology Service. Allambie Heights, New South Wales, Australia: The Spastic Centre of NSW.

Technotalk (1996). Newsletter of the Assistive Technology Service. Allambie Heights, New South Wales, Australia: The Spastic Centre of NSW.

Toll, M. F. (1993). Gifted learning disabled: A kaleidoscope of needs. *Gifted Child Quarterly, 16*(1), 34–35.

Tyler, J. S., & Colson S. (1994). *Focus on exceptional children.* Denver, CO: Love Publishing Co.

Vialle, W. (1993). Current theories in intelligence and the practice of gifted education. *Gifted, 77,* 11–14.

Whitmore, J. R. & Maker, C. J. (1985). *Intellectual giftedness in disabled persons.* Rockville, MD: Aspen Systems Corp.

Willard-Holt, C. (1994). *Recognizing talent: Cross-case study of two high potential students with cerebral palsy.* Storrs, CT: The National Research Center on the Gifted and Talented.

Autism: The Silent Mask

CHAPTER

10

USA PERSPECTIVE

INTRODUCTION

Overall, the purpose of this chapter is to establish that there are gifted children among those identified as having autism and that they are often denied appropriate support and opportunities. The chapter provides a detailed picture of individuals with autism, as this population is rarely discussed in tandem with gifted learners. A profile of the dual-labeled gifted/autistic, through analysis of case studies, is also included. Further, the chapter contains a discussion of connections between autistic and gifted populations, and concludes with suggestions for the best educational practices for this underserved group of learners.

In retrospect, it appears that my earliest instincts regarding autism fueled my interest in the subject, and ultimately directed my research into its potential links with giftedness. My preoccupation with the field and my empathy for individuals displaying autistic behaviors can be traced to my childhood. I was eight years old, and my family subscribed to several of the then-trendy news magazines of the 1950s (for example, *Life*, *Look*, and *Colliers*). My life was immediately opened to the worldly events, incidents, and theories that are traditionally absent from the minds of most children.

I was riveted to the details of an article describing case studies of autistic children who were unwilling to relate to their primary caregivers; the children frequently dominated the lives of their families with food preoccupations and unusual stereotypical behaviors such as echolalic speech (the repetition of words and phrases) and the closing and opening of doors. The image of the boy who would only eat McDonalds' hamburgers is still fixed in my mind. Years later, I would remember bits and pieces of the article when personal events stimulated my memory; this was the case when my one-year-old son curiously displayed a strong preference for bologna at every meal, and when he balanced, through cantilevering, numerous unusual objects.

I was also struck, however, by the recollection of children who demonstrated a quiet state of knowing, an underlying visage or intelligence in addition to a focus—not uncommon among children with autism. Over the years, as I have met and observed children with autism, I am spontaneously reminded of my earliest intuitions regarding this hidden state of awareness within them. Kanner (1971), in his follow-up study of the eleven children with autism he originally researched in 1943, recounted a 1940 diary entry from the mother of a three-year-old autistic boy. She stated, "He gave the impression of silent wisdom to me . . ." (p. 125). In fact, Kanner, in characterizing his autistic subjects, explained that "all had intelligent physiognomies, giving at times—especially in the presence of others—the impression of serious-mindedness or anxious tenseness . . ." (p. 142).

Much important research has been done in the field of autism since Kanner's initial investigation and description in 1943. However, even subsequent to Kanner's groundbreaking research, in the 1940s and 1950s, children with autism were usually not diagnosed appropriately. Temple Grandin is a high-functioning autistic who has a Ph.D. in animal sciences and is currently a professor at Colorado State University. She believes she was originally labeled as brain-damaged instead of autistic in the late 1940s because it took medical doctors and psychologists a long time to get the message (Grandin, 1995b). One can only wonder about the public's general awareness and sensitivity to the condition of autism today. In retrospect, it may have taken the movie "Rain Man," about an autistic savant, released in the 1980s and starring Dustin Hoffman, to bring sensitivity and understanding about the subject of autism to the general population. Psychologist Bernard Rimland, a noted expert in the field of autism and himself the father of a thirty-nine-year-old autistic son named Mark, believes that as a result of the film, "There is a much greater understanding, sympathy, and support now—a kinder, gentler awareness" (in King, 1989, p. 9). Further, according to King (1989), "One mother noted that since the film, fewer people now confuse the term autistic with artistic" (p. 9).

In 1990, the autistic syndrome was added to the list of designated handicapping conditions under the Individuals with Disabilities Education Act (IDEA), Public Law 101-476. Another law, Public Law 94-142, which governs the mainstreaming of children with handicaps into the public schools, defines them as "mentally retarded, hard of hearing, deaf, speech impaired, visually handicapped, seriously emotionally disturbed, orthopedically impaired or other health impaired children with specific learning disabilities who by reason thereof require special education and related services" (Davis & Rimm, 1989, p. 370).

Despite the heightened awareness and increased interest in the field of autism, few educational programs or courses of study have been introduced into the public schools or postsecondary institutions to accommodate this underserved population of learners. The mainstreaming definition contained in Public Law 94-142 fails to mention autism as a specific designated handicap, although a case would no doubt be made for the inclusion of children with autism by arguing that they fall under the category of "specific learning disabilities." Their specific exclusion from the list, however, may lend support to the notion held by some educators that public schools do not have to provide programming for students with autism.

In 1979, a Fact Sheet generated by the United States Office of Gifted and Talented estimated that possibly up to 300,000 children in the United States were both gifted and handicapped (Clark, 1992). Statistically, twenty to twenty-five percent of persons with autism are *not* mentally retarded, and have average to above-average intelligence (Donnelly & Altman, 1993; Rimland, 1978). In addition, research and clinical experiences over the years have documented the existence of gifted individuals with autism as well as autistic savants; their behaviors are frequently indistinguishable from those displayed by children who meet standard gifted definitions. Educators concerned with the dual label of gifted and disabled have long been aware of the backgrounds of such eminent individuals as Albert Einstein and Leonardo da Vinci whose "gifts" were mixed with autistic behaviors (Bireley, 1994). Examples of traits and characteristics sometimes shared by both gifted and autistic populations include eidetic (photographic) memory; limited communication and a desire to be alone; visual thinking; strong spatial skills; a facility with puzzles; and precocious math, art, and music abilities.

According to Grandin (1995b), autism occurs on a continuum from mild to severe, with each case being different. Likewise, gifted individuals also progress along a continuum from mildly gifted through highly gifted. Such a comparison lends support to the hypothesis that the two populations are matched at several points, a premise that will be developed in this chapter. It is well acknowledged, however, that while strengths and weaknesses of both groups may overlap, the sensory, verbal, and social perception difficulties of dual-labeled gifted/autistic are generally neurologically grounded and more severe (Donnelly & Altman, 1993).

Unfortunately, all too often children with autism fail to be identified for their gifts and are instead selected to be educated with those learning-disabled populations who are void of any exceptional learning abilities. The needs that loom the greatest are those that represent deficits, and remediation becomes the primary concern. Donnelly and Altman (1993) refer to gifted youngsters with autism as a "sub-group" and observe that "[b]y definition, these students have remarkable skills occurring alongside areas of deficit which cause test scores to be uneven or fall below gifted and talented program criteria" (p. 253). Similarly, Clark (1992) notes that even when giftedness is suspected, it is unusual for children already receiving special services to also find a place in a gifted program. These individuals may easily be misunderstood and become frustrated because "the strengths and weaknesses often mask each other" (Silverman, 1993, p. 159).

It is also interesting that once programming or protocols have been established for high-functioning, gifted/autistic individuals, minimal follow-up has been given to their adult development or accomplishments. According to Oliver Sacks, "[W]e almost always speak of autistic children, never of autistic adults, as if such children never grow up or were somehow mysteriously spirited off the planet, out of society" (in Grandin, 1995b, pp. 11–12). Researchers and teachers, however, are finding that among individuals with autism, there are those who, if there is high intelligence, understanding, and motivation along with early educational intervention, can live successful, even "exceptional," lives.

AUTISTIC POPULATIONS

Definitions

Autism is a perplexing physical disorder that is characterized by a large number of symptoms which vary in kind and severity with each individual. The population in the United States is estimated at approximately 300,000. Autism is generally thought to exist on a continuum from severe to mild, encompassing ranges of intelligence from mental retardation through giftedness (Rutter & Schopler, 1987). According to the Autism Society of America:

> Autism is a severely incapacitating life-long developmental disability that typically appears during the first three years of life. The result of a neurological disorder that affects functioning of the brain, autism and its behavioral symptoms occur in approximately fifteen out of every 10,000 births. Autism is four times more common in boys than girls. It has been found throughout

the world in families of all racial, ethnic, and social backgrounds. No known factors in the psychological environment of a child have been shown to cause autism. (in Gerlach, 1996, p. 1)

Individuals with autism may manifest the condition in a number of ways, including being unable to relate normally to people, objects, and events; displaying abnormal sensory responses (for example, hyper or mixed); exhibiting delays, deterioration, or the complete absence of the development of social, expressive, and responsive language skills, in spite of certain thinking capabilities; and displaying stereotypical behaviors such as arm flailing, twirling, and the ordering of objects with no tolerance for any outside interference with these ritualistic mannerisms.

Types of Autism

There are several different types of autism which, like the condition itself, are largely distinguished by their behavioral manifestations. At this time they are considered subgroups of the autistic label, but they are frequently confused and described in overlapping terms by different psychologists and researchers in the field, making a clear understanding difficult. Following is a list of the major autistic categories.

Kanner-type. This type of autism, which is sometimes called Early Infantile Autism or Classic Autism, was defined by Kanner in 1943 when he used case study methodology to investigate eleven children with autism. Basically, Kanner-type autism is characterized by the early onset of illness (usually before the first year), late speech, lack of eye contact, a paucity of interaction, a lack of proper pronoun usage (the substitution of *you* for *I*), stereotyped behaviors, and possible mental retardation. However, individuals do display normal mobility and coordination, along with relatively strong visual and thinking patterns.

Asperger Syndrome. This type of autism, which is sometimes called high-functioning autism, was researched by the Viennese psychologist Hans Asperger in 1944. Although he performed his research at approximately the same time as Kanner, his paper was not translated into English until years later, and no connection between the two studies was made. In Asperger Syndrome, the children have normal or near normal development until the age of eighteen months, after which there is a period of regression. The syndrome is characterized by somewhat formal speech with pseudo-adult qualities, expressed in a flat, monotone voice; poor motor coordination; late mobility; strong attachments to places; depression; echolalic speech; routinized obsessive-compulsive behaviors; difficulty in relating to people; a lack of empathy for others; poor eye contact; and a lack of intuition. These individuals often demonstrate normal sensory responses, strong islets of ability, and near normal or normal intelligence. They may also engage in untraditional and unorthodox thinking that can result in creative products.

Pervasive Developmental Disorder (PDD). This classification is used when the important defining criteria of autism is not met (for example, onset before the age of three), or when the condition appears atypical, inconsistent, and less severe. PDD is usually more aligned to Kanner-type autism than Asperger Syndrome. It is characterized by its early onset, aberrant language development, impaired social relationships, peculiar motor behaviors, and stereotypical behaviors.

Regressive/Epileptic-type. Temple Grandin, a gifted individual with autism and a researcher in her own right, categorizes high-functioning autistic under the Kanner/Asperger classification because of their similarities, and at the same time labels low-functioning autistic as being Regressive/Epileptic. This type of autism is characterized by coordination difficulties, the absence of receptive speech (the inability to understand others), modality mixing, epileptic seizures, abnormal EEG (electroencephalograph) readings, an undersized brain stem, high anxiety levels, and mental retardation. Somewhat normal thinking and emotions may be evidenced by these individuals at times.

Savants. Savants do not technically represent a separate form of autism; however, they do constitute a population that often exists in tandem with individuals who display autistic tendencies. Of the three savant categories—idiot savant, autistic savant, and crypto savant— the first is probably the best known because of detailed accounts in the media of individuals with retarded intellect who can perform mathematical feats or play complicated piano concertos. According to Morelock and Feldman (1991), the term *idiot-savant,* coined by Dr. J. Langdon Down of London in 1887, refers to "severely mentally handicapped persons displaying advanced levels of learning in narrowly circumscribed areas" (p. 357). Their advanced "islands of ability" sharply contrast with their disabilities, and the occurrence is rare. Although approximately ten percent of the autistic population displays savant behaviors, only one percent of them might be characterized as being extraordinary (Rimland, 1978); most savants would be found among those individuals with autism whose intelligence is in the normal or above-normal range.

Examples of savant brilliance include calendar counting (the ability to list specific dates and the days of the week on which they fall for thousands of years); musical knowledge (playing classical pieces perfectly after hearing them only once, or singing arias in foreign languages unknown to the individual); lightning mathematical calculations; artistic creations (painting, drawing, and sculpting); mechanical ability (dismantling and building televisions and cars); prodigious memory (mnemonism); unusual sensory discrimination (smell and touch); and extrasensory perception (Rimland, 1995). Some savants are also hyper-lexic, displaying the ability to read and spell without any understanding of the words; possess eidetic memory (photographic memory) skills; have extraordinary abilities to retain directions; or have the ability to balance items to an exceptional degree.

According to Donnelly and Altman (1993), those termed autistic savants are individuals with "remarkable areas of talent despite their pervasive disabilities in communication and social development" (p. 252). Autistic savants display intelligence in the range of near normal to above normal. Raymond, in the 1986 movie "Rain Man," is an example of an autistic savant. According to Rimland, "more than half of all autistic savants have two or more savant abilities" (in Blake, 1989, p. 1).

Crypto savants, a term coined by Rimland, refers to savants whose lack of ability or willingness to communicate prevents their talents from being shared with others, and ensures that they remain dormant. Rimland suggests that autistic individuals with savant abilities successfully ignore uncomfortable outside stimuli. Because these individuals are unable to broaden their focus of attention due to brain abnormalities, they block out any "drive for novelty" which then allows for continued repetition in the initial area of focus (in Blake, 1989). Another view is offered by Treffert who suggests that "savant skills may be due to a failure to forget rather than an enhanced ability to store" (in Blake, 1989, p. 7).

Characteristic Behaviors of Autistic Populations

Some of the behaviors displayed by individuals with autism have been mentioned in the descriptions of the different autistic syndromes and in the diagnostic definitions. Additional anomalies may be evidenced, and are elaborated on as follows.

Social. Individuals with autism may display an inability to control their attentional and emotional shifts, shyness, an inability to play or activate their imagination, few metacognitive behaviors, remoteness, a lack of accessibility, inappropriate moral or intellectual intensity, an inability to make friends, violent rages, poor social judgment, an inability to interact to emotional cues or nuances, an inability to comfort others, fixed facial expressions, a paucity of gestures, and an inability to explain themselves and their behaviors to others.

Language. Individuals with autism may be verbose and fill their environment with incessant, empty chatter; not remember verbal sequences, necessitating their being written down; use awkward and inappropriate language for social communications; use speech that has an abnormal pitch, rate, and rhythm; have idiosyncratic word usage; display a lack of emotional expression; and have a large memory bank of nouns as compared to other word forms.

Stereotypical. Autistic sometimes perseverate in their behaviors. These behaviors may include elaborate and compulsive rituals and routines, finger play, rocking, tics or Tourette's behaviors, humming, intense fixations, rigid body movements, unusual attachments to objects, self-abuse such as hitting their heads or biting themselves, stressing over small changes, incessant puzzle play, inappropriate manipulations of objects such as door slamming, and the licking or smelling of objects or wall surfaces.

Sensory. Individuals with autism frequently have hyper-vigilant nervous systems that can quickly become overwhelmed. As a result, they may experience spasms, extreme low or high pain tolerance, a need for tactile pressure, an aversion to hair washing or scratchy clothes, eating disorders due to the inability to eat noisy or heavy textured food, the mixing of sensory channels (touch to the face comes through as sound or a sound is seen as color), mono-channeling (an individual cannot hear speech and focus on outside stimuli at the same time), the visualization of air and dust particles, and panic attacks. They may also "hear" and "experience" noises and cars a far distance away and exhibit perfect musical pitch.

Research

It is highly probable that individuals with the condition described as autism have existed throughout history, and that, in the past, they were often institutionalized for their behaviors. Sacks (1993) suggests that autism "is a condition that has always existed affecting occasional individuals in every period and culture" (p. 106). Likewise, Schopler and Bristol (1980) believe that there have always been autistic individuals, citing accounts going back two hundred years; they suggest that the condition was improperly diagnosed. In the early 1940s, the syndrome was medically described by Leo Kanner in Baltimore and Hans Asperger in Vienna. They independently converged on the term *autism*, which emphasized the cardinal feature of "Mental aloneness" (Sacks, 1993).

Bettelheim's research in 1959 indicated behavioral similarities between feral (wild) children and the behavior of autistic (in Schopler & Bristol, 1980). Bettelheim believed that feral children had been abandoned by their mothers and judged that autistic children had been physically and psychologically neglected by their parents, as well. He concluded that the incidence of autism could be connected to poor parenting. This inaccurate, guilt-laden theory was not dispelled until 1964 when psychologist Bernard Rimland published his book *Infantile Autism: The Syndrome and Its Implications for a Neural Theory of Behavior*. Rimland's research suggested that operant response conditioning techniques could be successful in replacing some of the bizarre behaviors evidenced by autistic individuals.

Today, most researchers believe that there is no one etiology connected with autism and that it is probably the result of complex factors, including brain abnormality, biochemical imbalance, genetic factors, diet, birth complication, injury, and disease (Grandin, 1995a; Rimland, 1990; Schopler & Bristol, 1980).

Currently, the field of autism has expanded to include psychologists, educators, researchers, individuals with autism, and parents who are dedicated to understanding different autistic syndromes and autistic-like behaviors, and identifying effective methods of intervention that will help provide successful outcomes. Parents are writing books (e.g., Eastham, 1990; Gerlach, 1996; Hart, 1993) in order to focus on and explain the condition, and provide individual case histories. The field of autism has had a slow beginning, but support and interest are apparently growing.

CASE STUDIES

Coping with Autism

Accounts of the lives of gifted individuals with autism illuminate their private struggles and challenges; these stories present the outside world with unparalleled insights into their existence. They also create powerful profiles of individuals who do battle with the integration of their strengths and weaknesses on a daily basis. One such example is Donna Williams. Now an adult and an author (Williams, 1992), she continues to display a variety of autistic behaviors. She has strong expressive language mixed with weak receptive skills, which is partially due to sensory jumbling. In her autobiography, she explains how, as a child, she would withdraw into a state of mind filled with colors, rhythm, and sensations—a hypnotic state—similar to drug-induced states. There she felt in touch with her true nature, "softer." She explains that when she did not permit herself this luxury and instead remained alert to her environment, it sapped her energy and her life felt like a battle. Being in the normal world was hard and often painful; however, with great effort and motivation, she could do it for limited periods of time.

Golcomb's (1987) research compared the developmental stages during childhood of Nadia, a gifted, autistic artist, and Eytan, a gifted artist without autism. Nadia drew realistic horses between the ages of three and seven with mechanical precision, but with little or no personal response. Artistically, she appeared to rapidly pass through many developmental stages because of her intense ability to concentrate and draw for a seemingly endless number of hours. By comparison, Eytan, who drew tadpoles, cars, and helicopters in great detail, took much longer to go through stages. Nadia was able at age five to achieve the skills normally demonstrated by a skilled adolescent. However, as she was exposed to school and developed speech, and academic and social abilities, her fixation and her artistic gifts reportedly began to fade.

Bemporad (1979) recounts the story of Jerry Goldsmith, who was born in 1935 and, at the age of four, was diagnosed as autistic by Leo Kanner. According to Bemporad, Goldsmith's gifts were many at the ages of three and four, including having profuse speech (not used for communication), extensive knowledge of the alphabet, the ability to sing a variety of songs and recite their lyrics, an appreciation of classical music by Bach and Mozart, the ability to write, an interest in newspapers, strong math knowledge, the ability to draw and understand detailed maps, and acute hearing and smell. However, he was also grounded in rituals and sameness, a loner, echolalic, antisocial, without empathy, preoccupied, and rigid. According to Bemporad, despite his strengths, as an adult, Jerry is "unable to intuit the social nuances of behavior, and is therefore forced to retreat from a world that is persistently surprising and lacking in regularity" (p. 195). His case history represents a promise that remains largely unfulfilled.

Research on the prognosis for children with autism continues to suggest that the success rate is low (Bemporad, 1979; Lovaas, 1987). According to Bemporad, Lotter's 1978 research found that only 5 to 17% of the subjects in their samples achieved a "good outcome," which was interpreted to mean "a near normal social life with satisfactory functioning at school or work. In contrast, 61 to 74% of children who were previously labeled as having autism showed 'very poor outcomes' meaning they were unable to lead any kind of independent existence" (p. 193). There are, however, notable exceptions.

Temple Grandin

The extraordinary individual selected to be profiled in a detailed case study is Temple Grandin, a gifted/autistic with some savant-like abilities. Dr. Grandin, as she is professionally referred to in her position as assistant professor of animal sciences at Colorado State University, is a contradiction to the findings of many researchers regarding the dismal prognosis for individuals with autism. Her success is likely connected to the rigorous methods used by her parents in her upbringing, some of which parallel techniques that are currently used with children with autism, and that appear promising. In addition to her university position, she currently runs her own consulting business dealing with animal equipment and its design. According to Temple, "One third of all of the cattle that go to meat plants in the U.S. and Canada go through facilities and equipment that I've designed" (7/3/96).

Temple Grandin, who was born in 1947 and raised in the New England portion of the United States, was first brought by her parents to be evaluated when most doctors were not aware of the condition called autism. At age two, she didn't speak and was thought to be deaf; she was eventually diagnosed as being brain-damaged. She was rediagnosed in the early 1950s and labeled as suffering from Classic Infantile Autism.

Family History. Temple's family history is both impressive and "loaded" with unusual accomplishments and health conditions; such revelations often surface when thorough investigations are made into the families of those with autism (Kanner, 1971; Rimland, 1964). She came from a privileged background. Her mother, a visual thinker, is intellectually gifted, and her maternal grandfather invented the automatic pilot for airplanes. Her maternal grandmother was nervous and high-strung, and showed signs of acute sensitivity to sounds; reportedly, as a little girl, she complained that the coal going down the chutes was torture to her ears. In addition, a maternal great-uncle was probably schizophrenic. Temple believes that her father could probably have been classified as having mild Asperger Syndrome; he was clever with numbers, good at the stock market, and very remote, in addition to displaying a hair-trigger temper. Her paternal grandfather was also high-strung and temperamental, and her paternal great-grandfather, a pioneer, reportedly "organized the largest corporate wheat farm in the world" (Grandin, 1995a, p. 148). Temple is one of four children, and one of her sisters, an artistically talented interior decorator, is a visual thinker who is also dyslexic.

Behaviors. I was first introduced to Temple in 1994 when a mutual friend, Carol Lee Berger, a speech therapist and researcher specializing in working with individuals with autism, became aware of my research in the field. Two years later, I had arranged to do a telephone interview with her at 10 A.M., and was startled when the phone rang at 9:50. It was Temple; she was anxious to begin the interview. I soon realized that the precipitous phone call was just one of many behaviors that reflected Temple's strong preoccupation with being responsible and attending to task.

Temple displayed many of the classic signs of infantile autism. In her biography *Emergence: Labeled Autistic* (Grandin & Scariano, 1986), Temple writes that at six months, her body became stiff and unresponsive, and that at ten months, she clawed at her mother, like a trapped animal. She had trouble with expressive language—it all came out like a big stutter—and she did not begin to speak normally until she was almost four years old. Her responsive language was adequate, but she had difficulty in understanding when her parents spoke too quickly, as they did when "they went into what I used to call grown up talk" (7/3/96). She involved herself in stereotyped behaviors, including playing with supermarket doors, chewing on toys and spitting out paper, spreading her feces, and endlessly dribbling sand through her fingers. During the interview, Temple explained:

> When I did that, I would shut the world out. See, I think the reason why the autistic child withdraws is because sensory stimulation hurts. Touch hurts . . . sound hurts . . . so the child is going to withdraw. But the problem is, if you let the child withdraw, then the brain is not going to work. So what you've got to do is keep the kid connected with the world, but at the same time you've got to be careful not to overload his senses. (7/3/96)

Although Temple's sensitivity toward people was not keen—she was not empathetic—her other senses were hyper-vigilant: loud sounds hurt her ears, and certain kinds of touch, like the feel of a petticoat, she described as "sandpaper ripping off nerve endings" (7/3/96). She commented that it was like having "bionic senses" and added, "It drove me crazy!"

As a young child, Temple frequently threw tantrums, and could go from being calm to enraged in a moment. As she was growing up, she directed her antisocial behaviors at adults, and admits to once having bitten a teacher. As she entered puberty, she frequently felt depressed, and became more isolated from her classmates and few friends; she occasionally got into physical fights with them. Her adolescence, unhappily, was characterized by high anxieties and panic attacks. Scholastically, Temple struggled, as she was a late reader, poor at math, weak at controlling her motor functions, sloppy, disorganized, and clumsy in written expression.

Temple, however, was also gifted. Using an individualized test, her intelligence level was measured as 137 at the age of eight. She attributes some of her developed abilities to her many compensatory behaviors, including her autistic determination and passion for succeeding. She also "thinks" using strong visual memory, which means she is adept at seeing the whole picture complete with details; she sometimes visualizes what nobody else can. She explains that when she wants to think of the concept of "dog," or "house," or "chair," she must visualize the picture of one specific dog, or house, or chair—and then another, and yet another. The generic concept of the noun is too abstract and does not exist for her. Temple also has eidetic memory for things that are important to her—like memorizing a piece of top secret equipment for her business. She says it takes about fifteen seconds: "I push the button, and the picture is saved" (7/3/96). During the interview, Temple revealed that she also has some artistic strengths. She is a self-taught draftswoman, and she has perfect musical pitch.

Perhaps one of Temple's most impressive gifts is her empathy and understanding for animals. Her intense preoccupation with horses and cattle began in her adolescence and was later channeled into a career. As a teenager, Temple would visit her aunt's ranch and that of a neighbor's in Arizona, south of Tucson. She spent many hours observing and thinking about animals, and began to understand their behaviors. According to Temple, because some animals such as cattle also have hyper-vigilant senses, she became aware that the same things that scare her also scare them; some examples are shiny metal and loud noises. Later on, in college, she became interested in animal sciences and decided to make it her life's work. Her empathy for animals and deep concern for their fair treatment enabled her to design innovative chutes and other equipment that work efficiently, take into account the natural behaviors of animals, make sense, and are animal-sensitive.

Education/Treatment. Temple has a long history of formal education, beginning with her enrollment in a private nursery school at age two and one-half, and ending with her commencement in a Ph.D. program at the University of Illinois at the age of forty-two. She credits her mother with investing a great deal of time in her education, and extending the process into the home. According to Temple, her mother insisted upon maintaining a very structured environment for her. At the age of two and one-half, she spent over three hours a day with six other children in a private nursery school (a speech teacher worked with her one-half hour each day). She was also involved in a total of two hours of directed mealtimes daily where she remembers that "table manners were drilled into me" (7/3/96). In addition, a nanny was hired to play games and structure interactions with her and her sister after lunchtime.

When Temple needed help understanding numbers, her mother accommodated her visual learning style by placing grooves on colored blocks to correspond to the depicted numbers. The use of wood also strengthened her tactile learning and satisfied her affinity for grasping concepts in a concrete manner. When Temple had difficulty in reading, her mother taught her at home after school, using a defined phonics approach. In addition, both her mother and her teacher collaborated to speak with Temple's classmates in school, explaining to them about her condition, and instructing them how to provide her with support and assistance rather than ridicule.

Temple's formal education was comprised of a number of small, private schools. She described her elementary school as quiet, small (only thirteen students in a class), and traditional, with everyone doing the same thing. She candidly admits, "I wouldn't have liked ten things going on at once" (7/3/96). She explains, "Teachers used structure with me and put limits on my behaviors even though I was always testing them." Her middle school experience was less successful, as it occurred in a somewhat larger facility, and with the onset of puberty, "my hormones kicked in." She spent four and one-half years in a secondary boarding school immediately after being removed from the ninth grade for fighting. Luckily, she connected with a science teacher, a mentor named Mr. Carlock, who took a special interest in her. He directed Temple's fixations about herself, her autistic condition, and animals by teaching her skills (for example, library and index usage) for doing research in the area of animal science.

Temple's postsecondary education was done at Franklin Pierce College in New Hampshire where she initially sought a degree in psychology until she realized she was not on the same wavelength with her fellow students. She soon switched to the field of animals and eventually received her masters degree and Ph.D. in this area from Arizona State University and the University of Illinois, respectively. Temple reveals that she had some difficulties in meeting all of the requirements, but by getting tutoring help and taking her time, she successfully accomplished this educational milestone.

Present Status. During our interview and conversations, I found Temple Grandin to display few of the mannerisms associated with autism. She explained that her "behaviors" improve year by year, gradually, and that friends are often telling her how much she has changed. They point out that her voice is better modulated and that she stands more erect; she also appears less rigid and more relaxed when interacting with others. However, she admits to having to "rehearse" for most social situations and new experiences. Her recent encounter giving a deposition to an officious lawyer seemed to unsettle her because she had not previously prepared. "I didn't know how to handle the situation, and I finally called him an asshole" (7/3/96). In her latest autobiography (Grandin, 1995b), Temple explains that her autistic mannerisms, such as formal speech and directness, often cause others to prejudge her unfavorably. She recounts a story concerning two engineers who discounted her input and would not take her seriously until she impressed them with designs from her portfolio; now she always carries samples of her work with her for situations that necessitate that she validate herself.

Temple is very visual and descriptive in her explanations, and prone to using analogies. In describing the sensory processing of low-functioning, regressive epileptics, she compared their thinking to "a jammed radio station—full of static." She then continued the analogy by explaining that higher-functioning individuals with autism permeate "the jumbled information to get though the static, but the picture looks really blurry" (7/3/96). Temple always appears to be in search of the concrete and the tangible. Throughout our discussions, she literally used some form of the word structured dozens of times in relation to things that she supported or perceived to be good.

During our interview, I had the opportunity to speak to Mike, a friend of Temple's, who described her as being "motivated, easy to be with, humorous, and somewhat mischievous" (7/3/96). In fact, Temple's humor might be described as being dry. In discussing her annoyance with school requirements and the bureaucracy surrounding educational institutions, she complained, "You wonder why there are no Einsteins today? It's because they probably flunked the GREs!" (7/3/96).

Temple openly discusses her use of antidepressants. She uses Tofranil, although she recommends the use of newer drugs such as Prozac for anyone needing such medications. Although she believes these drugs are often necessary to help regulate individuals with autism, she recommends their use as a last resort, and only in moderation. She admits to sometimes missing her former intense drive and passion, but feels she now has more control from within (Grandin, 1995b).

Temple's goals are moral. She strives for tangible accomplishments, which she refers to as "good stuff." By comparison, she says, "I don't want to do bad stuff" (7/3/96). Temple believes that contributing to the world is an act of immortality. To this end, her goals are to improve the treatment of animals by creating sensible standards of animal care, and to further the understanding of autism. "I am what I do," Temple stated emphatically as we ended our interview. And if Temple is to be judged by her accomplishments—the dozens of papers and books she has written on various subjects relating to the fields of both autism and animal science, her plant and equipment designs, and her human squeeze machine which applies deep pressure stimulation to the body and relieves tension—she is doing impressively well.

CONNECTIONS BETWEEN GIFTEDNESS AND AUTISM

Overview

An increasing number of researchers (Donnelly & Altman, 1993; Rimland, 1995) are becoming aware that more and more high-functioning individuals with autism are also being recognized as being gifted and talented. There appears to be a heightened interest in the special abilities that coexist between the two populations. Individuals with autism often possess a strange mixture of talents interspersed with defects, and sometimes their behaviors differ from those of gifted populations only by degree. Grandin (1995b) believes that "[p]eople labeled autistic have an extreme form of traits found in normal people" (p. 176). In support of this belief, she cites work done on autism by Robin Clark:

> The disorder may occur if a person receives too big a dose of genetic traits which are only beneficial in smaller amounts. For example, a slight tendency to fixate on a single subject can enable a person to focus and accomplish a great deal, whereas a stronger tendency to fixate prevents normal social interaction. (in Grandin, 1995b, p. 177)

She concludes that genetic traits are responsible for both severe disabilities and the genius that has "produced some of the world's greatest scientific discourse" (p. 187).

According to Rimland (1978), researchers have observed that it is difficult if not impossible to distinguish autism from true genius at an early age, in some cases. He believes that until the limitations of the condition surface (for example, bizarre behaviors and social disconnectedness), sometimes all that is apparent are the extreme talents. Isabelle Rapin, a neurologist who specializes in autism, also sees the connections between autistic and gifted learners. In her analysis of many of the overlapping behaviors associated with these populations, she questions where autism ends, and oddness begins (in Sacks, 1993).

Shared Behaviors

Some gifted learners are described as working with "autistic singularity." Such a description underscores the notion that many similar behaviors are evidenced in both gifted and autistic populations. Autistic learners are well known for their preoccupations—for their ability to focus with intensity on activities, behaviors, and objects—that seemingly compel their attention. Yewchuck (1987) commented that "[t]heir minds take off on journeys that are beyond their control" (p. 221). Based upon their observations of individuals with autism, Cesaroni & Garber (1991) hypothesize that these individuals may be gifted in their ability to perceive and glean an extended spectrum of information from any given stimulus. By comparison, others filter out and discard subtle sources of stimuli that individuals with autism maintain.

Keeping this is mind, the question evoked is: Does the autistic population see too clearly, and does the rest of the population not see clearly enough? Rimland (1978) recognizes the benefits to gifted learners of being able to acutely concentrate, and concludes, "The ability to narrow attention to a tight focus and hold it there until the mind absorbs and comprehends the topic is a crucial requirement for students of law, mathematics, accounting, medicine and other professions" (p. 79). According to Morelock and Feldman (1991), precocious learners, including the gifted, savants, and gifted/autistic, are "highly attracted to and motivated by their respective areas of achievement" (p. 359). These behaviors and accomplishments can become self-stimulating and are later often sustained.

Lists of negative behaviors used to describe gifted students also run parallel to those characterizing autistic learners; they sometimes differ only in intensity. Both populations are often described as being stubborn, uncooperative, egocentric, discourteous, argumentative, indifferent to conventions of socialization and dress, and resistant to teacher domination. They are also similar in that they may display a rigid fascination in an interest; a compulsive preoccupation with words, ideas, and numbers; perfectionist personalities, and a need for precision; a lack of social skills; the need to monopolize conversations and situations; intellectual prowess; the ability to only visualize models and systems; a proclivity to learn in intuitive leaps; an intense need for stimulation; difficulties in conforming to the thinking of others; and a tendency toward introversion. As to the latter, seventy-five percent of individuals in the general population are extroverts, whereas seventy-five percent of gifted learners are introverts who tend to be loners (Silverman, 1993). It also has been observed that "[t]he tests given to diagnose hyperactivity, disruptive classroom conduct, or extreme withdrawal are often the very tests that spot gifted ability. The excessive energy that creates problems may also be behind the students' achievement in a few areas of interests" (Silverman, 1994, p. 221).

Individuals with autism, as well as gifted learners, are often known for their hyper-vigilant senses. In the 1800s, Galton measured giftedness, in part, based on visual, auditory, and tactile measures of acuity (Colangelo & Davis, 1991). Kanner's original characterization of eleven autistic subjects in 1943 also emphasized these individuals' acute senses. Dabrowski's theory of "overexcitabilities" refers to gifted individuals' heightened sensory awareness and capacity to respond to various types of stimuli due to a highly sensitive nervous system (Silverman, 1993). Piechowski reported in 1979 that one of the gifted subjects he and Dabrowski studied described his tactile, hyper-sensitivity that carried over into his adult life. He said, "My mornings were difficult, for my clothes had to exert the same pressure on both sides on my body. One stocking had to be exactly as tight as the other or I couldn't function" (in Silverman, 1993, p. 15).

Many individuals with autism are visual thinkers (Grandin, 1995b; Rimland, 1978). Grandin maintains her autistic tendency of seeing pictures of nouns in great detail; this is made apparent in the title of her latest book, *Thinking in Pictures and Other Reports from My Life with Autism* (Grandin, 1995b). Likewise, eminent individuals such as Thomas Locker, the illustrator/writer of children's books, and Albert Einstein are also examples of gifted, visual thinkers.

Finally, gifted individuals often complain that they have few friends or intuitive peers (Schopler & Bristol, 1980). In their biographies of their experiences with autism, Grandin (1995b) and Williams (1992) frequently attest to feeling lonely and having difficulties in associating with others. Williams recounts, with great pain, going from friendship to friendship as a child, as no one could understand her. Grandin preferred friends who shared her interests about animals, and still does.

Eminent Individuals with Autistic Traits

Researchers have frequently noted that gifted individuals who function within the normal population also occasionally exhibit characteristics associated with autism (Blake, 1989; Donnelly & Altman, 1994; Grandin, 1995b; Rimland, 1964). Dahlberg (1992), a child psychologist interested in the gifted, suggests that the highly precocious pursue their interests and, in the face of ostracism, become isolated and reclusive. Further, in an effort to escape, they retreat from the larger group and take refuge in "complex cerebration." Dahlberg concludes that they cannot win the praise typically received by others; although they, too, seek approbation; they usually find it in "the unusual, the esoteric, and even in what some would consider the bizarre. Isaac Newton was a perfect example of the latter. Albert Einstein was another" (p. 9). Following is a brief description of individuals who have displayed giftedness along with autistic behaviors. In addition to those listed here, other notable individuals have been mentioned as possibly displaying autistic traits, and future research might begin investigating the musical geniuses Mozart and Bartok.

Albert Einstein. As discussed in Grandin (1995b), Einstein, as a child, was thought to be a dullard; he was a nonspeaker until after the age of three, a loner, and a poor speller, and was often lost in a world of his own. He had a penchant for playing with jigsaw puzzles or making houses out of playing cards. As an adult, his thoughts were scattered, and his lectures were incomprehensible. She further quotes Howard Gardner, who described Einstein as a person capable of "returning to the conceptual world of a child" (p. 180). Einstein's account, as further reviewed in Grandin, was given in the biography *The Private Lives of Albert Einstein* by Highfield and Garter (1993), who believe he was probably an individual with mild Classical Autism or Asperger's Syndrome. Fortunately, he was able to connect his visual imagery with his motivational thinking, and perform productively. He was also fond of unconventional behaviors, including letting his hair grow wild and wearing inappropriately casual, and sometimes outrageous, clothes. She also states that Einstein's proclivity toward wearing loose-fitting clothing might suggest a hyper-sensitivity to touch.

Bill Gates. As an adult, Gates, the head of Microsoft, still perseverates in repetitive rocking and reportedly does so during business meetings and on airplanes. He displays poor social skills and a lack of eye contact; clothing styles and cleanliness are not highly valued. As a child, he demonstrated savant skills such as reciting difficult and long Bible passages while speaking in a monotone voice (Grandin, 1995b).

Bobby Fischer. Fischer, the world chess champion, has been known for his bizarre, antisocial behaviors and mannerisms both as a child and as an adult. As a youth, he was thought to be intense and introverted. According to Rimland & Fein (1988), he worked on a number board, figuring out chess problems, during the ceremonies honoring him at the world chess championship.

Howard Hughes. Hughes, the inventor and entrepreneur, was viewed as being intensely fixated and narrow-minded throughout his life. In his retiring years, he was known for his compulsive cleanliness, fear of diseases, unconventional dress, and odd mannerisms. Reportedly, he would measure the sides of the chocolate cakes he had delivered to his house on a daily basis to be certain they were exactly twelve inches high (Rimland & Fein, 1988).

Sir Isaac Newton. Along with his contributions to science, Newton was known for his profound abilities to concentrate and his "absent-minded professor" habits. He was able to hold mental problems in his mind seemingly endlessly until they were solved. Reportedly, he was once observed, while in deep concentration in a wine cellar, writing formulas in the collected dust (Rimland, 1978).

Vincent Van Gogh. As a child, Van Gogh was viewed as having no outstanding abilities and was instead known for his aloof behaviors. He was a loner who displayed tantrums and lacked social relatedness and responsive language. As an adult, he was poorly groomed, blunt, and lacking in tolerance. According to Vernon W. Grant, in his book *Great Abnormals* (1968), "He talked with complete self-absorption and little thought for the comfort or interest in his listeners" (in Grandin, 1995b, p. 184). His great artistic talent was not revealed until he was twenty-seven years old (latent talent discoveries are not uncommon in the history of autistic individuals with Asperger Syndrome). According to Grandin (1995b), the epileptic seizures he experienced after entering the asylum may have changed his perception and been responsible for some of his compositions. "The swirls in the sky in his painting 'Starry Night' are similar to the sensory distortions that some people with autism have" (Grandin, 1995b, p. 184). In addition, she also observes that the edges of objects are seen as vibrating and possibly "are not hallucinations but perceptual distortions" (p. 184).

Ludwig Wittgenstein. Austrian philosopher Wittgenstein's early childhood development was abnormal; he was considered a dullard, and did not speak until the age of four. Yet, he reportedly had unusual mechanical ability, as he constructed a sewing machine at age ten (Grandin, 1995b). His family profile included depression, and both of his brothers committed suicide. His language was formal and pedantic, and as an adult, he was ostracized for his rigid mannerisms and routinized behaviors.

Family Loading

Studies concentrating on the families of autistic and gifted individuals indicate that the family lineage often includes people displaying great genius as well as various emotional and mental handicaps including autism, schizophrenia, manic-depression, and dyslexia (Donnelly & Altman, 1993; Grandin, 1995b; Kanner, 1971; Rimland, 1964). Galton's early investigations in 1869 into genius and giftedness made note of the connections between eminent individuals and heredity. Gifted individuals were often viewed as coming from "succeeding generations of distinguished families" (in Colangelo & Davis, 1991, p. 6). Similarly, according to Grandin (1991), it is well documented that "autistic traits often show up in a mild degree in the parents, siblings, and close relatives of an autistic child" (p. 26). Temple Grandin's family history itself, lends support to this theory; many members within her immediate and extended family displayed both autistic and gifted traits. Similarly, Albert Einstein's family history, includes a high incidence of autism, depression, dyslexia, food allergies, high intellectual aptitude, and musical talent (Grandin, 1991). During a meeting with Temple Grandin, Einstein's second cousin revealed to her that she had one musically gifted, autistic child and one intellectually gifted child.

In Narayan, Moyes, and Wolff's (1990) survey, investigations of the parents and relatives of twenty-one high-functioning children with autism revealed that many displayed "social gaucheness" and a tendency toward the single-minded pursuit of special, often intellectual, interests. Their backgrounds also included dyslexia, schizophrenia, and high educational achievements. In addition, these authors cite a study done by Delong and Dwyer in 1988 in which the authors found that "in over two-thirds of the families with high functioning autistic children, a first—or second—degree relative had Asperger's syndrome" (p. 529).

Kanner's original case studies of children with autism in 1943 led him to believe that inheritance played a strong role in the condition. He felt that the parents and immediate relatives of these children represented a homogeneous group with regard to intellect and personality (Rimland, 1964). Both parents were frequently college-educated and often had professional occupations. They were physicians, lawyers, chemists, psychologists, successful businesspeople, journalists, and scientists. They were often clever, and several had relatives mentioned in *Who's Who*. Their personalities also tended to be homogeneous, as they were often removed, bookish, formal, preoccupied, detached, focused, unemotional, introverted, formally polite, dignified, and serious. A later study done by Kanner in 1949 investigated the backgrounds of fifty-five additional children with autism; it revealed that the pattern regarding exceptional parentage was consistent with previous findings (Rimland, 1964).

Rimland (1978), in noting that a disproportionate number of autistic learners came from families with high intellect and occupational attainment, concluded the following:

> Many seem to have inherited the neurological make-up that permits them to zero in on whatever attracted their attention. But these children lack the capacity to "zero out," to expand their focus and comprehend the context of whatever they are focussing on. (p. 80)

BEST EDUCATIONAL PRACTICES FOR AUTISTIC

Overview

Individuals among handicapped populations, including autistic learners, often feel discriminated against because they are not supported in the unique manner in which they learn, think, and contribute. Instead, they are unfairly penalized by educational systems that standardize outcomes to fit one pattern of learning. Perhaps the point can best be made by a gifted twenty-six-year-old with dyslexia who dramatically defended his disadvantage rather than his "disability" as follows:

> I have experienced firsthand the anguish, despair, and utter frustration of the inarticulate child who cannot tell the literal person that literacy is not the only level on which he exists; that he is a whole person with many ways of giving and receiving information other than reading and writing, and that the social environment demand for functional literacy tends to overshadow all the other potentials that an individual may possess. . . . The essence of my messages is that functional literacy is not the only measure

of an individual and never was. My argument is with the world of education which tends to forget the relative narrowness of its focus and thereby does some of us grave disservice. (Mindell, 1982, pp. 27–28)

In the study conducted by Lincoln, Courchesne, Kilman, Elmasian, and Allen (1988) describing the intellectual abilities of high-functioning individuals with autism, some of their subjects were perhaps unfairly characterized as having "thought disorders" rather than receptive or expressive language problems. In response to the question on an IQ measure "Who wrote Hamlet?," individuals gave responses such as "Hamster" and "Dr. Suess" (author of *Green Eggs and Ham*). Rather than representing a thinking disorder, such associations could also be considered the creative responses supplied by divergent thinkers to questions for which they do not have the exact answers, much like those stumped contestants give on quiz shows.

It has long been held that giftedness is domain-specific, and not a generalized endowment (Morelock & Feldman, 1991). In fact, one-fourth of the four hundred eminent adults mentioned in Goertzel and Goertzel's book *Cradles of Eminence* (1962) displayed handicapping conditions as well as strong gifts. It is clear that high-functioning individuals with autism, as well as other handicapped populations, package their gifts differently.

According to Colangelo and Davis (1991), Leta Hollingworth, a pioneer in the study of precocity, "argued that it is the business of education to consider all forms of giftedness in pupils in regard to how unusual individuals may be trained for their own welfare and that of society at large" (p. 7). Karnes and Johnson (1991) supported this notion, adding, "Failure to actualize one's potential creates a breeding ground for frustration and poor mental health" (p. 428). Research done by these authors suggests that there are many barriers to accurately identifying giftedness in problem learners and providing appropriate educational opportunities, including the lack of adequate tests, proper training of personnel, use of IEPs and appropriate equipment, adequate funding, career counseling for students, and successful models. In addition to helping gifted/autistic self-actualize and develop their talents for the benefit of society, more emphasis should be placed on providing them with educational programs that best meet their needs.

Early Identification and Screening

In addition to the federal laws that guarantee a free and appropriate education to all students with autism (PL 94-142 and IDEA, PL 101-476) in 1986, the Education of the Handicapped Amendment (PL 99-457) mandated early intervention services. As a result, "many states have begun early intervention programs for children from birth to age 3" (Gerlach, 1996, p. 27).

Psychologists, educators, and researchers interested in effective educational placement for autistic learners concur that early identification is crucial for successful outcomes (Baum, 1984; Bemporad, 1979; Clark, 1992; Gerlach, 1996; Grandin, 1995b; Karnes, 1984; Lovass, 1987; Rimland, 1990). Grandin (1995b) and others believe that the prognosis for individuals with autism improves if intensive education begins before the age of three. In fact, "[e]arly intervention in a good program can enable about 50% of autistic children to be enrolled in a normal first grade" (p. 59). Additionally, Grandin also believes that for those late onset individuals with autism who experience deteriorations, immediate educational intervention is required in order to reverse the patterns "before senses become totally scrambled" (p. 56). Similarly, Richarley, Carruthers, and Mitchell (1991) found that "[w]hen assessment was made in preschool years, intense specialized work with the child led to an adequate school adaptation" (p. 343). Finally, Bemporad's research (1979) underscores that it is easier to successfully mainstream those who are between the ages of two and four into a normal preschool group than to mainstream older children with autism into the primary grades.

Instruments

As there are no medical tests to diagnose autism, it must be behaviorally defined using qualitative measures such as checklists, observations, and family interviews. Accuracy of diagnosis may be difficult, as the behaviors of most children with autism are erratic; therefore, procedures must be done over time to provide a complete profile (Pledgie, 1982; Rutter & Schopler, 1987).

A few instruments are available for use in making a diagnosis, including the American Psychiatric Association's fourth edition of the *Diagnostic and Statistical Manual of Mental Disorders* (DSM-IV, 1994) (Gerlach, 1996). Twelve criteria listed under three major categories are provided. According to Gerlach (1996), "The diagnosis of autism is made if the child displays at least six of the 12 symptoms and a minimum number in each category" (p. 5). In addition, the onset of the condition must have occurred before the age of three. Another diagnostic checklist is available from the Autism Research Institute under the direction of autism expert Bernard Rimland and is known as Form E2 (in Gerlach, 1996). The form is used in combination with observations of speech and behavior patterns. A cumulative score is arrived at, and a cutoff point is set for identification purposes. A diagnosis of autism is determined only after additional tests have been performed that rule out other possible conditions.

When evaluating gifts in autistic populations, special attention must be given to the measures used. Instruments such as standard intelligence measures or Rorschach's often depend on strong verbal skills—expressive and responsive language. As some gifted learners with autism are not highly verbal, such tests should not be used exclusively. In addition, some intelligence measures, such as the WISC-III, give bonus points for speech, which also places handicapped populations at a disadvantage. Rimland (1978) recommends using a battery of tests in combination with observations for autistic populations. His research suggests that when autistic learners achieve IQ scores below 50, they usually remain stable during successive tests; however, when scores measure over 50, sudden improvements may be made even if performance levels remain low. Therefore, these individuals with autism should be evaluated more frequently.

Parent Support

Case stories of individuals with autism, as well as work done by researchers, attest to the invaluable importance of parent support, guidance, and involvement in the lives of gifted/autistic (Baum, 1984; Grandin, 1992; Kanner, 1971; Rimland, 1978; Silverman, 1993). In many instances, parents and teachers act as partners in the education of children with autism, and they are trained together so that the educational programs generated in school can be carried out in the home. Kanner (1971) advised that parents must be included in the therapeutic efforts of autistic learners rather than be viewed as etiological culprits. His longitudinal re-evaluation of eleven children with autism when they became adults revealed that although there were great similarities among the children at age four and five, major differences in treatments, including levels of parental support, the avoidance of institutionalization, and organized programs, shaped their destinies. All of the children he studied did indisputably better under the guidance of caring, trained parents and guardians than they did if they were institutionalized.

According to Piechowski (1989), it is important to stress that "[t]he great achievers and the eminent as a rule have a parent or mentor especially devoted to them" (in Silverman, 1993, p. 22). Further, he concluded "the nurturing generations appear to be necessary to the achieving ones" (p. 22). No smaller measure of support should be expected for capable children with autism whose gifts are just as real, but are often obscured by layers of cerebral and emotional confusion. Finally, in evaluating the importance of parent involvement for children treated in a Toronto Center for autistic learners, it was noted, "Very often an important motivating factor for parents was the poor prognosis given by the clinician who made the original diagnosis. This prognosis often motivated parents to do all that was possible in avoiding such an outcome" (Szatmari, Bartolucci, Bremner, Bond, & Rich, 1989, p. 222).

Training

Many researchers emphasize the importance of teacher training to the successful implementation of programs for autistic learners (Bireley, 1994; Clark, 1992; Maxwell, 1994). Rimland (1978) notes that, unfortunately, it is easier for the federal government to pass laws to mandate the education of all students, including those with autism, than to define methods to carry out this mandate through instruction and teacher training. However, some researchers offer suggestions. Bireley (1994) recommends that a three-way communication should be established among the special education staff, the gifted teachers, and the regular education teachers in order to best accommodate the needs of individuals who are both handicapped and gifted. Ideally, each teacher should be trained in the expertise of the others, and be aware of the best available educational practices. Clark (1992) believes that such training and team approaches are rare, but sees such efforts as distinguishing successful programs from those that do not work. However, caution must be taken to avoid using great amounts of energy for planning and discussing rather than for providing services directly to students. Rimland (1978) warns against "Cadillac" approaches, which he feels can become expensive, inefficient, and fragmented.

Russo and Koegel's (1977) study of the integration of children with autism into public school classrooms provides further evidence of the importance of teacher training to successful programs. Results showed that when classroom teachers from grades kindergarten and first grade were "properly" trained by the special education staff in behavior modification techniques, students with autism could be successfully mainstreamed into classrooms, and gains were sustained into the second and third grades. Training consisted of available readings, discussion, observations, and practice for ten hours prior to the classroom teachers' attempts to work with the students within the classroom. Progress in these students' behaviors were made in the three target areas of language development, social behaviors, and decreased stereotyped mannerisms. Yewchuck (1987) also stressed the importance of training, especially in the development of idiot savants; she recommended that educators look for islands of ability through which to teach.

In conclusion, it should come as no surprise that, as Newson, Dawson, and Everard (1982) have stated, "[a] skilled and imaginative teacher prepared to enjoy and be challenged by the child seems repeatedly to have been a deciding factor in the success and educational placement of high-functioning, autistic children" (in Grandin, 1992, p. 13).

Programming

Generally speaking, effective programs for individuals with autism involve early intervention; extensive teacher and parent training;

structured, full-day services; and behavior modification techniques. Such techniques might include reinforcement, praise, rewards, time out, substitutions, and the use of aversives in order to reduce problem behaviors and build skills (Gerlach, 1996; Grandin, 1995b; Rimland, 1964). In Lovaas's (1987) study, nineteen children diagnosed as autistic who were under the age of four were enrolled in an early intervention program using intense behavior modification treatment for approximately forty hours a week for two or more years. Parents and teachers were trained in the same operant techniques, such as time out, hand slapping, and reinforcement. Growth was seen in increased student responsiveness and expressive language, intelligence scores, social relatedness, abstract thinking, and emotional interactions. Stereotypical behaviors were decreased, and reading, writing, and math skills improved. After the study, treatment was reduced from forty hours to ten when students entered school. Results indicated that forty-seven percent of the students successfully went into normal classes, as compared to one student in the control group, which did not offer the intense treatment; no indications of spontaneous recovery were evidenced.

Structured programs for individuals with autism currently appear to represent best practice. In their follow-up study, Szatmari et al. (1989) investigated sixteen high-functioning individuals with autism eleven to twenty-seven years after their discharge from a Toronto Treatment Center designed for this special population. They found that as adults, eight individuals functioned completely independently, seven had received a high school degree, and seven others had gone ahead to receive a university degree.

Williams (1992) suggests that in dealing with uncooperative autistic learners, there should be "a strongly persistent, sensitive though interpersonal approach to teaching the child that the world will not give up on it, that it will relentlessly make demands of the child. Otherwise, the world will remain closed out" (p. 217). Bemporad (1979) also believes that intense behavioral programs are best for autistic and society. He believes that if an intense, forty-hour-a-week program continued for two years is successful for individuals with autism, as the research suggests, it should be undertaken. He rejects the idea that assigning a special education teacher to one student at a cost of one hundred thousand dollars is excessive compared to the more than two million dollars incurred by individual clients requiring life-long institutionalization.

Channeling

Researchers and individuals with autism who provide insights into their own autistic behaviors are aware of the positive gains that result when fixations are directed or channeled into worthwhile goals or careers. Grandin (1995b) insists that rather than stamping out fixations, the opportunity should be taken to turn a negative into a positive. Among Kanner's eleven original subjects with autism, the three most successful individuals were those who were encouraged to integrate their stereotypical behaviors into useful activities. For example, Donald T.'s preoccupation with measurement was made useful by having him construct and engineer the building of a well; his fixation with insects turned into a study of their classification.

Other gifted individuals have successfully channeled their preoccupations into careers, such as Thomas Locker, the artist and illustrator, who remembers doing little speaking or interacting as a child, as he was continuously thinking visually and communicating in pictures. Similarly, Temple Grandin channeled her fascination with animals and their movements into a career designing humane animal equipment and handling systems. Finally, Yewchuck (1987) reminds us that in some cases, the talents of individuals with autism may represent the only available avenue through which to develop their skills.

Medical Equipment

With advanced technology, a great many mechanical and electrical devices have been developed that can successfully augment services provided to gifted/autistic in educational settings. These devices include the use of computers for facilitated communication (FC). Another example is the Berard auditory training equipment. This system electronically distorts music at random intervals for a period of time in order to help reduce sound sensitivity in autistic learners (Gerlach, 1996). Treated glasses are also sometimes successfully used to filter out irritating color frequencies and vibrations. Grandin's deep pressure squeeze machine helps to make some individuals calmer, as does rolling individuals in heavy gym mats or having them wear weighted vests. Deep body massages and being stroked with soft surgical scrub brushes can also relax autistic individuals with hyper-vigilant senses (Gerlach, 1996). Other useful equipment might include mechanized swings, video cameras and tape recorders, and microcomputers.

Medical Attention

The use of medicine may be needed to help calm individuals who have attention deficits or who are otherwise unable to take educational instruction. Rimland (1978) believes in the early use of vitamin B6 and magnesium supplements for individuals with autism, especially with those displaying late-onset, regressive autism. Grandin (1995b) supports the use of drugs, but only in minimum doses and as a last resort. She believes they can help normalize electrical activity within the brain. Grandin's use of antidepressants has helped to calm her anxieties and modulate her speech. An individual's reactions to food substances should also be monitored carefully. Williams (1992) suggests that some symptoms of autism may be traced to allergies of foods such as milk, wheat, or eggs. Food intolerances may also interfere with the rate of absorption of minerals, vitamins, and toxic substances, and may affect brain function.

Miscellaneous

Additional recommendations for working with autistic learners have been made by a number of researchers and are worth noting. Grandin (1991) believes that teachers need to attend to sensory problems when working with autistic learners; however, educators must also realize that techniques that might be beneficial to some individuals may be painful to others. Minimizing background sounds, being enthusiastic, holding the child's chin, stroking, and using visual imagery and symbols might be excellent strategies for some, while at the same time proving ineffective and obtrusive for others. Sandpaper letters may be useful for teaching reading and writing skills under certain circumstances, and some nonverbal autistic learners can sing words they are unable to speak (Grandin & Scariano, 1986). Grandin also believes that individuals with autism should not be placed in classes with children evidencing severe learning disorders for long periods of time, as it produces poor modeling; instead, they should interact with normal children for as much of the day as possible. She recommends that teachers revisit treatments; what appeared unsuccessful two years ago might prove worthy at a later date (Grandin, 1992).

Gerlach (1996) recommends that the success of autistic learners in educational settings should be data-based and monitored with the use of charts, computers, observational diaries, and checklist evaluations. Others suggest that schools, rather than setting long-term goals for individuals with autism, should concentrate primarily on making daily and weekly gains; long-term objectives are sometimes unrealistic and represent little more than wish lists. It also appears that programs for gifted individuals with autism have a special obligation to capitalize on the strengths of the learners rather than their weaknesses. With this in mind, the Jacob K. Javits Gifted and Talented Students Education Act of 1988, under the auspices of the federal government, awards money to programs designed for a variety of gifted students; preferential treatment is given to minority and handicapped gifted populations.

CONCLUSION

Though at the age of three or four, it may seem that there is little hope for some youngsters with autism, "many develop into autonomous human beings, capable of life that may at least appear full and normal" (Sacks, 1993, p. 107). Similarly, in 1990, Grandin reflected:

> Aware adults with autism and their parents are often angry about autism. They may ask why nature or God created such horrible conditions as autism, manic depression, and schizophrenia. However, if the genes that caused these conditions were eliminated, there might be a terrible price to pay. It is possible that persons with bits of these traits are more creative, or possibly even geniuses. . . . If science eliminates these genes, maybe the whole world would be taken over by accountants (in Sacks, 1993, p. 124).

Grandin (1995a) emphasizes that when she works with animals, she does not try to fix a problem by forcing a solution, but instead inquires about why the animal behaves the way it does in the problematic situation. The lesson here for those working with individuals with autism is to try, at least in part, to get inside the autistic mind—the autistic world—in order to understand and best meet the needs of autistic individuals.

It is also clear that public schools are required to provide gifted individuals with autism with appropriate educational opportunities that address both their strengths and weaknesses. After Mindell (1982) studied the case history of R.D., the twenty-six-year-old gifted metalsmith with dyslexic and epileptic behaviors, she concluded "talent has many faces" (p. 28).

So, too, do the handicaps and disabilities that mask these talents and gifts. Autism is just one.

References

Baum, S. (1984). Meeting the needs of learning disabled gifted students. *Roeper Review,* 7(1), 16–19.

Bemporad, J. R. (1979). Adult recollections of a formerly autistic child. *Journal of Autism and Developmental Disorders,* 9(2), 179–197.

Bireley, M. (1994). The special characteristics and needs of gifted students with disabilities. In J. L. Genshaft, M. Bireley, & C. L. Hollinger (Eds.), *Serving gifted and talented students* (pp. 201–215). Austin, TX: PRO-ED.

Blake, A. (1989). Real "rain men": The mystery of the savant. *Autism Research Review International,* 3(1), 1–7.

Carlton, S. (1992). Fitting a square peg into a round hole. *Roeper Review,* 15(1), 4–6.

Cesaroni, L., & Garber, M. (1991). Exploring the experience of autism through first hand accounts. *Journal of Autism and Developmental Disorders,* 21(3), 303–313.

Clark, B. (1992). *Growing up gifted: Developing the potential of children at home and at school* (4th ed.). New York: Merrill.

Colangelo, N., & Davis, G. A. (1991). Introduction and historical overview. In N. Colangelo & G. A. Davis (Eds.), *Handbook of gifted education* (pp. 3–13). Needham Heights, MA: Allyn & Bacon.

Dahlberg, W. (1992). The childhood dilemma of unusual intellect. *Roeper Review, 15*(1), 7–10.

Davis, G. A., & Rimm, S. B. (1989). *Education of the gifted and talented* (2nd ed.). Englewood Cliffs, NJ: Prentice-Hall.

Donnelly, J. A., & Altman, R. (1994). The autistic savant: Recognizing and serving the gifted student with autism. *Roeper Review, 16*(4), 252–256.

Eastham, M. (1990). *Silent words.* Ottawa, Canada: Oliver & Pate.

Gerlach, E. K. (1996). *Autism treatment guide* (Rev. ed.). Eugene, OR: Four Leaf Press.

Goertzel, V., & Goertzel, M. G. (1962). *Cradles of eminence.* Boston: Little, Brown.

Golomb, C. (1987). *The graphic development of two artistically gifted children: The drawings of Nadia and Eytan.* Viewpoints. (ERIC Document Reproduction Service No. ED 281 622).

Grandin, T. (1987, January). Motivating autistic children. *Academic Therapy, 22*(3), 297–301.

Grandin, T. (1991). *My experiences with visual thinking sensory problems and communication difficulties.* Unpublished manuscript, Colorado State University, at Fort Collins, CO.

Grandin, T. (1992). An inside view of autism. In E. Schopler & G. B. Mesibov (Eds.), *High functioning individuals with autism* (pp. 105–126). New York: Plenum Press.

Grandin, T. (1995a). How people with autism think. In E. Schopler and G. B. Mesibov (Eds.), *Learning and cognition in autism* (pp. 137–156). New York: Plenum Press.

Grandin, T. (1995b). *Thinking in pictures and other reports from my life with autism.* New York: Doubleday.

Grandin, T., & Scariano, M. M. (1986). *Emergence: Labeled autistic.* Novato, CA: Arena Press.

Hart, C. A. (1993). *A parents guide to autism.* New York: Pocket Books.

Kanner, L. (1971). Follow-up study of eleven autistic children originally reported in 1943. *Journal of Autism and Childhood Schizophrenia, 1*(2), 119–145.

Karnes, M. B. (1984). A demonstration/outreach model for young gifted/talented handicapped. *Roeper Review, 7*(1), 23–26.

Karnes, M. B., & Johnson, L. J. (1991). Gifted handicapped. In N. Colangelo & G. A. Davis (Eds.), *Handbook of gifted education* (pp. 441–437). Needham Heights, MA: Allyn & Bacon.

King, A. (1989, March 28). "Rain Man" brings brighter days to autistic families. *The Hollywood Reporter,* 9.

Lincoln, A. J., Courchesne, F., Kilman, B. A., Elmasian, R., & Allen, M. (1988). A study of intellectual abilities in high-functioning people with autism. *Journal of Autism and Developmental Disorders, 18*(4), 505–524.

Lovaas, O. I. (1987). Behavioral treatment and normal educational and intellectual functioning in young autistic children. *Journal of Counseling and Clinical Psychology, 55*(1), 3–9.

Maxwell, E. (1994). The changing developmental needs of the gifted: Birth to maturity. In J. L. Genshaft, M. Bireley, & C. L. Hollinger (Eds.), *Serving gifted and talented students* (pp. 17–30). Austin, TX: PRO-ED.

Mindell, P. (1982). The gifted dyslexic: A case study with theoretical and educational implications. *Roeper Review, 4*(3), 27–28.

Morelock, M. J., & Feldman, D. H. (1991). Extreme precocity. In N. Colangelo & G. A. Davis (Eds.), *Handbook of gifted education* (pp. 347–364). Needham Heights, MA: Allyn & Bacon.

Narayan, S., Moyes, B., & Wolff, S. (1990). Family characteristics of autistic children: A further report. *Journal of Autism and Developmental Disorders, 20*(4), 523–535.

Pledgie, T. K. (1982). Giftedness among handicapped children: Identification and programming development. *The Journal of Special Education, 16*(2), 221–227.

Richarley, G., Carruthers, A., & Mitchell, M. (1991). Brief report: Biological factors associated with Asperger syndrome. *Journal of Autism and Developmental Disorders, 21*(3), 341–348.

Rimland, B. (1964). *Infantile autism: The syndrome and its implications for a neural theory of behavior.* Englewood Cliffs, NJ: Prentice-Hall.

Rimland, B. (1978, August). Inside the mind of the autistic savant. *Psychology Today,* 68–80.

Rimland, B. (1990). Autistic crypto-savants. *Autism Research Review International, 4*(1), 3.

Rimland, B. (1995). Reaching the gifted student with autism. *Autism Research Review International, 9*(2), 2.

Rimland, B., & Fein, D. (1988). Special talents of autistic savants. In L. K. Obler & D. Fein (Eds.), *The exceptional brain* (pp. 474–492). New York: Guilford Press.

Russo, D. C., & Koegel, R. L. (1977). A method for integrating an autistic child into a normal public school classroom. *Journal of Applied Behavior Analysis, 10*(4), 579–590.

Rutter, M., & Schopler E. (1987). Autism and pervasive developmental disorders: Concepts and diagnostic issues. *Journal of Autism and Developmental Disorders, 17*(2), 159–186.

Sacks, O. (1993, December). An anthropologist on Mars. *The New Yorker,* 106–125.

Schopler, E., & Bristol, M. (1980). *Autistic children in public school* (ERIC Document Reproduction Service No. ED 197 577). Reston, VA: Eric Clearinghouse on Handicapped and Gifted Children, Council for Exceptional Children.

Silverman, L. K. (1993). The gifted individual. In L. K. Silverman (Ed.), *Counseling the gifted and talented* (pp. 3–25). Denver, CO: Love Publishing Co.

Silverman, L. K. (1994). Highly gifted children. In J. Genshaft, M. Bireley, & C. L. Hollinger (Eds.), *Serving gifted and talented students* (pp. 217–240). Austin, TX: PRO-ED.

Szatmari, P., Bartolucci, G., Bremner, R., Bond, S., & Rich, S. (1989). A follow up study of high-functioning autistic children. *Journal of Autism and Developmental Disorders, 19*(2), 213–225.

Williams, D. (1992). *Nobody nowhere.* New York: Avon Books.

Yewchuck, C. (1987). Idiot savants: Retarded and gifted. In Baine, D., et al. (Eds.), *Alternative futures for the education of students with severe disabilities* (ERIC Document Reproduction Service No. ED 310 576). Edmonton, Canada.

AN AUSTRALIAN CASE STUDY

Adam's uneven developmental profile throughout infancy and toddler days foreshadowed the perplexing and enigmatic child he was to become. Physical milestones were those of a typical child; however, his emotional development was clearly delayed. He did not form the normal close attachments to his mother, other family members, or "significant others." He was highly dependent on routines, vigorously resisted change, and indulged in a range of obsessive behaviors. He demonstrated an early interest in numbers and written language, but his oral language did not progress past a babbling stage.

Adam's impaired social and communication skills resulted in referral to a child psychologist at three years of age. He was initially assessed (using the Stanford Binet) as being in the average to low average range of ability, and as having "autistic tendencies." Adam's parents were unimpressed with both the management and the outcome of this assessment, taking place as it did in a totally unfamiliar setting with unfamiliar people. This raises yet again the question of appropriate assessment of any child, but particularly a child with one or more exceptional abilities or disabilities.

While acknowledging that Adam clearly had special needs, his parents were also aware that he had some exceptional abilities, none of which had been detected or commented upon in his "assessment." They were determined that he would have as normal an education and environment as their other two children, and so placement in the local preschool followed by enrollment at a regular community school was planned. Adam became a familiar and accepted figure within his comparatively small community, and he gradually became accustomed to the school he was to attend because of his older brother's attendance there.

Adam's enrollment at the preschool from the age of four was relatively uneventful, although it was clear that he embodied a unique combination of strengths and weaknesses. He quickly focused on the computer and managed computer games that would challenge a child several years older. He did not, however, interact at all with the other children, continued to resist efforts to involve him in any social activity, and had great difficulty adapting to any change in routine. He also began speaking in a robotic "Nintendo-like" voice that was still largely incomprehensible to most people.

The principal of the school at which he was to enroll had the opportunity to observe Adam in the preschool setting, and also became familiar with him through various kindergarten orientation activities conducted late in the year prior to his enrollment. She was concerned about his poor language and social skills, and his lack of flexibility, but recognized that he also had strengths. The teachers at the school had a strong commitment to the philosophy of inclusion and were already meeting the needs of children with a diverse range of abilities and disabilities. Nevertheless, it was with some sense of trepidation that the teachers at the small community school welcomed Adam into kindergarten for his first year of formal education.

The teacher referred to the early weeks of kindergarten as "a blur," as Adam and the other kindergarten children adapted to the routines of "big" school. Adam initially found the transition from one activity to another difficult, even when prepared as much as possible; however, as the routines became established, Adam settled down and, within a few weeks, managed this aspect of school very well.

Adam did not respond effectively to verbal instructions, particularly those given to the group rather than to him as an individual. When the teacher included many more visual cues in her instructions, Adam was able to respond much more positively.

Although Adam was confidently reading aloud to his mother before he started school, he was unable to do this with his teacher at school. Adam's teacher was prepared to wait for him to develop the necessary trust in her, and within six months, Adam had the confidence to read aloud to her. Thus, many of Adam's early difficulties were overcome with patience and with small modifications to teaching style.

By the time Adam had concluded his first year at school, his oral language had developed to the point where he was generally understood by most people. His written language achievements were equivalent to those of a child one or two years older, and his number concepts were even more advanced.

There were, however, continuing challenges. It took considerable time for Adam to feel confident with new experiences. He avoided tasks that he found difficult because he constantly strived for perfection and that rarely happened on a first attempt. This reluctance to try new activities meant that it was difficult to extend him. His asocial behavior also meant that accelerating him would be problematic. He continued to have difficulty accepting correction or redirection, saying, "No! No!" repeatedly, babbling to himself, and withdrawing from any social contact on those occasions when he was corrected. He had not yet established any friendships and still avoided even superficial contact with others.

At the conclusion of his first year at school, the teachers reflected that, while it had not been without difficulties, Adam's introduction to the school had been successful. It is interesting to take note of the factors that appear to have contributed to this success.

A Philosophy of Acceptance

The most important factor appears to be that the school was willing to accept Adam, and acknowledged his right to an education in his local school. There was no time or energy spent debating whether or not he should be enrolled. Having established that he had a right to be at the school, the focus was on how to best meet his needs.

An Informed Approach

The teachers operated from a foundation of knowledge. They were able to gather important information concerning Adam from a range of sources, including:

- previous assessments: these focused on his areas of strength and need (although admittedly emphasized the needs rather than the strengths).
- Adam's parents: Adam's early ability to read and his strong number concepts were raised by his parents, which enabled Adam's teacher to prepare for him more effectively.
- preschool teachers: successful management strategies were passed on by the preschool teachers. One of the most important was the fact that Adam needed to be prepared before a preferred activity was to cease, thus giving him time to prepare for the change.
- their own earlier experiences with him: Adam's proficiency with computers, his facility with numbers, his written language ability, and his difficulty with changes in routines were all noted during early contact with Adam, and this information helped the school to prepare for him.

An Acknowledgment of Individual Learning Styles

Adam's teacher noted early in the year that Adam was a "visual child" and was able to adapt her instructional style to meet his needs. The use of less auditory input and more visual cues meant that instruction and directions were more accessible to Adam, thus reducing his frustration and increasing his ability to cope in the regular classroom.

An Acknowledgment of the Concept of Multiple Intelligences

The school was familiar with the concept of multiple intelligences and strived to nurture each individual's strength. This approach was ideal for a child such as Adam, who had clear strengths in addition to obvious areas of need. The school largely rejected the notion of formal intelligence tests, and believed such assessments to be particularly inappropriate for Adam because of the time he needed to establish rapport with any individual and his inability to cope with the change a testing situation would inevitably involve.

Staff Development

The staff at the school were aware that children with particular gifts were in regular classrooms and that they had a responsibility to nurture these gifts. The teachers at the school had been involved in, and continued to be involved in, regular staff development in the area of giftedness. They were sensitive to the needs of these children. They joined Adam's parents and the parents of other children in being strong supporters and advocates for all children with special needs.

Thus, although Adam was still at the beginning of his formal education, his early experiences revealed that a child with such a range of needs and abilities can be catered for in a regular classroom, if surrounded by people with the appropriate skills and, more importantly, a willingness to meet individual needs, whatever they may be.

Emotional Disturbance:
The Beguiling Mask

PART 5

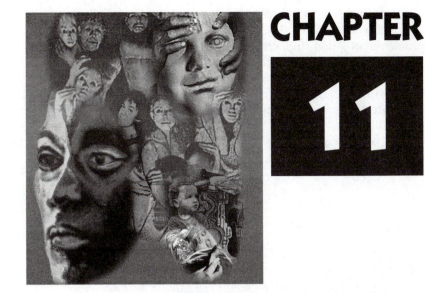

CHAPTER 11

USA PERSPECTIVE

Working with emotionally disturbed gifted children and youth can be energizing and uniquely rewarding. There are occasional down moments, but it is a world of challenge and thoughtful interaction. Patton, Blackbowen, and Fad (1996) expressed how they felt about working with emotionally disturbed students by stating that you can mourn because a rosebush has thorns or rejoice because a thornbush has roses.

Peter, a five-year-old highly gifted boy, arrived home from his first day of kindergarten. The mother, a university colleague, had asked that I be there when Peter returned from school. He characteristically bolted in, greeted us, and asked that I come see his new fish. His mother, barely able to contain herself, blurted out, "How was school?" He nonchalantly replied, "They had lots of toys and books, but a woman kept getting in my way!" His mother grimly smiled and said, "Tomorrow will be better for you." "Oh, I'm not going back," he replied. I murmured a silent prayer that he would soon adjust and do well in school. But, as with many gifted students, his giftedness soon had an overlay of emotional problems and behavior disorders.

Several years later, when I was directing the Office of Gifted and Talented in Washington, D.C., I was reminded of the immensity of the problem that gifted students have with school adjustment. One of the state consultants for gifted education called to tell me that she had just discovered a distressing problem. Fifty percent of the students referred by classroom teachers for the emotionally disturbed program in her state, after extensive psychological testing, were, in reality, found to be gifted students.

It is hard to know who is emotionally disturbed and who is not. In this chapter, I will use emotionally disturbed/behavior disordered (ED/BD) interchangeably.

DEFINITION

The federal definition of behavior disorders/emotional disturbances in the United States focuses on five areas: (1) educational development, (2) social and interpersonal responses, (3) behavioral adjustment, (4) emotional adjustment, and (5) adjustment to school-related events. The term *serious emotional disturbance* (SED) is defined as a condition in which the student exhibits one or more of the following characteristics, over a long period of time and to a marked degree, that adversely affects educational performance:

- inability to learn that cannot be explained by intellectual, sensory, or health factors;
- inability to build or maintain satisfactory interpersonal relationships with peers and teachers;
- inappropriate types of behavior or feelings under normal circumstances;
- a general pervasive mood of unhappiness or depression; or
- a tendency to develop physical symptoms or fears associated with personal or school problems. (34 C.F.R. ch. III, § 300.7)

A simple definition has been suggested by Whelan (1979): emotionally disturbed children do too much of that which children should not do (excess) and not enough of that which children should do more of (deficit).

PREVALENCE

In 1992, the United States Department of Education reported that about 400,670 students between the ages of six and twenty-one had been classified as seriously emotionally disturbed. However, teachers and other school personnel identify from twenty to thirty percent of the school-aged population as exhibiting behavior problems in a given year (Ruben & Balow, 1978). Another important piece of information to be considered is that two to four times as many males as females are identified as emotionally disturbed (Cullinan, Epstein, and Sabornie, 1992), although the ratio equalizes as they become adults. How many of these identified emotionally disturbed students are gifted is unknown.

In school, gifted students experience stress differently from other students because of the uniqueness of their developmental growth. They are often described as intense, and this intensity may be misunderstood by parents and educators. The intensity of gifted students may be directed toward global issues, or it can be turned inward toward personal concerns (Maxwell, 1995).

Terrasier (1985) used the term *Dyssynchronicity* to describe the dilemma of being a gifted student. He maintained that because of their advanced cognitive ability, the gifted are faced with the dilemma of experiencing different mental, emotional, social, and physical ages. This phenomenon, coupled with intensity, creates experiences that are qualitatively and quantitatively different.

An example of Dyssynchronicity can be noted in the behavior of a nine-year-old boy, whose parents brought him to the University of South Florida Gifted Child Center for an intellectual evaluation for entrance into a public school for the gifted. The mother stated that the boy had appeared in several television commercials and had participated in a number of community theater productions. When I met him, I saw an attractive, dark-haired, blue-eyed, high-energy young man. We exchanged greetings, and when I indicated that I was going to ask him some words and their meanings, he mischievously asked if he could have his friend answer for him because, he said, rolling his eyes, "I'm tired." I asked if the friend were there. He said, "Yes," and gestured toward his right hand. I decided to humor him by directing my questions in the direction of his hand, while he, of course, answered. He was assessed as highly gifted, and I recommended him for the gifted school. In an interview the following day with a group of teachers, he again said, "I'm tired and would like my friend to answer." Sadly, the teachers interpreted his behavior as immature and bizarre, and his application to the school was rejected. The teachers failed to see any value in his powerful imagination or his need to playfully interact with adults.

I began to counsel the family, particularly the boy. I found him to be very persistent, exceedingly curious, and capable of long periods of concentration. He had deep emotional sensitivity that allowed him to accurately portray characters far beyond his maturity level. His family shared many stories of great elation, but they also shared stories of great anguish in which the boy and the family had to deal with rejection or misunderstanding of his giftedness. This young man represents a gifted student who manifests emotional disturbances that, in turn, overshadow his giftedness, or one whose giftedness is perceived as being behavior disordered.

Where does the problem start? The problems arise when the social interactions and transactions between gifted children and their social environment, including school and the family, are inappropriate.

A RESEARCH-BASED THEORY OF EMOTIONAL DEVELOPMENT

Dabrowski (1964, 1972) theorized that intensity signals high potential for advanced levels of development. In his research, he found that intensity or superabundance of responsiveness to stimuli can be noted in five dimensions: (1) psychomotor, (2) sensual, (3) emotional, (4) imaginative, and (5) intellectual.

According to Dabrowski, gifted students may demonstrate intensity in all five dimensions, with some dimensions being more active than others. He called these energies, or intensities, overexcitability. Research comparing overexcitabilities (OEs) has found a greater incidence of OEs in gifted children and adults in comparison with other populations (Felder, 1982a, 1982b; S. Gallagher, 1985; Piechowski & Colangelo, 1984; Piechowski, Silverman, & Falk, 1988). When parents and educators fail to understand the overexcitability of gifted students, the students' behavior may become even more intensified and manifest itself in emotional disturbance or behavior disorders. Dabrowski's theory has four levels: (1) self-serving motivations, manipulations, self-protectiveness, exploitation, and wheeling and dealing; (2) struggle to attain one's inner sense of self; (3) struggle to live up to one's inner desire; and (4) self-actualization.

Dabrowki's theory of emotional development addresses a core of personal characteristics that distinguish gifted students' behavior. It is essential in the nature of many gifted students to valiantly fight for the principles that they believe in (level 3) and to attempt to be individuals who are true to themselves (level 2); however, the last level, level 4, is the most difficult—the attempt to self-actualize and, in the words of a gifted twelve-year-old, "to make a difference."

Silverman (1995) describes gifted students as demonstrating a persistent drive toward action; intense feelings, fears, joy, and caring; imagination and an extensive fantasy life; a deep and rich response to sensory stimuli; and a mind that is always responding because the world is full of so many exciting things to do, see, and experience. This intensity is reflected in the words of a gifted student who asked me, "Do you have trouble sleeping? I can't turn my mind off." When the feedback that gifted students receive from school personnel indicates that "they" are the problem, gifted students without appropriate coping mechanisms begin to feel estranged from classmates and school in general.

Characteristics That Cause Concern for Gifted Students

Persistence in gifted students is often viewed negatively by parents and teachers, and sometimes referred to as stubbornness. Parents state that if they do not take meals to their gifted children when they are deeply engaged in projects, the children simply do not take the time to eat. When persistent gifted students are forced to stop their work on projects, at home or in the classroom, they may be less than cooperative and viewed as willful or belligerent.

Another characteristic of gifted students' behavior that causes concern for parents and teachers is perfectionism. When gifted students are trying to complete a project to their satisfaction, they often become very frustrated. Some gifted students learn to refuse to try if the task cannot be accomplished in the manner that they want it to be. This reaction may be the beginning of persistent underachievement that can last throughout their schooling (Whitmore, 1980). One gifted student who was very frustrated with her artwork angrily shouted, "I have a picture in my head of how it should look and this isn't it." She then ripped the sketch into pieces.

Sensitivity of gifted students can also be viewed as a problem. However, Dabrowski (1964, 1972) viewed sensitivity as a power to enable gifted students to bring real change when appropriately addressed toward world problems. Yet sensitivity causes gifted students to perceive criticism and rejection of their ideas or behavior as very disturbing. This disturbance can lead to depression, and coupled with intensity, the sensitivity of gifted students can serve to magnify problems. When gifted students are unable to reconcile their behavior to expected norms, depression may also become a serious problem.

Measurement and Assessment

No test yields a mental health quotient; instead, careful observation, documentation, and descriptions of behaviors are used by professionals to gauge mental health. For example, an accurate record of the number of times a child is aggressive or runs around the classroom, when these events occur, and under what circumstances is very helpful in predicting behavior and deciding on appropriate intervention.

Quay (1975, 1979) and Van Issen, Quay, and Love (1980) compiled clusters of behavior ratings by teachers and parents and other information about children's responses to construct questionnaire items, resulting in the Revised Behavior Problem Checklist (Quay & Peterson, 1987). This checklist helps teachers and professionals identify six dimensions of behavior: (1) conduct disorder, (2) socialized aggression, (3) attention problems–immaturity, (4) anxiety-withdrawal, (5) psychomotor behavior, and (6) motor excess. Four of the clusters are listed in Table 11–1.

Kauffman (1993) attempted to link intervention and education strategies to classifications similar to those suggested by Quay and Peterson (1987). He calls them the facets of Disordered Behavior: (1) attention and activity disorders; (2) conduct disorder: overt aggression; (3) conduct disorder: covert antisocial behavior; (4) delinquency and substance abuse; (5) anxiety: withdrawal and other disorders; (6) depression and severed behavior; and (7) psychotic behavior.

Assessment also includes the use of projective tests, objective tests, behavior checklists, behavior observations, and interview schedules. Examples of instruments and discussion of their strengths and weaknesses are included the text *Educating Exceptional Children* (Kirk & Gallagher, 1983).

GOALS FOR WORKING WITH EMOTIONALLY DISTURBED/BEHAVIOR DISORDERED GIFTED

In working with emotional disturbances/behavior disorders in gifted students, it is essential that we help them learn to prioritize their goals, values, and investments of time and energy. A second goal is to help them develop coping strategies to manage and deal with daily life stress. As gifted students experience risks and pressures, their abilities can become detoured toward defensive and avoidance patterns (Rimm, 1987). Gifted students expect the world to make sense, and they react strongly when it does not. This need for precision is particularly characteristic of the highly gifted (Kline & Meckstroth, 1985). Hollingworth (1931) contended that highly gifted children (IQ above 145) were more prone to develop social adjustment problems than the mildly gifted. Terman and Oden (1947) also found this phenomenon in their research.

Dealing with Stress

Gifted students describe their stress as being out of control. This stress may manifest itself in physical symptoms such as a faster heart rate, perspiration, flustered complexion, stomach ache, back aches, and shortness of breath. In addition to the physical manifestations of stress, Kueczen (1987) states that students may also exhibit a range of antisocial behavior in response to stress. These behaviors include violence,

Table 11-1 Dimensions of disordered behavior

Conduct Disorder	Anxiety-Withdrawal
Fighting, hitting, assaultive	Anxious, fearful, tense
Temper tantrums	Shy, timid, bashful
Disobedient, defiant	Withdrawn, seclusive, friendless
Destructiveness of own or others' property	Depressed, sad, disturbed
Impertinent, "smart," impudent	Hypersensitive, easily hurt
Uncooperative, resistive, inconsiderate	Self-conscious, easily embarrassed
Disruptive, interrupts, disturbs	Feels inferior, worthless
Negative, refuses direction	Lacks self-confidence
Restless	Easily flustered
Boisterous, noisy	Aloof
Irritability, "blows up" easily	Cries frequently
Attention-seeking, "show-off"	Reticent, secretive
Dominates others, bullies, threatens	
Hyperactivity	
Untrustworthy, dishonesty, lies	
Profanity, abusive language	
Jealousy	
Quarrelsome, argues	
Irresponsible, undependable	
Inattentive	
Steals	
Distractibility	
Teases	
Denies mistakes, blames others	
Pouts and sulks	
Selfish	

Socialized Aggression	Immaturity
Has "bad companions"	Short attention span, poor concentration
Steals in company with others	Daydreaming
Loyal to delinquent friends	Clumsy, poor coordination
Belongs to a gang	Preoccupied, stares into space, absent-minded
Stays out late at night	Passive, lacks initiative, easily led
Truant from school	Sluggish
Truant from home	Inattentive
	Drowsy
	Lack of interest
	Lacks perseverance, fails to finish things
	Messy, sloppy

Note. From Quay Classification, in *Psychopathological Disorder of Childhood* (2nd ed., pp. 17–18, 20–21), H. C. Quay and J. S. Werry (Eds.), 1979, New York: Wiley. Reprinted with permission.

vandalism, aggression, boasts of superiority, criminal activity, dare-devil stunts, fire starting, impatience, negativity, rudeness, self-harm, self-abuse, stealing, testing or defying authority, use of bad language, difficulty in getting along with friends, jealousy of close friends and siblings, vicious acts against animals or other people, clinging dependency, dislike of school, downgrading of self, escapism, exclusive day-dreaming, regressive behavior, lying, overeating, and procrastination.

As a graduate research assistant to Hewitt, director of the UCLA Neuoropsychiatric Institute, I learned to look for patterns and search for approaches that would work. Hewitt and Taylor (1980) stressed the importance of working with the child and the family and used the metaphor of a baseball game to reinforce his point. He said that someone from another culture who was trying to understand baseball might decide to pay exclusive attention to the behavior of the first base-man. This observer would follow in great deal and report at length on the first baseman—how he fields, throws, bats, runs, and so forth. However, even with the most intense examination of one player, the observer could never understand the nature of the game. Consequently, to study a child in great detail without examining the social system in which the child exists is likely to inhibit full understanding of the child and his or her behavior (Hewitt & Taylor, 1980).

Hewitt and Taylor (1980) described the emotionally disturbed child as a socialization failure, whose behavior for whatever reason is mal-adaptive according to the expectations of the society in which the child lives. The child does things that teachers or parents want them to stop or, on the other hand, fails to do things that teachers and parents think they ought to do. This is particularly important in the case of gifted children, who often resist conforming or giving away their sense of autonomy. Payne et al. (1991) stated that emotionally disturbed/behavior disordered children behave in ways that teachers consider undesirable or inappropriate, and their behavior differs from that of normal children along three crucial dimensions: (1) severity, (2) chronicity, and (3) context.

Intervention Strategies and Models

There are different conceptual models to use with children with ED/BD that include assumptions about what the problem is, how it came about, and what can be done about it (P. Gallagher, 1988). Five models are displayed in Table 11–2. Some interventions are focused on the child, whereas others are focused on an interaction.

Behavior Analysis Model. Teachers and parents often discover when they are involved in behavior analysis that they have been reinforcing inappropriate behavior in their students. They may also discover that they have been teaching the children to misbehave by paying attention to and thereby reinforcing misbehavior.

Table 11-2 Five models and interaction of cause, assessment, and intervention

	Biophysical Model	Behavioral Model	Psychodynamic Model	Sociological Model	Ecological Model
Cause	Genetic factors, neurological damage, or biochemical problem	Environmental events, or antecedents and consequences of behavior	Effect of interactions between child and significant others on personality development and resolution of internal conflicts	Breaking rules that govern social interactions	Mismatch between child and environment
Assessment	Conducted by medical personnel; teacher serves as a screening and a referral agent	Teacher observes and identifies critical events in the environment, defines target behaviors, and identifies reinforcers	Conducted by qualified psychologist; teacher gives various observational data	Teacher provides information on how cultural values are transmitted to children and representativeness of minority values in curriculum	Teacher may identify his or her academic demands and ways in which child's behavior is disruptive in school setting
Intervention	Teacher monitors drug or diet therapy, notes side effects, and makes modifications in daily schedule if required	Systematic application of applied behavior analytic principles (positive reinforcement, extinction, time-out, overcorrection, and so on)	Teacher selects low-stress curriculum and materials; trained teachers may conduct play therapy	Teach individual coping behavior to match environmental expectations	Teacher changes physical organization of classroom (for example, carrels); teacher uses effective materials, predictable rule enforcement, and motivational feedback

Note. From *Educating Special Learners* (p. 347), by Cartwright et al., 1995, Belmont, CA: Wadsworth. Copyright 1995 by Wadsworth Publishing Co.

In my sixth grade class of gifted children, a young man would become distraught at school failure or perceived slights by peers or teachers and begin to weep profusely. At home, his parents were very solicitous when this behavior occurred. When he exhibited the same behavior in school, I would continue with the lesson and signal to his classmates that everything was alright. He would eventually begin to snuffle, wipe his face, and involve himself in the classroom work. He was an only child and overprotected; his parents drove him to and from school, and did not permit him to have friends over for visits or to play outside the home.

Psychodynamic Model. By emphasizing cognitive skills with students, as their academic accomplishment and self-concept improves, a side effect is a growing ability to cope with life situations. This approach has been referred to as psychodynamic and involves minimizing stress in the school environment and home. This model includes psychoanalytic ideas about unconscious motivation and puts a premium on the teacher/pupil relationship.

Another intervention is talking out the problem through play therapy, reflective listening, or reality interviewing developed by Glasser (1969). He suggests working with the entire class to hold classroom meetings of three types: (1) open-ended meetings in which any topic can be discussed, (2) social problem solving in which students bring up problems for discussions, and (3) educational diagnostic meetings in which students talk about educational goals and problems.

Ecological Model. Ecological strategy (Rhodes, 1967) maintains that human problems result from improper interaction between the individual and the environment, and the emphasis is on modifying stress in the ecology. It was adapted from research in biological ecology and ecological psychology. Every child is enmeshed in a complex social system. In the ecological model, education is concerned with the child in the classroom, with the family and the neighbors, and in all other areas of the social environment.

Biophysical Model. The biophysical model involves assessment by medical personnel. The teacher serves as a screening and referral agent and monitors the drug therapy or diet therapy prescribed by the physicians or psychiatrists.

Sociological Model. The sociological model stresses teaching the individual coping behavior to match environmental expectations. It is concerned with breaking rules that govern social interactions.

Sample Classroom Activity for Emotionally Disturbed Gifted Students

Perls (1973), the most notable contributor to Gestalt theory, was fond of saying, to lose your mind, you must come to your senses. Activities such as role reversal, in which a student takes on the role of another person; role-playing the indecisive parts of the self; spontaneously creating dialogue with an empty chair; and awareness-building exercises such as boundary breaking are activities based on Gestalt therapy to improve self-awareness and understanding.

Selected Classroom Activities Based on Gestalt Theory

The following activities are from *Leadership: Making Things Happen,* by Sisk and Shallcross (1986).

Activity 1. Think of musical instruments. Select one. List as many adjectives as you can to describe the instrument. Now, in front of each adjective, insert the words "I am . . .". As students describe the instrument, they become aware of clues about how they feel about themselves.

Activity 2. Still another way of becoming more aware of oneself is suggested by psychiatrist Bob Partridge, who asks students to look at where they might think they are in their lives by drawing the hands on an empty clock face. Where would you draw the hands on the clock face?

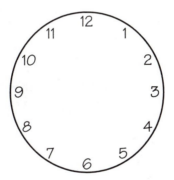

This is a very revealing activity. Although age needs to be taken into account, for most students, their responses reveal basic attitudes they hold about themselves.

Activity 3. *Book of Lives:* Ask students to get a blank bound book and, over a week or two, collect sixteen one-sentence autobiographies in the book. Have them approach people, tell them what they are doing, and ask them to contribute their life stories. Each autobiography is stated as a single sentence. The students can add their own autobiography as the sixteenth contribution. This activity is an invitation to accidental poetry, to fresh insight, and to self-revelation.

In activities like these, there are clues to how students feel about themselves in the way they talk about themselves: fat, lazy, slow, getting old, witty, healthy, on top of things, happy. Each student possesses a small voice inside that gives impressions, opinions, directions. These inner messages are either self-affirming or self-condemning, or in Gestalt language, they represent our Top Dog and Underdog subselves.

Cole-Whittaker (1979) suggests an effective format for building awareness of one's behavior and being in charge of oneself. There are four phases: (1) observe, (2) choose, (3) give up blame, and (4) create the way you want it. Gifted students who are emotionally disturbed/behavior disordered relate very positively to this approach because it helps to empower them to be in control of the situation.

CASE STUDY

Case Study of a Gifted Student with Emotional Disturbance/Behavior Disorder

A combination of interviews; observations in and out of school; anecdotes from family, teachers, and acquaintances; and formal assessments were used to complete this case study of a young man I choose to call Sam.

By parental account, Sam was remarkable from a very early age. By the age of two, he was reciting correctly numerous verses and poems that had been read to him, and by the end of his third year, he was spontaneously counting and computing. At four, he was dictating stories to his mother, and at age five, he was reading fluently on a third-grade level. From age six to age twelve, he showed a penchant for mathematics and puzzles. Sam was identified early as gifted, with a battery of standardized intelligence tests; translated into IQ terms, his scores ranged from 137 to at best 180.

Sam was born into a family that recognized, valued, and fostered intellectual ability. His two sisters were also highly gifted; both of them studied law. One became a judge, and the other an international corporate lawyer. The father was a very successful and well-respected businessman, and the mother was active in local politics and chairperson of the local school board. Early on, Sam experienced close parental involvement. The family was somewhat protective, but they were totally committed to his talent development. He was seemingly intuitive in math and described his advanced skill as "manipulating pictures in his mind." However, he was somewhat restricted emotionally and hesitant to interact with others. Sam was exposed to advanced teaching and instruction from teachers who valued his gifts, particularly in mathematics and science. Because of his ease in excelling in math, he was given progressively difficult material. His personal frustration resulted from the fact that he was better in math than other subjects, particularly creative writing.

As an adolescent, he was distressed with his difficulty in making friends and described himself as being more comfortable with adults. He expected a great deal from himself, and his teachers said that he was his own worst critic. He set high performance standards for himself and others. His parents rewarded these high standards and supported his efforts toward achieving. They encouraged him to challenge himself and rewarded reasonable rational behavior. They helped him seek out numerous outside opportunities, such as university gifted programs, service projects, and summer internships.

Sam was ambitious, pragmatic, and somewhat wary of people who were not highly principled. In an interview, he stated that he was fearful of people who might deter him from his career goals. He was passionately involved in the discipline of mathematics and planned to apply to the Massachuetts Institute of Technology (MIT). He scored at the 99th percentile on the ACT and 1540 on the SAT and applied to Johns Hopkins University, Boston University, and MIT. All three accepted him, and he selected MIT, where he began to work closely with a professor he described as a mentor. A major stress event occurred when Sam was in his first year of college; his father was convicted of a felony and sent to prison. He began to have difficulty studying, and because he was geographically and emotionally separated from his family, he keenly felt the loss and the perceived betrayal of his father. He began to have sleep disturbances, withdrew from his family, was restless, and had difficulty concentrating.

Still another trauma occurred when his major professor at MIT published a paper using Sam's ideas without giving any reference to or acknowledgment of his work. The professor also used several of Sam's ideas in a presentation at a national Congress on Mathematics. Sam experienced the first fruits of his talent appreciated, then appropriated. He had trusted his instructor and felt deeply betrayed. In Sam's mind, the professor replicated the father's betrayal. He was unprepared for dealing with this phenomenon, and his perception was that he had failed. He became deeply discouraged and found it hard to persevere and advance, and eventually he decided to leave the university.

At home, he began driving a taxicab. He felt alienated from his family and moved into an inner-city apartment. He stated that he had to pay a certain amount per day to use the cab, and because he had few fares, he was losing considerable money on a daily basis. When I last interviewed him at age nineteen, he indicated that he had lost his ability to realistically plan for his future, and he described feelings of vulnerability. Sam, shortly thereafter, committed suicide by leaping from an airport parking facility. Sam's failure to develop the adaptive techniques that he needed to cope with his increasingly perceived failure, problems, and progressive isolation from meaningful social relations all represent paths to his suicide.

CONCLUSION

Kirk and Gallagher (1983) state that suicide often represents an intense rage against more powerful adults and is seen by the child or young person as the only action that will have some impact on those at whom he or she is angry.

I would like to return to the rosebush metaphor. We can mourn because a rosebush has thorns or rejoice because a thornbush has roses. Parents and educators who cannot see the joy and humor in life's struggles will soon find that the thorns of the rosebush will drain their enthusiasm and strength to endure the difficult periods. Teaching and working with twice exceptional children, gifted and behavior disordered/emotionally disturbed, requires that teachers and parents modify and change the environment of the students. The goal is to teach and improve the students' ability to learn and execute more appropriate behavior, which will enable them to develop their gifts and talents to enrich not only their own lives, but the lives of others as well.

REFERENCES

Cartwright, G., Cartwright, C., & Ward, M. (1995). *Educating special learners.* Boston: Wadsworth.

Cole-Whittaker, T. (1979). *What you think of me is none of my business.* La Jolla, CA: Oak Tree Publications.

Cullinan, D., Epstein, M., & Sabornie, E. (1992). Selected characteristics of a national sample of seriously disturbed adolescents. *Behavioral Disorders, 17*(4), 273–280.

Dabrowski, K. (1964). *Positive disintegration.* Boston: Little, Brown.

Dabrowski, K. (1972). *Psychoneurosis is not an illness.* London: Gryf.

Felder, R. F. (1982a). *Responses of gifted education and chemical engineering graduate students on the OEQ and DRI.* Paper presented at the National Association for Gifted, New Orleans, LA.

Felder, R. F. (1982b). Identifying and dealing with exceptionally gifted children: The half blind leading the sighted. *Roeper Review, 8,* 174–177.

Gallagher, P. A. (1988). *Teaching students with behavioral disorders: Techniques and activities for classroom instruction,* Denver, CO: Love Publishing Co.

Gallagher, S. A. (1985). A comparison of the concept of over-excitability with measurement of creativity and school achievement in sixth grade students. *Roeper Review, 8,* 115–119.

Glasser, W. (1969). *Schools without failure.* New York: Harper & Row.

Hewitt, F. M., & Taylor, F. D. (1980). *The emotionally disturbed child in the classroom: The orchestration of success.* (2nd ed.). Needham Heights, MA: Allyn & Bacon.

Hollingworth, L. (1931). The child of very superior intelligence as a special problem in social adjustment. *Mental Hygiene, 15,* 1–6.

Kauffman, J. M. (1993). *Characteristics of emotional and behavioral disorders of children and youth.* New York: Macmillan.

Kirk, S., & Gallagher J. (1983). *Educating exceptional children.* Dallas, TX: Houghton Mifflin.

Kline, B. E., & Meckstroth, E. A. (1985). Understanding and encouraging the exceptionally gifted. *Roeper Review, 8,* 24–30.

Kueczen, B. (1987). *Childhood stress.* New York: Delta.

Maxwell, E. (1995). The changing developmental needs of the gifted: Birth to maturity. In J. Genshaft, M. Bireley, & C. Hollinger (Eds.), *Serving gifted and talented students* (pp. 17–30). Austin, TX: PRO-ED.

Patton, J., Blackbowen, J., & Fad, K. (1996). *Exceptional individual in focus.* Englewood Cliffs, NJ: Prentice-Hall.

Payne, J. S., Patton, J. R., Kauffman, J. M., Brown, G. B., & Payne, R. G. (1991). *Exceptional children in focus.* Columbus, OH: Merrill.

Perls, F. S. (1973). *The Gestalt approach and eye witness to therapy.* Palo Alto, CA: Science and Behavior.

Piechowski, M. M., & Colangelo, N. (1984). Developmental potential of the gifted. *Gifted Child Quarterly, 28,* 80–88.

Piechowski, M. M., Silverman, L., & Falk, R. F. (1988). Comparison of intellectually and artistically gifted on five dimensions of mental functionality. *Perceptions and Motor Skills, 60,* 539–549.

Quay, H. C. (1975). Classification in the treatment of delinquency and anti-social behavior. In N. Hobbs (Ed.), *Issues in the classification of children* (Vol. 1) (pp. 377–392). San Francisco: Jossey-Bass.

Quay, H. C. (1979). Classification. In H. C. Quay, & J. S. Werry (Eds.), *Psychopathological disorder of childhood* (2nd ed.) (pp. 17–21). New York: Wiley.

Quay, H. C., & Peterson, D. R. (1987). *Manual for the revised behavior problem checklist.* Coral Gables, FL: Author.

Rhodes, W. C. (1967). The disturbing child: A problem of ecological management. *Exceptional Children, 33,* 637–642.

Rimm, S. (1987). Why do bright children underachieve? The pressures they feel. *Gifted Child Today, 10,* 30–36.

Ruben, R., & Balow, B. (1978). Prevalence of teacher identified behavior problems: A longitudinal study. *Exceptional Children, 45,* 102–111.

Silverman, L. (1995). Highly gifted children. In J. Genshaft, M. Bireley, & C. Hollinger (Eds.), *Serving gifted and talented students.* Austin, TX: PRO-ED.

Sisk, D., & Shallcross, D. (1986). *Leadership making things happen.* Buffalo, NY: Bearly Ltd.

Terman, L., & Oden, M. (1947). *Genetic studies of genius: Vol IV. The gifted child grows up.* Stanford, CA: Stanford University Press.

Terrasier, J. C. (1985). Dyssynchronicity—Uneven development. In J. Freeman (Ed.), *The psychology of gifted children* (pp. 265–274). New York: Wiley.

Van Issen, A., Quay, H. C., & Love, C. T. (1980). Interrelationships among three measures of deviant behavior. *Exceptional Children, 46,* 272–276.

Whelan, R. J. (1979). The emotionally disturbed. In E. L. Meyer (Ed.), *Basic readings in the study of exceptional children and youth* (pp. 329–330). Denver, CO: Love Publishing Co.

Whitmore, J. (1980). *Giftedness, conflict and underachievement.* Needham Heights, MA: Allyn & Bacon.

CHAPTER 12

AUSTRALIAN PERSPECTIVE

Mark: A Case Study

Mark is the older of two boys in a middle-class family, currently living in a medium-sized country town in New South Wales, Australia. His father holds a clerical position, as did his mother before she became a full-time homemaker.

Mark demonstrated many characteristics of a child with great gifts from a very young age: he read before he walked, quickly developed a fascination with numbers, and could occupy himself for hours at a time from an early age. It was not these traits, however, which prompted Mark's parents to seek advice, but rather his violent tantrum behavior, his inability to relate to family members, and the range of antisocial and obsessive-compulsive behaviors in which he indulged. Mark's behavior was causing great anxiety and tension within the immediate and extended family, rapidly eroding his mother's confidence in her parenting ability, and putting him at risk of both physical and emotional harm from family members who loved him but who could not understand, manage, or even tolerate his behavior.

Early visits to educational psychologists resulted in the focus being placed on Mark's behavioral symptoms, which were viewed as the result of poor parenting. Reports of Mark's extraordinary abilities were ignored, and requests for specific testing of Mark were inexplicably denied. The patronizing and unhelpful attitudes of those professionals with whom Mark's parents first came into contact caused a long-term distrust of, and cynicism about, the so-called "helping professions."

When Mark was almost four, his parents became aware of an early intervention unit in the local area designed to cater to preschool children with a range of difficulties, and they arranged to visit there with Mark. After a short time, the teacher suggested that the parents leave Mark at the center for a couple of hours, to enable the staff to see how Mark operated in that setting. This was the first occasion on which Mark, rather than the parents, was observed and in any way assessed. Mark's significant social and emotional problems were immediately apparent, but more significantly, the highly experienced early intervention teacher was able to identify Mark as a boy with high levels of ability, a fact that was confirmed shortly after when he scored within the top 0.03% of the population when assessed on the WISC-R.

The positive response of the particular early intervention teacher at this time not only helped put into place an appropriate program for Mark, but did much to restore his parents' confidence in educational professionals and, to use his mother's words, "saved Mark's life and our sanity."

Within six months of being placed on both a behavior modification program and a suitable learning program, Mark's obsessive-compulsive behavior reduced dramatically, and there were fewer tantrums. Mark was then able to enroll early in kindergarten.

Mark's experiences throughout his early years at elementary school depended very much on his particular grade teacher. In grade 1, a program was tailored to meet Mark's highly individual needs. He was accelerated for both mathematics and language into upper elementary grades, but spent significant time with age peers as his social skills developed. In subsequent years, however, and following some staff changes, Mark was enrolled in an "age-appropriate" class where he would "learn how to conform," despite the strong advocacy of his parents. Not surprisingly, his behavior and achievement levels deteriorated rapidly.

With the help of the local media and other concerned parents and teachers, but with significant resistance from local educational authorities, the plight of the gifted children in that small country region was highlighted. This resulted in some large-scale assessments being carried out, which identified forty-six gifted children whose educational needs were not being met, and a class for gifted children was established.

The special class enabled the teacher to plan each of the children's educational programs in a much more individualized manner. Mark began receiving an appropriate education for the first time in several years. At eight years of age, he was working at secondary levels in mathematics and language, and reports referred to his highly developed problem-solving skills, his understanding of sophisticated sociological concepts, and his innovative ideas in the science and technology areas. Of great interest and significance, also, were reports of his involvement in class discussions and his increasing acceptance of class rules and routines.

Although Mark was still most content when involved in focused, individual academic activity and often resisted the intrusion of others into his private world, he was now able to live and work within the normal boundaries of a classroom and a family, a goal that had appeared to be beyond his reach just a few years before.

DUAL EXCEPTIONALITY

Mark's story raises a number of key questions concerning students with dual exceptionalities. Are gifted children, particularly those in the highly gifted range, at greater risk of emotional or behavioral problems than their nongifted peers? Do the characteristics that are typical of gifted children predispose them to social and emotional difficulties? How often do behavioral or emotional problems mask a gift such as Mark's? How can children like Mark be assessed appropriately, when their behavioral symptoms form such an overwhelming barrier, and when they are unlikely to cooperate in testing situations? What constitutes an appropriate curriculum for gifted children? How can we prepare teachers and other professionals to meet the specialized needs of a child such as Mark? How can the families of gifted children be supported in the management and development of their children? And, finally, how can all the people involved successfully meet the affective needs of these gifted children so that their great potential can be realized, and they are able to lead productive and fulfilling lives?

In this chapter, each of these questions is addressed in turn, within the context of some broader issues. First is an examination of the literature, both theoretical and empirical, relating to the factors that may put gifted children at risk of emotional difficulties, and thereby mask their gifts. The special needs of those children who are already classified as "twice exceptional" and the particular risks they face are examined. A discussion of the need for improved identification and assessment procedures is followed by consideration of the special problem of suicide, as this is of increasing concern to the Australian community. Some guidelines for developing a curriculum that will facilitate the affective development of gifted students and minimize the chances of emotional problems developing are presented in the context of broader issues, such as the critical role parents and parent education programs can play, the need for a collaborative approach to the education of these children, and the necessity of improved teacher and counselor education programs if the emotional, as well as the cognitive, needs of our gifted children are to be effectively met.

RELATED RESEARCH

Readers will be familiar with the popular perception of the highly intelligent "mad professor" or the bespectacled and introverted school "dork." Portrayals in literature and other forms of media have perpetuated the idea that gifted individuals lack appropriate social skills and that they may be expected to behave in a highly idiosyncratic, and possibly even dangerous, manner.

Theorists in the area of the emotional development of gifted individuals have differing views on their susceptibility to social and emotional problems. Hollingworth's work during the 1940s (in Grossberg & Cornell, 1988) suggested that gifted individuals are, in fact, more at risk of both social and emotional adjustment difficulties. Other theorists who have supported the view that giftedness itself may make individuals more vulnerable to social or emotional difficulties include Altman (1983); Betts (1986); Buescher (1985); Delisle (1992); Freeman (1983); Levine and Tucker (1986); Mallis (1986); Meyers and Pace (1986); Webb, Meckstroth, and Tolan (1982); and Whitmore (1980). Roedall (1984) went further, putting forward the view not only that gifted individuals are more likely to have adjustment problems, but also that the more profound the giftedness, the more likely it is that the individual will experience emotional problems.

Some empirical research in the field, however, has presented a more optimistic view. Oram, Cornell, and Rutemiller (1995) directly refuted Roedall's claim. They found no significant differences between the psychosocial adjustment of academically gifted students and their nongifted peers, nor did they find that the more gifted an individual is, the more chance there is of that individual having adjustment difficulties. The longitudinal research of Terman earlier this century (in Cornell, 1984) suggested that the incidence of emotional problems in gifted individuals is comparatively low. Janos and Robinson (1985) reported superior levels of social knowledge and psychosocial adjustment, greater courtesy, higher self-esteem, higher levels of trustworthiness, and fewer aggressive and withdrawal tendencies in gifted children. Reynolds and Bradley (1983) and Scholwinski and Reynolds (1985) found that gifted children are usually less anxious than their nongifted peers; and Kaiser and Berndt (1985) reported that gifted students are less likely to experience loneliness. The research of Grossberg and Cornell (1988) supported the view that gifted children are at risk of emotional problems for precisely the same reasons as are nongifted children—that is, for family and individual reasons, rather than because they are gifted.

Other researchers (Baker, 1995; Hayes & Sloat, 1989) believe that there is insufficient evidence to determine whether or not gifted individuals are at greater risk of serious emotional disturbance, and that much research, particularly into adolescent adjustment, such as that of Reynolds (1990) and Kovaks (1989), is not sensitive to the individual differences that identify the gifted child. Clearly, there is a need for further investigation into the emotional development of gifted children and any special risks they may face.

Whatever theory is accepted about the relationship between giftedness and the risk of emotional disturbance, it should nevertheless be remembered that approximately nine to ten percent of *all* children suffer some form of emotional disturbance (Gallucci, 1988). Thus, at least this percentage of gifted children are at risk. Further, children like Mark are certainly out there, struggling with enormous social and emotional difficulties that are depriving them—and the rest of us—of the great advantages that the full realization of their potential can afford.

POTENTIAL RISK FACTORS

Particular personality factors or characteristics typical of gifted individuals have been identified in the literature as those that signify potential strengths but that, in some circumstances, can also be the underlying cause of significant adjustment problems.

Increased Sensitivity

The first of these personality factors is increased sensitivity (Silverman, 1994; Whitmore, 1980), a trait mentioned more than any other by parents, when asked to describe their gifted child (Silverman, 1993). This sensitivity may take the form of strong reactions to sensory experiences, of being extremely compassionate or protective, or of being easily hurt and unduly affected by criticism. Whitmore (1980) adds the fact that this often leads to a tendency to perceive rejection, even when it does not exist. This "supersensitivity" can lead to social difficulties and problems in emotional adjustment, as the normal "give-and-take" of social interactions becomes more problematic.

Intensity of Feelings

Related to sensitivity is the intensity of feelings experienced by many gifted individuals. This factor is cited frequently in the literature as one that makes gifted children vulnerable to personal stress and resulting emotional problems (Betts, 1986; Levine & Tucker, 1986; Mallis, 1986; Meyers & Pace, 1986; Silverman, 1994; Webb, Meckstroth, & Tolan, 1982). As Piechowski (1991) points out, this emotional intensity makes gifted children "acutely aware of the precariousness of human existence and the precarious condition of our world. Because of this, and because others understand it so little, gifted children can be extremely vulnerable and at risk" (p. 301).

Perfectionism
Perfectionism is also considered to place the gifted child at risk of emotional problems (Adderholt-Elliot, 1987; Parker & Adkins, 1995; Silverman, 1994; Whitmore, 1980). This can clearly be a potential strength, as the gifted individual continually endeavors to achieve beyond that which has been achieved before, but, as Parker and Adkins (1995) stress, it is not always easy to distinguish between a focused and committed striving toward excellence, and the obsessive and destructive pursuit of a standard that does not exist. The latter would make the gifted individual extremely vulnerable to emotional stress and subsequent adjustment difficulties. Parker and Adkins cite a number of studies that link perfectionism to depression, anorexia nervosa, obsessive-compulsive disorders, migraines, panic disorders, and even suicide.

Introversion
Introversion is a further characteristic of giftedness that may place these individuals at risk of emotional problems (Silverman, 1994; Whitmore, 1980). Gifted individuals tend to have a more reflective and introspective personal style than is typical (Gallagher, 1991). An overly reflective style may lead to preoccupations with the more negative aspects of life, which could militate against balanced and healthy emotional development. Whitmore (1980) adds that a preference for solitary activity often leads to gifted children having fewer opportunities to develop their social skills, which may hamper their social and emotional development.

Unrealistic Expectations
The tendency to set unrealistic expectations for themselves and others can lead to problems adjusting to performance in the real world, where actual achievement rarely matches the ideal (Maker, 1977; Swesson, 1994; Whitmore, 1980). This tendency may also be accompanied by extreme and critical self-scrutiny, which places additional stress on the gifted child.

Asynchronicity

The well-acknowledged "asynchronicity," or uneven development, evident in many gifted individuals may lead to an inability to cope emotionally with many of the issues their intellect or social conscience raises for them (Dise-Lewis, 1988; Whitmore, 1980). Delisle (1992) added that the impotence to change the "real world" was an additional stressor facing gifted individuals, who could see the problems around them, but not always the solutions.

Environmental Factors

To these characteristics must be added risk factors that operate outside the individual personalities of the gifted children. One such factor is the high expectations of parents and teachers. While generally contributing to high achievement, high expectations can be detrimental if they are unrealistic or if the child believes they are irrelevant.

An additional critical variable that may put the gifted child at risk is the lack of appropriate educational provision. If the teaching and learning programs are not relevant and motivating, if they lack challenge, if the evaluation methods are not meaningful to the children, there is the risk of adding to the stress that operates in the lives of these children. The issue of what constitutes a relevant curriculum for gifted children is developed at a later point in this chapter.

RISKS FOR THE TWICE EXCEPTIONAL CHILD

Deserving particular mention are the gifted individuals who are perhaps most at risk of developing social or emotional problems—the so-called "twice exceptional," who already face the challenges of living with a complex combination of strengths and weaknesses.

Gifted Children with Learning Disabilities

The largest of these twice exceptional groups is the group of gifted children with learning disabilities. There is increasing interest from both research and theoretical points of view in the development and progress of these students. Students with dual exceptionalities face even greater asynchronicity than "normal" gifted children. The "erratic arrangement of strengths and weaknesses" evident in these students (Swesson, 1994, p. 14) is emphasized by the learning disability, leading to an even greater discrepancy between potential and actual achievement, and consequently to feelings of instability and disequilibrium. Schiff, Kaufman, and Kaufman (1981) found that gifted learning-disabled students often referred themselves for psychological assessment, which highlights their own awareness of their vulnerability to emotional difficulties. As early as 1968, when this category of exceptionality was still greatly misunderstood, Krippner warned of the difficulties in adjustment faced by students who operate at the upper limits of some areas of achievement and the lower limits of others, with social immaturities being one possible result—but with psychopathic, neurotic, or psychotic tendencies being the more worrying possibilities.

Frustration was found to be a common characteristic of gifted learning-disabled students in a study completed by Vespi and Yewchuk (1992) and in work carried out by Hishinuma (1993). Clearly, underachieving, or being accused of being "dumb" or "lazy," when believing you are capable of high achievement can be a source of great frustration. They also found that gifted learning-disabled students had a fluctuating self-image and highly inconsistent social skills, both of which place the child at risk of emotional problems. Baum and Owen (1988) found that gifted learning-disabled students had even lower self-esteem than their learning-disabled peers. There is also evidence that if gifted learning-disabled children are in programs that focus only on their deficits, that is, remedial programs, self-esteem is lowered even further (Baum, 1988; Nielson & Mortoff-Allen, 1989).

Swesson (1994), Hishinuma (1993), and Doney (1995) found that the gifted learning-disabled child often has poor motivation and suffers from depression, anxiety, withdrawal, and feelings of inadequacy. Yewchuk and Bibby (1989) reported that gifted learning-disabled students tend to be extremely self-critical and to be acutely aware of the criticism of others.

It is often the case that gifted learning-disabled students are so resourceful that they can work around their poor organizational skills and processing problems, and still achieve quite well, although not to their potential. This raises the difficulties associated with the identification and assessment of these students. Most identification procedures place an emphasis on high test scores, which disadvantages the child who may have an extraordinary ability to manipulate abstract ideas but who lacks the organizational skills and memory for facts that can be so important in some assessment instruments (Maker, 1977). Assessment issues are discussed in greater detail at a later stage; however, the issue is worth raising at this point because of the particular problems faced by the gifted learning-disabled group.

Gifted Students with Physical Disabilities

Although research into the particular challenges faced by the gifted learning-disabled is now quite well established, research into the problems faced by gifted students with other disabilities, particularly low-incidence handicaps, is still in its infancy. Underachievement is clearly a great risk in students who, to quote Moon and Dillon (1995), have a "unique constellation of gifts and disabilities" (p. 111), and who face many obstacles in achieving their potential.

Children with physical disabilities, particularly those disabilities that have an impact on communication such as cerebral palsy, need to be assessed extremely carefully. The effect of having no way to give expression to a highly creative or reflective mind can be devastating on both cognitive and affective performance.

Other groups, such as gifted individuals with visual or hearing impairments, also face special difficulties in achieving their potential, with consequent vulnerability to social and emotional difficulties (Vernon & LaFalce-Landers, 1993).

Gifted Females

Girls may also be seen as constituting a group that is at particular risk of developing social or emotional difficulties. Reis (1987) claims that gifted females receive more mixed messages from their parents, their teachers, and their peers than any other group. Pressure to conform to society's expectations of a woman's role and the effects of sexism and discrimination may make girls particularly vulnerable to emotional stress (Hickson, 1992). There is reportedly a higher incidence of depression (DeMoss, Milich, & DeMers, 1993; Hayes & Sloat, 1989; Silverman, 1993; Weiss, 1990) and of low self-esteem and learned helplessness in gifted female populations than in gifted male populations (Berndt, Kaiser, & Van Alst, 1982; Worell & Remer, 1992). Killian (1983) reported that gifted girls also experience more tension and frustration than gifted boys.

IDENTIFICATION AND ASSESSMENT ISSUES

When children display the characteristics of emotional disturbance, particularly when the behavior is bizarre or threatening, it is perhaps understandable that the focus of attention will be on the symptoms, rather than on the underlying reasons for the behavior. Aberrant behavior, whether it be aggressive or passive, is almost always a "distress signal" or a call for help, and a strong indicator that the motivation behind it needs to be addressed.

The behavior can be an indicator that the child is struggling to come to terms with a gift that is being unrecognized or lacking in nourishment. Teachers need to search out possible reasons for such behavior. What characteristics does the child have that may provide clues? Great curiosity or an unusually large knowledge base about a favorite topic may indicate a passion that is not being recognized or that is, in fact, being thwarted. Other characteristics of giftedness, such as sensitivity to criticism and personal frustration at failing to live up to unrealistic personal expectations, may also be behind the "acting out" behavior of children (Swesson, 1994). The tendency for gifted girls to hide their potential due to cultural and/or peer pressure is another signal that educators need to be particularly vigilant if these girls are to be identified and receive an appropriate education.

Ellston (1993) highlights the importance of early identification because of the risk of long-term depression, lowered self-esteem, and aggressive or disruptive behavior in gifted students who are not in appropriate programs. This is a particular risk in those gifted children who have another area of special need, because the range of needs is so diverse (Toll, 1993).

As stated previously, most identification procedures place an emphasis on high test scores. Moon and Dillon (1995) caution against the use of standardized test scores alone. Emotional problems may lead to frustration throughout the test that depresses the score. Many emotionally disturbed children lack the coping skills that help develop persistence, and so performance in tests may be affected (Coleman, 1992). Low self-esteem, which is a common characteristic of students with emotional disturbances, can also have an impact on performance in assessments of all types (Van Tassel-Baska, Olszewski-Kubilius, & Kulieke, 1994).

Moon and Dillon (1995) believe that some tests, specifically the WISC-R, have too low a ceiling to accurately assess high levels of verbal giftedness. In the case of gifted students with other disabilities, such as a learning disability, low scores on specific subtests may depress the overall score and thus mask the child's real level of ability. When giving such multicomponent assessments, careful analysis of the individual test scores must be made to identify those with gifts in particular areas.

The complexity of these individuals demands particularly careful assessment (Gallagher, 1991; Hickson, 1992; Whitmore, 1989). A multidimensional approach is essential. Continuous and long-term observation of these children yields more useful results than most standardized assessment instruments. Questionnaires for teachers and parents, student interviews, and self-concept scales also have a part to play in the assessment of these children. Cohen and Frydenberg (1993) highlight the importance of listening to children. While most teachers act in the way they believe to be best for these children, much can be learned from the insights and observations of the children themselves.

THE PROBLEM OF SUICIDE

A chapter on the social and emotional needs of gifted children must include some discussion of the distressing subject of suicide. The risk of suicide must not be underestimated in our young people. Australia currently has the highest rate of youth suicide in the Western world. There is no evidence to suggest that being gifted protects a young person from seeing suicide as a solution to life's problems.

Dixon, Cross, Cook, and Scheckel (1995) believe that some characteristics of giftedness, such as excessive sensitivity, divergent thinking, excessive introspection, extreme emotionality, and, for some, a preoccupation with negative themes, can be directly associated with the risk of suicide. A further problem is related to the fact that gifted individuals may believe that, with their many resources, they should be able to "fix themselves" if they are feeling depressed, and so they may be reluctant to ask for assistance (Peterson, 1993). It must be made clear to these young people that everyone, without exception, needs other people, and that it is no admission of weakness to seek help.

There are things that can be done to minimize the risk of suicide in depressed young people. They need someone to show that they care. They may try to alienate you, but you must persevere. Peterson (1993) reports the case of an adolescent called Genna who, after experiencing long battles with depression and thoughts of suicide, spoke of her need for people at the times when she knew she was pushing them away from her with great determination. The willingness of those around her to keep trying was the evidence she needed that people still cared for her, and this was what persuaded her to keep living.

Listening to young people without trivializing their problems is one of the most valuable things that can be done to help. They may need to be asked directly if they wish they were dead or are thinking about killing themselves. Hayes and Sloat (1989) point out that they may need help to understand that the only way they can continue to have options is to keep living—an obvious point, but the individual concerned is usually too distraught to perceive it. If possible, some commitment should be drawn from them to put off whatever they may be contemplating until they have discussed their problems with a professional—after all, they have nothing to lose when the alternative is the loss of their life.

Appleby and Condonis (1990) list a number of indicators of suicide that must never be ignored:

- An actual suicide threat or statement indicating a desire to die is often overlooked as a bid for attention and disregarded. It is, in fact, a cry for help and should never be disregarded.

- An unsuccessful attempt may be seen as merely another bid for attention, with no real desire to die. The fact is that many successful suicides come after one or more unsuccessful attempts.

- Signs of mental depression, such as low energy levels, and expressions of hopelessness and worthlessness, are often ignored by others who see only an individual's high performance and cannot believe that anything could really be of concern to that person.

- Changes in eating or sleeping patterns, more time spent alone, or less interest in previous passions may all indicate an individual who is losing contact with those around him or her.

- Making arrangements, such as giving away prized belongings, is a serious sign that must be responded to without delay, because it suggests impending action.

People often feel that if a suicide threat is revealed in confidence, they are honor-bound not to break the confidence. This is particularly true of adolescents. What must be stressed is that the concern for the person's life must override any breach of confidentiality, and the threat must be passed on to a trained professional immediately.

Fortunately, there are things that teachers can do to minimize the chances of serious social, emotional, or behavioral problems emerging, and many of these relate directly to the curriculum that is offered to these children. The next section examines factors that should be considered in the development and implementation of an appropriate curriculum for gifted students, particularly for those who may be especially vulnerable to emotional difficulties.

RECOMMENDED COMPONENTS OF AN EFFECTIVE CURRICULUM

There is growing recognition of the fact that educational programs need to meet the needs of the whole child, rather than address only cognitive potential or the area of giftedness. The most successful programs for gifted students are those that also address the affective needs of these children (Bailey & Sinclair, 1992; Hishinuma, 1991; Hollingworth in Silverman, 1990; Mendaglio, 1995; Silverman, 1993; Vespi & Yewchuk, 1992).

The literature has identified ways in which the affective needs of children may be met through appropriate curriculum provision. Coleman (1992) uses the conceptualization of coping resources put forward by Compass in 1987 to highlight the importance of teaching coping strategies to gifted students. These strategies include personal strategies like problem-solving skills, interpersonal skills, and the development of positive self-esteem, in addition to environmental strategies such as using a supportive social network. Hammer (1988) states that coping resources may be cognitive, social, emotional, spiritual or philosophical, or physical, and makes the point that the wider the variety of coping strategies possessed by a student, the greater the chance of that student's successfully managing stressful experiences.

Clark (1992) recommended the Integrative Education Model (IEM), which incorporates strategies to develop self-esteem and an internal locus of control. The Autonomous Learner Model (ALM), developed by Betts and Knapp (1980), also emphasizes social and emotional development through activities to develop self-understanding, self-acceptance, and interpersonal communication.

Included at this point are some strategies that, if included in the curriculum for gifted children, will assist their development in four critical areas:

- self-awareness, understanding, and acceptance;
- social and interpersonal skills;
- the effective management of stress; and
- self-management skills.

Strategies to Develop Self-awareness, Understanding, and Acceptance

Examine Personal Beliefs and Feelings. Mendaglio (1991) points out that gifted children may need assistance in expressing the strong emotions that are characteristic of so many, because emotional reactions often determine how one copes with personal and environmental stressors. Worell and Remer (1992) found that examining personal beliefs and attitudes did much to enhance the self-esteem of gifted adolescents. Discussions of such intensely personal issues need to take place within an atmosphere of complete trust, as students are placing themselves in an emotionally vulnerable position. It is important for teachers to express their own feelings in a genuine manner during these discussions, to demonstrate to the students a willingness to share the vulnerability.

Certain ground rules need to be established with the class to facilitate this climate of trust. Schmitz and Galbraith (1985) suggest the following:

There's no such thing as a dumb question or a dumb answer.

It's good to have a mind of your own.

None of us is perfect.

Children need to understand that feelings are neither right nor wrong—behaviors resulting from them can be more or less helpful, but the feelings themselves have an integrity of their own, and certainly cannot be denied. Teachers need to demonstrate that they accept the students' emotions, even if they do not agree with them.

Gifted children also need to understand their strengths, abilities, and limitations. Individual children's special gifts should always be discussed in the context that many people have special talents, and that all people are equally valuable, whether they have particular gifts or not. Differences need to be accepted, and valued, as part of the human condition.

These children should also be helped to understand that they do not have to be perfect—that nobody is perfect. Adults should share their own mistakes with the children, and demonstrate that mistakes and risks are part of learning. Positive beliefs, attitudes, and goals will emerge from understanding and acceptance of individual strengths and limitations.

Incorporate "Values Clarification" Activities. Values clarification exercises have long been used to assist students in exploring their beliefs and feelings. These procedures can raise awareness of affective and behavioral problems, help students understand why some values and behaviors are good and others are not, assist in the development of empathy and positive attitudes toward others and themselves, and assist students in making a commitment to positive behaviors (Davis & Rimm, 1989).

Values clarification exercises can center on a discussion of certain attitudes and behaviors where students brainstorm why they believe they would or would not do certain things, such as kill in self-defense or cheat on an unfair test. Discussions may center on whether individuals see themselves as "lions" or "pussycats," and the advantages and disadvantages of each. Sentence completion exercises (such as "I feel good when . . ."; "I feel frightened when . . ."; "I feel proud when . . ."; "I can make someone else feel good by . . ."; and so on) stimulate active thoughts about feelings and beliefs.

Davis and Rimm (1989) also suggest the use of *analogical thinking* strategies during which students try to make imaginative comparisons, such as "How is a good friend like a favorite book?" or "How is alcohol like fire?" There are many sources of these exercises, and these exercises can contribute greatly to an affective curriculum. Cohen and Frydenberg (1993) refer to this as the process of "synectics," which was developed by William Gordon as a way of approaching problem solving in a creative way. They provide a step-by-step guide to its use in the classroom, which demonstrates how this strategy can be used to help resolve personal issues (pp. 156–159).

Strategies to Develop Social and Interpersonal Skills

Discuss Social Behavior. Teachers need to discuss social behavior with gifted children and help them explore the consequences of certain actions and the impact of their behavior on other people. There are many relevant questions that can promote active discussion of social behavior. Why do we need to have successful relationships with other people? What are the characteristics of a good friend, and how might these be developed? A very useful exercise is one in which each student comments on a positive quality in another class member. Thus, a statement like "I like the way Rod shares his resources—he's really unselfish" affirms this quality in Rod and highlights for the speaker how worthwhile this attribute is, and how such attributes elicit a positive response in others.

Discussion of moral issues can also be included. What should be done if a friend becomes involved in dangerous or illegal activities? How should you respond if you are encouraged to join friends in such activities? If these topics are discussed within the safety of an accepting and tolerant classroom, students feel able to explore different options, which assists them in developing a range of strategies to use in social situations.

Acknowledge Appropriate Behavior. An important part of developing social skills is to acknowledge in a very positive way when the student supports a friend, shares something, or demonstrates self-control, patience, or tolerance. These are some of the "life skills" that contribute so much to personal development and success in such situations.

Provide Specific Strategies. Educators should also provide some specific strategies on how to improve social relationships. They should talk about the importance of smiling and of being a good listener. They may discuss with the class different conversation starters, such as asking about hobbies or favorite sports. Students can be encouraged to role play different responses to situations where teasing may occur, or when a great disappointment is experienced. Teachers should allow the students to practice their responses and debate the consequences of different reactions.

Use Cooperative Groupings. Cooperative learning activities have been shown to develop a range of skills in students of all ages (Ford, 1994; Johnson & Johnson, 1990). Elmore and Zenus (1992) successfully incorporated students' affective needs into a mathematics curriculum after it became apparent that their students were experiencing great difficulties in personal interactions and that several had very low self-esteem, despite the fact that they were making excellent academic gains in their mathematics program. One of the most effective strategies used by Elmore and Zenus was the use of *Jigsaw* cooperative learning groups. Before this program could be implemented, the students had to be taught how to praise and encourage each other, how to listen effectively, how to seek assistance appropriately, and how to make group decisions; in other words, how to behave as responsive group members. Assumptions cannot be made that students already know how to behave in cooperative groups. Students had many opportunities to practice these skills and had to evaluate how well each strategy was used throughout the lessons.

In the Jigsaw model, each group of students learns a component of work, or a new process, thereby becoming the "expert." The individual groups study together, highlight key points, and discuss and clarify any problems that arise. Groups are then reallocated, so that each new group consists of members of each of the expert groups. Individual group members then teach the rest of the group their particular component or process. Important points are listed, and when the class comes back together as a group, the major points are noted and any issues discussed. In the study by Elmore and Zenus (1992), the social skills of all the students increased, although the lower and moderately achieving groups appeared to gain most.

Many gifted individuals, both with and without co-occurring disabilities, report the use of social resources to help them cope with the stressors in their lives (Coleman, 1992). This appears to be a major factor that is missing from the lives of those gifted individuals who develop serious social and emotional problems, and highlights the need for parents and teachers to find ways of facilitating the social skills and, therefore, the social support networks of gifted students.

Strategies to Develop Stress-management and Coping Skills

Use Journals. Gifted students themselves have identified journal writing as an excellent way in which to air frustrations and develop views (Lim, 1994). Doney (1995) and Sands and Howard-Hamilton (1994) also report favorably on the use of writing, particularly journal writing, to develop student self-esteem. Journals may be used for a range of different purposes. A two-way journal, which moves between the teacher and the student, allows each person to reflect on personal and/or world events, and respond in a private and considered way to the other. Journals may also be used to record personal achievements or to monitor progress toward a goal—this can be extremely valuable for the student who is losing motivation. Journal writing assists the student to articulate feelings, explore new ideas, and clarify thoughts, all of which promote healthy social and emotional development.

Teach Relaxation Skills. Relaxation exercises are useful at all times, but are particularly useful for periods of high anxiety. Yoga techniques, such as that of breathing in and out very slowly, first to the count of three but building up to a count of ten, require the individual to focus only on breathing and have a greatly calming effect. Other techniques can also be taught, such as visualization, in which the students visualize relaxing or calming scenes, or picture themselves in control, responding appropriately in situations that they normally find stressful. Step-by-step guidelines for activities of this nature may be found in Sisk (1987).

Develop Positive "Inner Dialogue." Teachers can help the students to become aware of the power of inner dialogue and how it affects behavior and feelings. Talking to oneself mentally is one way in which people evaluate what they have done, and gifted children tend to do this earlier than most children. The child should be encouraged to engage in positive rather than negative self-talk by practicing such thoughts as "It's okay to have problems," "Nobody's perfect," and "I did a good job of that," rather than the more damaging "I'll never get this right" or "Why am I surrounded by idiots?"

Use Humor. Humor can be an extremely effective way of managing stress. The various types of humor should be discussed with students. They should be encouraged to use humor to overcome frustration and disappointment, to deal with mistakes, to combat teasing, and generally to take themselves less seriously.

Use Bibliotherapy. Bilbliotherapy is essentially the use of books to solve problems (Sisk, 1987, p. 264). Students are encouraged to identify with book characters who are experiencing similar problems. When used in conjunction with directed discussions, the reading of books that confront social or emotional issues that are of concern to the student (for example, divorce, unemployment, death) is an extremely useful and safe way to explore alternatives, test personal hypotheses, assess different value systems, clarify feelings and expectations, discover how one's actions can impact on other people, accept consequences of choices, and come to terms with disappointments and setbacks. Discussion questions can stimulate thinking in a variety of areas and operate at different levels, in order that a range of individual personal and cognitive needs may be met.

Encourage Physical Activity. Physical activity can often do a great deal to reduce stress and provide an alternative to some less productive way of expending energy (Plucker, 1994). Young gifted children, particularly those whose gifts lie in cognitive areas, may neglect this important aspect of their lives. Both individual and team activities can contribute to personal development, confidence building, and stress management, in addition to physical fitness, and strength and endurance—all of which contribute to a more productive lifestyle.

Teach Problem-solving Skills. Problem-solving approaches can be used to manage difficulties in cognitive, affective, or social domains; most often, they incorporate moving through a specific series of steps, as the issue is identified and solutions are explored. What is the exact problem? Can the problem be broken down into smaller steps? What are some different ways we could approach this? What are the positives in this situation? What can we learn from this that will help us next time? Is this problem really in our sphere of influence?

Cognitive appraisal, where one evaluates a situation and decides upon an appropriate coping strategy, is a problem-solving skill that is not often used by children—it is perceived to be much more of an adult strategy (Dise-Lewis, 1988). Using Lazarus's conceptualization of cognitive appraisal as either problem-focused or emotion-focused, Sowa, McIntyre, May, and Bland (1994) reported on the ways in which their sample of gifted children used cognitive appraisal strategies to cope with stress. They provide an example of a problem-focused strategy when they report how a boy described why he altered the way he argues. "He said, 'One minute I was arguing and the next minute, (I thought) why not try to do something different? . . . If you argue people are going to get mad and . . . it is going to mess your chances of getting exactly what you want' " (p. 96). By changing his behavior, the child attempts to influence the environment, which is a productive way to manage a stressful situation.

Sowa et al. (1994) also reported how one child used an emotion-focused strategy to overcome disappointment at not attending a summer program: "Well, okay, I wanted to go, but it is only two weeks out of my summer . . . I'll find something else to do" (p. 96). By changing his or her interpretation of the situation, the child manages the disappointment in a way that helps reduce stress.

This is simlar to cognitive restructuring or reframing, which involves consciously changing the way you think about something. Plucker (1994) found that reframing allowed students to deal with stress more effectively.

Strategies to Develop Self-management Skills

Gifted children need to learn that the only behavior over which they have genuine control is their own. They cannot control the behavior of others; therefore, their energies are best spent in developing personal skills that will help them to manage the stress they will inevitably encounter.

Incorporate Self-evaluation Strategies. Students will increase confidence levels if they learn how to evaluate themselves. Therefore, teachers should replace external evaluation strategies with those that rely more on individual evaluation of performance. Further, when teachers need to give feedback, it should be process feedback, which rewards effort, rather than product feedback. This reduces the pressure to perform at a high level on all occasions and increases the chances that the student will risk trying something new.

Model Calculated Risk Taking. Gifted students who are suffering from social or emotional problems may need to learn how to take calculated risks. Often feelings of depression lead to an inability to see options and alternatives (Appleby & Condonis, 1990). Students need to learn how to weigh risks, assess probable consequences, and value unusual alternatives. This can best be taught through a modeling process. In as many situations as possible, teachers should "think aloud" as they weigh alternatives and decide upon courses of action.

Teach Goal Setting. Goal setting is an important strategy that may be applied to any aspect of one's life. It can be a particularly useful way to address problems, as setting short-term goals reduces a large problem to a more manageable one. Goal setting also assists the development of independence and self-management skills, both of which are significant in the development of emotional health.

It is important for students (and teachers!) to set realistic goals, as goals that are either too high or too low will lead to feelings of failure. Goals also need to be explicit to aid both achievement and evaluation.

Schmitz and Galbraith (1985) recommend the use of a Personal Growth Contract with gifted children, which is a form of goal setting aimed at emotional development. In using this strategy, the children identify an area of personal growth, such as decreasing the number of negative comments about a sibling, and then specify, in point form, the strategies that can be used to reach that goal. Resources that will assist achievement, any anticipated problems that may prevent progress, and the time frame for achievement of the goal are listed. Specific ways of evaluating achievement of the goal should also be included, such as:

How will I know when things are better?

How close did I come?

Did I achieve what I hoped?

It is also helpful to specify ways in which progress toward the goals may be measured and rewarded, as this provides continued motivation.

Use Individual Student Contracts. Contracts increase student choice and do much to empower the students in their learning. All of us need to feel that we have some control over our lives. This is perhaps more true of the gifted individual. Students should also be encouraged to develop their own learning contracts, in which they plan their own goals, select their topics, conduct their research, organize their resources and time, and take part in the evaluation procedures. It is often helpful to have the students develop their own set of evaluation criteria, so that their teachers can come to a better understanding of what they value in the learning process.

Encourage Record Keeping. Keeping a log or other record of achievements or progress toward a goal can be a highly empowering tool. When motivation drops, or setbacks cause particular disappointment, a log of achievements provides a gratifying record of past successes.

Analyze Motivation. Teachers should discuss with the students times when they felt particularly motivated or were particularly successful, and try to recreate those conditions, in order to help them to understand the conditions that motivate them to produce their best. Were they working alone or with someone in particular? What project was being worked on? Was the project a small or large one? Over what period of time was the project managed? Did the project relate to something that was extremely important to them?

Model Decision-making Skills. Teachers can model the processes necessary to make good decisions. The particular steps of defining the problem, identifying alternative courses of action, identifying criteria by which to evaluate the alternatives, managing the evaluation procedures, making the decision, and understanding the implications of that decision can be incorporated into many classroom activities. Students need to understand that in making most important decisions, compromises need to be made, which is why decision making is so often difficult, and also why it is such an important life skill. Gifted children need to have the autonomy to make decisions and, importantly, they need to be allowed to live with the consequences.

Use a Temperature Scale. Some children, particularly those with a "short fuse," benefit from using an emotional temperature scale. Wragg (1989) suggests the following procedure. The first step is to discuss the types of situations that provoke the child. This is valuable because even being aware of potentially problematic situations may help the child understand the need for self-control mechanisms. Students should imagine various situations and rate how they would make them feel, ranging from "calm and under control" at number 1, to "loss of control" at number 9, and "boiling point" at number 10. This leads into a discussion of the sorts of things that might make the temperature rise quickly and the consequences if the "loss of control" line is crossed. Finally, teachers and students discuss a range of strategies that could bring the temperature down. Wragg's book details the process of "talking sense to yourself," where such strategies as using calming and coping statements like "I can handle this," "I can stay in control," "I'm not going to let this get out of control," and "It's not worth getting upset over" allow the child to regain control and avoid boiling over.

SOME RELATED ISSUES

If educators are serious about providing for the total development of their gifted students, there are several issues that are worthy of discussion at this point, because they have broad implications for the planning, implementation, and evaluation of programs for gifted children.

Need for a Collaborative Approach

The diverse needs of gifted students who experience social or emotional problems demand an integrated approach to their educational programming (Hishinuma, 1991; Van Tassel-Baska, 1991). A collaborative model that uses the skills of a group of people with expertise in varying areas, but with a shared vision of support for gifted young people, is going to be more effective than the isolated efforts of concerned individuals. Counselors, psychologists, parents, and mentors need to work with teachers in true collaborative style if the best possible programs are to be offered to children.

Use of Mentors and Role Models

Several writers emphasize the fact that mentors and role models may be particularly useful in nurturing the emotional health of gifted individuals (Doney, 1995; Noble, 1989; Van Tassel-Baska, 1991). Van Tassel-Baska, Olszewski-Kubilius, and Kulieke (1994) point out that mentors and role models feature consistently in the lives of eminent individuals. Noble (1989) reported that mentors had played an important role in the development of the one hundred gifted women in her study. The ability of mentors to support, enthuse, and encourage a developing mind clearly has an impact on the emotional development of these individuals. Gifted students, particularly those with disabilities, receive particular validation from contact with mentors who have experienced the same challenges.

Need for Vocational Education

Some gifted students, because of the range of their capabilities, need vocational guidance in order to select the option most likely to fulfill them. In the case of gifted students with emotional difficulties, vocational guidance appears to be even more imperative, for lack of personal fulfillment can have extremely damaging consequences for this group.

Those gifted children who have co-occurring disabilities may assume that their vocational options are restricted. This assumption may need to be challenged, and the personal beliefs and attitudes that generated it may need to be examined as part of the vocational program.

The Role of Parents

Healthy family relationships and parent-child interactions are critical for the social and emotional health of any child, and this does not change if the child happens to be gifted (Cornell & Grossberg, 1987; Janos & Robinson, 1985; May, 1994). Gifted children certainly bring much joy and stimulation to family life, but there is no doubt that they can also bring tensions, challenges, and frustrations.

Parents need to provide a place of security and unconditional love for their children. They need to be good listeners, and to provide an environment in which it is safe to discuss problems and explore solutions. Parents have many opportunities to model considerate behavior, sensitivity to others, how to apologize, how to share happiness and sorrow, to forgive, to renegotiate, and to solve problems, but not all parents can develop these skills without help or direction, and they may look to teachers for support and guidance.

Parent training has been shown to assist the development of positive and encouraging home environments, student motivation, and academic achievement (Hickson, 1992), so they are worthy of consideration in any program for gifted children. Programs such as those developed by Gordon (1970), Dinkmeyer and McKay (1989, 1990) and Dinkmeyer, McKay, and Dinkmeyer (1989) provide detailed strategies for parents in managing children of all ages.

Need for Counseling Programs

Counseling should be an essential component of educational programs for all students, but especially for those students who are at particular risk, such as those described in this chapter. While the daily curriculum can provide much to assist the social and emotional development of children, some children require the assistance of a more specialized counseling program.

St. Clair (1989) recommends the client-centered counseling approach of Carl Rogers because gifted students are generally ready for self-appraisal at quite young ages. Ford (1994) claims that many "at risk" gifted children need to be specifically taught skills that promote resilience, such as a positive and proactive approach to daily life, flexibility, task persistence, divergent thinking, and problem-solving skills. People with these skills tend to have an internal locus of control, personal autonomy, high self-esteem, and positive peer relationships, all of which are indicators of strong emotional health and stability.

Need for Teacher and Counselor Education

There is disturbing evidence of negative attitudes toward gifted students among both teachers and counselors (Landrum & Landrum, 1995; St. Clair, 1989). Some teachers do not know how to respond to the gifted child who may be very lonely, immature, or socially inept. The oppositional behavior of other gifted students, their resistance to control, and their quick-witted responses may all contribute to the fact that they will not be the regular teacher's favorite students!

It is imperative that the particular needs of gifted students, and their right to receive an appropriate education, are recognized by these two important groups. This has implications for teacher- and counselor-training programs in Australia, which currently do not contain compulsory units on the education of the gifted. Increased knowledge about gifted children should contribute to more positive attitudes toward gifted children and also to the development of more appropriate curricula. Sensitizing these two groups to the characteristics of the full range of gifted students seems critical, if for no other reason than the fact that they are the potential leaders of our society. We will all benefit if their social and emotional needs, as well as their cognitive needs, are addressed.

CONCLUSION

This chapter has examined ways in which social, emotional, and behavioral problems may mask the potential of a great poet, a revolutionary thinker, or an inspirational leader. It has highlighted the need to be wary of traditional identification and assessment methods, and to continually explore new ways of bringing to light the gifts that may lie hidden behind the mask of emotional disturbance. An examination of the literature has directed the way to the provision of a curriculum that meets the affective, as well as the cognitive, needs of these children, and emphasized the importance of utilizing the full range of available expertise to ensure that gifted students with emotional difficulties have the opportunity to fully realize their potential.

Supplee (1989) reminds us that there are no short-term solutions to many of the problems faced by our gifted emotionally disturbed students. Their difficulties have often taken years to develop and will not disappear overnight. Parents, teachers, and counselors need to make a serious commitment to the continued support of these students, so that they may successfully overcome their problems and lead productive and fulfilling lives.

REFERENCES

Adderholt-Elliott, M. (1987). *Perfectionism: What's bad about being too good.* Minneapolis, MN: Free Spirit.

Altman, R. (1983). Social-emotional development of gifted children and adolescents: A research model. *Roeper Review, 6*(2), 65–68.

Appleby, M., & Condonis, M. (1990). *Hearing the cry.* Sydney, Australia: Rose Educational Training and Consultancy.

Bailey, S., & Sinclair, R. (1992). Out of sight but not out of mind. *Gifted Education International, 8*(2), 114–116.

Baker, J. A. (1995). Depression and suicide ideation among academically gifted adolescents. *Gifted Child Quarterly, 39*(4), 218–223.

Baum, S. (1988). An enrichment program for gifted learning disabled students. *Gifted Child Quarterly, 32*(3), 226–230.

Baum, S., & Owen, S. V. (1988). High ability/learning disabled students: How are they different? *Gifted Child Quarterly, 32*(3), 321–326.

Berndt, D. J., Kaiser, C. F., & Van Alst, F. (1982). Expression and self-actualization in gifted adolescents. *Journal of Clinical Psychology, 38,* 142–150.

Betts, G. (1986). Development of the social and emotional needs of gifted individuals. *Journal of Counseling and Development, 64,* 587–589.

Betts, G., & Knapp, J. (1980). Autonomous learning and the gifted: A secondary model. In A. Arnold (Ed.), *Secondary programs for the gifted* (pp. 29–36). Ventura, CA: Ventura Superintendent of School Office.

Buescher, T. M. (1985). A framework for understanding the social and emotional development of gifted and talented adolescents. *Roeper Review, 8,* 10–15.

Clark, B. (1992). *Growing up gifted.* New York: Macmillan.

Cohen, L. M. & Frydenberg, E. (1993). *Coping for capable kids.* Melbourne, Australia: Hawker-Brownlow.

Coleman, M. R. (1992). A comparison of how gifted/LD and average/LD boys cope with school frustration. *Journal for the Education of the Gifted, 15*(3), 239–265.

Cornell, D. G. (1984). *Families of gifted children.* Ann Arbor, MI: University of Michigan Research Press.

Cornell, D. G., & Grossberg, I. N. (1987). Family environment and personality adjustment in gifted program children. *Gifted Child Quarterly, 31,* 59–64.

Davis, G. A., & Rimm, S. B. (1989). *Education of the gifted and talented.* Englewood Cliffs, NJ: Prentice-Hall.

Delisle, J. R. (1992). *Guiding the social and emotional development of gifted youth: A practical guide for educators and counselors.* New York: Longman.

DeMoss, K., Milich, R., & DeMers, S. (1993). Gender, creativity, depression and attributional style in adolescents with high academic ability. *Journal of Abnormal Child Psychology, 21,* 455–467.

Dinkmeyer, D., & McKay, G. D. (1989). *Systematic training for effective parenting (S.T.E.P.): The parents' handbook* (3rd ed.). Circle Pines, MN: American Guidance Service.

Dinkmeyer, D., & McKay, G. D. (1990). *Systematic training for effective parenting (S.T.E.P.): Parenting teenagers* (2nd ed.). Circle Pines, MN: American Guidance Service.

Dinkmeyer, D., McKay, G. D., & Dinkmeyer, J. S. (1989). *Systematic training for effective parenting (S.T.E.P.): Parenting young children.* Circle Pines, MN: American Guidance Service.

Dise-Lewis, J. E. (1988). The life events and coping inventory: An assessment of stress in children. *Psychosomatic Medicine, 50,* 484–499.

Dixon, D. N., Cross, T. L., Cook, R. S., & Scheckel, J. L. (1995). Gifted adolescent suicide: Data base versus speculation. *Research Briefs, 10,* 45–49.

Doney, C. J. (1995). Creating opportunities, or what is it like to be a WHALE? *Journal of Learning Disabilities, 28*(4), 194–195.

Ellston, T. (1993). Gifted and learning disabled: A paradox? *Gifted Child Quarterly, 16*(1), 17–19.

Elmore, R. F., & Zenus, V. (1992). Enhancing social-emotional development of middle school gifted students. *Roeper Review, 16*(3), 182–185.

Ford, D. (1994). Nurturing resilience in gifted black youth. *Roeper Review, 17*(2), 80–85.

Freeman, J. (1983). Emotional problems of the gifted child. *Journal of Child Psychology and Psychiatry, 24,* 481–485.

Gallagher, J. J. (1991). Personal patterns of underachievement. *Journal for the Education of the Gifted, 14,* 221–233.

Gallucci, N. (1988). Emotional adjustment of gifted children. *Gifted Child Quarterly, 32,* 273–276.

Gordon, T. (1970). *Parent effectiveness training.* New York: New American Library.

Grossberg, I. N., & Cornell, D. G. (1988). Relationship between personality adjustment and high intelligence: Terman versus Hollingworth. *Exceptional Children, 55,* 266–272.

Hammer, A. (1988). *Manual for the coping resources inventory.* Palo Alto, CA: Consulting Psychologist Press.

Hayes, M. L., & Sloat, R. S. (1989). Gifted students at risk for suicide. *Roeper Review, 12*(2), 102–107.

Hickson, J. (1992). A framework for guidance and counseling of the gifted in a school setting. *Gifted Education International, 8*(2), 93–103.

Hishinuma, E. S. (1991). Serving the needs of the gifted/learning disabled. *Gifted Child Today, 14*(5), 36–38.

Hishinuma, E. S. (1993). Counseling gifted/at risk and gifted/dyslexic youngsters. *Gifted Child Today, 16*(1), 30–33.

Janos, P., & Robinson, N. (1985). Psychological development in intellectually gifted children. In F. Horowtiz & M. O'Brien (Eds.), *The gifted and talented: Developmental perspectives* (pp. 180–187). Washington, DC: American Psychological Society.

Johnson, D. W., & Johnson, R. T. (1990). Social skills for successful group work. *Educational Leadership, 47*(4), 29–33.

Kaiser, C. F., & Berndt, D. J. (1985). Predictors of loneliness in the gifted adolescent. *Gifted Child Quarterly, 29,* 74–77.

Kennedy, D. M. (1995). Glimpses of a highly gifted child in a heterogeneous classroom. *Roeper Review, 17*(3), 164–169.

Killian, L. M. (1983). Personality characteristics of intellectually gifted secondary students. *Roeper Review, 5*(3), 39–42.

Kovaks, M. (1989). Affective disorders in children and adolescents. *American Psychologist, 44,* 209–215.

Krippner, S. (1968). Etiological factors in reading disabilities of the academically talented, in comparison to pupils of average and slow learning ability. *Journal of Educational Research, 61,* 275–279.

Landrum, M. S., & Landrum, T. J. (1995). Perceived problem behaviors in intellectually gifted children. *Research Briefs, 10,* 39–43.

Levine, E., & Tucker, S. (1986). Emotional needs of gifted children: A preliminary phenomenological view. *The Creative Child and Adult Quarterly, 32*(2), 245–247.

Lim, T. K. (1994). Letters to themselves: Gifted students' plans for positive lifestyles. *Roeper Review, 17*(2), 85–89.

Maker, C. (1977). *Providing programs for the gifted handicapped.* Reston, VA: Council for Exceptional Children.

Mallis, J. (1986). *Diamonds in the dust.* Austin, TX: Multimedia Arts.

May, K. M. (1994). A developmental view of a gifted child's social and emotional adjustment. *Roeper Review, 17*(2), 105–109.

Mendaglio, S. (1991, September 26–28). *Facilitation of emotional expression in gifted students.* Paper presented at the SAGE Conference, Edmonton, Alberta, Canada.

Mendaglio, S. (1995). Sensitivity among gifted persons: A multi-faceted perspective. *Roeper Review, 17*(3), 169–172.

Meyers, R., & Pace, T. (1986). Counseling gifted and talented students: Historical perspectives and contemporary issues. *Journal of Counseling and Development, 66,* 548–551.

Moon, S. M., & Dillon, D. R. (1995). Multiple exceptionalities: A case study. *Journal for the Education of the Gifted, 18*(2), 111–130.

Nielsen, M., & Mortoff-Allen, S. (1989). The effects of special education service on the self-concept and school attitude of learning disabled/gifted students. *Roeper Review, 12*(1), 29–36.

Noble, K. D. (1989). Living out the promise of high potential: Perceptions of 100 gifted women. *Advanced Development, 1,* 57–76.

Oram, G. D., Cornell, D. G., & Rutemiller, L. A. (1995). Relations between academic aptitude and psychosocial adjustment in gifted program students. *Gifted Child Quarterly, 39*(4), 236–244.

Parker, W. D., & Adkins, K. K. (1995). Perfectionism and the gifted. *Roeper Review, 17*(3), 173–176.

Peterson, J. (1993). What we learned from Genna. *Gifted Child Today, 16*(1), 15–16.

Piechowski, M. M. (1991). Emotional development and emotional giftedness. In N. Colangelo & G. Davis, *Handbook of gifted education* (pp. 285–306). Needham Heights, MA: Allyn & Bacon.

Plucker, J. A. (1994). Issues in the social and emotional adjustment and development of a gifted, Chinese American student. *Roeper Review, 17*(2), 89–94.

Reis, S. M. (1987). We can't change what we don't recognize: Understanding the special needs of gifted females. *Gifted Child Quarterly, 31,* 83–89.

Reis, S. M. (1995). Talent ignored, talent diverted: The cultural context underlying giftedness in females. *Gifted Child Quarterly, 39*(3), 162–170.

Reynolds, C. R., & Bradley, M. (1983). Emotional ability of intellectually superior children versus non-gifted peers as estimated by chronic anxiety levels. *School Psychology Review, 12,* 190–194.

Reynolds, W. M. (1990). Depression in children and adolescents: Nature, diagnosis assessment and treatment. *School Psychology Review, 19,* 158–173.

Roedall, W. C. (1984). Vulnerabilities of highly gifted children. *Roeper Review, 6,* 127–130.

Sands, T., & Howard-Hamilton, M. (1994). Understanding depression among gifted adolescent females: Feminist therapy strategies. *Roeper Review, 17*(3), 192–195.

Schiff, M., Kaufman, A. S., & Kaufman, N. L. (1981). Scatter analysis of WISC-R profiles for LD children with superior ability. *Journal of Learning Disabilities, 14*(7), 400–404.

Schmitz, C. C., & Galbraith, J. (1985). *Managing the social and emotional needs of the gifted: A teacher's survival guide.* Minneapolis, MN: Free Spirit.

Scholwinski, E., & Reynolds, C. R. (1985). Dimensions of anxiety among high IQ children. *Gifted Child Quarterly, 29,* 125–130.

Silverman, L. K. (1990). Social and emotional education of the gifted: The discoveries of Leta Hollingworth. *Roeper Review, 12,* 171–178.

Silverman, L. K. (1993). Techniques for preventive counseling. In L. K. Silverman (Ed.), *Counseling the gifted and talented* (pp. 81–108). Denver, CO: Love Publishing Co.

Silverman, L. K. (1994). The moral sensitivity of gifted children and the evolution of society. *Roeper Review, 17*(2), 110–116.

Sisk, D. (1987). *Creative teaching of the gifted*. New York: McGraw-Hill.

Sowa, C. J., McIntyre, J., May, K. M., & Bland, L. (1994). Social and emotional adjustment themes across gifted children. *Roeper Review, 17*(2), 95–98.

St. Clair, K. L. (1989). Counseling gifted students: A historical review. *Roeper Review, 12*(2), 98–102.

Supplee, P. L. (1989). Students at risk: The gifted underachiever. *Roeper Review, 11*(3), 163–166.

Swesson, K. (1994). Helping the gifted / learning disabled. *Gifted Child Today, 17*(5), 14–16.

Toll, M. F. (1993). Gifted learning disabled: A kaleidoscope of needs. *Gifted Child Today, 16*(1), 34–35.

Van Tassel-Baska, J. (1991). Serving the disabled gifted through educational collaboration. *Journal for the Education of the Gifted, 14*(3), 246–266.

Van Tassel-Baska, J., Olszewski-Kubilius, P., & Kulieke, M. (1994). A study of self-concept and social support in advantaged and disadvantaged seventh and eighth grade gifted students. *Roeper Review, 16*(3), 186–191.

Vernon, M., & LaFalce-Landers, E. (1993). A longitudinal study of intellectually gifted deaf and hard of hearing people. *American Annals of the Deaf, 138*(5), 427–434.

Vespi, L., & Yewchuk, C. (1992). A phenomenological study of the social / emotional characteristics of gifted learning disabled children. *Journal for the Education of the Gifted, 16*(1), 55–72.

Webb, J., Meckstroth, E., & Tolan, S. (1982). *Guiding the gifted child*. Columbus, OH: Psychological Publishing.

Weiss, D. E. (1990). Gifted adolescents and suicide. *The School Counselor, 37*, 351–358.

Whitmore, J. R. (1980). *Giftedness, conflict and underachievement*. Needham Heights, MA: Allyn & Bacon.

Whitmore, J. R. (1989). Voices of experience . . . Four leading advocates for gifted students with disabilities. *Roeper Review, 12*(1), 5–13.

Worell, J., & Remer, P. (1992). *Feminine perspectives in therapy: An empowerment model for women*. New York: Wiley.

Wragg, J. (1989). *Talk sense to yourself*. Melbourne, Australia: ACER.

Yewchuk, C., & Bibby, M. (1989). Identification of giftedness in severely and profoundly hearing impaired students. *Roeper Review, 12*(19), 42–48.

CONCLUSION
Potential Unmasked: Lessons from this Book

The chapters in this book explore the myriad ways in which the potential giftedness of individuals and groups is masked by the collective, myopic vision of our society. While the perspectives reflect the differing experiences of educators from the United States and Australia, there are more similarities than dissimilarities in the situations they describe and the solutions they support. Most importantly, it is clear that the cost for individuals and society of the unrealized potential of so many can no longer be borne by societies that claim to foster the equitable development of all their members. The stories of the individuals in these chapters remind us of the outstanding achievements of those who have had to overcome prejudice regarding their abilities and who have had to struggle to receive an education commensurate with those abilities. The question remains as to how many individuals have failed to reach their potential because the masks imposed by our society have not been lifted. It is our belief that all our children have the right to an education that is appropriate to their particular pattern of strengths and weaknesses; and it is the responsibility of all